Path of Light
Volume I
Introduction to Vedic Astrology

Path of Light
Volume I

Introduction
to
Vedic Astrology

James Kelleher

AHIMSA
San Francisco

The Path of Light: Volume One © 2006 by James Kelleher

All rights reserved under International and Pan-American Copyright Conventions

This book is sold under the condition that it shall not be circulated, traded, resold, reproduced or transmitted in any form or by any means, electronic or mechanical, including photocopying, recording, or by any information storage and retrieval system, without the publisher's prior written consent, except by a reviewer who may use brief quotations in articles and reviews.

Published by Ahimsa Press

Printed in the United States by Thomson-Shore, Inc.

Book design by JTC Imagineering
Editors: Debra Infante and David Goldstein Ph.D.
Astrological Chart Designer: Marga Laube
Nakshatra Art: Arun Sharma
Nine Planet Art: Susanta Sarangi

James Kelleher's website is www.jameskelleher.com. All questions related to this book should be emailed to james@jameskelleher.com.

First Edition

Library of Congress Control Number: 2006920731
ISBN-10: 0-9774480-0-2
ISBN-13: 9780977448005

To M. K. Gandhi,
for taking me in,
treating me like a son,
and passing on the light.

Acknowledgements

The Path of Light has only been made possible by virtue of the generous efforts and blessings of the following people, to whom I am deeply grateful:

Debra Infante, for her consistent editing, researching, formatting, and modifying the text, as well as helping to create the index and glossary.

David Goldstein Ph.D., for editing and reviewing the text, as well as giving advice regarding key modifications and additions to the manuscript.

Ken Miller, for reading and reviewing the final text, and for lively discussions related to the book on the trail from Gangotri to Kedarnath.

Sat Siri Khalsa and Hank Friedman, for their helpful insights after reviewing the final manuscript.

Marga Laube, for assistance with the book design, research assistance, and creative layout of the horoscopes.

Dr. K. S. Charak, for his insights regarding key technical points.

Rajiv Tomar, for his assistance during my many trips to India, as well as coordination in obtaining the artwork for this book.

Dr. David Frawley, for his suggestions pertaining to ancient Vedic history and the nakshatras, and for his support and encouragement.

Terri Schwaderer, (my wife) for frequent advice related to grammar and design, as well as her constant encouragement, understanding, and support.

Swami Sivanandamurthy, for his encouragement and blessings during the writing of this book.

Sarah's chart is borderline betw. Cancer and Leo, and this impacts her Navamsa (potential). The Navamsa that shows up at www.mywebastrologer.com is significantly better than the one calculated by Solar Fire.

Moon
Exalted in rasi

Mars
Ruling own sign - rasi   Exalted - Navamsa

Jupiter
Exalted - rasi

Venus
Exalted in Navamsa   Rules own sign rasi

Saturn
Exalted in Navamsa

① play poker
② back rub
③ throw him a surprise party
④ sexy voice mail at work
⑤ barber shop shave
⑥ tie his tie for him
⑦ Godfather lines - Leave the gun. Take the cannoli!

Jemis Navamsa
Ruling Jup in Pisces in 3rd
Ruling mars in Aries in 4th
Ketu is in the 4th with mars

Joseph's Vedic chart is borderline betw. Gemini and Cancer

Sun
Ruling in rasi

Moon
Fallen in rasi - aspected to Saturn

Mars
Fallen in Navamsa

Jupiter
Ruling in rasi

Contents

TABLES AND ILLUSTRATIONS   15
HOW TO USE THIS BOOK WITH THE "VEDIC CHART CALCULATOR"   17
FOREWORD   19
CHAPTER ONE: INTRODUCTION   22
    What is Vedic Astrology?   24

    The Veda: Rig Veda; Sama Veda; Yajur Veda; Atharva Veda   24
    Jyotish is a Vedanga   25
    Branches of Vedic Astrology   25

    The Four Aims of Life   26

    Astronomy and Mythology   26
    History of Jyotish   27

    Great Jyotishis of the Past: Time Line   28

    The Zodiac   31

    Ayanamsha: The Precession of the Equinox   32

    Yugas -The "Big Picture" of Time   33
    Cycles of Creation and Dissolution   35

Author's Journal: Pack Light   38

CHAPTER TWO: THE LAW OF KARMA   43
    Influx/Bondage/Outflux   44
    Doing Good Doesn't Get Rid of Karma!   45
    The Key to the Karmic Riddle   46
    Equanimity Stops the Influx of Karma   46
    Fate vs. Free Will: Three Types of Karma   47

Three Intensities of Prarabdha Karma   47
Jyotish Promotes Equanimity and Enhances Free Will   48

Author's Journal: Nimitta and the Three Glasses of Milk   50

Chapter Three: Signs   52

Aries   53
Taurus   55
Gemini   57
Cancer   59
Leo   61
Virgo   63
Libra   65
Scorpio   67
Sagittarius   70
Capricorn   73
Aquarius   75
Pisces   77

Author's Journal: The Lagna and the Jain Monk   81

Chapter Four: The Planets   84

Sun   88
Moon   91
Mars   93
Mercury   96
Jupiter   99
Venus   102
Saturn   104
Rahu   108
Ketu   110

Judging the Strength of Planets   113
Planetary Strength or Weakness (Three-Step Assessment)   114

1. Sign Placement
   Own Sign   114
   Exaltation   114
   Moolatrikona   115
   Debilitation   115
   Friend's Sign   115

Contents

    Enemy's Sign   115
    Zero Degrees   116
    Retrograde Planets   117
    Vargottama   117

2. House Placement   118
    Placed in a Kendra (houses 1, 4, 7, or 10)   118
    Placed in a Trine (houses 1, 5 or 9)   118
    Placed in a Dusthana (houses 6, 8, or 12)   118
    Directional Strength   118

3. Association with Other Planets   119
    Conjunct or Aspected by Natural Benefics or Malefics   119
    Hemmed In Between Benefics or Malefics   119
    Combustion   119
    Planetary War   120

Author's Journal: Jupiter's Children   121

Chapter Five: Houses   124

    Signs Equal Houses   124

    House – Sign Overlays   125

    Midpoint – Equal House   127

    House Rulers   128

    Houses and the Four Aims of Life   129
    Dharma Houses (1, 5, 9)   129
    Artha Houses (2, 6, 10)   130
    Kama Houses (3, 7, 11)   131
    Moksha Houses (4, 8, 12)   132

    Kendra Houses (1, 4, 7, 10)   133
    Kona Houses (1, 5, 9)   133
    Minor Dusthana Houses (3, 11)   135
    Upachaya Houses (3, 6, 10, 11)   135

    Orientation to the North Indian Chart   135
    The Numbers Represent Signs, Not Houses   136

Putting the Planets in the Signs   138

(Classical Significations; Physical Correspondences; The Ruler of Each House Placed in the Twelve Houses; Each of the Planets Placed in the House)

The First House (Thanu Bhava)   140
The Second House (Dhana Bhava)   155
The Third House (Sahaja Bhava)   168
The Fourth House (Sukha Bhava)   180
The Fifth House (Putra Bhava)   194
The Sixth House (Roga Bhava)   209
The Seventh House (Kalatra Bhava)   223
The Eighth House (Mrityu Bhava)   238
The Ninth House (Dharma Bhava)   254
The Tenth House (Karma Bhava)   270
The Eleventh House (Labha Bhava)   286
The Twelfth House (Vyaya Bhava)   301

Judging the Strength of Houses   315

The Three-Part House Analysis   315
1. House Occupants   315

   House Occupied by Natural Benefics or Malefics   315
   House Occupied by a Temporal Benefic or Malefic   316
   House Occupied by the Yogakaraka   317

2. House Ruler   317

   House Ruler Placed in Its Own House   318

3. Planetary Influences on a House   318

   Aspects   318
   House Ruler Aspecting Its Own House   319
   Benefic and Malefic Aspects on a House   319
   Unoccupied Houses   321
   Kartari Yoga (House Hemmed In)   321

Author's Journal: "Do You Want to Fly?"   322

CHAPTER SIX: NAKSHATRAS   327
    1. Ashwini   329
    2. Bharani   333
    3. Krittika   336
    4. Rohini   340
    5. Mrigashira   344
    6. Ardra   348
    7. Punarvasu   352
    8. Pushya   355
    9. Ashlesha   358
    10. Magha   363
    11. Purva Phalguni   366
    12. Uttara Phalguni   369
    13. Hasta   371
    14. Chitra   375
    15. Swati   379
    16. Vishakha   382
    17. Anuradha   385
    18. Jyeshtha   388
    19. Mula   391
    20. Purva Ashadha   394
    21. Uttara Ashadha   396
    22. Shravana   399
    23. Dhanishtha   403
    24. Shatabhisha   405
    25. Purva Bhadrapada   409
    26. Uttara Bhadrapada   411
    27. Revati   414

Author's Journal: The Swami and the Dead Girl   416

GLOSSARY   418

BIBLIOGRAPHY   424

INDEX   428

AUTHOR   435

Andrea's Navamsa
- Held back by her ignorant   Mercury, Mars, Sat, Rahu in 9th
- Lots of limitations in higher institutions
- Fallen Venus in 11th
    - Limits earnings from her job
    - Limits her friends

Denai's Navamsa
- Venus, Sun, Mars, Rahu in the 5th

Jenni's Navamsa
- Mars/Ketu in 4th - Mars is ruling
    - lots of luck with homes, cars, boats
    - powerhouse in the home
    - has the help she needs at home
- Venus
    - ruling in 3rd - teaching kids goes well
    - a sibling does very well

Tables and Illustrations

HISTORY OF VEDIC ASTROLOGY   29
TIMELINE OF THE YUGAS (ACCORDING TO *Manu Samhita*)   34
PLANETS

    Sun   88
    Moon   91
    Mars   93
    Mercury   96
    Jupiter   99
    Venus   102
    Saturn   104
    Rahu   108
    Ketu   110

Judging the Strength of Planets   113
Planetary Strength or Weakness (Three-Step Assessment)   114
Table of Sign Strength   116
Table of Planetary Friendship   116
Directional Strength   119
Table of House Rulers   128
Table of Temporal Benefics, Malefics, and Yogakarakas for Each Ascendant   317
Table of Aspects of the Planets   319

NAKSHATRAS

    1. Ashwini   329
    2. Bharani   333
    3. Krittika   336
    4. Rohini   340
    5. Mrigashira   344
    6. Ardra   348
    7. Punarvasu   352
    8. Pushya   355
    9. Ashlesha   358

10. Magha   363
11. Purva Phalguni   366
12. Uttara Phalguni   369
13. Hasta   371
14. Chitra   375
15. Swati   379
16. Vishakha   382
17. Anuradha   385
18. Jyeshtha   388
19. Mula   391
20. Purva Ashadha   394
21. Uttara Ashadha   396
22. Shravana   399
23. Dhanishtha   403
24. Shatabhisha   405
25. Purva Bhadrapada   409
26. Uttara Bhadrapada   411
27. Revati   414

How to Use This Book
with the
"Vedic Chart Calculator"
(for the beginner)

Although *Path of Light* is intended for students of Vedic astrology, it is also appropriate for the non-astrologer or beginner in Vedic astrology. *Path of Light, Volume I* is particularly appropriate in this case. Most students of Vedic astrology have their own astrological software for calculating horoscopes. This makes it possible to apply the astrological principles found in this book to the charts of friends and family members. Non-astrologers, however, may not possess their own astrological software. For this reason, I have installed a free "Vedic Chart Calculator" on my website. This is intended to assist those students who do not have software, by providing them with a free method to calculate horoscopes. The chart calculator uses state-of-the-art Vedic astrology software, which includes a complete world atlas. The atlas automatically computes the latitude, longitude, and adjusts for various time zone issues including daylight savings time, and war time.

To use the "Vedic Chart Calculator" go to my website at www.jameskelleher.com and click on the "News" tab at the top of the home page. On the side-bar of the News page, click on the link that says "Vedic Chart Calculation." This will activate the chart calculator. When entering the birth data for the horoscope, note that the day is listed first (DD), then month (MM), and finally the entire year (YYYY). For birth time, note that the hour is listed first (HH) and it is in military time, then minutes (MM), and finally seconds (SS) only if known. Please note: When selecting the city of birth it may be necessary to push and hold the (ctrl) key while clicking on the button that says, "Click here to locate city."

Once you have calculated a chart, it will be displayed in a North

Indian chart style. Below the chart is a table labeled "Basic Planetary Details," which will list the positions of the Ascendant (abbreviated "Asc"), as well as each of the planets by degree and sign. The sign position of the planets will assist you while reading the chapter on the signs. Next to the "Position" column is the "Nakshatra" column, which gives each planet's nakshatra. This will be helpful when reading the chapter on the nakshatras. The "Ruler" column next to the "Nakshatra" column lists the planet that rules that particular nakshatra.

Continuing to the right there is another table labeled "House Details." This table will be helpful for reading the chapter on the houses. The first column, labeled "House," lists the twelve houses of the horoscope. The middle column of this table is labeled "Ruler," and gives the ruler of each of the houses for the chosen horoscope. The last column is labeled "Ruler Placement," giving the house placement of each of the rulers of the twelve houses of the horoscope. This will give you the information necessary to read the interpretations given for house ruler placement in the chapter on the houses.

At the top of the page there are three orange tabs. Clicking on the tab labeled "Vimshottari Dasha" will give a complete list of dashas (major periods) and bhuktis (sub-periods). Clicking on the "Divisional Chart" tab gives the standard divisional charts (vargas). These pages will be helpful when reading *Path of Light, Volume II*.

Foreword

Vedic astrology now commands an important presence in the astrological world, both East and West. It is recognized as one of the most accurate predictive systems, notable for delineating specific events in our lives in a stunningly precise manner. Yet, at the same time, Vedic astrology is admired as one of the most spiritual and insightful forms of the discipline with its deep understanding of the law of karma and its many tools for connecting us with our higher Self. Interest in the subject is growing rapidly, along with its interface with other Vedic disciplines like Yoga, Ayurveda, Tantra and Vastu, which are similarly widely gaining in popularity.

There are several introductory books on the subject and a few more technical volumes published in the West. In India a large number of books on Vedic astrology are available in English, including very technical volumes, many written over the past decade, providing an extensive literature for the serious student to examine.

Various associations of Vedic astrology now exist in the western world like the Council of Vedic Astrology (CVA) centered in the United States, which has a worldwide following, and the British Association of Vedic Astrology (BAVA). Many such modern Vedic astrological organizations can be found in India, starting with the Indian Council of Astrological Sciences (ICAS), founded by Dr. B.V. Raman. A full-fledged western Vedic astrology school has recently emerged through the American College of Vedic Astrology (ACVA). Vedic astrologers regularly teach at western astrological conferences and have hosted many conferences of their own as well, with the depth of teaching increasing on a yearly basis.

We could perhaps call this a renaissance of Vedic astrology as well as its worldwide spread. It is quite a change from the situation fifteen years ago when Vedic astrology was almost unknown in the West and information on it was very hard to find, much less finding any skilled practitioners of it. Vedic astrology will likely continue its growth for many years to come as one of the most important sciences for the planetary age.

James Kelleher was one of the first Americans to study Vedic astrology in depth, a pursuit he has dedicated himself to over the past thirty years. His quest for Vedic astrological wisdom has led him on a wide range of interesting travels and studies with notable Vedic astrology teachers and gurus. Kelleher has also been one of the main founders of Vedic astrology organizations in the West and a popular teacher at many classes, conferences and seminars.

Yet more importantly, James has been one of the most successful Vedic astrology practitioners, having read thousands of charts from his home in northern California and in his travels throughout the country. He has maintained a full time practice for the last fifteen years, with an unflagging enthusiasm. Kelleher is able to examine all aspects of a person's life, from the most mundane to the most spiritual, using the entire range of Vedic astrological tools, from the basic birth chart to divisional charts, annual charts and ashtakavarga. He has examined the symbolic basis of Vedic astrology in great detail and brings that into his readings as well.

James is considered to be a Vedic astrologer's astrologer and is clearly one of the best practitioners among the American born Vedic astrologers. I have known James over the last fifteen years and observed the many sides of his astrological skills and studies. Kelleher's *Path of Light* reflects these many years of study and practice. It is clearly a book that has taken a great deal of time, patience and consideration to finish, with much thought having gone into its every page. It is not just the work of someone passing on knowledge gained from other sources, but reflects what the author has actually found to be valid through his own reading of many charts.

The book is digested wisdom, not just standardized information or New Age fluff. It covers nearly everything the beginning Vedic astrologer would want to know, in both depth and detail. It is an excellent reference volume for those seeking to understand what the planets mean in various signs and houses. Notably, Kelleher examines the Nakshatras or lunar mansions, one of the more unique and esoteric aspects of Vedic astrology, in some detail.

Kelleher describes the foundation of Vedic astrology as a tool for understanding our karma. He adds many interesting stories from his own life-experience. In this regard, Kelleher has traveled more times to India and met with more Indian Vedic astrologers than perhaps any other astrologer in America. He could produce an entire book on his travels alone.

The *Path of Light* is the foundation for what is likely to be a whole set of books on Vedic astrology by the author. Readers can look forward to Kelleher's work as providing a good foundation for a new western Vedic astrology that is in harmony with classical sources and Indian gurus and also made relevant and verified by application in the charts of people today. This makes the book not just an introduction to Vedic astrology but a textbook for the serious student as well.

—Dr. David Frawley (Pandit Vamadeva Shastri)
   Author of *Astrology of the Seers* and *Yoga and Ayurveda*
   Director, American Institute of Vedic Studies

Chapter One

Introduction

As long as human beings have been on earth, they have been engaged in an eternal quest for happiness. At the core, all people want to be happy, yet most people do not know how. Modern western civilization has become quite sophisticated in terms of science and technology, yet it is plagued with drug addiction, crime, depression and other cultural diseases. Clearly, the scientific and technical paradigms of western society have fallen radically short of delivering the fulfillment that they promised. They have utterly failed to address the subjective side of the human condition. As a result, the average person still suffers.

Over the past few decades, many westerners have looked to the paradigms of the East to fill in this gap. One such paradigm is found in the writings of the yogis and sages of ancient India and is called the Veda. Vedic science not only speaks to the subjective side of the human condition, but also describes outer aspects of life in great detail. The Vedic seers had profound insight into many branches of knowledge such as mathematics, astronomy, architecture, healing, and of course, astrology. All of these branches of knowledge can be used to enhance the outer condition of life. Unlike western science, however, Vedic science also focuses on the subjective experience. In fact, the inner condition of the human mind is the primary focus of Vedic science, which not only clearly describes the root cause of suffering, but also provides effective tools for eradicating it.

It is in this context that Vedic astrology has been presented to the world. It is part of a complete and integrated system. This idea is sometimes hard for the western mind to comprehend. We are more used to taking isolated techniques out of their contexts and practicing them independently. One example of this might be found in the western approach to herbal medicine. Here in the West we sell single Chinese herbs such as ginseng over-the-counter in health food stores as cures for lethargy, fatigue, and sexual inadequacy. It never occurs to us that there might be a reason why, in Chinese Medicine, such herbs are usually only prescribed in combination with other herbs. Such is the western mind. We are always engaged in the quest for the quick fix. With such a strong tendency to isolate, separate, and eliminate context, it is no wonder that so many westerners feel isolated, lonely, and depressed.

Vedic astrology is both an art and a science, which helps people achieve wholeness in life. It accomplishes this by first showing the person how his seemingly isolated and random experiences actually make sense when taken in the context of the overall cosmic plan. It shows the person how his past actions, thoughts, words and deeds manifest in this lifetime in terms of karmic patterns that are reflected in the horoscope. It clearly describes these karmic impressions, giving the person insight into his own unique physical constitution, psychological make-up, talents and abilities, which helps him to find purposeful work, prosperity, meaningful relationships and good health. Vedic astrology gives him a schedule upon which these karmic impressions will fructify, and thus allows him to gain greater understanding and perspective during the up and down periods of life. It also shows the person how to cultivate inner detachment and equanimity, the one sure method of eradicating karma and gaining final liberation.

This book is intended as an introduction to Vedic astrology. More than that, however, it is intended to introduce a way of thinking about life that is radically different from conventional western thought. This alternative paradigm is contained in the theory of karma, which is described in the first part of the book. Without this understanding of how karma binds the soul, how it determines our life tendencies, and how it is eventually eradicated, it is not possible to comprehend the essence of Vedic astrology. Practiced in the overall context of Vedic science, this astrology contains the knowledge of how to gain happiness in life on both material and spiritual levels. For this reason, the *Brihat Samhita* says, "A person who studies astrology and divines the course of people's destiny will never be found in hell. On the other hand, he will attain a permanent status in the world of Brahman."

What is Vedic Astrology?

Vedic astrology is the astrology of India. It is said to have been intuitively perceived thousands of years ago by the same ancient mystics who developed the various techniques of meditation and yoga for which India is so well known. It is called Jyotish, which means "the lord of light," because it is used to illuminate life, providing both practical and spiritual insight.

The Veda

The term Vedic comes from the word "veda," which literally means knowledge. True knowledge is said to be transcendental, and the real experience of "the Veda" can only be directly perceived by the enlightened mind. Out of compassion for mankind, however, ancient seers composed four sets of hymns called the Vedas, which are expressions of various aspects of knowledge such as philosophy, yoga, meditation, healing, and other sciences. They are designed to help humanity in the quest for happiness, peace and fulfillment. The first and greatest of the Vedic texts is called the *Rig Veda*. It was followed by the *Sama Veda*, the *Yajur Veda*, and the *Atharva Veda*.

Rig Veda

The *Rig Veda* is the mother of all Vedas. It is the oldest and the first of the Vedas. It is made up of more than 1,000 hymns that include knowledge related to many branches of learning and aspects of life. The writing of the *Rig Veda* probably took place over a long period of time but it came to conclusion around 3730 BC.

Sama Veda

The *Sama Veda* consists of some of the hymns of the *Rig Veda* put to a meditative, musical style. Just listening to a pundit of *Sama Veda* chant a hymn will put the mind in a meditative state. In the *Sama Veda*, the sound and rhythm of the mantras is used to create ecstasy and awaken higher consciousness.

Yajur Veda

The *Yajur Veda* deals with rituals and techniques for purifying and elevating consciousness. Some of these rituals are used as remedial techniques in Vedic astrology, and can effectively diminish the effects of difficult planetary influences.

Atharva Veda

The *Atharva Veda* is the Veda of rituals, incantations, and other practices used to diminish negativity and to enhance the positive aspects of life. It also contains a great deal of practical information related to various sciences. Some *Atharva Veda* mantras are used in the daily Hindu rituals in order to increase prosperity, health, and happiness.

Jyotish is a Vedanga

Besides the four main Vedas, the ancient rishis also developed some auxiliary disciplines which help us to understand the Vedas properly. These subjects are called Vedangas. A Vedanga is a limb. In this respect the Veda is seen as a living being and the body of that being is said to have six limbs. These limbs are the sciences of grammar, intonation, meter, etymology, ritual, and astrology. Jyotish, therefore, is a Vedanga. It is said to be the eyes of the Veda, which are necessary to perceive the light of knowledge.

Branches of Vedic Astrology

Just as the Veda has six limbs, Jyotish also has limbs. They are Gola—observational astronomy, Ganita—astronomical and astrological calculations, Jataka—natal astrology, Prashna—horary astrology, Muhurtha—electional astrology, and Nimitta—the study of omens.

Gola (observational astronomy): At the foundation of astrological interpretation is the observed movements of the grahas or nine planets. This branch of Jyotish focuses on the movements of the Sun, Moon, Mars, Mercury, Jupiter, Venus, Saturn, Rahu and Ketu. It does not include the outer planets, Uranus, Neptune and Pluto.

Ganita (astronomical and astrological calculations): Ganita is the branch that deals with computations. In ancient times there were no computers, so astrologers had to compute the positions of planets by hand. The calculation of a single horoscope could take hours and involved a great deal of mathematical understanding, as well as an understanding of astronomy. A great classic in this field is the *Surya Siddanta*.

Jataka (natal astrology): This is the branch with which most people are familiar. The interpretation of birth charts is the focus of this branch. Most of the great classics, such as the *Brihat Jataka*, and most modern books on Vedic astrology primarily deal with this branch.

Prashna (horary astrology): This limb deals with how to accurately answer questions. There are a variety of techniques employed for this purpose, but most of them center around the exact moment when the question is asked. The great classics *Shat Panchasika* and *Prashna Marga* deal with this subject. This is a huge field which has been especially developed in the state of Kerala in South India.

Muhurtha (electional astrology): Muhurtha is the branch of astrology which is used to select an auspicious time to begin any undertaking. Modern astrologers are frequently asked to select a good time for marriage, starting a business, travel, building a house and many other important endeavors. One of the great classics in this field is *Kalaprakashika*.

Nimitta (omens): This branch of Jyotish is one of the least understood and least practiced and yet it is one of the most important. It relies on the intrinsic connectedness of all things. In the past, astrologers relied on the use of omens extensively to make accurate predictions for their clients. In modern times, however, the use of omens in astrology has gone out of vogue.

The Four Aims of Life

The ancient seers who developed Jyotish possessed deep wisdom, but they were also very practical. They sought to solve the age old problem of human suffering by providing tools such as yoga, meditation, ayurveda and Vedic astrology, which assist men and women in their quest for happiness and fulfillment. Ultimately, all of these tools aim at producing enlightenment, a state of consciousness that is characterized by infinite bliss, unbounded awareness, deep abiding peace, and freedom. Yet the ancient seers understood that, for the average person, the path towards enlightenment need not be one of austerity and deprivation. They outlined four worthwhile aims of life: dharma (law, duty or purpose), artha (material wealth), kama (desire, pleasure, affection, emotion), and moksha (liberation or spiritual freedom). They designed Jyotish as a tool to help people achieve all of these aims, so that life, in both spiritual and material aspects, can be a joyous event culminating in enlightenment.

Astronomy and Mythology

The original jyotishis were both expert astronomers and enlightened sages. They made their calculations directly, by looking up at the heavens. Using stone observatories, sundials and various other simple astronomical tools, they mapped the heavens and accurately plotted the movements of planets. For thousands of years they watched the night sky and divided the zodiac into various divisions, including signs (sections of 30 degrees), nakshatras (sections of 13 degrees 20 minutes), navamshas (sections of 3 degrees 20 minutes) and even shashtyamshas (tiny sections of 1/2 degree). They went on to describe the forms and symbols they could see in the heavens and they linked each planet, sign and constellation with a particular god or goddess. They meditated deeply and began to tell the stories of the gods based on the symbols they saw in the heavens. These stories were told and retold down through the ages around campfires, in temples, and eventually, some of them were written down. The myths and stories are full of symbolism, which illuminate basic psychological archetypes. In this way, Jyotish has always had a strong storytelling foundation. Mastering Jyotish requires more than a mere technical understanding of the subject. It requires a thorough grounding in Vedic philosophy and mythology, an undertaking that, by itself, could take a lifetime. The artful use of storytelling by the Vedic astrologer will touch the deepest chord within the client, linking him to his own personal mythology.

History of Jyotish

Ancient India, which produced the Vedas, was located in the northwestern section of modern India which is now called the Punjab. While most conventional historians assign the Vedas to the period between 1500 and 900 BC, modern archeological evidence suggests that they are much older, and that the Vedic culture may even be more than 8,000 years old.

This ancient civilization centered around seven rivers, the largest of which was called the Saraswati. This was a fertile agricultural land, where crops thrived and trade flourished. As villages and cities began to grow, two cities in particular, Harappa and Mohenjodaro, became great centers of civilization. These cities were highly developed, with an organized political structure. They were laid out in a meticulous geometric pattern. They had brick houses, some with bathrooms, where the inhabitants bathed using a pitcher of water that drained out of the house into an intricate drainage system. Only the Roman drainage systems, more than 2000 years later, can compare with those of ancient India. The inhabitants of these cities were multi-ethnic, and spoke several languages. The people were also skilled in mathematics. They were farmers, merchants, seafarers, priests, artisans, and crafts people of various kinds. In short, the cities of ancient India were quite sophisticated by ancient standards.

Around 2000 BC, however, due to catastrophic geological changes, the Saraswati River and its tributaries dried up. This led to a migration to the Ganges River Valley, which became the center of cultural development that produced modern India. The *Rig Veda*, the most ancient of the four Vedic texts, was written well before this cataclysm. Its text constantly refers to "the land of seven rivers" and specifically to the Saraswati. The life of Krishna and all the events depicted in the great epic, The *Mahabharata*, also took place in this region, probably about 3000 BC. The *Rig Veda* also mentions specific astronomical configurations which suggest that Vedic culture might even have existed as early as 6000 to 7000 BC.

Although there is no archeological evidence that Vedic texts were in existence at that time, it is well known that Vedas were originally preserved through an oral tradition. At first, fathers taught their sons. The secrets of Vedic astrology were memorized and jealously guarded within families. Later, many astrological works were written down, first on palm leaves, and then later in books.

One of the most important ancient astrological works is the *Brihat Prashara Hora Shastra*, which is attributed to the great sage, Parashara, who lived at the time of the Mahabharata War, about 3000 BC. Although Parashara is accepted by many astrologers to be the Father of Vedic astrology, references in the *Rig Veda* suggest that Jyotish was a developed science even before Parashara's time. It is also more likely that Parashara's *Hora Shastra* was a compilation of the writings of astrologers who belonged to Parashara's lineage and it was actually written down much later, probably evolving into its present form a few thousand years after Parashara's time.

Great Jyotishis of the Past: Time Line

While it is unlikely that Vedic astrology originated with Parashara, it is clear that his methods have come to define the most popular style of astrology practiced in India today. Parashara is not, however, the only great jyotishi of the past. In fact, since his time, there have been many astrological luminaries who have contributed their knowledge in either oral or written form. One such astrologer was Jaimini, who might have been a contemporary of Parashara and may have lived slightly after Parashara's time. Jaimini had a unique method of analyzing a horoscope and making predictions, which while not currently in vogue in India today, is still practiced by many astrologers. Like Parashara, it is also probable that Jaimini's methods were originally transmitted orally and were written down later by members of his lineage.

Another, more recent astrological giant was Varahamihira, who lived around 500 AD. Varahamihira was a court astrologer who became famous due to his formidable intellect and numerous astrological works. He also was known as an expert predictor. It is said that he got his name by predicting the death of the son of a king. In his role as the court

History of Vedic Astrology

4,000 B.C.	
3928 B.C.	Vedic Astronomer Atri records an eclipse that fell one day before the summer solstice on 03/26/3928 B.C.
	The *Rig Veda* finalized
	The Age of Vasistha and Visvamitra
	The Age of Rama
3,800-3,700 B.C.	The Battle of the Ten Kings
3,100 B.C.	Krishna and the Mahabharata War; approximate time of Parashara
3,000 B.C.	
3,100-2,000 B.C.	The Sutra-Brahmana period
2,000 B.C.	
1,900 B.C.	The Saraswati River dries up, causing a migration to the area surrounding the Ganges River
1,000 B.C.	
599-520 B.C.	Life of Mahavir, 24th Tirthankara of Jainism
566 B.C.	Birth of Gautama Buddha
327-325 B.C.	Invasion of India by Alexander the Great
0	
100-200 A.D.	Rise of Buddhism
505 A.D.	Varahamihira composes the *Brihat Samhita*
600-700 A.D.	Rise of Tantrism
650-725 A.D.	Life of Kalyanavarma, Author of *Saravali*
788-820 A.D.	Life of Shankara, Founder of Advaita, non-dualist Vedanta
1,000 A.D.	
1,030 A.D.	Al-Biruni, the Arabic scholar comes to India and studies Vedic astrology, later translating the *Brihat Samhita* into Arabic
800-1,400 A.D.	Multiple Islamic invasions
1,649 A.D.	*Prashna Marga*, the great South India classic on horary astrology is written by an anonymous Brahmin astrologer from Kerala India
2,000 A.D.	

astrologer, Varahamihira predicted that on a certain date and time, the king's son would be killed by a pig. Aware of the prediction, the king took every precaution to protect his son, sequestering him in the palace, away from all pigs. When the date and time of the prediction arrived, the young boy was playing safely in the palace courtyard when a statue of a pig accidentally fell on him, killing him instantly. Varaha means "pig," which was the name given to Varahamihira by the king.

Introduction

The Zodiac

In the West, it is common for people to ask, "What's your sign?" Most people understand this to mean the zodiacal sign that the Sun was passing through at the time of the person's birth. Most people also have a rudimentary astronomical understanding that the zodiac is a band of sky filled with constellations of stars. These constellations form the background for the planets as they move through the heavens. Determining the Sun sign appears to be quite simple. It would seem that all you have to do is look up in the heavens on the person's day of birth, find the Sun, and determine which constellation of stars falls in the background of the Sun. That constellation is obviously the Sun sign, right?

Unfortunately, it is not that simple, or at least in the case of Western astrology it is not that simple. First, when you read in the newspaper that you are a Cancer or a Leo, this does not mean that the Sun was actually in the sign of Cancer or Leo when you were born. In fact, most of the time when a Western astrologer says that you are a Cancer, the Sun was actually in the sign of Gemini. This is because Western astrology uses what is called the Tropical zodiac.

The Tropical zodiac, as the name suggests, is a zodiac which is oriented to the seasons. There is a symbolic relationship between the seasons and the signs. Aries, for example, symbolizes new beginnings. Spring also symbolizes new beginnings. According to Tropical astrology, the first day of springtime is always considered to be the first day of Aries. In astronomy, however, the Sun entered the sign of Aries on the first day of springtime only about fifteen hundred years ago. Since then, the date of the Sun's entry into the sign of Aries has actually changed slightly each year. Since Tropical astrology is based on the symbolic relationship between the signs and the seasons, it continues to place the Sun in Aries, beginning each year on the first day of spring, regardless of where the Sun is actually located in the sky.

Vedic astrology, on the other hand, uses a Sidereal zodiac. The Sidereal zodiac is aligned with the stars in the heavens. The Vedic astrologer places the planets in the positions that are closer to the real positions viewed in astronomy. These planetary placements are not exactly identical to astronomical coordinates, but are approximations. Thus, there are two zodiacs. The zodiac you read in the newspaper is the Tropical zodiac, which is used by westerners and corresponds to the seasons, not what you see in the heavens. The zodiac which is used by Vedic astrologers is the Sidereal zodiac, which corresponds to what you actually see in the heavens on your birth date.

Ayanamsha

The distance in degrees and minutes between the Tropical and Sidereal zodiacs is called the ayanamsha. Most Sidereal astrologers agree that the ayanamsha value is currently between 22 and 25 degrees. The method of calculating the ayanamsha, however, is a subject of some debate among astrologers. Intelligent arguments are put forth by proponents of each ayanamsha. In the end, it is up to each astrologer to decide which ayanamsha he or she will use, based on his or her own experience. All of the Vedic astrology computer programs offer optional ayanamshas. This author uses Lahiri ayanamsha, which is the most common ayanamsha used in India. It is also the official ayanamsha adopted by the Indian government. All charts in this book will be calculated using Lahiri ayanamsha.

Popular Ayanamshas
Calculated for January 1, 2000

Lahiri   23° 51
B. V. Raman 22° 24
Sri Yukteshwar 22° 30
Fagan – Bradley 24° 49

The Precession of the Equinox

The reason that the two different zodiacs are so far apart is an astronomical phenomenon called the precession of the equinox. The precession of the equinox is a slow wobble in the Earth's spin which causes the first day of spring to occur at a point when the Sun is approximately 50 seconds farther back in the zodiac each year. This means that over the course of hundreds or even thousands of years, the distance between the zodiacs actually becomes quite pronounced. In 285 AD (using Lahiri Ayanamsha), for example, the first day of Aries and the first day of spring were actually the same. As a result, the Tropical and the Sidereal zodiacs were the same at that time. Since then, however, the precession of the equinox has separated the two zodiacs by more than 23 degrees.

The precession of the equinox has another value as well. As the equinox moves through the zodiac, it defines the world-age through which we are passing. Most people have heard of the Age of Aquarius. This is supposed to begin when the vernal equinox (the first day of spring) moves through the sign of Aquarius. Some astrologers feel that this has already begun. It does not take much astronomical knowledge, however, to tell that the vernal equinox is currently taking place in the sign of Pisces. Looking at it this way, we can say that we are in the Age of Pisces. Currently (in 2005) the equinox takes place when the Sun is at about 6 degrees of Pisces, so "The Age of Aquarius" will not begin until 2439 AD.

Yugas -The "Big Picture" of Time

Although the equinox is currently moving through the sign of Pisces, Vedic astrology does not actually emphasize these sign-oriented ages. "The Age of Aquarius" was actually a western invention, popularized more than 30 years ago by western astrologers, with a little help from the 60's rock musical, *Hair*. The concept, however, is valid, and there is no real problem with calling this current period, The Age of Pisces. Vedic astrology actually uses these precessional ages in a larger way to define yugas, or longer ages of mankind.

In his book, *The Holy Science*, Sri Yukteshwar describes the method for calculating these yugas based on the *Manu Samhita*, a classical Vedic text. According to Sri Yukteshwar, the yugas are linked to the precession of the equinox through the zodiac. There are two cycles, each lasting about 12,000 years. The first cycle began at the time when the vernal equinox was at 0 degrees of Aries, which took place about 285 AD. From that point onward, the equinox precessed (moved backwards). At the moment it is close to seven degrees of Pisces. This phase is an ascending phase, starting with complete spiritual darkness and ignorance and gradually increasing until it reaches the highest point of spiritual light, a Golden Age, which culminates in 12,000 years. As this ascending cycle progresses, the world passes through four ages or yugas. The first is Kali Yuga which began in the year 285 AD (using Lahiri Ayanamsha) and continued for 1200 years. Kali Yuga is characterized by complete ignorance and darkness on the spiritual level. In 1485 AD we entered Dwapara Yuga, an age of increasing intelligence and awareness. This age brings science, technology, the development of the arts, academic knowledge and even spiritual awakening for some people. Dwapara Yuga lasts for 2400 years. We are currently in the beginning portion of Dwapara Yuga. Next comes 3600 years of Treta Yuga in which the spiritual atmosphere allows human beings to perceive deep spiritual truths and to live in a state of inner absorption and spiritual bliss. Finally, Satya Yuga, a period of 4800 years, brings the world to the zenith of spiritual awareness. This period is characterized by the highest levels of truth, purity, and spiritual realization. •

After the ascending phase is over, a descending cycle of 12,000 years begins. It also has four yugas, beginning with Satya Yuga and moving through Treta, Dwapara and Kali Yugas. The total precessional cycle, at least according to the ancient sage, Manu, is 24,000 years. This is very close to the 25,900 years which modern astronomy allots to the precessional cycle.

Timeline of the Yugas
(according to *Manu Samhita*)

```
                    |
          0 A.D.    |
                    |
        285 A.D.    | KALI YUGA
                    | 285 – 1485 A.D.
                    |
       1485 A.D.    | DWAPARA YUGA
                    | 1485 – 3885 A.D.
                    |
              ●     | (you are here)
                    |
       3885 A.D.    | TRETA YUGA
                    | 3885 - 7485 A.D.
                    |
       7485 A.D.    | SATYA YUGA
                    | 7485 - 12285 A.D.
                    |
   SATYA YUGA       | 12285 A.D.
 12285 - 17085 A.D. |
   TRETA YUGA       | 17085 A.D.
 17085 - 20685 A.D. |
  DWAPARA YUGA      | 20685 A.D.
 20685 - 23085 A.D. |
    KALI YUGA       | 23085 A.D.
 23085 - 24285 A.D. |
                    | 24285 A.D.
                    |
```

(Left side: Ascending Phase; Right side: Descending Phase)

Although it makes a great deal of sense, the idea of linking the yugas to the precession of the equinox, elaborated in the *Manu Samhita*, it is not the currently accepted concept of yugas in mainstream Hinduism. Normally yugas are considered to be part of the bigger picture of the cycle of creation and destruction of the universe. This cycle has been elaborated in the classical literature of India that follows.

Cycles of Creation and Dissolution

In the beginning, it is said that Mahavishnu, whose name means the all-pervading, asked the questions, "Who am I? Who created me? Why was I created? What is my work?" As soon as he asked these questions, the answers came, "I am everything. I am eternal, and nothing else exists except for me." Then a voice told him, "The universe is repeatedly subjected to creation, sustenance and destruction. Each time this happens, you are born by the power of the almighty, for the purpose of sustaining the universe. Your attribute is sattva (purity and virtue)."

Out of Vishnu's navel, a lotus grew and in the lotus flower, Brahma (the creator) took birth. His attribute is rajas (activity or passion). Brahma did penance before Vishnu and was granted all the boons he wanted. After that Brahma began to create.

From the middle of the eyebrows of Brahma, Rudra (Shiva) took birth. His attribute is tamas (darkness) and he destroys the world at the end of creation. It is said that when he was born, he cried. Brahma said, "Ma Ruda," which means do not cry, and named him Rudra.

According to the Vedic theory of time, the universe is repeatedly created and destroyed. The span of time from creation to destruction of a universe is called a day of Brahma. Another term for a day of Brahma is a Kalpa. After a day of Brahma is over, he is said to rest for an equal amount of time, which is called a night of Brahma. So two Kalpas equal one Ahoratra (a day and a night of Brahma). After each Ahoratra, another day of Brahma begins. In this way, the universe repeatedly expands and contracts to a total of 120 years of Brahma. After that, Brahma's life comes to an end and the whole process begins again.

One Human Year = One Ahoratra (day of the gods)
360 Ahoratras = One Devavatsara (year of the gods)
12,000 Devavatsaras = 1 Mahayuga
71 Mahayugas = One Manvantara
14 Manvantaras = One Kalpa
2 Kalpas = One day and One Ahoratra (a day and a night of Brahma)
360 Ahoratras = One Brahma Varsh (year of Brahma)
120 Brahma Varsh = One Mahakalpa (lifetime of Brahma)

Our place in the current day of Brahma:

1 Kalpa (day of Brahma) = 4,320,000,000 years = 14 Manvantaras
1 Manvantara = 71 Mahayugas

1 Mahayuga = 4 Yugas (Krita Yuga, Treta Yuga, Dwapara Yuga and Kali Yuga) = 4,320,000 years
Krita Yuga – 1,728,000 years
Treta Yuga – 1,296,000 years
Dwapara Yuga – 864,000 years
Kali Yuga – 432,000 years

In this scheme, the popular belief among most Hindus is that we are presently passing through the seventh Manvantara. So we are in the middle of the present day of Brahma. In the present Manvantara, we are in the twenty-eighth Mahayuga. In the present Mahayuga, we are in the last Yuga. As mentioned above, the last yuga of each Mahayuga is Kali Yuga, which began more than 5,000 years ago, (about 3102 BC) when Krishna's time on earth ended. This leaves more than 400,000 years before the present Kali Yuga ends.

The Yugas begin with Krita Yuga, which is characterized by the predominance of virtue and purity. As the yugas progress, the spiritual atmosphere in the world becomes progressively less conducive to the practice of virtue. This degeneration culminates in Kali Yuga.

Kali Yuga, which is the current Yuga, is characterized by the predominance of tamas or darkness. During this period, human awareness is at a low level and unable to perceive its true nature. As a result, human behavior during Kali Yuga is not in harmony with Divine Law. It is said that in Kali Yuga, sin prevails. In fact, in the *Vana Parva*, the famous Sage Markandaya put it this way, "Kali Yuga will bring dishonesty. Charity and sacrifices will only be done for show. Brahmans (the highest caste) will not do their duties. Sudras (the lowest caste) will become prosperous. Sinners become kings. The life span of people will be shorter. The stature of people will be shorter. There will be an increase of people who have animal-like natures. The sense of taste and smell will diminish. Women will sell their vaginas. Cows will give less milk. No one will observe asramas (the four vows) correctly. Students will sleep with their teacher's wives. Rainfall will be erratic and in and out of season. Trees and plants will diminish. Murder will be common. Merchants will be dishonest. Good people will decrease and sinners will increase. Girls of seven or eight will become mothers. Young boys will become fathers. Old men will still try to practice the habits of young men. Wives will have sex with their employees or servants. Wives will become prostitutes even when their husbands are alive. Masses of people will die of hunger."

Of course this description is not meant to characterize the entire human condition during Kali Yuga. It only describes the negative side of it. During Kali Yuga, it is said that darkness predominates. There is still great goodness and virtue in the world, but it is a rarity. Truly virtuous people are uncommon. We are all used to seeing corruption, violence, and other negative qualities around us constantly, so we are actually surprised when we find a truly honest or kind person. Such is the condition of life during Kali Yuga. It is a time of darkness. During a time of darkness, a little light goes a long way. This is one reason that during Kali Yuga, those who do practice virtue have a tremendous influence on the rest of the world. Ironically, taken in this way, Kali Yuga becomes an excellent time for spiritual development.

Author's Journal:

Pack Light

"*I used to live on a handful of chickpeas and a cup of milk a day. I slept on the ground with no pillow or mattress. I had no possessions except the shirt on my back.*" My guru, Gandhiji, was up to something. Whenever he wanted me to learn a lesson, he would invariably take the indirect approach. He would make his point first with a few cryptic statements about his own life, and after that, my own life experience would take over and teach me the lesson first hand. On this occasion, we were in the middle of India, in a long, narrow boat, on our way upriver to Siddhavarkoot, an ancient temple complex sacred to the Jains.

I sat there mulling over Gandhiji's words as he fell back into his characteristic silence. The boatman skillfully pushed his long pole into the muddy river bottom and moved the gondola upstream. I looked at my suitcase, nestled in amongst the other baggage in the front of the boat. It was obviously much larger than any of my Indian companions' suitcases. My Jain philosophy teacher, Hem Chandji, for example, had only taken a small briefcase, in which he had packed his toothbrush, a change of underwear and his dhoti, a white cloth, which he wore when visiting temples and participating in pujas. He did his laundry in a bucket each morning. Over the course of the one-month pilgrimage, he always seemed to look clean and fresh and always seemed comfortable. "*I wonder if Gandhiji thinks my suitcase is too big,*" I was thinking.

After a couple of hours in the boat, I could see the long staircase of Siddhavarkoot in the distance up ahead, descending from the temple complex down to the river's edge. The boat glided to the landing and we disembarked. As I went to pick up my suitcase, Gandhiji stopped me. "Let the porter do it," he said. "It's much too heavy. You might strain yourself." He was acting completely serious, but I had come to know his style of teasing. "I'm surprised he didn't actually offer to carry my suitcase up the stairs himself," I was thinking. These little humorous jabs were Gandhiji's way of making a point. He was letting me know the more you carry with you, the more it weighs you down and holds you back. This is a concept that the Jains and also the Hindus call aprarigrah, the principle of non-attachment. The fewer possessions you have, the less you have to worry about in life.

As I entered the temple complex at Siddhavarkoot, I immediately felt a wave of relaxation and peace. This pilgrimage sites has been the focus for hundreds of thousands of devout Jains who have chanted mantras, practiced pujas and offered prayers here for thousands of years. Over the years, Siddhavarkoot has taken on a tangible spiritual vibration that evokes peace and tranquility in anyone who visits. Its relative inaccessibility, as well as the scenic boat trip which carries the spiritual traveler to its steps, adds to the ambiance. Located on the banks of the Narmda River, Siddhavarkoot is made up of a series of ancient, finely carved Jain temples intermixed with simple, open-air brick accommodations for visitors. I stowed my things on a cot in my room and spent the rest of the day experiencing the silence of the temples, reading, and walking by the river.

While I was sitting next to the river that afternoon, I noticed someone walking on the opposite shore. He was a tall, blond westerner. I watched him as he washed his face in the river and then walked up the bank of the river to the place where the ancient temple-ruins stood. He seemed to be camping there in the temple ruins. "Strange!" I thought. "This guy is really austere, with no real shelter under this scorching sun." My curiosity was piqued. At dinner that evening, I mentioned this to Gandhiji. Gandhiji said, "Oh yes, that fellow was over here earlier today and I met him. He is a very spiritual man!"

That night, a group of villagers from a nearby village came to the temple to sing bhajans, (hymns). They were simple people, who lived in grass huts with dirt floors, and had few possessions and little material security. One had a harmonium (an air pumped portable keyboard instrument) and another had a set of tablas (drums). Gandhiji and I went over to the temple when we heard the singing begin at about 9:00 p.m. We all sat on the floor of the temple and joined in with the villagers as they sang their bhajans. I was immediately struck by how bright and relaxed the villagers seemed to be. There were no pompous, "better than thou" types here. They laughed together, sang, and as the stars began to fill the sky, they began to dance. They had a large streamer-type ornament on a string that resembled a pompom used by cheerleaders in the United States. One person would take the streamer and whirl it around while doing an improvised devotional dance in front of the statue of Mahavira (the last Jain prophet). Everyone else sang at the top of his lungs while the drums and harmonium provided the background. When the dancer finished, he passed the streamer to someone else. Whoever he passed it to would be required to get up and dance.

Being the only western person in the group, I clearly stood out, so it was inevitable that I would get the streamer passed to me. At first I tried to get out of it, saying, "Uh . . . I don't dance . . . no thanks . . . no really. . . ." But the villagers would not take no for an answer so I had to comply. The music started. "Mahavira Bhagavan ki jai. . . ." I took the streamers, and stood in front of the statue. Slowly I began to sway back and forth, getting the feel of the streamer moving in circles. I felt a little awkward at first but then quickly realized that nobody here was self-conscious. These villagers were uncomplicated. Self-consciousness is an attribute of over-abundant and sophisticated societies. These people were simply overjoyed to sing and watch the dance, and they would be happy with anything I did. I started to move in bigger circles, now swinging the streamers to the beat of the music. The villagers sang louder, belting out the chorus. The drummer wrenched his whole body as he beat the tablas and drove the entire group into a rhythmic frenzy. Soon I was completely caught up in the movement, rhythm and music. My body took on a new energy and began to flow effortlessly. Then I lost all awareness of my body as my heart and mind began to soar in a devotional stream of consciousness. At the end of the dance, laughing and filled with a playful energy, I walked over to Gandhiji, and handing him the streamers said, "Your turn."

Gandhiji took the streamers and quickly immersed himself in a dynamic and passionate devotional dance. I was amazed to see how fluidly he moved. The whole group continued to belt out the bhajans with even more energy than before. While the dance was going on, I got up and moved outside the temple to a place where I could watch him dance and also see the bright canopy of stars in the moonless night sky. Outside the temple I could see the river moving silently, revealing its winding form in the reflected starlight. The music from the temple pulsated as the sound of the bhajans, drums, and clapping reverberated out over the water and onto the opposite shore. Except for the lights and music in the temple, everything for miles around was black and silent. On the opposite shore, however, I could see a single campfire, and imagined what magic the bhajans must be creating for the lonely camper who stoked its flames. I thought about the simple way in which the villagers lived, and wondered about their uncomplicated and happy way of life. "They know how to live, and they sure know how to throw a party!" I thought.

The next morning Gandhiji suggested that he, another fellow named Jayasen, and I go for a boat ride. It was about 11:00 a.m. as the three of us got into the boat. The boatman took up his long pole and we began to *glide silently across the river. The day was heating up. The temperature was already above 90 degrees. I dragged my hand in the cool current of the river and watched a child swimming downstream. "A swim in the river would be refreshing right now," I thought.* As we neared the opposite shore, Gandhiji announced, "Jim, you can get out of the boat now and go talk to that western man who is camping in the temple ruins. I need to talk to Jayasen in private." Without saying anything, I stood up and moved carefully to the bow of the boat as it moved onto the sandy shore. I jumped onto the shore, then turned around and gave the bow an energetic push, sending the boat back out into the river.

"What is Gandhiji up to?" I was thinking as I walked up towards the temple ruins. I could see the rubble of the ancient temple ahead. The blond western man was sitting on a rock eating a piece of fruit. He was about six-feet tall, with longish hair. He was in cut-off shorts, and wore no shirt or shoes. "Hello there," I said as I approached. "Hello," the man responded. "My name is Jim, I'm staying with the group on the other side at the temple complex." The man smiled and said, "I'm Eric." I could tell that he had an accent, but I could not place it. Eric simply sat there smiling and looking at me. I continued, "You have picked an interesting place to camp out!" "Yes, I like it here, it's very peaceful," Eric said. I was looking around to find signs of supplies, camping gear, a tent possibly, a backpack, anything that might buffer the obvious discomfort of camping out in such a rocky, craggy place. "Uh . . . you don't have much baggage with you!" I said. "No, I try to travel light. I have all of my things in this daypack," he responded. I looked at the bag near his feet. It was a very small daypack, the kind students use for school. "You do travel light!" I said. "How long have you been in India?" I asked. "About two years," Eric said, "I started out with a backpack, traveling on trains, staying in ashrams, but then I found that I did not need so many things, so I began discarding more and more things. Now I have a smaller load to carry, and I am much happier."

I spent the next half-hour talking to Eric about his travels and about his lifestyle. I was in awe of the utter simplicity and lack of clutter in his life. He had come from Sweden and had spent the last two years traveling throughout India. When he started out he stayed in ashrams, but he had also become accustomed to camping out whenever he was traveling in rural areas. The thing that struck me was that in spite of the austerity of his life, he was a bright light. He seemed happy, at peace with himself, and fully self-sufficient. He had one pair of sandals, one shirt, a pair of shorts, a small cooking pot and a container for water. That was it! He had put the principle of aprarigrah into direct practice in his life and was living a life free of worry and strain. He slept under the stars, bathed in the river, and let God take care of the rest. "What a life!" I thought.

Back in the boat, I excitedly described my discovery to Gandhiji and Jayasen. Gandhiji said, "Yes, he is a very spiritual man. Too much baggage in life weighs a man down and holds him back. Mahatma Gandhi understood this too. His motto was, 'Simple living, high thinking!' This is the way to live." I sat back in the boat and began thinking about my own cluttered life. As we pulled up to the boat landing, I could see three small children playing joyfully in the water as their mother washed the family laundry in the river. I noticed the bright smiles on their shining faces as they splashed and shouted. Even the mother seemed to take great pleasure in the simple act of living. As she laughed and joked with her kids, I thought about the simple way of life that I had witnessed here in Siddhavarkoot. I thought about the villagers singing bhajans the previous evening, and about Eric and his minimalistic way of traveling. "I've gotta get a smaller suitcase!" I thought. As I looked up, I saw Gandhiji looking at me. He was nodding and laughing!

Chapter Two

The Law of Karma

Jyotish is much more than a simple divination system. It is a great vidya (spiritual science), which is deeply imbedded in a profound philosophy of life. The study of Jyotish, therefore, requires an understanding of eastern philosophy, especially the law of karma, which is the underlying mechanism upon which astrology rests. The law of karma is also the foundation of the eastern concept of spiritual development. Properly understood, it provides the astrologer with a necessary context for explaining the cause of suffering, and more importantly, the mechanism by which suffering can be eradicated.

When asked to explain the term, karma, most people explain it this way, "as you sow, so shall you reap." Although this a good departure point for discussing karma, it does not go far enough in explaining the intricacies of karmic bondage, nor does it show how karmic impressions can be eradicated. In fact, a superficial understanding of karmic law as mere cause and effect, leaves one with the erroneous idea that the whole point of the theory of karma is to do good and avoid doing evil. Actually, nothing could be farther from the truth! Yet most people persist in thinking that doing good will eventually bring them enlightenment, union with God, and ultimate freedom from suffering. This is not to say that doing good and avoiding evil is without benefit. In fact, virtuous conduct is very beneficial, because it results in good health, prosperity, and other favorable circumstances. Similarly, wrong action brings ill health, poverty and other miserable conditions. Doing good and avoiding evil is, therefore, the only intelligent choice. Unfortunately, this approach alone does not solve the problem of how to get rid of karma and gain enlightenment. It only gives a means to have a more comfortable and enjoyable life in this world or the next. This point can be understood more clearly by first understanding the way in which karmic impressions are incurred, how they cause bondage, and also how they are shed.

The most fundamental spiritual principle is the transcendent self. Most people identify with their bodies, minds, and egos. The real self, however, is unbounded, un-manifest, and pure consciousness. The condition which causes people to suffer through life thinking that they are bound and limited by physical, emotional, and psychological conditions, rather than living a life of freedom and bliss, is called bondage. Bondage is the result of the soul's association with karmic impressions, incurred through various thoughts, words, and deeds in the past.

Each person has several levels to his individuality. On the surface, there is a physical body. On an invisible level, however, there is also a subtle, karmic body called the causal body, which holds karmic impressions. The causal body incurs karmic bondage in the following way:

1. *Influx* – The individualized consciousness or self is constantly generating various passions such as anger, pride, deceit, and greed. Each new passion or desire is characterized by a distinct vibratory quality that creates an impression in the causal body. Each karmic impression carries the same vibratory signature as the passion, desire, or thought from which it originated. The constant process of creating new impressions in the causal body we will call influx.

2. *Bondage* – When a karmic impression stays in the causal body, it is called bondage. Each karmic impression carries the quality of the state of consciousness that produced it. If, for example, the karma was generated by an experience of overwhelming greed, then the impression will be colored by greed. If, on the other hand, the karmic impression was generated by a sentiment of overwhelming generosity, then it will have a positive quality of generosity. In this way, karmic impressions lodge in the causal body, binding the soul in either negative or positive modes. The two general modes of karmic bondage are punya (positive karma) and papa (negative karma). In either case, the result is called bondage, a state of limited perception in which the soul is incapable of realizing its infinite blissful nature.

3. *Outflux* – Each karmic impression is incurred with a certain quality (e.g. greed, a negative impression). Each impression also has a certain intensity (e.g. mild, medium, or intense), which depends on the quality

and intensity of the conscious state which generated the impression. Similarly, each karmic impression also has a life span, or a duration of time during which it will remain in the causal body. When its time is up, then the karmic impression will naturally be released and will exit the karmic body. As it exits, it causes the soul to vibrate in a way that is similar to the quality of consciousness which caused the karmic impression in the first place. If the karmic impression was initially incurred by an experience of greed, then an experience related to greed will result at the time the impression is released. The problem here is that if the feeling of greed overshadows the person, and if he becomes involved in the experience, then he will bind a new impression in the causal body. This sets up a vicious cycle where involvement in the emotions produced by shedding karmas simply causes them to be re-incurred.

The preceding description makes the prospects for eventually getting rid of karmic impressions seem quite dismal. Everything in Vedic philosophy centers on solving this karmic dilemma. It is karma that binds the soul to ignorance, suffering, and limitation. It is karma which dupes the consciousness into forgetting that it is infinite and blissful. This sorry state of affairs can be likened to a mirror that is covered with dust. The sun shines brightly in the sky illuminating everything with radiant omnipresent light, yet the mirror, which is covered with dust, fails to reflect the infinite sunlight. If there could be some way to remove the dust, then the mirror would be able to realize its unlimited potential to reflect the sunlight. Similarly, the soul, shrouded in karmic impressions, fails to realize its potential to reflect the transcendent light of pure consciousness. If there could be a way to get rid of karmic impressions, then eventually the soul would realize its true nature as unbounded energy and bliss.

Doing Good Doesn't Get Rid Of Karma!

Karma has two varieties, punya (positive) and papa (negative). Similarly, karmic bondage also comes in two types, positive and negative. Bondage by karmic impressions that are predominantly negative causes the person to experience a life of pain and misery. Karmic bondage that is predominantly positive brings wealth, intelligence, good health, pleasure, and other experiences which are generally cherished. Of the two, any intelligent person will obviously choose to create positive karma over negative karma. After all, doing good karma will ultimately produce desirable life experiences. It is the great key to temporal happiness. As you sow, so shall you reap! This, of course, is the way most of us think. In fact, many people base their entire approach to spirituality on this principle of doing good in order to attract good experiences and avoiding evil in order to avoid suffering. The only problem with this idea, of course, is that it does absolutely nothing to address the problem of getting rid of karma. Doing good only causes us to incur positive karmic impressions (punya), which results in a positive state of bondage later on. In other words, through lifetimes devoted exclusively to doing good, we succeed only in insuring that in the future we will be reborn in chains of gold rather than chains of iron. Unfortunately, a person can be just as ignorant of his unbounded nature when living in a mansion as when living on a dung heap!

The Key To The Karmic Riddle

The sages who revealed the Vedas had deep and practical wisdom. They knew that no lasting happiness could be gained by simply adopting an approach to life which placed primary importance on doing good action. They recognized that even the results of good karma would eventually fade. After being born into a life of good health, affluence, and comfort, a person eventually becomes ill, suffers, and dies. Although the sages encouraged virtuous conduct as a means for producing a happy, healthy, and prosperous life, they recognized that the ultimate solution to the karmic dilemma had to be found elsewhere. They knew that a real solution had to provide a means to eliminate the cause of bondage altogether. It is for this purpose that the Vedas and all their supportive texts were written. Every word of every manuscript was intended to provide the world with a key to unlock the riddle of karmic bondage. That key is called equanimity.

Equanimity Stops The Influx Of Karma

It was described earlier how the shedding of karmic impressions causes a vibration in the causal body which in turn attracts new karma, resulting in a vicious cycle of karmic bondage. In order to interrupt this cycle, the Vedic rishis recommended the cultivation of equanimity in the mind. Equanimity is a state in which the various positive and negative vibrations of consciousness are stilled. By keeping the mind tranquil at the time of karmic fructification, karma is shed without generating new impressions. The absolute form of equanimity, called samadhi, is the state of total absorption in the absolute stillness of pure consciousness, which is the product of deep meditation. This form of equanimity produces the most profound silence in the mind and results in the most intense shedding of karmas. On a relative level, however, equanimity can also be practiced by keeping the mind relatively detached and tranquil in the midst of difficulty or success. This kind of equanimity can be facilitated in various ways, including the study of astrology, which brings about an intellectual understanding of life experiences against the background of the theory of karma. Of course, the best idea is to approach equanimity from both angles, which is why the ancient sages recommended that the studies of philosophy and astrology be grounded in the regular practice of meditation. The result of this two-fold approach is that the mind quickly becomes more serene and the cycle of karmic bondage is inevitably broken. The person is more able to remain calm, neutral, and happy, in the midst of the ups and downs of life. As a result, karma leaves and is not replaced with new karma. Eventually the karma that overshadows self-awareness is completely exhausted and enlightenment dawns.

Fate vs. Free Will: Three Types of Karma

There are three types of karma. The total pool of karma that has been stored up from all past actions is called sanchita karma. The portion of karma that has been set in motion and which is scheduled to be shed in this lifetime is called prarabdha karma. It is the prarabdha karma that is reflected in the horoscope. The astrological chart is a map of prarabdha karma. It not only shows the particular type of prarabdha karma which will manifest, but also provides a schedule for its fructification. The third kind of karma is called kriyamana karma. This is new karma created in this lifetime by our own free will. Our ability to create kriyamana karma (free will) is constantly being offset by the prarabdha karma (fate), which is shedding at any given time.

Three Intensities of Prarabdha Karma

The prarabdha karma that is reflected in the horoscope comes in three varieties, mild, medium, and intense. If the prarabdha karma that is shedding at a particular time is mild, then it will not be able to overpower the person's free will. As a result, he will find it easy to use his free will in order to create a reality of his choosing. If the karma that is shedding is of medium intensity, then the person's free will may be partially blocked. In this case, he will still be able to use his free will to some extent, but will also have to accept some inevitable results of the prarabdha karma. If the karma that is rising is intense, however, inevitable events will result. In the case of intense karma, the person may just have to accept his fate.

The relationship between prarabdha karma (fate) and kriyamana karma (free will) is interactive. It is obvious that our own efforts to improve the quality of life are very important to the overall experience of happiness and progress in life. On the other hand, there are some things in life that just have to be accepted. The great Christian mystic, Saint Frances of Assisi, elegantly summarized the theory of karma in his prayer of serenity. "God grant me the serenity to accept the things I cannot change; the courage to change the things I can; and the wisdom to know the difference."

In the actual practice of Jyotish, it becomes quickly apparent that most of the karma reflected in the average horoscope is either mild or medium in intensity. Truly intense karma is rare. In general, people tend to believe that their problems are much more intractable than is actually the case. A good astrologer can usually reveal for the client areas where his own misunderstandings, doubts or fears inhibit the expression of his full potential. In most cases, a little intelligently directed free will can have a tremendous impact on improving the quality of life.

Jyotish Promotes Equanimity and Enhances Free Will

People go to astrologers for all kinds of reasons. Many go because it is exciting. The thought that an astrologer can tell them all about themselves by looking at their chart is intriguing. This causes astrology to be used like a parlor game, placing it into the category of trivial entertainment. Sometimes, though, even when a person approaches the astrologer out of a desire to be entertained, the astrologer surprises him by revealing some deep insight. This can have the effect of awakening the person's mind to the fact that there is deeper wisdom in life that goes beyond the mechanistic paradigms of western science. It leaves the client with a sense of wonder and awe, and sows the seeds of spiritual interest.

Many people are simply curious to know what will happen to them in the future. They especially want to know when they will get more money, love, prestige and professional success. Sometimes, this sort of person only wants to look at the positive elements of his chart and is afraid of looking at anything negative. The mere thought that a future experience could be uncomfortable or difficult makes him afraid. This has caused many astrologers to give in to the subtle pressure to tell only sweet truths and to make only positive predictions. This approach, of course, simply reinforces the root cause of suffering, which is the person's desire for pleasure and the fear of pain.

Of course, there are also people who approach astrologers with only a desire to know themselves better. They are not afraid of challenging experiences in life because they have already accepted the undeniable fact that life is both positive and negative. They also know that a little astrological insight into a challenging period can sometimes help to transform the period into one of success and empowerment. Although this approach to astrology is less common, it is definitely the highest road. Used this way, astrology becomes the greatest reflective tool. In combination with the practice of meditation, its power to promote spiritual growth is tremendous. Through meditation, the person brings the mind to a state of absolute equanimity, which causes a powerful shedding of karmic impressions. Through understanding the horoscope, the person gains clearer insight into the numerous ways in which his own karmic impressions are scheduled to manifest. This produces both a greater ability to handle life's ups and downs with an even mind and a sense that life is happening according to an overall cosmic plan.

Ironically, once a person stops running after pleasure and avoiding pain, life actually becomes more pleasurable. Similarly, as a person begins to use his horoscope as a tool for self-reflection and spiritual growth rather than as a parlor trick, he begins to be able to actually capitalize on astrological insights in very practical ways. The chart gives insights into how to best actualize one's potentials in career, health, relationship, and other important areas. Besides providing the person with more equanimity, Jyotish also enhances the use of free will, producing greater success and happiness in the practical, material world.

Author's Journal:

Nimitta and the Three Glasses of Milk

People often ask me how astrology works. How do planets influence us? Is it gravity? What makes it possible for the positions of planets in the sky to have anything whatsoever to do with the experiences of individuals on earth?

There are different ways to answer this question. Interestingly, however, the gravitational pull of planets is not one of them. Astrology works on principles that are far more subtle than those which govern the physical universe. In fact, ancient literature suggests that planets may actually radiate a form of subtle energy which affects the human aura. However, there is an explanation which makes it unnecessary to look for a cause and effect relationship between the planets and human life. C.G. Jung called it synchronicity. Jain philosophy calls it crammbadda paryaya, seriated modification. According to this theory, every event in the universe has its own unique moment and is not caused by any external factor. The apparent causes which we usually attribute to these events are called the Nimitta karan, instrumental or coincidental causes. So when we see Mars retrograding through Cancer and predict civil unrest, it isn't because Mars is causing it. Rather, Mars is simply coinciding with the predicted events, symbolizing them.

The word "Nimitta," then, means an omen, a sign of what is to come. If you want to know what is going to happen in the future, look around for signs. If you are good at reading signs, you will be a good predictor. It is really not so esoteric. Before sophisticated meteorological equipment, for example, people used to apply this approach for weather prediction. This is expressed in the familiar quote, "Red sky at night, sailor's delight, red sky in the morning, sailors take warning." Astrology has always been a science of reading omens. In fact, there is an entire branch of Vedic astrology called Nimitta, devoted to this subject exclusively.

Here is an example which will illustrate how Nimitta is actually used in astrology: Once I was invited to dinner, along with two other astrologer friends, by a popular lady-guru in Delhi. Before we sat down to eat, she asked us a question, "Will I return to live in India?" Apparently, she had been residing in the United States for some time and wanted to return to India. She was obviously expecting us to "sing for our supper," so one by one, each of us gave his astrological opinion. While listening to my two friends analyze her horoscope, I scanned the room for any signs that might pertain to the question. The time of an astrological reading is an important moment. Even small, seemingly insignificant things happening at that time, can be very meaningful. Suddenly, while one of my friends was giving his predictions, the guru asked the cook to bring three glasses of milk for the three astrologers. When the milk arrived, there was also a knock at the door. It was the ex-Consul General to India who had come to visit the guru. I had what I needed. When my turn to interpret the chart came, I said, "I don't need to look at your chart. The signs coinciding with this reading suggest that you will return to India in three years." Then I explained my reasons. The three glasses of milk given to the astrologers represented the fulfillment of the question in three years. The ex-Consul General coming to visit clinched the matter. After hearing my comments, the guru commented that the whole reason for asking had been because she was building a big ashram in India. She would not come to reside there permanently until it was finished. It was supposed to be completed in two to three years.

Chapter Three

Signs

In Jyotish, as in other forms of astrology, the ecliptic is divided into twelve equal sections of 30 degrees. These sections are called rashis (signs). As a whole, the zodiac is called the Kalapurusha, the god of time, and each sign represents one of the limbs of the Kalapurusha's body. From this global perspective, the zodiac is seen as a cosmic clock, a visual history of the evolution of the universe.

On the level of individual horoscopes, however, the rashis are used to describe and modify various elements of the individual's personality and disposition towards life. Classical texts categorize the rashis in different ways such as how they rise, their element, their constitutional type, their fertility capacity, and tendency towards motion. Unlike western astrology, the psychological traits of rashis have not been emphasized by ancient authors. This may be due to the cultural context in which ancient Jyotish was practiced. In the past, astrologers may not have been as concerned with describing the personality traits of their clients, as with making accurate predictions about the events in their lives.

In modern, western civilization, however, people are not only interested in accurate predictions, but are also thirsty for psychological insight. They want to understand their personality traits through the symbols provided by the horoscope. Therefore, this text offers a more psychological description of the signs than is usually found in Vedic astrology texts. I hope this will contribute to filling a gap in modern jyotish literature, as well as assist the modern student in making the reading of the horoscope more meaningful to his clients. The following interpretations are modern applications of traits described in classical texts.

Aries

Classical:

Round eyes, popular, spends money, travels, talkative, eats little, likes walking, wise, gets recognition in large groups, bilious, liked by women, few children, angry, courageous, oldest amongst siblings, stingy, problems with relatives.

Interpretation:

Aries is the sign of the self. It is the first sign of the zodiac and so it is related to independence. When the Ascendant, Sun, Moon, or other focal planets are in Aries, life takes on a major theme of self-discovery.

Because Aries is the first sign of the zodiac, Aries people like to be first. They can be aggressive, competitive and even selfish at times, desiring fame, recognition and money. They usually try to be the best at everything. They have strong personal desires and ambitiously work to fulfill them, sometimes putting their own desires above those of friends and family. But their assertive and fiery natures, combined with good planning ability, often contribute to success in the outer world. They have sound ideas and usually do well at science, math, or other technical areas.

Because Aries is a martial sign ruled by Mars, Aries people can be fiery and even angry at times. They are forceful, impulsive and bold. Although they usually like physical exercise, Aries people also enjoy activities that mentally challenge them. They tend to be planners and schemers and are willing to take a chance on a new venture or a new idea. Because of their martial natures, their ideas rarely stay in the mental realm. Instead, Aries people are constantly proving themselves by actualizing their plans. In this respect, their impulsive, headstrong natures can sometimes get in the way, causing them to act impatiently, in spite of good advice from others.

Aries people also love things that are artistic or beautiful, so they tend to be attracted to physically beautiful and refined romantic partners. In the relationship department, they are learning to balance their assertive, self-oriented approach to life by adjusting to others. They usually attract partners who have a more developed sense of compromise and relational harmony. Through a little awareness and much trial and error, they can learn to bend, yield, and consider the feelings and desires of others. Partnership teaches them, sometimes the hard way, to move beyond their egocentric tendencies and open their hearts to love. On the positive side, they contribute leadership and direction to their relationships, compensating for their partner's tendencies to be a little indecisive.

On the spiritual level, the self-discovery motif of the Aries person is seen as a search for self-realization. All of the independent, individualistic tendencies ascribed to this sign are really only a reflection of an underlying desire for pure, spiritual awareness. Understanding this clarifies and also validates the Aries "me first" process in life, redefining it as "I am." The self-orientation, which may seem to be selfishness, or even narcissism to others, is actually an integral part of a much deeper search. In fact, for the Aries person, it is the most important part of a unique trial and error process, through which they first strengthen, and ultimately transcend the ego in order to become self-realized.

Taurus

Classical:

Pleasant appearance, good digestion, does well in farming, lucky, prosperous, likes the opposite sex, selfless, works hard, has daughters, attracts lasting friends, ambitious, affectionate, sometimes stubborn, loves pleasure, artistic or musical, noble, charitable, generous, strong, possessive, intuitive, sharp intellect.

Interpretation:

Taurus is the sign of material life. Those born with a strong Taurus theme in the chart will have important lessons to learn about money, possessions, and other material attachments, especially if the Ascendant is Taurus.

Taurus people are earthy. They love the comforts of life. Because Venus rules this sign, they love everything that is beautiful and artistic. They make good artists, musicians and cooks. They are very tactile and sensuous, loving pleasures of all kinds. In fact, even their natural attraction to money is usually related to the comforts that money can provide.

With Taurus, there is always a strong relational tendency. They are usually strongly attracted to the opposite sex and vice-versa. Again, because Venus rules this sign, they are usually good-looking, charming, and have smooth social skills. They attract good, long-lasting friends and tend to be very steadfast in their affections toward others. They are slow to boil, but when angered, they are also slow to forgive. Like all Venusians, Taurus people love harmony and peace in their relationships with others. They usually have fixed ideas and can be quite stubborn at times.

On the spiritual level, people with a Taurus theme are being asked to learn to transcend the material aspect of life. This may sound as if they are supposed to renounce their possessions and go off to a cave to meditate, but this is not the case. Generally speaking, Taurus people are not suited to be monks or nuns. There may be exceptions, of course, but even Taurus monks tend to be very sensuous, love to eat well, become the financial directors of their hermitages, and are constantly struggling with material desires. The idea is that they are being asked to learn about money, possessions, comfort and luxury through direct experience. Simply renouncing the world and going to a monastery will not allow the Taurus person to avoid his inevitable date with the material world. The Taurus person's karma, positive or negative, usually propels him into many confrontations with material life. Taurus people frequently become bankers, merchants, artists, and investment brokers. They usually live comfortable lives, but in some cases they may also go through financial struggles, poverty, or other uncomfortable material situations. This depends on whether positive or negative karmas are dominating the horoscope. Regardless of the quality of their material experience, the lesson is still the same. They are being asked to directly experience the ups and downs of material life in order to gain insight into its purpose and ultimately, to let go of their attachment to it. In the end, the enlightened Taurus person becomes a prime example of being "in the world but not of it."

Gemini

Classical:

Articulate, educated, humorous, fun-loving, enjoys singing and dancing, sexual, voluptuous, fickle, witty, wealthy, good at astrology, charming, versatile, generous, handsome, creative, open-minded, nervous, restless, likes food.

Interpretation:

Gemini is the sign of communications. Those who have Gemini prominent in their charts usually have active, creative minds and are constantly processing information. They have diverse interests, are versatile, and lead very busy lives.

Mercury's rulership of Gemini causes the Gemini-born to be communication and information-oriented. They make good teachers, sales people, high-tech workers, and writers. They are quick learners and are usually able to demonstrate anything they see or hear immediately. Sometimes this gives them the appearance of being experts, or at least knowledgeable in subjects about which they know very little. They are very curious, constantly on the lookout for new information. When they learn something, they immediately communicate or teach it to someone else. They find the whole process of taking in and giving out information tremendously stimulating, and they receive plenty of positive feedback from others who are mesmerized by their cleverness or apparent expertise. However, as Gemini's symbol (twins) would suggest, Geminis are better at mimicking and imitating than they are at truly original thinking.

At their worst, Geminis can be jacks-of-all-trades and masters of none. They can be dilettantes, preferring the excitement of new experiences to the consistent study of a single subject. Their cleverness with communication can cause them to be slippery and manipulative. They also tend to put their eggs in too many baskets, getting strung out and overwhelmed by their many exciting activities.

Because of the synthetic quality of this sign, Geminis are very creative. They are said to be less original and more imitative. They can, however, display a particular style of originality that puts diverse pieces of seemingly disjointed information together into unique and original creative statements. They make great writers, artists and musicians. They usually display their talents at a young age, but sometimes can burn out prematurely in their youth.

In the area of relationships, the changeable quality of Gemini expresses itself. Some astrological writers say that Geminis are fickle. This of course is not always the case and mainly depends on other factors in the horoscope. Actually, Gemini people make charming and affectionate romantic partners. They are usually very sexual, but communication is an indispensable key to their sexuality. They tend to attract spouses who are straightforward, outgoing, and well educated. It is true, however, that Geminis need lots of excitement and change. They are restless and get bored with repetition. Without other stabilizing factors in the chart, they can move from relationship to relationship and tend to marry more than once.

From the spiritual angle as well, Geminis become aware of the self through learning and communicating. As they become more interested in the development of consciousness, they study literature that facilitates the process. They make good astrologers and become eclectic philosophers, usually more inclined to study several philosophies than to go deeply into one. Their inquisitive minds become the tool they use to unfold the deeper layers of consciousness and ultimately transcend the mind altogether. As the mind becomes more subtle, they begin to recognize their intuition at work. They become detached from their clever and eloquent communication process and begin to simply witness it. Communication, errands, and creative projects become objects of meditation. In this way they find God amidst the hustle and bustle of daily life, recognizing the divine presence in the intuitive flow of their unlimited creative activities.

Cancer

Classical:

Intelligent, likes to live near water, cultivates friendships, talkative, has few sons, has many ups and downs, easily influenced by women, wise, scholarly, nervous, restless, talented, charming, diplomatic, gains through travel, difficulties in marriage, close to mother and home, has occult tendencies, good at astrology, interest in music, frugal, industrious, affluent, owns real estate, intuitive, perceptive, sense of justice.

Interpretation:

The motivation towards security is the driving force behind the sign of Cancer. Those who have focal planets in this sign are motivated to create security and stability in every aspect of their lives. They create relationships, homes, families, institutions, and other foundations for the purpose of feeling stable. At the core, however, they are actually seeking a deeper kind of security.

Cancereans are homebodies. In childhood, they experience their mothers, their families, and their homes in terms of care and support. The level of nurturing and care they receive in early life makes an important contribution to their level of happiness and peace of mind later in life. This is true for all signs, but Cancer people are especially sensitive to their environments and particularly attached to their mothers. The watery nature of Cancer makes them intuitive and impressionable. Each impulse from the environment registers within them causing ripples of emotion. As a result, they usually become somewhat dependent on their physical and emotional environment for their peace of mind. Consciously or unconsciously, they spend their lives pursuing relationships, money, and careers, all for the purpose of feeling peace.

In relationships, Cancer people are caring and nurturing. Their own sensitivity and need for security cause them to give support and understanding to others, a quality that often backfires on them when other people become overly dependent. Moreover, Cancerians sometimes feel a distinct sense of responsibility for those close to them and they sometimes develop unhealthy, dependent relationships. On the other hand, Cancer types are quite capable of healthy relationships as well. They are dependable and responsible. They are very intuitive regarding the feelings of others, but often get their own feelings hurt if they sense hostility or criticism. When criticized, they may become defensive, shut down or withdraw altogether. They also find it hard to hide their emotional reactions because most of their feelings register immediately on their faces or in their expressive and sensitive eyes. In all of their relational interactions, however, they are looking for peace and security, so they are oriented towards marriage and family. They like people, have a knack for public relations, and are usually quite social and popular.

In the spiritual realm, Cancer people enjoy the benefit of their watery nature. They are naturally intuitive and sensitive, giving them an edge in this department. Their basic spiritual dilemma boils down to the security issue. Ultimately, Cancers are looking for lasting security and stability, a quality that is unattainable in outer life. Nevertheless, they spend most of their lives trying to find it through various worldly pursuits. They build homes and change their residences, get married and divorced, succeed and fail at careers, all in the pursuit of that elusive sense of peace. As Cancers become more aware, they begin to see that they are chasing a rainbow. They understand that they are depending on things that don't last. They realize that their endless attempts at creating peace have ultimately failed. They begin to look within themselves and focus attention on their own inner consciousness for happiness and security, thereby breaking the grip of their attachment and the cause of their suffering in life.

Leo

Classical:

Proud, determined, fiery temper, mother's favorite, courageous, heroic, victor, violent, enthusiastic, sober, talkative, rich, famous, ambitious, kind, self-employed, finds it hard to serve others, loyal to father, likes sports, popular, respected, calm, good organizer, mountaineer, landlord.

Interpretation:

Ruled by the Sun, Leo is a sign of pride, confidence and self-respect. Leo people are here to express themselves and to get recognition. Because they have a deep sense of their own greatness, they evolve along a channel that enables them to develop positive personality traits like nobility, generosity, and bravery. As a result, they spend their lives trying to express themselves in ways that validate this internal feeling of being magnificent.

Leo people feel they have good reason to think they are great. After all, they are very special people with a divine heritage. The only difference between Leos and the rest of humanity is that Leos have a clear sense of their royal status and the confidence to own up to it, while the rest of the world is more unsure and timid. Leos are born to shine. They are proud, noble and have strong wills. They have character. They also have a flair for the dramatic. They make good actors, musicians, athletes, directors, and leaders of all kinds. They feel the need to be an example, which is appropriate because it is actually part of their purpose in life. In fact, when a Leo is at his best, he is an inspiration to others, reminding them that they are also capable of true greatness.

At their worst, Leos frequently expect to achieve greater things in life than they actually accomplish, which usually results in disappointment. If they have not come to terms with their egos, they may seem egotistical, self-centered, or even obnoxious. They may find it hard to follow instructions given by other people, and may try to dominate their families, classrooms, or social groups. But what some people see in the Leo as an unhealthy egotistical quality, may actually be a simple and positive celebration of personal value, appropriate to the Leo's astrological nature.

In relationships as well, Leos seek to magnify their self-images. They are proud of their own physical appearance and are also impressed by the appearance of others. Initially, this leads them to cultivate friendships with people because they are handsome or beautiful. The same issue is true with personalities. Leos like lively, self-confident and creative people. However, they don't like to share the spotlight even though they like to associate with other charismatic, creative, or beautiful people. Instead they gravitate towards more permanent relationships that revolve around themselves. They like physically attractive romantic partners, and are themselves demonstrative and passionate lovers. They are usually the dominant partner in their relationships, asking for constant attention and admiration from their mates. In return, they are generous, protective, and loyal to a fault.

On the spiritual level, Leo people realize the self by directly confronting their egos. As the sense of self begins to grow, Leos develop stronger and stronger egos. They seek to validate their sense of inner divinity through an endless stream of creative, physical and professional self-expression. This, of course, causes many disappointments in life as they find out directly that self-aggrandizing only leads to alienation and suffering. Eventually, they get the point. They become aware that the ego is only a knot, a constricted or limited expression of the true, transcendent self. They learn to detach and become a witness to the creative dance of the ego, rather than a slave to it.

The enlightened Leo, however, does not become the soft-spoken humble sort of person that we read about in so many books about saints and sages. On the contrary, self-realized Leos become even more outgoing, expressive, and fiery. As a detached witness to their own self-expression, spiritually developed Leos allow the full brightness of this solar sign to shine. They become true spiritual examples. They do not retire into caves, but instead become gurus, acharayas, or avatars, spiritual lights to guide the rest of humanity.

Virgo

Classical:

Learned, discriminating, intelligent, shy, weak, writer, instrumental musician, artist, craftsperson, Vedantist, good memory, happy life, honest, polite, speaks slowly, tends to have more daughters than sons, lives far from the place of birth, benefits from other people's wealth and houses.

Interpretation:

Virgo is the sign of analysis. Along with Gemini, it is ruled by Mercury, the planet of the intellect, so Virgo people display the analytical side of this mental planet.

Virgos are organizers. They love to put things into compartments and boxes. They are neat, meticulous, orderly, and sometimes fussy. Their analytical natures cause them to constantly break things down into parts in order to categorize them. Assisted by good memories, they tend to have an eye for detail and can be a veritable storehouse of facts. This talent can be of great benefit in the professional world where their ability to analyze and remember plays an important role in developing expertise in almost any field. It also gives them a deep understanding of the mechanics of language, helping them to become very articulate speakers or writers. Furthermore, they are very practical and completely capable of applying their knowledge. They make great teachers, researchers, linguists, writers, artists, craftspeople, instrumental musicians, scientists, accountants and experts of any kind. It is no wonder that Virgos become such influential people.

In spite of their versatility and tendency to become accomplished, Virgos do have a negative side. They can be fussy, critical, and demanding. They also tend to worry, a spin-off from their tendency to analyze everything. If they get sick, for example, negative Virgos sometimes fuss and worry about their illnesses to such a degree that they make their problems worse. Since they are constantly running such a high level of mental energy, they also tend to have vulnerable nervous systems. For this reason, it is very important for Virgos to take care of their bodies by regulating their diet, exercise, and rest routines. Otherwise, they are prone towards digestive disorders, constipation, and other problems stemming from worry and excessive mental activity.

In relationships, Virgos are communicators, true to their association with the planet Mercury. Even here they tend to analyze, putting their spouses, friends, and especially themselves, under their intellectual microscopes. This, of course, can be a blessing or a curse. In some cases, spouses complain that their Virgo partners are too analytical and detached, instead of simply expressing their emotions. In other cases, their talent for self-criticism and self-analysis gives them a distinct advantage in emotional relationships. More than most signs, they are able to recognize their faults and communicate with their partners in ways that promote or even deepen marital harmony. In sexuality, an area where Virgos, "the Virgins," usually get off to a late start, they tend to become sensitive and attentive lovers. This is because the sexual relationship is essentially a form of communication, an area of expertise for Virgos. Since Virgos are good at self-analyzing, they are often able to overcome the psychological hang-ups that so often stifle sexual relations. As they get older and their relationship "expertise" develops, they also tend to become more sexually active.

The spiritual orientation of Virgo is usually mental, analytical and service-oriented. They tend to pursue intellectual spiritual paths that emphasize virtue and detachment. Due to the negative nature of their intellects, they sometimes become masters of the process of "Neti Neti," or "not this, not this," where the spiritual reality is discerned through a process of elimination. They may become "karma yogis," growing spiritually through service to others. As with any sign, however, Virgos evolve spiritually according to their natural tendencies. They use the intellect to transcend the intellect. They discriminate and negate in order to find the truth. Along the way, they continue to gain expertise, becoming pundits, philosophers, and theologians. They are praised and admired for their spiritual knowledge, which is frequently mistaken for real wisdom by their admirers. In the end, however, spiritually evolving Virgos are forced to confront the futility of the negative intellect. Trapped and frustrated by the perception that nothing in the phenomenal world, including intellectual knowledge, is worthwhile, they ultimately give up their attachment to the intellect and retreat into the transcendent self, where they are released from the pain of negation, gaining freedom and lasting peace.

Libra

Classical:

Intelligent, soft spoken, peace-loving, balanced, courteous, clean, warm, agreeable, sensual, idealistic, ambitious, politically inclined, good mediator, impartial, just, musical, artistic, skillful, very active, few sons, good merchant, wealthy, comfortable life, has more success in the last part of life, has movable property, does well through partnership, successful in love and marriage, loves to travel.

Interpretation:

Libra is the sign of balance and harmony. Those born with a strong Libra orientation are learning to manifest these qualities in their lives and in the outer world. In the process, they create relationships of all kinds with other people.

Librans are usually charming. They are gentle, soft-spoken, and congenial. Ruled by Venus, they have natural charisma and an ability to inspire people. They love truth, fair play, and can be objective and wise mediators. They love music, art and everything that brings beauty to life. They are sensual, loving, and romantics at heart.

Even though balance and harmony are the central themes for Librans, they can also be very intense, passionate and idealistic to a fault. They usually have an extremely refined sense of beauty and harmony that causes them to perceive a wide gap between the actual, physical world and their idealistic, mental world. They become motivated to express their idealism in the outer world through romance, art, politics, and religion. As a result, Librans get very unbalanced and even fanatical at times. They can become romantics in relationships to the point of losing perspective, sacrificing everything for love. They sometimes become so devoted to political causes that they become ruthless. They can become starving, brooding and passionate artists. As spiritual aspirants, they sometimes become fanatics, leaving everything behind in order to pursue their spiritual ideal. As lofty and romantic as all this seems, however, the intensity and passion of the Libra person is frequently misspent, throwing them off center and actually preventing them from achieving their ideal. The point here is that in spite of having a theme of balance, Librans are frequently out of balance. They are, instead, learning to become balanced by directly experiencing the opposite.

Not all Librans are out of balance. Developed Librans have incredible skill at creating balance, not only in their own lives, but those of others. They are great with people and pursue relationships in order to practice their art. They are natural partners and love to harmonize with a spouse or lover. They are passionate, sensual, loving, and very sensitive to the needs of their spouses. They become influential and charismatic leaders. They gain recognition or even fame for their ability to manifest their ideals in the mundane world.

On the spiritual level, Librans are learning to create heaven on earth, without getting off center. They are willing to go to the extreme for their spiritual goals, but usually learn how to walk the middle path the hard way. There are exceptions to this rule. Ramana Maharshi, one of India's greatest saints, had a Libra lagna. He achieved his spiritual status through extreme renunciation. Yet, in his case, he had rare insight into his true spiritual center, which gave ultimate balance to his life later on. Most Librans, on the other hand, learn through trial and error that extremism sometimes gets in the way of spiritual development. Instead of renouncing the world, they learn to embrace it.

Librans have a relational philosophy. They are constantly creating relationships with others in an attempt to break down the barriers that separate and isolate them. As they develop, their emotional perception becomes more refined. They sometimes become great Bhaktis, following a path of devotional surrender to some aspect of God. Here they form a divine relationship in order to express a higher aspect of emotion. Even in this case, they are motivated by a deep sense of separateness. As the devotional relationship refines and develops through an attitude of surrender, the ego drops away. They become aware that separateness was only a product of the ego. They realize their unity with the divine, and life becomes an expression of supreme wholeness, balance, and harmony.

Scorpio

Classical:

Forceful, impulsive, cruel, sarcastic, sick as a child, respected by king or government, successful in business, traveler, artistic, independent, determined, devoted to mother, interested in occult.

Interpretation:

Scorpio is the sign of transformation, change, and rebirth. Like its counterpart, the eighth house, it is a sign of tremendous energy and power. Those born with Scorpio prominent lead lives of passion and metamorphosis.

Scorpios never have dull lives. They are intense and passionate, so they do not like routine or static conditions. When life begins to stagnate, Scorpios shed their old skins and regenerate themselves. This is not always a conscious process, however. Sometimes they are surprised by the many upheavals and changes in their lives, not realizing that these changes are life's way of breaking them free so that their evolution can continue.

Psychologically, Scorpios have a deep sense of their unconscious minds. Perhaps more than any other sign, they sense the various aspects of their inner power clearly. Their desire to realize and express this inner power, in the form of charisma, sexual energy, or physical prowess, becomes a motivating factor in their lives. They like to make up the rules as they go along because adhering to rules would mean limiting their ability to express their power. They also sense the dark side of their natures and are usually on friendly terms with it. As a result, many Scorpios thrive on taking risks, crossing lines of safety, and experimenting with the forbidden. They are usually very sexual and sometimes enjoy the sense of power that comes from defying conventional sexual taboos. The same is true in business, where Scorpios are sometimes willing to cross norms and ethical boundaries in order to achieve success.

On the other hand, not all Scorpios are so comfortable with the dark side of their natures. Many are afraid of it. Sometimes this takes the form of fears and other troubling emotions. Many Scorpios actively avoid the disturbing psychological effects of television programs or movies that are gruesome, violent, or frightening. It is also true that drugs and alcohol are particularly bad for them.

In their personal relationships Scorpios are charismatic. They like to influence others with their mind, body and emotions. They have deep insights and like the feeling of power that comes when others benefit from them. On the most positive level, they can be motivating forces in the lives of other people, catalyzing change and revolution within them.

On the negative side, they frequently impose themselves on others in the form of friendly advice or subtle manipulation, in which case others resist them. Being so passionate, they frequently suffer in relationships as a result of negative emotions like jealousy, possessiveness, guilt and anger. Nevertheless, their emotional power, combined with tremendous determination and will, can allow Scorpios to channel their passions in very positive directions as well. Positive Scorpios are capable of unmatchable selflessness, devotion, or even heroism.

Because this sign rules sexual energy Scorpios are also very sexual. They sometimes use their sexual energy as a way of influencing other people in order to validate their own sense of power. They like to make their partners feel powerful or supremely potent and sometimes praise them for their sexual attractiveness or prowess. The payoff here is that when Scorpios see their partner's ego swell with pride, they feel their own charisma and attractiveness more deeply. They love to "turn on" others in order to be the source of the other person's peak experience. They also have a unique ability to use their subtle sexual and charismatic energy, outside of their romantic relationships, in order to charm others into fulfilling their personal agendas.

As emotional partners, Scorpios can be intense. They seek profound and connected relationships. At the core, they are passionate, so their relationships and marriages tend to have big highs and lows instead of stability and peace. Sometimes this leads them to dramatic changes, power struggles, divorces, or in extreme cases, domestic violence. They would rather upset a relationship or marriage than become complacent. Yet, herein lies their relationship power. When they approach their relationships with awareness, Scorpios are capable of miraculously infusing them with life and depth. The passionate flow of deep emotional energy becomes an object of meditation, rather than something to be controlled or stifled, bringing profound healing and transformation to their relationships.

As with every sign of the zodiac, the spiritual path of Scorpios matches their natural astrological energy. They are passionate and powerful by nature. To deny or suppress this power would be a mistake. Scorpios learn to confront, experience and channel their power. At some stages of their evolution, this may mean freely exploring the whole range of their sexual or charismatic energies. This can be a painful process, however, like putting your finger in a flame to find out if it is hot. Direct and usually painful experiences force them out of their egos and teach them how to express their emotional-sexual powers in more selfless, life-supporting ways. As their awareness is refined, Scorpios learn to transcend the egocentric quality of emotional, charismatic, and sexual energy. The practice of yoga and meditation frequently enhances this process, facilitating the experience of deeper aspects of consciousness as they awaken and raise the kundalini, the primal spiritual energy which resides at the base of the spine. Here they develop a whole new level of power, spiritual power. Patanjali, in his classic work on yoga called The Yoga Sutras, described various siddhis, or powers, which come to those who are able to access and harness the immense power of the subtle mind. Yet he also described that in the end, even these super-normal powers are not actually spiritual. They are still relative, and therefore are material abilities, having nothing whatsoever to do with true spirituality. This is the ultimate realization of Scorpios. As they progressively refine and evolve their power-nature, they finally confront the uselessness and utter absurdity of the ego's obsession with control and power. They recognize that at every stage of development, even the level of yogic power, they have experienced pain and misery as a result of their egocentric approach to life. In the end, they give up the ego altogether in one final liberating act of sublime metamorphosis, realizing their unity with the divine.

Sagittarius

Classical: (The only one with wholly positive descriptives)
Religious, good speaker, devoted, sharp, strong, warrior, prevails over enemies, charming, intuitive, philosophical, interested in the occult, good predictive abilities, just, humane, active, ambitious, conventional, conservative, sympathetic, honest, wise, cheerful, positive, righteous, integrity, restless, affluent, noble, courageous.

Interpretation:

Sagittarius is the sign of truth, knowledge, freedom and abundance. Many who are born with this sign prominent become devoted to all that extends their understanding of life and allows them to live in accord with universal law. Others devote their lives to the principles of freedom and abundance. They are ruled by Jupiter, the prime benefic, so they generally find solutions to problems easily and tend to succeed in life. They are straightforward, open, honest, gregarious, restless, and love nature.

In their relationships, Sagittarius people are generous and optimistic partners. They frequently bring sound judgment, integrity, foresight, prosperity, knowledge and even luck to a marriage. In fact, at their best they are capable of very successful marriages or relationships, based on all the qualities of virtue and abundance natural to their astrological sign. They also demand the truth, even though they don't always realize it. When their relationship or marriage breaks down, for example, it is sometimes because either they or their partner has failed to be completely honest. Most often, however, the Sagittarius person has no doubts about telling the truth. The problem instead is how to tell it without moralizing, patronizing, or sounding self-righteous. Never intending to be cruel, they sometimes hurt the feelings of their partners, who are frequently less enthusiastic about absolute frankness, preferring a sweet truth or a white lie to the sometimes tactless observations of their Sagittarius mates.

On the intellectual level, Sagittarius people usually seek knowledge in traditional academic institutions, where they are frequently able to achieve high degrees. They gravitate towards professional status, becoming doctors, lawyers, philosophers and other types of knowledgeable experts. They also make great teachers, naturally able to express whatever knowledge they have amassed. In other words, they tend to use whatever expertise and knowledge they have gained to help enrich the lives of others. This process gives them a distinct sense of purpose and elevates their feelings of self-worth.

Those born with Sagittarius prominent are also righteous and virtuous. They love tradition and often follow traditional religious or spiritual paths. This provides them with convenient and time-tested systems of morality and ethics within which they can easily aspire to virtue, truth, justice, integrity, and all that is right and good.

Of course, herein lies the downfall of Sagittarius. On one hand, they derive tremendous benefit from treading a traditional cultural, spiritual or religious path. Adherence to moral and ethical codes brings order to life, promoting health, prosperity, and self-esteem. On the other hand, Sagittarians are often blind to the tremendous ego-payoff imbedded in their practice of virtue and righteousness. The positive sense of self-esteem that comes from the feeling that their beliefs are the "real truth" and that their actions are somehow in accordance with the "real universal principles of conduct" inherent in that truth, becomes an alluring and irresistible drug to the Sagittarians. This can produce a subtle disease of the ego. In its advanced stages, this kind of negative Sagittarius quality can express itself in the form of self-righteousness, intolerance, and rigid adherence to rules. They can become critical and judgmental of others. In many cases, however, they mask their spiritual egotism with an appropriate dose of "token tolerance," managing to avoid any meaningful confrontation of their egos.

On the other hand, the ability to discriminate is also the great strength of this sign. Sagittarius people are constantly separating truth from fiction, right from wrong, and good from evil. This makes them natural philosophers and moralists. They are adept at the path of discrimination, the use of the intellect in the process of spiritual evolution. They develop broad philosophical outlooks and their ability to understand and utilize traditional philosophies allows them to see how their life experiences fit into a deeper, more expansive scheme of life. Their instinctive awareness of the underlying truth, however, makes them rely only on the intellect as a tool for confirming what they intuitively know. More than any other sign, perhaps, Sagittarius people sense that they already possess absolute knowledge and truth. Thus, they are usually ready and willing to stand up for what they believe, vilifying heretics, castigating the unrighteous, and generally criticizing all those who do not share their perception of the truth. Standing up for the truth, or what they believe to be true, is a very important part of the Sagittarius process. Even though it makes them prone to self-righteousness and spiritual egotism, there is no better way for them to actualize what they believe. For the aware Sagittarian, it becomes a way of testing the validity of beliefs by getting their judgments out in the open. This also allows them to watch the ups and downs of the spiritual ego in the process.

Their spiritual path becomes one of progressively unfolding more subtle layers of knowledge in the constant pursuit of inner and absolute truth. They chase a mirage, a shadow of truth in the form of information, rules, tenets, and elaborate explanations. Each belief seems to temporarily resonate with some aspect of deep inner perception. If they are paying attention, however, they notice that their beliefs ultimately fall flat, leaving them unfulfilled. In the end, they are forced to let go of beliefs altogether and directly confront knowledge in its abstract form. It is here that enlightenment dawns as the self-aware Sagittarian realizes his nature as the knower. No longer seeking knowledge, he realizes that pure and absolute knowledge is the nature of his very being.

Capricorn

Classical:

Ambitious, persevering, good stamina, works hard, efficient, learned, logical, progressive, articulate, talented, rational, reserved, fortunate, prosperous, tactful, diplomatic, takes advice well, sexual, devoted to spouse and children, problems in romance, likes poetry, likes travel, likes walking, gloomy, serious, cruel, feels no guilt, discontented, succeeds after struggle.

Interpretation:

Capricorn is the sign of actualization, the ability to bring mental and spiritual aspirations into concrete form. Those born with this sign prominent are hardworking, ambitious, persevering, patient, and usually achieve well in life. They value action and results. They are down to earth, organized, and pragmatic. They frequently get off to a slow start in life, but they begin to shine as they get to middle age. They value status and authority and usually take themselves seriously.

At their worst, Capricorn people can be demanding, cold, stiff, or overly formal. They sometimes take themselves so seriously that they become depressed. They frequently work too hard. They can also become very materialistic, valuing status, recognition and material affluence above all else.

On the emotional and romantic level, Capricorn types are devoted spouses and parents. They bring a down to earth practicality to their relationships that grounds their families, promoting prosperity and security. They love structure and understand the value of patience, hard work, and determination in the process of relationship. This sometimes translates as a constructive willingness to work on a marriage, take advice, or consider criticism. On the other hand, Capricorns can also get stuck in structure and formality. Out of a natural desire to provide security for their families, they can become so devoted to their careers that they may forget, or be unwilling, to attend to the personal or emotional sides of their relationships.

The spiritual approach of Capricorn types is also that of action and work. This can be seen on two levels. For most Capricorns, work means career. Here they thrive on fulfilling their dharma (natural life purpose) through working in a career. Although this may seem far removed from traditional spirituality, it may be the best and in fact the only approach for many Capricorn people. Remember that their natural tendency is to bring their mental and spiritual impulses into the concrete world. Regular, mundane, day-to-day work gives them that opportunity. Consciously or unconsciously, they learn to bridge the gap between spirit and matter, working their way towards a very concrete form of self-actualization. As this process refines, a second type of "work" begins to emerge. Here, the growing inner awareness of evolving Capricorn people motivates them to practice mental or even spiritual disciplines. Turning their hard-working nature inward, they can become mentally strong and spiritually detached. They have a natural understanding of the value of austerity in the process of spiritual development. This, however, can easily get out of hand causing them to forget that excessive austerity can also hinder their progress.

In other words, Capricorns, like those dominated by other signs of the zodiac, remain true to their zodiacal nature to the end. Even as they near the enlightened stage, their process is one of accomplishment and achievement. They want to see practical results of their spirituality expressed through action in the outer world, and they are willing to work very hard on both inner and outer levels to make this a reality. Eventually they realize the utter futility of the effort. They understand that their efforts to achieve, even on the spiritual level, only serve to reinforce the ego. Out of despair and frustration they are forced to give up the struggle and allow the work to be done for them. In this final act of sublimation, they withdraw their claim as the author of their actions and become free. They realize their unmoving, silent nature and finally come to rest, absorbed in the infinite stillness and bliss of pure awareness.

Aquarius

Classical:

Philosophical, sympathetic, helpful, good memory, grateful, charming, independent, interest in science, interest in astrology, kind-hearted, logical, sociable, convincing, stubborn, hard-working, good at handling and benefiting from the money of others, likes flowers and scents, avaricious, ups and downs in life.

Interpretation:

Those born with Aquarius prominent in their charts are progressive thinkers and humanitarians. They are interested in all that is new, scientific, technological, metaphysical, and unconventional. Their minds are capable of understanding abstracts and alternatives, so they are open minded and innovative. They have a strong sense of friendship and community, but maintain a certain detachment and independence. This characteristic, combined with the ability for innovative and progressive thinking, can make the Aquarius person a good leader. They can be selfless and devoted to their friends, families, or societies. They do not like convention, so they sometimes make friends among the eccentric, alternative, or socially outcast. They are champions of the underdog and unpopular causes.

Aquarians can also be very self-critical. They work hard, but sometimes become limited and oppressed by their many responsibilities. They can procrastinate, but once they start they work tirelessly, picking up momentum as they go. Aquarians can also be so open-minded and interested in alternatives that they sometimes become down right flakey. This sometimes leads them to develop extremely eclectic philosophies that have no direction or continuity. As a result, they sometimes find it hard to commit to any particular spiritual path because they can relate to so many.

In relationships and marriage, Aquarius types are devoted, yet independent. They like community, so they enjoy creating families and working for the collective good. They are loyal friends, selfless parents and supportive partners. They enjoy people and like to socialize, yet they can also be impersonal, detached, and cerebral. This cerebral tendency causes some Aquarius types to live in the abstract which can sometimes get in the way of meaningful connection in personal relationships. In some cases, this tendency, along with their openness to alternatives, causes them to have difficulty staying in a single relationship.

On the spiritual level, the Aquarius path seems to be one of progressive relationalism. They have a strong need for community and seek out others with whom they can share their spiritual journey. They are also very open-minded and unwilling to adhere to convention. This presents them with a dilemma because the very nature of groups is to form rules, regulations and conventions. Some Aquarians resolve this dilemma by getting involved with groups that have alternative or unconventional agendas. Others involve themselves with conventional groups and then play the role of the radical or the dissenter, hoping that their group or society will expand as a result. Still others simply pursue offbeat life styles, seeing themselves as different, yet not realizing that they can only be different in relationship to others. Even here, they are using group consciousness as a vehicle for their spiritual development, viewing themselves as pioneers and radical adventurers who somehow lead the rest of humanity a little closer to real freedom. From the Aquarius point of view we are all one, joined karmically at the hip, evolving together and becoming enlightened together. Although they may seem independent or even detached, their philosophy actually has no room for pure isolationism. They seek to actualize themselves through constantly expanding and evolving their sense of collective consciousness.

As the Aquarian sadhana (spiritual practice) refines, their tendency to break the boundaries of conventional thinking becomes increasingly more cerebral and intuitive. They gradually refine their capacity for experimental and abstract thinking to include notions so subtle that even they have a hard time defining them. Some become highly intuitive, getting solutions and insights in flashes. At the end of this process, Aquarians, like their other astrological counterparts, are faced with their own unique spiritual crisis. They inevitably see that treading a path devoted to alternatives and the expansion of conventional boundaries only leaves them in a subtler form of relative bondage. They finally realize that their fascination and attachment to ideas that are new, unique, inventive or exciting only ends in a more refined state of mental agitation. They also realize that their constant need to expand the consciousness of humanity through perceiving dissonance and working for resolution is an endless and ever-restless journey. As a result, they are forced to give up their identification with the spiritual process, replacing it with the ultimate abstraction, pure consciousness, the unbounded ocean of being.

Pisces

Classical:

Intuitive, philosophical, spiritual, devotional, prophetic, affectionate, generous, humanitarian, good-humored, many disappointments, ups and downs in romance, big-hearted, wealthy, likes clothes, attached to spouse, influenced by women, overcomes enemies, earnings connected with water, gets wealth without much effort, grateful, drinks lots of water.

Interpretation:

The Pisces-born run on inspiration. They are idealists in the truest sense of the word. They are romantics, dreamers, travelers and very intuitive.

Pisces people are ruled by Jupiter so they tend to be philosophical. Unlike Sagittarius, the other sign that Jupiter owns, they do not love their philosophy simply for its ability to reveal the truth. They see truth instead as a vehicle which can deliver the ultimate inspiration, so they are sometimes more religious or spiritualistic than purely philosophical. Their perceptions are usually colored by a healthy dose of idealism and inspiration. As a result, they are not long on seeing the stark realities of life. Nevertheless, they make virtuous and inspired devotees of any cause or path.

Ruled by the twelfth sign of the zodiac, which is similar to the twelfth house of the horoscope, Pisces people are introspective and sensitive. They can be shy and sometimes lack self-confidence. They are also frequently disappointed and sometimes do not fully realize their ambitions. This occurs because they are looking for ideal values and life rarely satisfies their expectations completely. But because of their ability to project their creative and inspired mental energy, they often become extremely good at visualizing their goals and manifesting what they see.

Those born under this sign are kind, sensitive and intuitive. They are natural psychics and healers. They are empathic and compassionate. However, they sometimes pick up the negative thoughts and emotions of others unintentionally. If, for example, they hear that someone else is suffering, floundering in an ocean of misery, they tend to want to jump right in and feel miserable with them. This brings total disempowerment for the Pisces. Their lesson is to learn how to empathize rather than sympathize with others. Sympathy in this context means to feel bad when one hears that someone is suffering. Empathy means compassion, which is impersonal and detached. When Pisces people learn to empathize rather than sympathize, they gain real power. They give selflessly to others, healing or helping them without losing their own mental peace. They give themselves permission to remain happy, while helping someone who is suffering. The image is one of remaining in the boat and simply throwing a raft to the drowning man, rather than jumping in the sea and drowning along with him.

In relationships, Pisceans are romantics. They are very emotional. They love the feeling of being in love. However, they frequently feel the other side of the romantic coin-depression, disappointment or even despair. This is the price they pay for their intrinsic attachment to the romantic drug. They learn the hard way that there is no up without a down, no elated high without a low. The aware Pisces person finally realizes that the process of creating personal attachments always falls short of giving them the love and joy they desire. They become disillusioned with personal romance, and begin to seek impersonal or unconditional love in its place. They realize that the ecstasy which they seek does not exist in attachment and fantasy. They become selfless and detached, free from the grip of personalized relationships. Ironically, this actually makes them much more capable of experiencing fulfilling personal relationships.

The spiritual path for the Piscean is one of transcending illusion, fear, doubt, and moodiness in order to experience boundless consciousness and bliss. In order to transcend the imagination they must use the imagination as a vehicle.

They frequently start their journey with a desire to develop virtue. They make real efforts to give selflessly, create pure art, heal the world, or find God. They enjoy the whole process of trying to become the ideal, feeling the sense of gratification that comes with good and virtuous or idealistic conduct. Virtue, after all, has its rewards. When one gives, the world responds in kind. There are subtle, yet tangible rewards for the practice of virtues, such as the gratitude and admiration of others, the attraction of disciples, the feeling of purity and holiness, and the positive self-regard which all this engenders. There is nothing more powerful and attractive than virtue. Yet, it is here that Pisceans meet their deepest obstacle, the illusion of their goodness, the spiritual ego. In fact, many never get beyond the practice of virtue. They build their own private religions to propagate it, becoming psychics, artists, musicians, healers, humanitarians, teachers, or simply devoted parents in order to feel the mood of these various spiritual personas.

The main point is that the desire to be ideal is no less illusory than the desire to be a dark character. In fact there is a whole range of negative personas, with traits such as deception, seduction, and addiction, which are also part of the Pisces repertoire. And even in these cases, Pisces people are looking for a mood, a style, or a sense of self, based on image. Whether positive or negative, virtue or vice, both approaches bind the soul in illusion and ego. And more than most signs, Pisces is prone to the seduction and illusion of the spiritual ego. Of course, one has to act, and there are only two choices—virtue or vice. So, given the choice, virtue is always preferable. But are there only two choices? Actually, there is a third. One can do good karma or bad karma. But one can also do "no karma." Action done from detachment, without an agenda, without subtly identifying with one's persona as a saint or a sinner breaks the vicious cycle of karmic bondage. This "no karma" approach brings a relationship to virtue and vice which is different. Virtue is seen as that action which leads to positive feedback and is therefore the only intelligent choice. Vice is seen as unintelligent action that leads to negative outcomes according to karmic law. So the Pisces person who is pursuing a "no karma" approach gives up his attachment to "being good," and simply prefers good because it is the only intelligent choice. The attachment to being good, holy, intuitive, or spiritual is difficult for Pisceans to release. It is a subtle addiction to the mood produced when they see themselves in these spiritual roles. Like any addiction, it comes along with serious denial, which Pisceans must confront before they can manage to free themselves from the spiritual ego.

This does not mean that Pisceans should try to reject their moods. They actually use inspiration, falling in love, devotion, fears, self-doubts, idealism and all other elated or depressed mental states as their tools. They learn how to maintain a thread of detached self-awareness in the midst of experiencing the swings of their emotions and moods. They begin to realize that the imagination is only a projection of the mind. They start to see that the self is the unchanging screen upon which they project their imagination, thoughts and feelings. But they never lose these mental fluctuations completely. How could they? It is the nature of a Pisces person to have them.

In fact, as they mature spiritually, they begin to realize that the infinite projections of their mind are simply the joyful and creative play of consciousness. Instead of hoping for inspiration and trying to push out depression, they embrace both as equally important parts of life's melodrama. Their hopes and expectations drop away as they experience the mind and its dance as a natural expression of the essentially blissful inner self. Instead of being an instrument of delusion, the mind becomes intuitive, spontaneously expressing reality rather than fantasy. They also realize that they have always been intuitive, but their conditioning and attachments have simply prevented them from seeing it, warping and distorting the natural expression of the mind. They see that imagination and intuition are simply different ways of experiencing consciousness. With imagination, consciousness is filtered through a complex web of wishing and hoping, attachment and aversion. Intuition is an unfiltered, spontaneous expression of an innocent mind with no agenda. Their ultimate transcendence of projection, mood-making, fear, fantasy, and illusion brings them the understanding that they have always been capable of accessing their inner truth. They become aware of the limitless possibilities they have always possessed. Their enlightenment dawns in the realization that they have only attained that which was already there—freedom, bliss, and peace.

Author's Journal:

The Lagna and the Jain Monk

"Rickshaw, rickshaw," the rickshaw driver shouted as we got down from the train near Patna. He was a thin, weathered man, about thirty years of age. He was looking for a customer and we looked like good prospects. My Jain philosophy teacher, Hem Chandji, and I had just arrived at Rajagiri train station after a night spent rocking gently back and forth, listening to the clatter of the tracks below, and nodding in and out of sleep as we traveled from Bhopal to Patna by second class sleeper train. We were on our way to Parasnath, a Jain pilgrimage site, where it is said that eighteen of the twenty-four Jain Tirthankaras (prophets) attained moksha. This particular morning we were breaking our journey to take a side trip to Rajagiri, another Jain pilgrimage site.

"Take us to the Jain Mandir," Hem Chandji told the rickshaw driver. Hem Chandji and I climbed aboard the passenger seat of the rickshaw and the driver hopped onto the seat of the bicycle that powered it, standing up to pedal at first in order to gain momentum. It was a nippy December morning, about 5:00 a.m., and the streets of Rajagiri were relatively empty. I zipped up the collar of my fleece jacket and put my hands in my pockets to get warm. As we rode through the narrow lanes, I noticed signs of life, a man sweeping the dirt outside his house, a woman holding a baby in the doorway of her grass hut. The driver moved to the center of the lane as we passed three women in colorful saris, carrying the day's supply of water in large pots on their heads. The sun was just peaking over the eastern horizon as another day of life began in this little Indian town.

We arrived at the Jain temple, got down from the rickshaw and paid the driver. Hem Chandji led the way. He was looking for a Jain monk named

Jinendra, an old friend who lived in the ashram and managed the temple. We followed a footpath around to the back of the temple complex to the monk's quarters. Hem Chandji found Jinendra's room and we entered. The room was bare, with only a cot, a wooden table with a couple of books on it, and a single chair. On a hook by the door was a white dhoti, one of only two pieces of clothing owned by Jinendra. When we arrived, Jinendra was outside in the communal bathing area, where he was dowsing himself with cold water. I couldn't help but admire his simple, austere way of living. Jainism is known for its adherents practicing what Mahatma Gandhi called "simple living, high thinking." The Jains call it "aprarigrah," or non-attachment. They seek to limit their possessions in order to free the mind for more spiritual pursuits.

When Jinendra entered the room after his bath, he was wrapped in his other white dhoti. I was struck by his beaming smile, as well as the joyful greeting he gave to Hem Chandji as he folded his hands and saluted him with the traditional Jain greeting "Jai Jinendra!" Although still in his mid-thirties, Jinendra seemed to radiate a silence, peace, and serenity far beyond his years. "What a great way to live," I thought to myself, "totally free from the attachments of the world."

Hem Chandji introduced me as an astrologer from the United States, and Jinendra immediately became very interested. He went to the drawer of his table, took out a pen and paper and sketched out his chart. Like many Indians, Jinendra knew enough about his chart to sketch it out correctly without the degrees of the planets. He then asked me to sit down and discuss his chart. Not having the planetary periods available, I used the current transits as a point of departure. I noticed that Jinendra had a Scorpio Ascendant. I said, "Saturn is currently passing through your fourth house where it is opposing your Moon. In the past two years, you might have been feeling some pressure from your community or foundation. You might have felt some frustration in your work here in the temple." I was secretly thinking, "What kind of problems could a monk have? Look at the peaceful life he is leading!" To my surprise, Jinendra said, "Yes! I am the manager of this temple. The community and board of directors of the temple are using political tactics to undermine my authority. This has been going on for exactly two years." Then Jinendra proceeded to fill me in on the complicated political infighting and power struggles, to which he was a part. He was reacting to the challenging transit of Saturn in a style completely consistent with his Scorpio Ascendant.

After discussing Jinendra's chart and making a prediction on when his frustration might abate, we had some chai, while Jinendra and Hem Chandji caught up with each other on their lives. Then Hem Chandji and I made a brief stop to visit the temple and returned to the rickshaw. It was now 9:00 a.m. and the Sun was fully up. I watched as the rickshaw man strained to get the rickshaw going, peddling us slowly into the alleyway and then towards the main road. I took off my fleece jacket and sat back on the rickshaw bench, bracing myself against the seat as we jogged in and out of potholes. I thought about Jinendra and his life. In spite of years of meditation, fasting, austerities, and a general life of renunciation and detachment, he still had moments when he lapsed into the weak side of his astrological patterning. The Ascendant, or Lagna, sets a major theme for life. No matter how evolved we become, we always retain this deep-rooted astrological signature. In the case of a Scorpio Ascendant, power struggles, complicated relationship problems and secret intrigues are typical. Karmas continue to rise. Life continues to challenge us, even if we renounce the world and move to the mountains or to an ashram. "Where then can we retreat?" I thought. At that moment the rickshaw bolted as the driver hit a bigger than average hole in the road, nearly knocking me out of the seat. "Nowhere," I muttered to myself. "The bumps in the road find you no matter where you try to hide. Sometimes all you can do is hang on and try to enjoy the ride!"

Chapter Four

The Planets

There are nine planets in Vedic astrology. They are called grahas in Sanskrit, which means "grasper." It is important to note that the concept of a planet, from a western scientific point of view, or even from the point of view of Western astrology, is very different from that of Jyotish. In India, the grahas are considered to be living beings, deities who possess consciousness and great power. On the surface they all have physical bodies, which are the planets we see in the sky, but this is not the level from which the planets influence us.

Planets, Cause and Effect

Nobody really knows exactly how the planets in the heavens affect human life on earth. Some people think that it is the gravitational pull of planets that influences us. This is not likely, because the actual effect from the gravity of planets on the earth is infinitesimal. It is probably more likely that, if the planets affect us at all, they do so on a much more subtle level. In fact, if you think of a planet as a sentient being, it is easy to understand the possibility of a subtle influence.

Sentient beings, through the various expressions of their consciousness, affect other sentient beings, without the use of their physical bodies. Most people understand that expressing either good or ill will towards someone will have a definite impact. Once, while driving in heavy traffic with my Guru in London, I cut in front of a pedestrian who was walking in the crosswalk. Gandhiji said, "You should be very careful not to cut people off in traffic. You will incur their curses." "A curse?" I thought. Like most westerners, this word had been relegated to the realm of superstition in my mind. What Gandhiji was saying was that all thoughts have an impact, even those momentary thoughts of anger that arise when someone cuts you off in traffic. By being more conscious of how my actions impact the feelings of others, he was telling me that I could avoid the negative influence on my life, caused by negative emotions projected in my direction.

Of course it is not only possible to influence other beings with negative thoughts, you can also direct positive thought energy towards other people with noticeable effects. In 1982, a double blind study was conducted at San Francisco General Hospital on the effects of prayer on patients recovering from heart surgery in the coronary care unit. One group of patients was prayed for regularly and the other was not. The results showed a statistically significant outcome in the group that received prayers, resulting in fewer deaths, shorter recovery time, and fewer side effects.

In a similar, but possibly even more subtle manner, it is quite likely that the noticeable effect of planets on our lives takes place on an etheric level, rather than on the gross physical plane. In this respect, the word "grasper" signifies the planets' ability to hold us in its positive or negative grip from an energetic point of view. The grahas are thought of as deities, gods who have personalities and consciousness. They interact with us and they influence us. In this respect they can be likened to teachers in a high school. Each has a different personality and a different subject to teach. When a student enters the classroom of one of these teachers, his positive or negative experience is determined by two things. First, the personal chemistry between the teacher and the student plays a role in the student's capacity to learn. Second, and most importantly, is the student's ability to surrender his mind to the teaching style of the particular teacher, whether he likes the teacher or not. While it is true that a student might complain that a teacher "has me in his grip!" It is more likely that the student is simply having a hard time absorbing the knowledge that the teacher is offering.

From this perspective, the planets become the dispensers of knowledge and awareness on our gradual journey towards moksha, or spiritual liberation. The problems we have in our interaction with certain planets are not because the planet is bad or negative, anymore than the failing grade received in your sophomore calculus class was because the math teacher was evil. Planets are deities, gods who have the capacity to bless us with strength, good fortune, knowledge, pleasure, and higher awareness. How could any of them be anything but a blessing to our lives!

On the other hand, there is another way of looking at the planets' grasping potential and at the apparent influence of planets on human life. The horoscope is a map of one's karma, which is a collection of impressions lodged in the causal body. These karmic impressions are generated and bound by impulses of attachment in our consciousness. When their time is up, they simply rise and fructify, generating new experiences of pleasure and pain, attraction and aversion. This cycle of karma was explained earlier. From this vantage point, what role do the planets play? In fact, what role do any beings outside of us play?

An example will illustrate the point. Let's say someone comes up to you and insults you. As a result, you become outraged and punch the person in the face, giving him a black eye. In the usual way of thinking, the man says, "You gave me this black eye! You caused me great pain." You respond, "Well, you started it! You insulted me and caused me to get angry!" While these perceptions seem obvious from a common sense point of view, according to the law of karma they do not hold up. The law of karma says that the black eye resulted from the man's own karmas, incurred in the past, which happened to be rising at just the same moment as your fist connected with his eye. Similarly, your anger resulted from the rising of your karmic impressions, and had nothing to do with the man's insults.

How then do we explain the role of outside agencies, like the fist or the man's insults, in producing ups and downs in life? The answer to this question can be understood very clearly in a term the Jains call the Nimitta karan or instrumental cause. According to this perspective, any event can be looked at from many points of view (nayas). From a common point of view, it is true that your fist caused the man's black eye. From a deeper point of view, however, the underlying cause of the black eye is the rising of the man's own karma. In this case, the fist is seen as an instrumental cause, a coincidental event that only apparently caused, but did not really create the black eye.

In the case of planets, their causative effects on people's lives can be seen in the same way. Even though, when seen from a practical point of view, planets may express some sort of subtle influence on human beings, the real cause of ups and downs in life is the fructification of karma. Planets become the Nimitta karan, or instrumental cause, which means that they are merely coincidental to the events of life, giving the illusion that they have us in their grip when in fact they do not. With this in mind, the word, "grasper", may be a term that more correctly describes the planet's symbolic relationship to the person's inner tendency to grasp or be attached. This viewpoint has the effect of placing the primary responsibility for the ups and downs in life on the shoulders of the person himself, thus freeing him from the illusion of being somehow at the mercy of outside forces. Planets do not influence you, nor do they have you in their grip. The only one who influences you is you, and this means that you are also the only one who has the power to change your life for the better.

"Thus, the planets possess a consciousness, have power to act. They have presiding deities whom they obey. They give to the living beings the fruits of their good and bad deeds." (Karapatri, *Sri Visnu Tattva Siddhanta*) Alain Danielou, *The Myths and Gods of India*.

Sun

Classical:

Soul, self, father, will, government, authority, public life, strength, hostility, courage, confidence, leadership, power, glory, fame, honor, respect, influence, kings, self-realization, east.

Physical:

General health and vitality, the body, heart, stomach, bones, right eye. In Ayurveda, the Sun is bilious (pitta).

The Sun represents the self. It is the core of the horoscope. On the deepest level it is the soul, the individualized form of pure consciousness that reincarnates lifetime after lifetime exerting its will toward ultimate liberation. On the outer level, however, it represents the individuality and expresses itself in the form of unique physical and psychological traits, revealing the secrets of the ego, the body, and the personality.

The first and most obvious expression of the Sun is on the physical level. It not only symbolizes the body in general, but also represents the digestive fire which gives energy, heat and vitality to the entire system.

A strong Sun in the chart means a strong body, good vitality and a high level of physical confidence. A weak Sun can suggest poor health, low energy, weak digestion, or a poor physical self-image.

The Sun is also the most fundamental male energy in the chart. It represents the father, our relationship to him, and everything that we receive from him. Inasmuch as the father is a role model, our relationship to him includes learning about our power to act with confidence and create an influence on our environment. For this reason, the Sun is one of the key factors in determining our career tendencies and is also the main astrological symbol of self-esteem.

If you consider some of the classical significations of the Sun, it becomes clear that self-esteem is one of its central themes. Power, glory, respect, and honor are only outer manifestations of a giant sense of self. Here the ego projects itself in attempt to realize its greatness. A strong Sun in the chart means a strong sense that "I am great." Of course, the greatness that one senses is actually an inner quality of consciousness. In an attempt to realize it, the ego sometimes goes out of balance. Attention getting, boasting, and other egotistical qualities can get in the way of success in life and are sometimes a sign of an imbalanced solar energy in the chart. In fact, sometimes this is a way of compensating for a lack of self-esteem, indicated in the chart by a weak or afflicted Sun. A strong sense of personal worth, on the other hand, is a sign of a healthy ego and a balanced Sun in the horoscope. In this case the self-esteem stems from an awareness that everyone shares the same transcendent greatness. It is the realization of this inner reality that is the underlying purpose of the Sun.

No other planet is as important as the Sun. In spite of the fact that most of the techniques of muhurtha, prediction and chart compatibility are based on the Moon, it is only the Sun that occupies the position of greatest importance in Vedic astrology. This is because it represents Agni, primal fire, the inner light of consciousness that illuminates life. It is the Sun's light, which is reflected in each of the numerous planetary combinations in the horoscope. As a result, even the name given to Vedic astrology, Jyotish, means "light."

Sun in Mythology:

Once in ancient times, the demons had conquered heaven. Aditi, the mother of all the gods, prayed to the Lord for help in restoring her children to their rightful abode. As a result of her prayers, she gave birth to Surya, the Sun, who reestablished righteousness in the world, allowing the gods to reclaim heaven.

Surya married Sanjna, the daughter of Vishvakarma, the divine architect. Surya's brilliance, however, was so dazzling that Sanjna couldn't stand it. She desperately needed a break from her husband's heat and brightness, so she devised a plan. Without telling her husband, she created a double of herself from her own shadow. Her double was called Chaya, which means shadow. Then Sanjna went home to her father. When her father saw her he asked her why she had come, but when he found out, he scolded her. Sanjna took the form of a mare and ran off to the north, where she grazed in the pastures there.

In the meantime Surya made love to Chaya, who he mistakenly thought to be his wife. Out of their union, Saturn was born. But after some time, Surya, through his deep intuition, realized that Chaya was not his real wife. He was about to curse her when she broke down and told him the truth about the whole charade. So Surya went to Vishvakarma's house looking for his wife. Vishvakarma told him that she had become a mare and was grazing in the north. Surya then took the form of a horse and went to find Sanjna. When he found her, she was shy at first because she didn't recognize him. When she finally realized that the horse was her husband, they made love and she later gave birth to the Ashwini Kumaras, the gods who rule the first nakshatra of the zodiac. The symbol for Ashwini is the horse's head.

[handwritten note: Is this why Saturn is fallen in Ashwini?]

Moon

Classical:

The mind, renown, mother, women, public, moods, peace, domestic life, receptivity, sociability, friendships, dependency, water, fluids, silver, happiness, white, reputation, middle age, eating, northwest.

Physical:

Body fluids, heart, spleen, belly, face, mind, blood, left eye, emotional disturbances, eating, sleep. In Ayurveda, the Moon is phlegmatic (kapha).

The Moon represents the mind. Just as the Sun is the inner light of the soul, the Moon is the reflector of that inner light in the form of the mind. As a symbol for the mind, the Moon represents the deepest, most fundamental aspect of mental awareness, including emotions, feelings, creativity, imagination, and moods. It indicates receptivity and the capacity to absorb knowledge, so it is a prime factor in determining intelligence level and forming the foundation of the intellect. The Moon represents the generalized, fluid mind, which distinguishes it from Mercury, the planet that signifies the more objective aspects of the intellect, such as logic, analysis and the capacity to deal with abstract thought.

The Moon is also the deepest female archetype in the chart, representing the maternal quality in nature, the Divine Mother. In this capacity, it also represents one's human mother, as well as one's relationships with females in general. It is the mother who cares for us and nurtures us in early life, creating a sense of safety and security. Related to this, the Moon also symbolizes childhood. It shows how secure and safe we feel within, reflecting both the level of psychological stability and the depth and quality of inner peace.

Extending the Moon's receptive and nurturing qualities further, it also becomes a prime factor influencing relationships with people in general. It shows the level and quality of our warmth, as well as the degree of openness and hospitality we extend toward others. It can give great insight into the types of friends we choose, as well as the way our friends respond to us. In this regard, it becomes an important element in determining reputation, popularity, or even fame.

Moon in Mythology:

Once a great rishi named Atri had a great desire to have soma, the nectar of the gods. In ancient times it was not uncommon for great sages to do very intense austerities in order to please the gods and fulfill their desires. In order to have his soma, Atri stood perfectly still, without blinking, with his hands raised to the heavens, and concentrated on soma for three thousand years! As a result, his body became saturated with soma and he levitated into the sky. He became so completely filled with soma that the soma began to spill out his eyes, sending out luminous rays into the heavens. Then the goddesses of the ten directions got together and formed a collective womb, in order to catch the soma. After a short time, the fetus fell out of the womb to the ground and became the Moon. Lord Brahma then took the Moon into the heavens on his chariot.

Path of Light – Introduction to Vedic Astrology

Mars

Classical:

Energy, desire, ambition, independence, brothers, courage, anger, violence, athletic ability, stamina, prowess, virility, scandals, enemies, disagreements, arguments, weapons, mechanical things, technical ability, military, real estate, gold, south.

Physical:

Vitality, energy level, head, bone marrow, bile, blood, muscles, leanness, adrenal glands, accidents, injuries, surgery, burns, inflammations, fevers, acute disorders. In Ayurveda, Mars is bilious (pitta).

Mars is the planet of energy and vitality. It is also a planet of power. Because of its ownership of Scorpio, a sign related to the kundalini, or primary life force, it acts to animate life by providing us with energy and power on every level.

On a purely physical level, Mars represents the general energy and stamina of the body, as well as specific contributing factors such as the adrenal glands, the blood, and the muscles. This is why Mars is a dominant influence in the charts of athletes and others interested in physical fitness.

Mars is also the great energizer of the emotions, playing an important part in our overall emotional vitality and stamina. Through Mars, emotion is projected outward in the form of desire. It is the primary ingredient of our ambitions, aspirations, and passions, and a major reason for taking an interest in life.

As a natural malefic, Mars can also be difficult. The difficulties it brings, however, are not because Mars is bad by nature. On the contrary, like all of the planets, Mars is essentially a celestial influence and, as such, its qualities are inherently divine. In this day and age, however, most people have some "Mars karma" to work through, and are incapable of completely attuning themselves to its finer qualities, especially if Mars is weak or imbalanced (poorly placed) in the horoscope. If Mars is imbalanced in the chart, then desires can be a major source of suffering. An inability to smoothly accomplish desires produces frustration and anger, leading to a wide range of personal and professional problems. Similarly, a weak or badly aspected Mars can sometimes produce a total lack of interest in life as a result of low vitality. In this case, life takes on a quality of inertia, lacking enthusiasm and direction.

Clearly, Mars is a key planet in determining our general level of happiness and fulfillment in life. Learning to "tune in" to Mars means learning to accomplish desires in smooth and life-supporting ways. It also means learning to deal with anger, recognizing that it is simply a result of unfulfilled desires. In this way, reflecting on the placement of Mars in the chart can become a method of spiritual development. As the planet of desire, Mars is at the root of all attachment in life, and learning to deal with attachments and desires is what life's all about!

Mars in Mythology

Once, when the entire world was comprised only of water, because the earth had been submerged below the sea, Brahma, the Creator, woke up from a long sleep. He gave birth to Swayambhuva Manu and his wife Shatarupa. He told them to create, but there was nowhere for them to sit, because there was only water everywhere. Brahma meditated on this dilemma and while he was deeply absorbed, he spontaneously gave birth to a tiny boar (Varaha, the boar avatar) from his nostril. This boar, Varaha, levitated in the air, grew as huge as a mountain, and started snorting and roaring with great power. He sniffed around to smell the earth and located it deep beneath the ocean. Then he plunged deep into the ocean, creating a roaring sound, and lifted the earth up in his jaws.

While he was lifting up the earth, a great demon named Hiranyaksha challenged him saying, "Hey you! You animal! Where have you come from? You pig of a god! You can't succeed without first fighting me." Varaha ignored him and continued bringing the earth up to the surface, where he set her floating again in her rightful place.

The Earth Goddess, of course was very grateful. A mighty hero had saved her and now she was very attracted to him. She approached him for intercourse and the two made love for one year. At the end of the year, the earth was pregnant. She gave birth to Mars, who was later given the status of a planet by Lord Shiva.

Mercury

Classical:

Intellect, discrimination, logic, analysis, speech, linguistic ability, education, mathematics, astrology, communications, publishing, writing, dance, drama, sense of humor, family prosperity, profession, business, trade, north.

Physical:

The mind and its effects on the body, skin, throat, nose, lungs, nervous system, ears. In Ayurveda, Mercury is vata, pitta, and kapha.

Mercury is the planet of the intellect, the logical and rational mind. It is this aspect of our intelligence that organizes and synthesizes thought. This not only gives us the ability to categorize and manipulate our environment, but also allows us to communicate about it.

As the ruler of the sign of Virgo, Mercury is an analyzer. It breaks things into their component parts, putting them into compartments and boxes. In this respect, Mercury represents the part of the intellect which discriminates between various bits of information in the process of discernment. This duality of mind is also the foundation of the ability for critical thinking. At its worst, analytical Mercury can cause us to be fussy and critical, finding fault with everything, and being dissatisfied. On the other hand, the same "negative intellect" can be used to sort out what is the real self from what is not, in a process of spiritual discernment.

On another level, Mercury also rules Gemini, the sign of the logical synthetic mind. Here the intellect functions in a more positive way, putting information together to give birth to completely new ideas. This is what a writer does when he takes separate words and puts them together to create a sentence. It is also what we do every time we speak, paint, dance, write a mathematical equation, or communicate in any other form. In this way, Mercury becomes one of the most important significators in the chart, ruling qualities of intellect that give us the ability to synthesize and communicate ideas and information.

Extending the mercurial qualities of analysis and synthesis to the practical world, Mercury becomes an important significator for some of our most important outer activities. Our interests, hobbies, and the type of education we receive, and even the kinds of careers we pursue are all greatly influenced by its disposition in the horoscope. With a powerful Mercury in the chart, a person becomes a mathematician, a logician, a teacher, a merchant, a writer, a dancer, a musician, an astrologer, or pursues some other occupation that requires a logical, organized mind and the ability to communicate well. A weak Mercury, on the other hand, can make getting ahead in the world quite difficult. In a world where learning, processing and communicating information has become such a dominant feature of life, the mental abilities represented by Mercury have become almost essential for survival.

On the personal level, Mercury's blessing makes life much easier. Since communication is such a fundamental aspect of how we interact with others, Mercury's disposition has a profound impact on relationships. If Mercury is well placed, for example, then communication in marriage tends to be smooth. A badly aspected or poorly placed Mercury will make it very difficult to resolve conflicts, share interests, or even express feelings to your spouse. Of course, this also extends to every other kind of interpersonal relationship as well.

Mercury in Mythology

Brihaspati (Jupiter), the guru of all the gods, had a beautiful wife named Tara. One day Tara went to bathe in the Ganges River. On her way home, Soma, the Moon, saw her and was struck by her incredible beauty. Soma was so intensely attracted to Tara that he completely disregarded her status as the wife of Brihaspati, and tried to seduce her. He said, "Best of women, you are so young and beautiful. It is a cruel twist of fate that you have to waste your voluptuous beauty on such an old and austere fellow like your husband. Your beauty won't last forever, so why not make good use of it while you have it. Come away with me and we will experience sensual pleasures and physical ecstasy."

At first Tara resisted Soma, but he was totally filled with lust for her. He picked her up and carried her off in his chariot. They traveled together to many beautiful places, and constantly made passionate love. When Brihaspati found out about the affair, he repeatedly sent the gods to get back his wife. But each time the Moon refused to give her back. Then Brihaspati personally demanded her return, but Soma told him that Tara was staying with him of her own choice and that he would not give her back.

Eventually, under great pressure, the Moon returned Tara. But by this time she was pregnant, and later she gave birth to a handsome, charming, articulate, and talented child named Mercury. (For further details, see Pushya nakshatra.)

Jupiter

Classical:

Wealth, guru, truth, spiritual path, belief system, philosophy, astrology, reputation, faith, duty, spiritual devotion, teachers, divine grace, wisdom, law, logic, good karma, luck, generosity, respect, husband, children, close friends, mantras, scriptures, northeast.

Physical:

Liver, gall bladder, thighs, knees, spleen, ear, fat, large body. In Ayurveda, Jupiter is phlegmatic (kapha).

Jupiter is the planet of truth and abundance. It is an expansive and benevolent planet that blesses anything it touches in the horoscope by supporting and promoting its significations. As the prime benefic, Jupiter represents everything which brings us more knowledge, prosperity and, ultimately, spiritual wisdom.

On a material level, Jupiter represents prosperity. It is the significator of wealth or money. Its expansive nature encourages us to move toward more and more abundance in life. Although it is the planet of luck, the good fortune represented by Jupiter actually results from positive actions and thoughts done in the past. Jupiter represents a portion of our "good karma" from past lives. Wherever it is placed in the chart becomes an area of potential prosperity or fortune.

Jupiter is also the planet of knowledge. It is intimately linked with academics and education, but usually indicates the higher forms of knowledge. It represents teachers and others who are authorities on various subjects. It also symbolizes professions that require high academic achievement, like medicine and law. Jupiter is a planet of intelligence and creativity, conferring the capacity to grasp broad philosophical principles, and to formulate our belief systems. In this respect, Jupiter represents our relationship to conventions, traditions, and other philosophies received through the family, religion, or society. In other words, anything that contributes to our pursuit of higher knowledge in life is usually related to Jupiter in some way.

The pursuit of knowledge, as symbolized by Jupiter, has a higher form as well. Jupiter represents the quest for ultimate truth along the spiritual path. Its Sanskrit name is Guru, the teacher, so it indicates priests, philosophers, and spiritual teachers of all kinds. Jupiter also represents the enlightened teacher, the one who is capable of leading us to the perception of inner truth. Even the enlightened teacher, however, is only a reflection of our own inner truth, which is what Jupiter really represents. On the highest level, Jupiter shows how we access the truth and the divine grace which naturally flows from that contact. When its deepest value is realized, Jupiter becomes a source of steadfast inner knowledge, which blesses life with freedom and unlimited potential.

Jupiter in Mythology

Jupiter is named Brihaspati, the guru of the gods. He was the son of a great sage, Angiras, who was the son of Brahma, the creator. He instructed and protected the gods, and taught them how to get their share of the soma (divine nectar), by using mantras to drive away their enemies, the asuras.

Brihaspati and Sukra (Venus), who was the guru of the demons, were constantly at odds. Once Sukra went deep into the Himalayas in order to do austerities to Lord Shiva for a thousand years. His purpose was to gain a secret method from Shiva that would enable him to destroy the gods. In the meantime, Indra sent his daughter, Jayanti, to take the method from Sukra by "hook or by crook." She masqueraded as his disciple and, once Venus learned the incantation, she got him to marry her. Venus couldn't say no to Jayanti because she had been such a devoted disciple, and he also agreed to stay sequestered with her as her husband for ten years.

During this time, Brihaspati capitalized on the absence of Sukra by going to the demons, disguised as Sukra. He said, "My dear students, I have returned. Now I will teach you the secret knowledge I learned from all my years of austerity." Naturally, the demons thought he was their teacher, Sukra, and he stayed with them for the entire ten years.

When Sukra came back, of course, he was astonished to find Brihaspati masquerading in his place. He tried to convince his students that he was the real Sukra, but they would not acknowledge him or accept him as their rightful teacher. As a result, Sukra cursed them saying, "You idiots, you don't realize my wisdom when I try to help you. So you will have to be defeated by the gods in a great battle!"

Brihaspati was quite amused that he had tricked Sukra into cursing his own students. He went home, having accomplished his purpose.

Venus

Classical:

Love, sensual pleasure, sex, wife, marriage, enjoyment, comfort, luxury, income, vehicles, charisma, artistic or creative pursuits, poetry, dancing, music, humor, wealth, water sports, beauty, clothing, scents, jewelry, silver, flowers, buying and selling, southeast.

Physical:

Face, eyesight, semen, kidneys, sexual organs, urinary system, tear glands, part of the pancreas. In Ayurveda, Venus is a combination of vata and kapha (phlegmatic and windy).

Venus is the planet of joy, so anything which can be enjoyed comes under its heading. This means that it rules the senses and all of the various pleasures we derive through them. At its deepest level, however, it represents universal love.

On the surface level, Venus represents our capacity to experience pleasure through the senses. Food, entertainment, artistic appreciation, creative ability, and beautiful things of all kinds fall under its domain. Sexual pleasure, for example, is one of its main significations. It not only shows how we experience and express the sensual side of sexuality, but also the entire range of relationship energy. Venus represents the capacity to feel and project romantic love, as well as denotes the emotional and physical attractiveness of the sexual partner.

Romantic love and sexuality, however, are only a part of its relational energy. Venus also represents all types of personal relationships. Friendships, relationships with co-workers, and diplomatic skills are also part of its repertoire. In fact, Venus reflects one of the most fundamental aspects of our personal energy, our capacity to feel love and express love. As we begin to tune in to this quality, we initially express it in terms of a capacity for laughter, charm and grace. People who have a strong Venus in their charts are sociable, have a firm understanding that other people love them, and easily love other people in return. As this capacity reaches maturity, however, it produces an ability to love in a much more expansive way. Here Venus represents universal love, which unites the diverse aspects of life and heals the isolation and loneliness produced by human birth.

Venus in Mythology

Once a great rishi named Bhrigu had a son named Ushana. Ushana became a great sage, and practiced meditation constantly. He was a great devotee of Lord Shiva, and constructed a Shivalinga (a phallic symbol representing Shiva) to which he prayed and performed various rituals constantly. He continued this practice intensely for five thousand years, with the purest desire to have a vision of Shiva. Shiva, however, did not appear to him. This did not stop Ushana, and he kept up his rigorous devotion until he completely conquered his senses and steadied his mind. He gave himself up in complete surrender to Shiva. He also fasted severely, living on nothing but thin air for many years.

After another thousand years went by, Shiva finally relented and appeared to Ushana. He said, "Great Sage, you are devotion itself, ask for any wish and I will grant it." Ushana was completely immersed in his devotion to Shiva and asked only to have his prayers and devotion accepted by Shiva, nothing else. His complete surrender pleased Shiva very much, so Siva gave Ushana the Mrita-Sanjivini, the secret power of raising the dead and restoring life. Siva told Ushana, "While you are alive in a physical body, you will be able to bring the dead back to life. You will also be able to conquer the gods and none will be able to conquer you. You will glow in the sky like a star." After giving this boon, Shiva disappeared, and Ushana turned into the planet Venus. He became the guru of the demons, and gained the knowledge of raising the dead, which came in handy in his various battles with the gods.

Saturn

Classical:

Longevity, death, laziness, obstacles, limitations, misery, perseverance, gaining strength over time, cruelty, iron, downfall, misdirected strength, wood, disease, poverty, work, service to others, servants, bad conduct, study of foreign languages, farming or agriculture, minerals, oil, things buried in the earth, theft, cruelty, malice, old people, west.

Physical:

Legs, feet, nerves, lymph system, chronic diseases, teeth, bones, immune system. In Ayurveda, Saturn is a vata planet.

Saturn is the planet of strength. It is also understood to be the chief indicator of adversity and problems in life. It represents diseases, obstructions, calamities, poverty, resistance, delays, cruelty, frustration, and many other types of suffering. Having acknowledged Saturn's association with difficulties in life, it is important to understand its nature. Like all the other planets, it is an essentially divine entity.

To deny that bad things happen in life would be ridiculous. It is equally obvious from a study of astrology that Saturn is associated with much of what we call suffering. It is a fact, however, that Saturn's purpose in the chart is not to cause misery. Suffering is only the result of a lack of awareness. In fact, Saturn brings equanimity, life's most valuable tool for overcoming unhappiness.

The way this works can be understood through analogy. Think of a bodybuilder lifting a weight. Every day he lifts the weight in a regular routine of exercise. In this process, he has two choices. He can moan and groan about the fact that he has to drag himself out of bed each day at 5 a.m. in order to work out, and complain about the fatigue and sore muscles he experiences after his exercise routine. With this attitude, he could become averse to his weights, dreading the sight of them and eventually quitting his exercise routine.

His other choice can be to tune into the process, accepting and enjoying the feeling of applying his will and his muscular energy to lift the weight. He can feel himself getting stronger day by day. After some time, he can appreciate his increased ability to calmly deal with any physical challenge, due to his well-conditioned body. He begins to look at the weight he lifts, not with disgust, but with attraction. He even delights in being able to increase the weight he lifts, because he knows that this will mean increased strength later on.

In the same way, Saturn is like the body builder's weights. It gives pressures, frustrations, stresses, diseases, and other problems for only one purpose, to bring strength. If we choose to tune into the challenges presented by Saturn, it eventually produces accomplishment, success, steadiness and a definite sense of enjoying the process. If we resist these challenges, however, we reinforce our own weakness, lapsing into a cycle of suffering and limitation. The choice is simple: we either accept and take responsibility for the things Saturn touches in the chart, or we fear and avoid them. Unfortunately, most people in the world today fall into the "fear and avoid" category. As a result, Saturn is usually associated with suffering.

At its best, Saturn represents organizational ability, patience, perseverance and the highest forms of spiritual responsibility. However, a strong Saturn in the chart does not insure happiness. When strong, it can sometimes be out of balance, producing qualities of intense responsibility which cause us to become workaholics or overly austere. If a strong Saturn is balanced, though, it produces real wisdom, born of detachment and equanimity. Once we have tuned in to the challenges presented by Saturn, there is no chance for life to disappoint us. Challenges are overcome through hard work and discipline. Success and adversity are accepted with indifference and life becomes filled with peace.

Saturn in Mythology

Sanjna was the wife of Surya, the Sun. Because of Surya's intense heat and brightness, she needed to get away from him for a while. So she created a duplicate of herself from her shadow. She called the duplicate Chaya, which means shadow. Then she ran off to her father's house. Her father, however, was very annoyed that she had left her husband and scolded her. Sanjna became upset and, taking the form of a mare, ran away to the north to graze in the pastures there.

In the meantime, the Sun made love to Chaya, whom he thought was his wife, and she gave birth to Shani (Saturn). Shani became a great devotee of Lord Krishna. He was always meditating on Krishna and praying to him constantly. When he grew up, Shani got married. His wife was also very spiritual and spent most of her time in prayer and also serving her husband.

One day Shani's wife was feeling very amorous and sexual. She bathed, put on perfume, and dressed in her most beautiful clothes. Then she went to her husband, and with a seductive, passionate tone in her voice said, "Look at me!" Shani, however, was completely absorbed in meditation on Krishna at the time. Normally, he would have been very interested in the sexual advances of his wife, but at that particular moment he was oblivious to anything but Krishna. So he ignored his wife, who was deeply hurt. As a result she cursed him, saying, " You fool. You aren't interested in looking at me, and you don't want to satisfy me! From now on, anything you look at will perish!"

When he came out of meditation, Shani found out what had happened and was very concerned. His wife apologized to him and they made love, but it was too late. The curse had already taken hold. So from that time onward, Shani, who really only wanted to do good for others, kept his eyes down in order to keep from harming anyone.

The destructive power of his glance was realized in full, at the time when Ganesh (the elephant-headed god) was born to Shiva and his consort, Parvati. After the birth a great celebration was held and many guests, including Shani, were invited. The proud mother, Parvati, wanted Shani to see her baby, who was sitting on her lap. Shani, however, insisted that, because of the curse, he should keep his eyes down. Parvati was very insistent, however, and Shani eventually relented, looking straight at the newborn child. Immediately, Ganesh's head disappeared. When Parvati saw this, she fainted. In fact, everyone in Kailash fainted, including Shiva himself. When Mahavishnu saw this, he got on his celestial bird, Garuda and flew off to the north. There he found a herd of elephants and beheaded one of them. He brought the head back and put it on the headless body of Ganesh. Parvati was very relieved.

Then Parvati turned to Shani. Now poor Shani had intended no harm, and was only following the insistent wishes of Parvati. Nevertheless, even though he was obviously very apologetic, Parvati cursed him saying, "You will be a cripple!" Everyone who heard this curse thought it was totally unfair and they all protested. So Brahma intervened and got Parvati to give him a blessing to make up for the curse. She said, "You will become the king of the planets, beloved of God, will live long, and will be a great yogi. You will have deep concentration and total absorption in your meditation on God. My curse will still have to manifest, however, so you will still have some lameness."

Path of Light – Introduction to Vedic Astrology

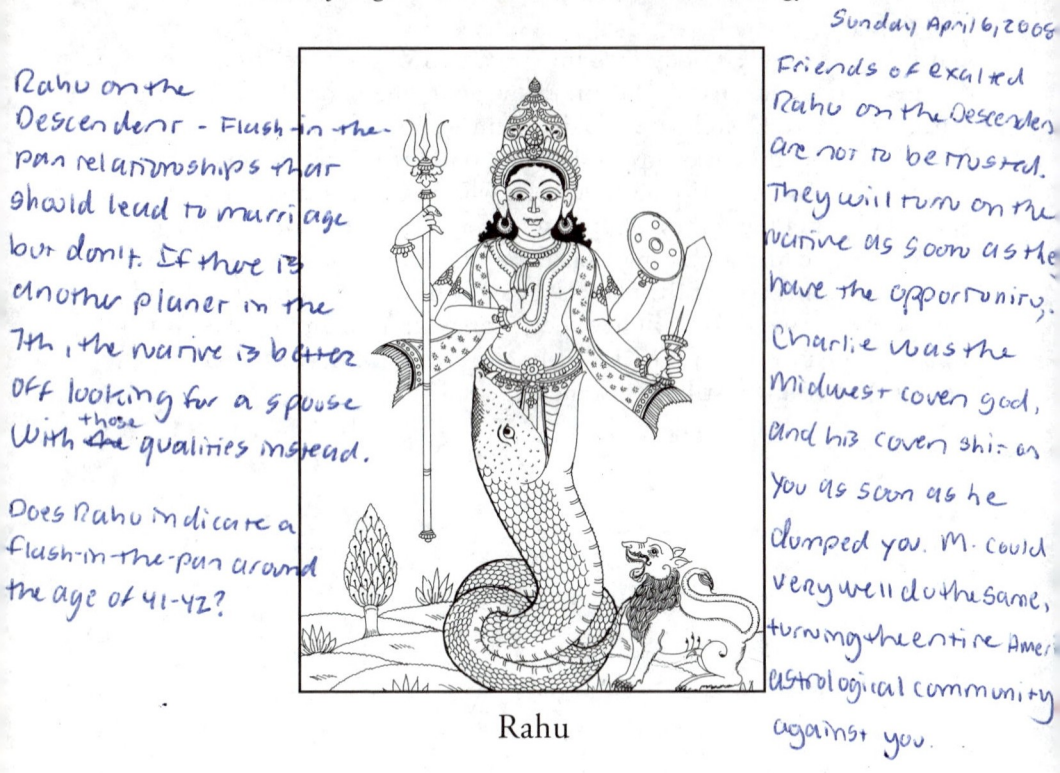

[Handwritten left margin: Rahu on the Descendent - Flash-in-the-pan relationships that should lead to marriage but don't. If there is another planet in the 7th, the native is better off looking for a spouse with those qualities instead.

Does Rahu indicate a flash-in-the-pan around the age of 41-42?]

[Handwritten right margin: Sunday April 6, 2008
Friends of exalted Rahu on the Descendent are not to be trusted. They will turn on the native as soon as they have the opportunity. Charlie was the Midwest coven god, and his coven shit on you as soon as he dumped you. M. could very well do the same, turning the entire American astrological community against you.]

Rahu

Classical:

Paternal grandfather, gambling, outcasts, foreigners, snakes, theft, widows, the unconventional, dream interpretation, astrology, insanity, possession by spirits, unfounded fears, compulsions, perversions, science, southwest.

Physical:

Accidents, hiccups, leprosy, debility, hemorrhoids, chronic boils, ulcers, incurable diseases, poison, snakebites, foot diseases, skin diseases, swellings. In Ayurveda, Rahu is vata.

Rahu represents change and the unexpected. Supposedly Rahu functions like Saturn, bringing adversities to life. Like one of its significations, the black serpent, Rahu is capable of injecting a potent venom. Accidents, acute pains, and incurable diseases all fall under its heading. It also brings an astral awareness, which sometimes results in mental disturbances, including paranoia, neurosis, psychosis, or even possession by spirits.

Rahu is also a symbol of compulsion. It usually gives a sense of urgency about the matters of the house or sign of its placement. In the fourth house, for example, Rahu may create restlessness in one's place of residence as well as a deep desire to own a home. Sometimes these strong desires are insatiable, creating a strong inner yearning for the things represented by the house or sign Rahu occupies. In some houses, such as the tenth, Rahu's compulsiveness can have positive consequences such as fame or accomplishment in the career. Even in this case, however, satisfaction is usually lacking, as the individual restlessly seeks even greater accomplishment and prestige.

As a chaya graha, or shadow planet, Rahu is hard to pin down. Frequently, the problems it brings have strange or uncertain sources. Rahu-type diseases sometimes defy diagnosis or are misdiagnosed. This is usually because the doctor is looking for a biological source, when the actual cause originates from an astral or psychic disturbance. In this situation, the intelligent patient will seek alternative medical care and often experiences better results.

A deeper look at Rahu reveals its more positive side. As an astral influence, it can also bring abstract, inventive and creative ideas to the awareness, resulting in progressive or sometimes even genius-like thinking. In this respect, it represents the unconventional and innovative aspects of life. Classically, Rahu is one of the primary indicators of astrology and the occult. Many modern Vedic astrologers, however, have related it to science, electronics, and cutting-edge technology.

The classics associate Rahu with foreigners and heretics. In modern times the word "heretic" can either mean a person who has a false belief, or a person who has a different belief system from you. Similarly, the word "foreigner" can either bring feelings of fear and mistrust (due to cultural differences) or feelings of interest and enthusiasm (arising from an interest in the new and the unknown). The bottom line is that Rahu acts to open the awareness to influences outside of the ordinary. In the process, it can be an important motivator of personal and spiritual evolution.

Perhaps this is also the key to Rahu's deepest significance. Represented by the mystical symbol of the serpent, Rahu has the capacity to shed an old skin and bring metamorphosis and new birth to life. It brings changes to anything it touches. The restlessness and lack of satisfaction Rahu produces point to areas of life that need spiritual transformation. On the other hand, being a shadow planet, perhaps Rahu's ultimate significance will always remain a mystery.

Ketu

Classical:

Moksha, meditation, divine knowledge, recitation of mantras, observing silence, prediction, fanaticism, philosophy, pilgrimage, salvation, fate, Ayurveda, healers, intuitive perception, renunciation, detachment, providential help, unexpected misfortune, doubt, anger, ambition, black and white magic, maternal grandfather, consumption, begging, pilgrimage, greed, backbiting, disputes, southwest.

Physical:

Hard-to-diagnose diseases, fears, anxiety, psychological disturbances, depression, parasites, viruses, infections, chronic itching and rashes, surgery, accidents, hiccups, incurable diseases, poisons, deafness. In Ayurveda, Ketu is pitta.

Ketu is related to moksha, liberation from karmic bondage. Among the planetary influences, it occupies the place of ultimate release from the karmic impressions, which keep the soul in a constant process of transmigration. As a result, all of the attitudes and practices that lead to moksha also fall within its domain.

Ketu represents spiritual release, and so signifies renunciation. A monk, for example, becomes disappointed with the world and leaves it in search of spiritual freedom. He spends his time in retreat and meditation, reciting mantras or just experiencing silent communion with the Divine. For this reason, mantras, meditation, retreat and deep silence are all prime qualities symbolized by Ketu. Similarly, pilgrimage, which is also an effort to reach a spiritual transcendence, is a Ketu signification.

In spite of Ketu's relationship to spirituality, it is not a benefic in Vedic astrology. Most people have not cultivated "good Ketu karma" in the past. In other words, the everyday person is not usually interested in the idea of letting go of conditions, expectations and worldly attachments. Most people want a comfortable life where their many expectations and needs are easily provided. For these people, Ketu is experienced as a negative influence, since its very nature is to bring dissatisfaction with the material world. This is the reason it can be related to narrow thinking, backbiting, disappointment and even depression. Since Ketu is related to Mars, it is also associated with arguments and disagreements. Ketu is also quite critical. At the most basic level, what Ketu really seeks is perfection and spiritual release, moksha. For those who have no inclination towards enlightenment, Ketu teaches its lessons the hard way, by demonstrating that the material world will always fall short of providing complete fulfillment. The resulting disappointment forces the person to discard, at least to some degree, his dependency on the outer world as a source of inner fulfillment. If he is unwilling to let go, real unhappiness and even depression can result.

Like all malefics in Vedic astrology, Ketu is not bad by nature. It is simply a divine messenger with the capacity to teach us the lessons of detachment and introspection, ultimately leading to spiritual freedom. From this perspective, Ketu can be associated with limitless positive experiences. In the lives of the spiritually-inclined, it functions to provide the deepest fulfillment, through meditation, reflection and the cultivation of an attitude of unconditional surrender to life. Instead of giving misery and suffering, it reveals the opposite, moksha-marga, the internal path towards enlightenment and final liberation.

Rahu and Ketu in Mythology

Once a great Sage named Durvasa, visited Indra, the king of the gods, in heaven. When Durvasa arrived, Indra was seated on a beautiful white elephant, about to leave on a trip. Durvasa went to Indra and offered him a garland of flowers that would never wilt. Indra accepted the garland and put it on his elephant. Unfortunately, the elephant took the garland in his trunk and dropped it on the ground. Then he stepped on it and thoroughly crushed it. As a result, Durvasa became furious and cursed Indra. He said, " It seems that your great wealth has made you too proud. Because of this, you will now lose all the wealth of the three worlds!"

Needless to say, Indra was very shocked and upset, and he even begged the forgiveness of Durvasa, but it was too late. Durvasa said, "I am Durvasa. It is not my nature to forgive." Immediately the goddess of wealth, Lakshmi, disappeared from heaven, which made all the three worlds become impoverished. Of course this made living on earth, heaven or even the underworld, totally unbearable. So the inhabitants of all three worlds got together and went to Brahma, the Creator, to ask for help. Brahma took them to Vishnu, and everyone prayed for his help. Vishnu told them, "When times are difficult, living beings need to rely on each other. If you want Lakshmi to return, and to have a prosperous life again, then you need to drink the amrita, the nectar of life. In order to get the amrita, you should put various plants, medicines, shrubs and vines in the great ocean. There is a huge mountain called Mandarachala. You can use it as a rod for churning the ocean. Use the king of the serpents, Vasuki, as a rope. Suspend the mountain from the rope and rotate the mountain in order to stir the ocean. When you do this, many things will come out of the ocean and you will regain your prosperity."

With Vishnu's encouragement, the gods and the demons joined together and did exactly as Vishnu instructed. As they churned the ocean, using the mountain as a giant churning rod, the first thing that came out was a powerful poison, which began to kill everything in all three worlds. When this happened, all the gods and demons ran, leaving Vasuki, the serpent god, alone to suspend the mountain. In the darkest hour, when all seemed totally hopeless, Lord Shiva displayed his compassion by stepping in and drinking the poison. The poison lodged in his throat, turning it blue. To this day he is called, Neelakantha, the blue-throated lord. He gained victory over death, so he is also called Mahamrityunjaya, the great conqueror of death.

After that, the gods and demons returned and began the churning process again. The next thing to come out of the ocean was Daridra, the older sister of Lakshmi. She is the goddess of misery. She asked the gods how she could help them and they said, "Please go stay in the homes of people who fight with their family members, use foul language, lie, and sleep at the hour of sunset." She agreed.

After braving these initial negative manifestations, the effort of the gods and demons was rewarded and the Moon god came out. The next to come out was Varuni Devi, the goddess of intoxication. Then many other auspicious things continued to come out of the ocean until, finally, Lakshmi herself rose from the ocean. At last, a radiant man with a dark complexion, decked in shimmering gems, and holding a pitcher of amrita, came out. This caused the gods and the demons to fight over the amrita, and the demons grabbed the pitcher and took it to the underworld.

The gods, of course were very disappointed. After all this work, the demons had stolen the amrita for themselves. Vishnu, however, would not allow this to happen. He took the form of Mohini, an enchanting, seductive woman. He went to the demons and danced for them. The demons were so consumed with lust that they became hypnotized by Mohini. She then called in the gods and had them sit in a row on one side, while the demons sat in a row on the other. As she kept the demons mesmerized with the seductive movements of her scantily clad body, she served amrita to each of the gods.

It was at this point, that Rahu, a giant and powerful demon, saw through her ploy and disguised himself as a god, in order to partake in the divine nectar. He sat down between the Sun and the Moon. When his turn came, he began to drink. At that moment, the Sun and the Moon guessed his true identity and immediately told Mohini. She instantly resumed the form of Vishnu and threw a discus at the demon, cutting off his head. The head became Rahu and the tail, or the rest of the severed body, became Ketu. Because of their betrayal, Rahu and Ketu continue to bear a particular grudge against the Sun and the Moon.

Judging the Strength of Planets

In Vedic astrology there are many different angles from which a planet's strength is judged. The most classical approach examines the planet from six points of view and is known as Shadbala. According to this method, the planet's strength is determined according to the following six points:

1. Sthana Bala – Positional Strength
2. Dig Bala – Directional Strength
3. Kala Bala – Temporal Strength
4. Chesta Bala – Motional Strength
5. Naisargika Bala – Inherent Strength
6. Drik Bala – Aspect Strength

Other texts on Vedic astrology have dealt with this system in depth.

Though complex and time consuming, Shadbala is an essential part of any serious study of Vedic astrology. In this book, however, I will simplify the process by suggesting a list that includes various elements of Shadbala.

Planetary Strength or Weakness (Three-Step Assessment)

1. Sign Placement

Each planet, except for the Sun and the Moon, has two signs that it owns, a sign of exaltation, a sign of debilitation and a moolatrikona sign. The Sun and the Moon own only one sign, but also have exaltation, debilitation and moolatrikona signs. These sign placements determine the strength or weakness of each planet.

Own Sign

When a planet is placed in the sign it owns it is strong. This means that it functions in its most natural way. This is similar to a person living in his own house; he feels most at home there and is willing to simply be himself. Similarly, a planet in its own sign radiates its most natural and comfortable energy.

Exaltation

When a planet is located in its sign of exaltation it expresses its greatest power. The sign of exaltation is different from the planet's own sign. It is a place where the planet's energy is amplified. This is like a person who is living in the house of a wealthy friend who is giving him the royal treatment, allowing him the run of the house. He may not really be able to totally be himself at the friend's house, but he actually has more advantages and power than being in his own house. Thus, a planet in exaltation radiates an energy that amplifies its significations and brings out its positive qualities. It is also true, however, that exalted planets are not always totally positive. As a matter of fact, they can sometimes contribute to a strong dose of ego. A person with an exalted planet in his chart will usually express that planet's strength to a fault. An exalted Saturn, for example, might make a person very responsible and hard-working. This is no doubt a virtue or strength, yet this can also cause the person to become locked into his sense of responsibility to the point of overworking. Each planet has its own peculiar ego tendencies when it is exalted.

Moolatrikona

Each planet also has a portion of a sign in which it is particularly strong called the moolatrikona. In all cases except for the Moon, the planet's moolatrikona will be a portion of one of it's own signs. The easiest way to understand this is to think of the planet's moolatrikona as a placement in which it is even stronger than its own sign. In the case of the Moon, the moolatrikona sign will be a portion of its sign of exaltation.

Debilitation

A planet in its sign of debilitation is in its weakest place. Here the planet functions with qualities very much unlike, and sometimes even opposite, its inherent nature. This is like a person living in the house of someone who is not only antagonistic towards him, but is also his complete opposite. For example, a patient, methodical and responsible person living in the house of an impulsive, rude and brash person might feel totally inhibited. Since the debilitated planet behaves in a way that is contrary to its nature, difficulties are often experienced with areas naturally symbolized by the planet, as well as the significations of the houses it owns. It is important to note, however, that planets in debilitation are not always bad. In fact, the classical texts often describe the personality qualities given by these planets in glowing terms. This is probably due to the fact that when a planet is debilitated, it does not contribute so much power to the ego. Usually, a person with a debilitated planet in his chart will be relatively free from the kind of ego problems associated with that planet.

Friend's Sign

If a planet is in a sign owned by a friend, it also gains strength. This is like a person who is living in the house of a friend who is sympathetic and supportive. This environment may not be his own natural place, but it is a place where he feels free and easy. In the same way, a planet in a friendly sign thrives and expresses its energy in a positive way.

Enemy's Sign

If a planet is placed in the sign of an enemy, it is weakened. This placement makes the planet uncomfortable, much like a person living in the house of someone who does not like him. In this situation, the person feels inhibited to express himself. He feels antagonized and may even feel threatened. In the same way, a planet located in the sign of an enemy becomes aggravated or restricted.

Table of Sign Strength

Planet	Own Sign	Debilitation	Exaltation	Moolatrikona
Sun	Leo	Libra 10°	Aries 10°	Leo 0°-20°
Moon	Cancer	Scorpio 3°	Taurus 3°	Taurus 4°-20°
Mars	Aries, Scorpio	Cancer 28°	Capricorn 28°	Aries 0°-12°
Mercury	Gemini, Virgo	Pisces 15°	Virgo 15°	Virgo 16°-20°
Jupiter	Sagittarius, Pisces	Capricorn 5°	Cancer 5°	Sagittarius 0°-10°
Venus	Taurus, Libra	Virgo 27°	Pisces 27°	Libra 0°-15°
Saturn	Capricorn, Aquarius	Aries 20°	Libra 20°	Aquarius 0°-20°

Table of Planetary Friendship

Planet	Friend	Enemy	Neutral
Sun	Moon, Mars, Jupiter	Venus, Saturn	Mercury
Moon	Sun, Mercury	None	Mars, Jupiter, Venus, Saturn
Mars	Sun, Moon, Jupiter	Mercury	Venus, Saturn
Mercury	Sun, Venus	Moon	Mars, Jupiter, Saturn
Jupiter	Sun, Moon, Mars	Mercury, Venus	Saturn
Venus	Mercury, Saturn	Sun, Moon	Mars, Jupiter
Saturn	Mercury, Venus	Sun, Moon, Mars	Jupiter

Zero Degrees

When a planet is close to zero degrees it is considered weak. This occurs when a planet is between 0 and 1 degree and also when a planet is between 29 and 30 degrees. As a result of this placement, the planet's energy does not express itself confidently. During the dasha of such a planet, the person often feels that he is not sure where he is headed, and finds it difficult to project himself into the areas of life signified by that planet.

Retrograde Planets

A retrograde planet is one that is apparently moving backward in a sign. This is actually an optical illusion because the planet is really moving in its usual direction. The phenomenon is very much like riding in a car at 40 miles per hour, next to a car that is going 30 miles per hour. Although it is actually going forward, the car next to you seems to be going backwards.

A planet becomes retrograde when it is very close to the earth. As a result, its influence is stronger. This means it gives a stronger dose of its significations. Being extra strong is not always good, however, especially if a planet is malefic. A retrograde Mars, for example, can be more aggressive, violent or angry. Even when the retrograde planet is a benefic and produces its positive significations in a stronger dose, there can sometimes be negative side effects.

A good way to understand the concept of retrograde is by thinking of a retrograde planet as being like a cup that is overflowing. The retrograde planet overflows with its own energy. This may be good in some ways, but it can also be excessive. For example, a retrograde Mercury can be excessively mental and verbal. The problems it produces in a person's life are not because the person has a weak intellect. On the contrary, the problems stem from over-activity of the intellect. Similarly, a retrograde Venus can become excessively sensual; a retrograde Mars can become excessively ambitious, aggressive, angry or violent. In addition, the excessive energy of the planet often causes the person to obsess internally about the significations of the planet. Strength can be good in some cases, but "strength to a fault" can also cause problems.

Vargottama

A planet placed in the same sign in the Navamsha chart as in the Rashi chart is called vargottama. It is said to behave like an exalted planet. Although the term "vargottama" has traditionally been reserved for the Navamsha chart, the vargottama principle can be applied to other divisional charts as well. The vargottama condition is particularly important in the Navamsha chart because the Navamsha chart is used to indicate all areas of life, as well as the area of marriage. When a planet is vargottama in the Navamsha chart, then it can be interpreted as an extra strong placement for the horoscope in general, and will promote the significations of the planet and the houses it rules. An exception to this rule occurs when a planet is vargottama but is also debilitated, indicating a considerably less beneficial effect than other vargottama placements.

2. House Placement

Placed in a Kendra (houses 1, 4, 7, or 10)

If a planet is placed in the angular houses, (first, fourth, seventh, or tenth), it is strengthened, allowing its qualities to manifest fully. This is true for the natural qualities and values signified by the planet, as well as the qualities of the houses owned by the planet.

Placed in a Trine (houses 1, 5 or 9)

If the planet is placed in the first, fifth or ninth house, then it is also strengthened, bringing fortunate experiences relative to what the planet symbolizes and whatever is symbolized by the houses it owns. Please note that the first house is both an angle and a trine house.

Placed in a Dusthana (houses 6, 8, or 12)

The sixth, eighth and twelfth houses are challenging houses. A planet placed in one of these houses is usually weakened. This means that the qualities and values symbolized by the planet are somehow difficult for the person to actualize in his life. It also means that the things symbolized by the houses ruled by the planet may be weakened. This will produce negative results in most cases. However, in the case of the rulers of the sixth, eighth and twelfth houses placed in the sixth, eighth or twelfth houses (other than their own houses) will produce a positive yoga called Vipareeta Raja Yoga. An example of this is the ruler of the twelfth house (losses) placed in the eighth house (upheaval, change, death). The eighth house placement weakens the ruler of the twelfth, thereby weakening the twelfth house. Since the twelfth house signifies a negative value (loss), the outcome is to have fewer losses. This yoga also tends to give the ability to overcome problems generally.

Directional Strength

The houses are each related to certain directions. The first house is east, the fourth house is north, the seventh house is west, and the tenth house is south. Each of the planets has a direction and therefore a house that gives it strength. The house opposite to its place of directional strength will be its place of directional weakness. This measurement is called Dig Bala. The house of strength and weakness for each of the planets is shown below.

Directional Strength

Planet	Directional Strength	Directional Weakness
Sun	10th house	4th house
Moon	4th house	10th house
Mars	10th house	4th house
Mercury	1st house	7th house
Jupiter	1st house	7th house
Venus	4th house	10th house
Saturn	7th house	1st house

3. Association with Other Planets

Conjunct or Aspected by Natural Benefics or Malefics

If a planet is conjunct (placed in the same sign) a natural benefic planet, such as Jupiter or Venus, it is generally strengthened. If, on the other hand, the planet is conjunct a malefic, such as Saturn, Mars, Rahu or Ketu, then the planet, as well as everything it signifies will be weakened. A similar result is produced when the planet receives the aspect of natural benefics or malefics.

Hemmed In Between Benefics or Malefics

If a planet is placed between two natural benefics it is strengthened. This condition is called Shubha Kartari Yoga. If the planet is placed between two natural malefics, it is weakened and is called Papa Kartari Yoga. For example, if Mars is placed in the tenth house, with Venus in the ninth house and Jupiter in the eleventh house, then Mars is hemmed in by benefics, producing good for all of the significations of Mars, such as brothers, ambitions, energy, etc.

Combustion

A planet which is closely conjunct the Sun is combust or burnt up. This is supposed to render the planet weak. In practice, however, this condition does not actually render the planet totally useless. Instead, it seems to give idiosyncratic problems related to the planet. If Venus is combust in the chart of a man, for example, he might have a beautiful wife and be a talented artist. These are not symptoms of Venus' weakness.

On the contrary, they are signs of its strength. On the other hand, the same man may also experience some problems in marital life that make him unable to really enjoy his marriage. He might find his career interfering with the practice of his art and again be unable to fully enjoy his creative gifts. The same sort of idiosyncratic experience will be connected with those things symbolized by the houses ruled by the combust planet.

Planetary War

Except for the Sun and the Moon, if two planets are placed within one degree of each other, they are in the condition called planetary war. This means they are competing for dominance. The winner is the planet with the highest latitude. Planetary war is supposed to render the winner stronger and the loser weaker. This will strengthen or weaken both the natural qualities of the winning or losing planet, as well as the things symbolized by the houses the planet owns.

Author's Journal:

Jupiter's Children

Do you ever think about how astrology first began? The first horoscope certainly was not calculated on a computer. In fact, if the founding fathers of astrology could see how their modern counterparts mechanically produce horoscopes on their laser printers, they would probably roll over in their graves. In ancient times, astrologers were actually astronomers, and they made their calculations directly, by looking up at the heavens. For thousands of years, these ancient seers watched the night sky and grouped the stars into crabs, centaurs, twins, deer and other symbols. They meditated deeply and began to tell the stories of the gods they saw in the heavens. These stories were told and retold down through the ages around campfires, in temples, until finally, some of them were written down.

I was reminded of this story-telling foundation of astrology once when I went camping with three friends at a remote mountain lake in the California Sierras. One of the three, Marc, brought his telescope and was hoping to take advantage of the high visibility caused by the thin mountain atmosphere. We were all looking forward to seeing Jupiter, Saturn, and possibly a few distant galaxies through the telescope, so we only put up a minor fuss when Marc announced that we would have to get up at 3:30 a.m. for the privilege.

And get up we did. By the time we had wiped the sleep away, donned our sneakers, and groaned a few disparaging remarks in Marc's direction, he was ready. He had already zeroed in on Jupiter, set the tracking device on his telescope so that the earth's rotation would not pull it out of the field of view, and was prepared to give us each a peek. I yawned and gently pressed my eye to the telescope. What I saw was a pleasant surprise. Jupiter was shining clearly, as expected, in the center of the field of vision, but around it I could also see eight of its moons. Jupiter, the ruler of progeny, seemed to be surrounded by his children. I was reminded of how important children were to Jupiter in the ancient myths, and how he once even lost his balance over the infidelity of his wife and her illegitimate child.

As the story goes, Jupiter, the preceptor of the gods, had a very beautiful wife named Tara. One day she was out walking when she came to the Moon's house. When the Moon saw her, he fell in love with her immediately. Tara also fell in love with the Moon and decided to move in with him. When Jupiter found out that Tara was with the Moon, he sent his disciples to bring Tara back, but Tara refused. Jupiter sent his disciples back several times, but each time they returned without Tara. Even when Jupiter went personally and tried to convince Tara to return, she would not come back to him.

This caused Jupiter to become very angry. He called the Moon, "The Brahman killer, gold thief, drunkard, he who marries another's wife." He also told the Moon that he was not fit to reside in the abode of the gods. "Unless you return my wife," Jupiter said, " I will curse you!" The Moon was not impressed and did not give in. He told Jupiter that Tara had come to him on her own and would leave him when she was no longer satisfied. This made Jupiter furious, so he went to Indra (the king of the gods) and asked him to help. Indra agreed and ended up going to war with the Moon.

Eventually, Brahma the Creator intervened and convinced the Moon to return Tara to Jupiter. By this time, however, Tara was pregnant, and later gave birth to the beautiful, articulate, and charming child, Mercury. Of course, Jupiter is the significator of children in astrology, and he was particularly infatuated with Mercury. He convinced himself that Mercury was his own child and tried to convince the Moon as well. But the Moon also loved the golden-colored child. This resulted in the world's first custody battle, with Jupiter and the Moon arguing over who was the real father of Mercury. They demanded that Tara name the real father. Tara would not, because Mercury was illegitimate. Finally Brahma (the Creator) questioned her and she confessed that the Moon was Mercury's real father.

As I continued to scan Jupiter's periphery for hints of another moon, I couldn't help but think of the wisdom of the ancient sages who intuited this story and those of other planets and constellations. These stories are part of a living mythology, linked personally to each of us through our horoscopes. They are not only stories of lust, greed, jealousy, and hatred, but also stories of courage, equanimity, compassion and enlightenment. They are stories about human foibles and virtues, meant for telling around campfires and for sharing with our children. I sat back from the telescope. The full Moon *was reflecting off the mountain peaks and its cool light was dancing gently on the mirror-calm alpine lake. I felt intoxicated, expanded, hypnotized by some ancient storyteller. "Maybe this is how it all started," I thought, "in campsites like this, on nights like this."*

Chapter Five

Houses

Just as signs are a way of dividing the heavens into twelve sections, houses are a way of dividing the horoscope into twelve sections, representing twelve compartments of life. There are literally dozens of house systems, and astrologers do not always agree on which is the best. The basic idea of house division begins with the ascendant, the exact degree of the zodiac that is on the eastern horizon at the time of birth. This degree marks the first house. In western astrology, most house systems take this degree to be the beginning of the first house. In the Vedic system, the ascendant degree is usually taken as the midpoint of the first house. From here the rest of the zodiac is divided into twelve sections or houses. It is also at this point that the debate over which house system is correct begins. This is because you can conceptualize the zodiac in many ways, and each makes sense from its own point of view. Instead of comparing and contrasting all of these house systems, however, I will simply describe two important ways of dividing the chart into houses.

Signs Equal Houses

Probably the easiest and the most flexible way of dividing the chart into houses is to simply take the sign in which the ascendant falls as the first house, regardless of which particular degree is on the horison. Then take the next sign as the second house, the next as the third house, and so on. If 10 degrees of Cancer is rising, for example, all 30 degrees of Cancer is taken as the first house, all 30 degrees of Leo (the next sign after Cancer) is taken as the second house. All 30 degrees of Virgo is taken as the third house. This sequence continues through Gemini, the twelfth house. This method is probably the most commonly used because it is so quick and easy. Usually, the first chart a Vedic astrologer examines is divided this way. It is called the rashi (sign) chart.

House – Sign Overlays

For example, if the ascending degree is 10 degrees of Cancer, then the sign of Cancer occupies the first house. The sign is a particular grouping

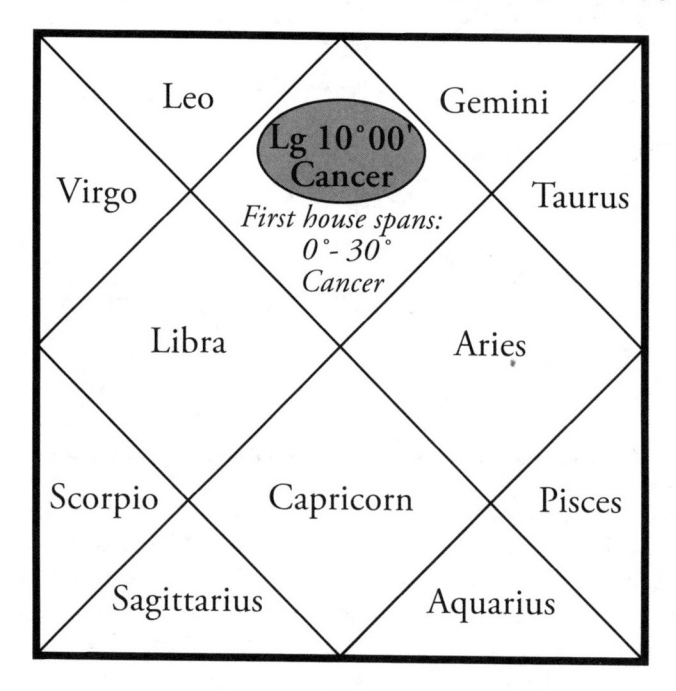

	Leo		Gemini	
Virgo		Lg 10°00' Cancer		Taurus
		First house spans: 0°- 30° Cancer		
	Libra		Aries	
	Scorpio		Capricorn	Pisces
		Sagittarius	Aquarius	

of stars, which happen to fill in that space. A house is simply a division of space, relative to a particular location and time. So the sign actually fills in the house like water filling up an empty cup. Since we are going to be using a system in which the sign is taken as equivalent to the house, we will simply say that, in this example, Cancer is the first house. All of the other signs fall sequentially in the eleven remaining houses. In other words, Leo will be the second house. Virgo will be the third house and so on. Signs follow a natural sequence in the sky. The ascendant simply marks a particular sign in the natural sequence as the first house. The following signs fill in the rest of the houses sequentially.

Just to be sure that this point is clear, let's take another example. If the ascending degree is 25 degrees of Libra, then Libra is the sign that occupies the first house. So we say Libra is the first house. The next sign

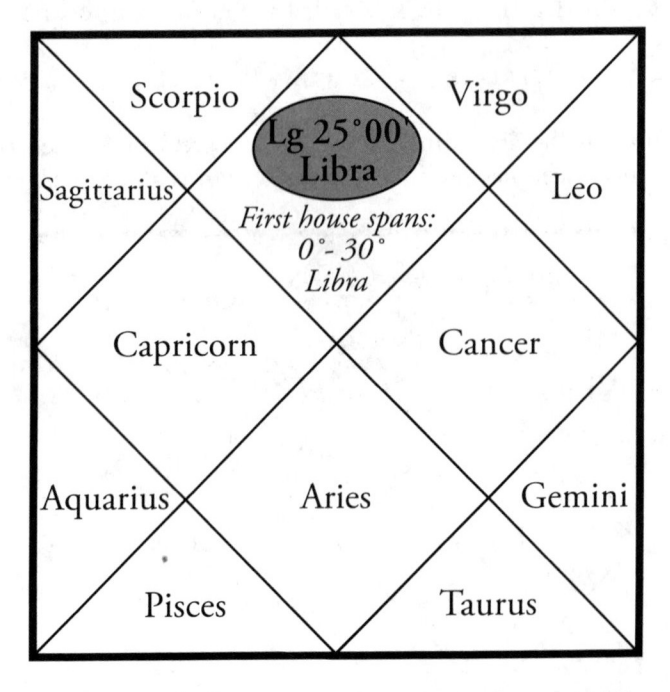

```
                Scorpio              Virgo
                          Lg 25°00'
                            Libra
        Sagittarius                         Leo
                        First house spans:
                              0°- 30°
                               Libra
              Capricorn            Cancer


        Aquarius           Aries           Gemini


                 Pisces              Taurus
```

to Libra in sequence is Scorpio, so Scorpio is the second house. The third house is Sagittarius. The fourth house is Capricorn, etc. Notice that the sequence is the same but the houses start from Libra, the ascendant. In the first example, the houses progress as follows: Cancer, Leo, Virgo, Libra, etc. In the second example, the houses start from Libra, then Scorpio, Sagittarius, Capricorn, etc. Depending on the rising sign or the ascendant, each chart has a different overlay of signs in houses.

Midpoint – Equal House

In this system of house division, the ascending degree becomes more important. It is taken as the midpoint of the house and the edges of the house are taken as 15 degrees on either side. If for example, 10 degrees of Cancer is the ascendant, then the first house will extend from 15 degrees in front to 15 degrees behind 10 degrees of Cancer. In other words,

Lg 10°00' Cancer

First house spans: 25° Gemini - 25° Cancer

All subsequent houses follow suit; 10° of the next sign becomes the midpoint of the next house

the first house will extend from 25 degrees of Gemini to 25 degrees of Cancer, (remember, there are 30 degrees in each sign) with 10 degrees of Cancer as the center, or most powerful point. This method is intended to be used in association with the rashi chart mentioned above. It can help the astrologer fine-tune the house placements of planets in order to reveal more detail. A chart divided this way is called a bhava (house) chart.

Many astrologers use both types of charts. In order to keep things uncomplicated, we will use only the rashi (sign) chart. A point to remember, however, is that just because the rashi chart is simple and easy, doesn't mean that it is sloppy and inaccurate. In fact, many Indian astrologers use the sign chart, without the support of a bhava (house) chart and sometimes even without divisional charts, and get very accurate results. Each astrologer has to decide for himself which combination of charts to use. The main one, however, will always be the sign chart.

House Rulers

Each house has a ruler. The ruler of a house is the planet that rules the sign which happens to fall in that house. If, for example, the ascendant is Sagittarius, then the planet that rules the sixth house is Venus. This occurs because the first house will be Sagittarius and, counting sequentially, the sixth house will be Taurus. Since Venus rules Taurus, it becomes the ruler of the sixth house.

Table of House Rulers

House	Ari	Tau	Gem	Can	Leo	Vir	Lib	Sco	Sag	Cap	Aqu	Pis
1	Mar	Ven	Mer	Moo	Sun	Mer	Ven	Mar	Jup	Sat	Sat	Jup
2	Ven	Mer	Moo	Sun	Mer	Ven	Mar	Jup	Sat	Sat	Jup	Mar
3	Mer	Moo	Sun	Mer	Ven	Mar	Jup	Sat	Sat	Jup	Mar	Ven
4	Moo	Sun	Mer	Ven	Mar	Jup	Sat	Sat	Jup	Mar	Ven	Mer
5	Sun	Mer	Ven	Mar	Jup	Sat	Sat	Jup	Mar	Ven	Mer	Moo
6	Mer	Ven	Mar	Jup	Sat	Sat	Jup	Mar	Ven	Mer	Moo	Sun
7	Ven	Mar	Jup	Sat	Sat	Jup	Mar	Ven	Mer	Moo	Sun	Mer
8	Mar	Jup	Sat	Sat	Jup	Mar	Ven	Mer	Moo	Sun	Mer	Ven
9	Jup	Sat	Sat	Jup	Mar	Ven	Mer	Moo	Sun	Mer	Ven	Mar
10	Sat	Sat	Jup	Mar	Ven	Mer	Moo	Sun	Mer	Ven	Mar	Jup
11	Sat	Jup	Mar	Ven	Mer	Moo	Sun	Mer	Ven	Mar	Jup	Sat
12	Jup	Mar	Ven	Mer	Moo	Sun	Mer	Ven	Mar	Jup	Sat	Sat

Houses and the Four Aims of Life

The karmic impressions, which are mapped out in the horoscope, exist in the form of vibration. On a psychological level, we can say that these impressions are simply desires of one sort or another that overshadow the soul, giving us the illusion of being limited. In Jyotish, we group and describe the karmas in various ways. One way is according to four aims of life (broad categories of desires), which are considered worthwhile. Along these lines, the houses are grouped into dharma, artha, kama and moksha houses.

Dharma Houses (1, 5, 9)

Dharma is defined in many ways. The most popular meaning is probably "purpose." It is the purpose for which you were born. Unfortunately, most of us in the West have defined dharma as the job we were meant to do as a profession. This is undoubtedly partially due to watching too much television, where the hero or heroine proclaims, "I know I was born for some great purpose!" It is very common for a client to ask a Vedic astrologer "What's my dharma?" Everyone wants to feel that he has some great work to do in the world. Everyone wants to be able to say that he has fulfilled some important role in life. Unfortunately, not everyone was born to lead an army, heal the sick, or to be the President. In any case, dharma is not synonymous with one's profession.

Dharma in its pure form is an attribute of consciousness. It is abstract, pure purposefulness, the very nature of consciousness. Real dharma needs no great action to validate it. It is self-fulfilling, self-validating. As dharma expresses through the individual personality, however, it takes different outer forms, according to the karmic patterns in the individual chart. So expressed dharma is different for each person, comprising the totality of actions that are natural expressions of the personality. Being in your dharma means acting according to your wiring, so doing the dishes, mowing the lawn, or even taking out the garbage can be just as dharmic as the so called "mission from God."

The dharma houses in the chart show the particular avenues through which dharma expresses itself. Although, in one respect, the total horoscope reflects the individual's dharma, there are also certain houses which show how the attribute of dharma awakens in the consciousness. Planets, which fall in dharma houses, via their natural significations and rulerships, show the kinds of activities and involvements that promote the growth of purposefulness in the life. Similarly, the rulers of houses 1, 5, and 9, by virtue of their house placement, show areas of life through which the person actualizes dharma.

Another word that can be used to describe dharma is integrity. Dharma houses reflect a certain sense of what is true, right, fair, real, and just. The first house shows physical integrity. All sense of purpose is rooted in the awareness of self. The physical body is the first experience of self. Physical integrity in terms of health and vitality is a primary expression of dharma. Similarly, the character traits as well as the level of self-confidence signified by the first house are fundamental ways in which dharma is expressed.

The fifth house shows mental integrity, the righteous and creative use of the intellect. The fifth house shows how the person rises to a more purposeful level of life through using his mind. This is also the house of children, which gives the person a link to a collective dharma of preserving the species.

The ninth house shows the highest, most evolved form of dharma in terms of higher spiritual truth. Here the person seeks wisdom. This is the house of higher education, where the person first begins to reflect on the broader philosophies of life. This is the also the house of the guru, the spiritual teacher, who leads the soul to higher knowledge. It is the house of beliefs and religion. It is the highest of the dharma houses and is called the house of dharma.

Artha Houses (2, 6, 10)

Artha usually means wealth. In the context of Jyotish, it is probably more appropriate to think of artha as sustenance. The most basic signification of the second house is the mouth. As a result, the second house is related to food. It also signifies the money we use to purchase food. The sixth house is a higher octave of the second, in the sense that it represents service to others, a more complex and purposeful way of getting food or sustenance.

The tenth house elevates this value to its highest level and makes the process of obtaining sustenance a vocation. Being the ninth house from the second, the tenth house is a dharma houses relative to the second house. As a result it carries the food-getting process to its highest level, giving it a higher purpose.

Kama Houses (3, 7, 11)

Kama means desire. Kama houses promote the fulfillment of various desires. They are also houses that are intimately linked to our relationships with other people.

The third house signifies basic communication skills and siblings. Our siblings are our first and most basic relationships. The individualized ego, which is a product of the first house, for the first time encounters others through the third house, in the form of brothers and sisters. Relationships formed through this house are fairly rudimentary, mostly pertaining to exchange of information. Desires encountered here generally relate to the many bits and pieces of information we process daily, as well as the many simple activities we perform in the process of moving closer to our desires.

The seventh house takes relationship to a higher level. Being the fifth from the third, our relationships become more purposeful, focusing on one other person. Here we partner with others in business or find a romantic partner. Desires we experience through the seventh house are also more complex, mostly involving other people. Sexual desire, desire for mutual business goals, as well as the desire for harmony in various types of relationships, are all indicative of this house.

The eleventh house brings our relational development to its highest point. Here we move beyond the idea of having a single partner, and expand our relationships to include groups, society, community, and even humanity at large. Desires experienced through this house are similarly more far-reaching. Whereas the third house reflects the simple desires that drive our basic daily activities, the eleventh house signifies our higher visions and life goals. Being the ninth house from the third, the eleventh house gives our desires a certain purposefulness. This is also why the eleventh house signifies the fruits of our desires, and our ability to reach our goals in general.

Moksha Houses (4, 8, 12)

Moksha means liberation. It is the state of consciousness that results when all the karmic impressions have been released and the soul experiences freedom and unbounded bliss. The moksha houses are spiritual houses. They signify different octaves of consciousness in the process of spiritual evolution.

The fourth house signifies the mother, the home, peace of mind, and happiness. Here the mind seeks peace, repose, comfort and security. The spiritual process of this house is at its peak when the mind is at rest, like a still lake.

The eighth house, on the other hand, stirs things up. The evolutionary process never lets things stay in a state of equilibrium, but always acts to upset the status quo. So the eighth house is that aspect of the spiritual nature which causes upheaval, change, and evolution. Usually this process is painful. Like a butterfly coming out of a cocoon or a woman giving birth, the eighth house has a gut-wrenching side to the transformation it produces. This is due to the fact that the eighth house represents the area of the mind that houses our papa karma, our sins from past lives. This is the area of the mind that psychologists probe, hoping to uncover some dark secret that is at the basis of our suffering. This house also signifies the kundalini, the fundamental shakti or spiritual energy which is symbolized by a coiled serpent at the base of the spine. No wonder that the eighth house, once activated, can unleash limitless transformational power.

The twelfth house is actually called the house of moksha. It represents the highest aspect of spiritual freedom. It is the culmination of the spiritual process. The basic property of this house is to dissolve boundaries. In this respect, the twelfth house is the house of unbounded awareness. Here the individualized ego loses its boundaries and merges with infinite, transcendent bliss. Again, being the ninth house from the fourth, the twelfth house shows a higher purposefulness in the spiritual process. The tranquil consciousness represented by the fourth house goes through a metamorphosis and change in the eighth house, and attains final liberation in the twelfth house.

Kendra Houses (1, 4, 7, 10)

The kendra houses, the first, fourth, seventh and tenth, are called angular houses or the angles of the horoscope. Planets placed here are strong. They have the tendency to produce noticeable qualities in the personality and noticeable events in a person's life. They stand out in the horoscope. A planet placed here generally strengthens the house it rules as well.

Natural benefics placed in kendras generally protect the person and soften the personality. Natural malefics placed in kendras tend to produce more negative personality traits and also promote discontent.

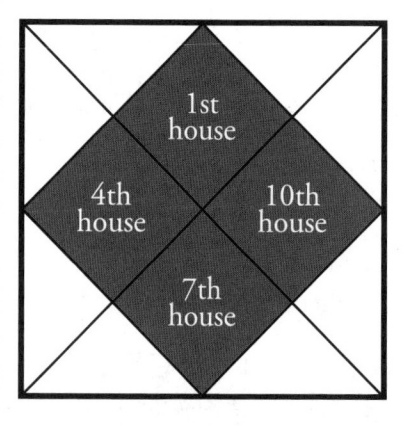

The tenth house is the most powerful kendra. Planets in the tenth will become conduits of action, propelling the person into noticeable vocational and avocational directions. The seventh, fourth, and first houses have progressively less capacity to produce externalized events in life.

Kona Houses (1, 5, 9)

The first, fifth, and ninth houses are kona houses. Sometimes called trikonas, these are houses of luck, good karma, and beneficence. Planets placed here tend to prosper, thrive and produce beneficial results. Similarly the houses ruled by planets placed in konas will thrive and prosper as well.

The strongest of the kona houses is the ninth house. This is the house of abundance, wealth, dharma, and the guru. It is a house of ultimate benefit. The fifth house follows in level of beneficial energy, being the house of purvapunya or good karma. Both the fifth house and the ninth house have a quality that seems like good luck. This is because both are related to good karmas coming from the past and easily produce beneficial results.

The first house is both a kendra and a kona. It is the cornerstone of the horoscope and has special significance as a result. Even though it is the weakest of the kendras and konas, this does not mean that it is a less significant house. As a kona, it simply has less of the power attribute that enables konas to produce outward results. As a trikona house, it has less of the luck and prosperity attribute that goes with konas. On the other hand, being both a kendra and a trikona house, the first house has the benefit of both, and becomes more significant than any other house in the horoscope. Planets placed here will have the most important impact on a person's life by directly affecting the individual's personality, health and general life experiences.

Dusthana Houses (6, 8, 12)

Sometimes called trik houses meaning "three," these houses represent difficulties, challenges, and suffering. Planets placed in dusthana houses usually go through problems. Similarly the houses ruled by planets placed in dusthana houses usually suffer in some way.

The sixth house is a house of enemies, disease, disputes, struggles, and effort. The eighth house is a house of upheaval, change, metamorphosis, and even death. The twelfth house is a house of losses, disappointment and dissolution. A planet placed in one of these houses suffers according to the characteristics of the particular house. For example, Venus, the significator of marriage, placed in the eighth house might suggest that the person's marriage could go through upheaval and change.

All three dusthanas, on the other hand, also have a positive side. The sixth house is connected to health and service. The eighth house is connected to metamorphosis and personal growth. The twelfth is a house of introspection, reflection and spiritual freedom. Using the same example of Venus in the eighth house, the person might go through upheaval and change in his relationship, which causes him to go to a marriage counselor and gain insights that regenerate the marriage. So there are methods for working with dusthanas that bring about positive results. The process, though, is usually painful, regardless of the end result.

Minor Dusthana Houses (3, 11)

The third house is the eighth house from the eighth house, so it carries some of the qualities of the eighth. It tends to produce changes, although less pronounced than the eighth house. The eleventh house is the sixth from the sixth and also the twelfth from the twelfth, so it also produces problems at times. It is a secondary health house, so malefics here can produce health problems at times. Neither of these houses is as potent in producing problems as the sixth, eighth, or twelfth houses.

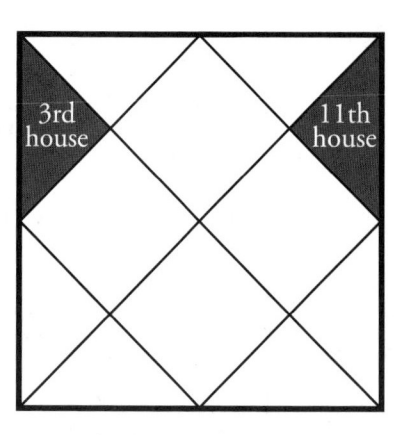

Upachaya Houses (3, 6, 10, 11)

Upachaya means growing or improving. These houses promote the growth and improvement of the significations of planets placed in them. This process takes place over time. When a planet is placed in an upachaya house it will give minimum of positive results early in life. In the case of the third house and the sixth house, there may be some negative results related to the planet's significations in early life. As time goes on, however, the significations of the planet grow stronger and more beneficial, allowing the person to realize the planet's best results in later life.

Orientation to the North Indian Chart

There are several chart styles used in India. Each style has its advantages and disadvantages. In this book the North Indian chart style will be used.

The first step in orienting to any horoscope, is to locate the Ascendant or lagna. In the North Indian chart the lagna, and therefore the first house, is located in the upper central diamond as shown in the example. Each of the other houses follows sequentially, counter clockwise.

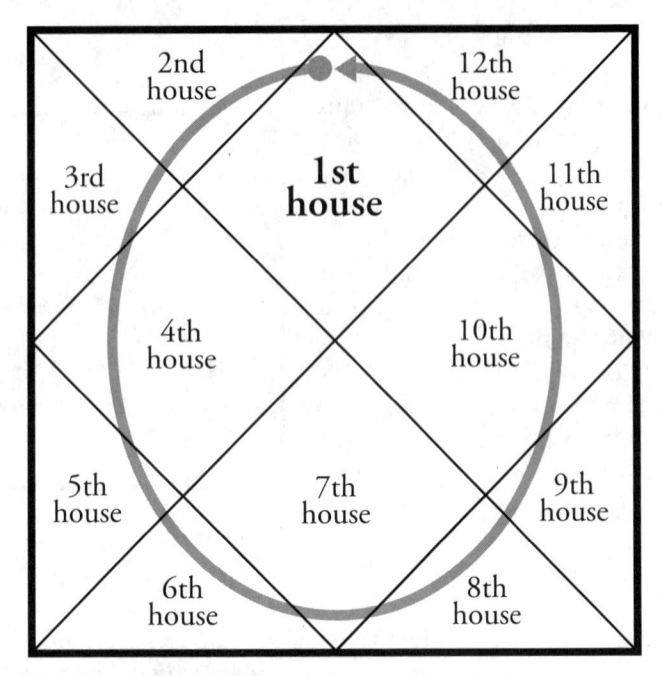

```
            2nd              12th
            house            house
   3rd                              11th
   house      1st                   house
              house
              4th        10th
              house      house
   5th       7th              9th
   house     house            house
            6th        8th
            house      house
```

The Numbers Represent Signs, Not Houses

In the North Indian chart form, the houses are always in the same place. The signs will fall in different places depending on which sign is the Ascendant. Since the houses are always in the same place, this makes the North India chart is very easy to use for the purpose of locating houses. There is no need to identify the houses by any symbol or number, because each of the twelve houses is always stationary. We use numbers, then, to identify the signs (not the houses). One of the most common mistakes that students make when beginning to work with the North Indian chart style is to assume the numbers in the chart indicate the houses, and not the signs. This can be avoided by simply practicing locating the houses of the chart using a blank chart. After becoming comfortable with the location of each of the houses using a blank chart, practice identifying the signs by their sequential numbers, starting from Aries. The signs are given here according to their number.

1. Aries
2. Taurus
3. Gemini
4. Cancer
5. Leo

6. Virgo
7. Libra
8. Scorpio
9. Sagittarius
10. Capricorn
11. Aquarius
12. Pisces

Putting the Signs in the Houses

The number that corresponds to the lagna sign goes in the first house. For example, if Gemini, the third sign of the zodiac, is the lagna, then the number "3" goes in the first house. The second house will then be occupied by the sign of Cancer, so number "4" goes in the second house. The following houses will each be occupied by the next signs in their natural order. The example chart illustrates the layout for the Gemini lagna.

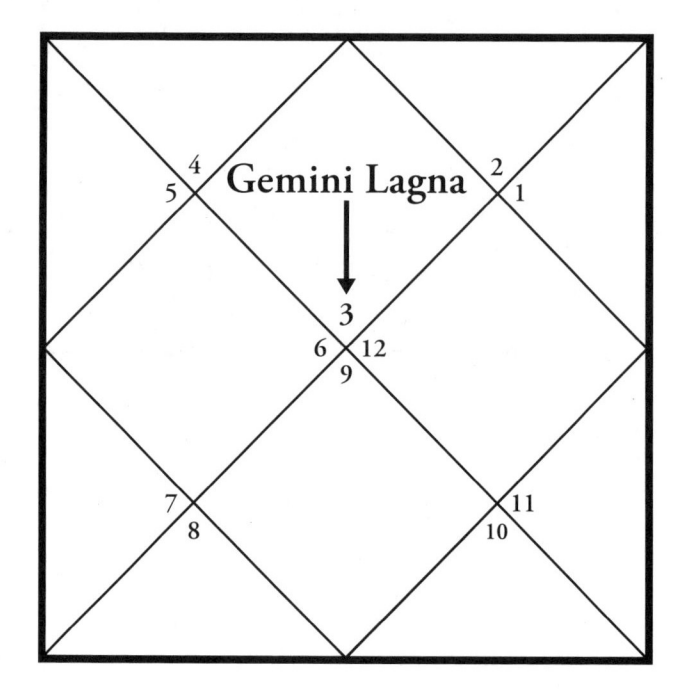

Putting the Planets in the Signs

The planets are each located in a particular degree and sign on the date and time of birth. If the planet Venus is located at 26 degrees of Libra, then it will be shown in the chart in the house that is identified by the number "7" (sign of Libra). The number of degrees (26) will be indicated along with the abbreviation or glyph for the planet Venus.

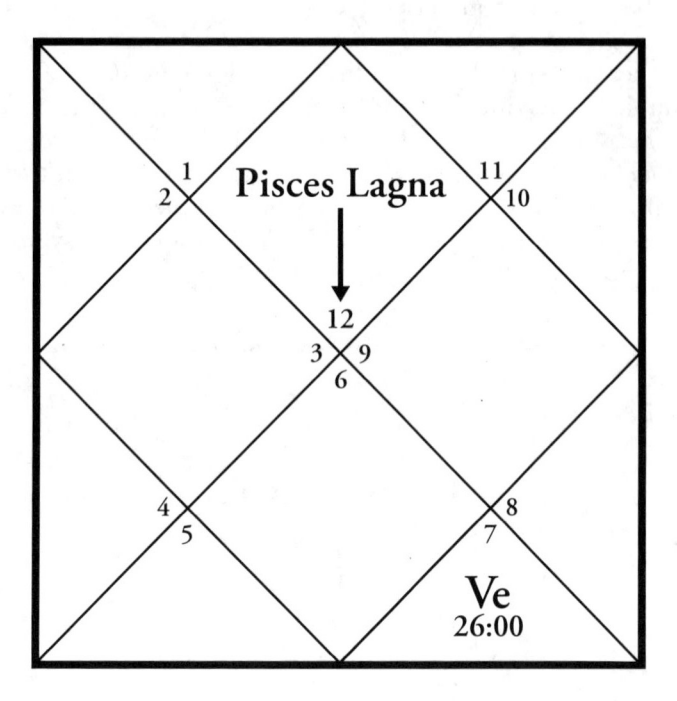

Pisces Lagna

Ve
26:00

The First House (Thanu Bhava)

The first house, sometimes called the ascendant, is the house of individuality. Everything that pertains to the self can be located here. It represents the orientation towards life, how we interact with the world, and how the world views us.

Since the experience of self begins with physical awareness, this house naturally signifies the body. Physical constitution, strength, and appearance are all represented here in seed form. General health and the nature of diseases are also shown by the sign and planets located in the first house.

The self is further expressed through personality. In this respect, the first house shows psychological traits, especially those which contribute to the persona, that part of ourselves we show the world. Rather than a complete picture of the psychology, the first house shows the basic temperament, the core personality style, the level of self-confidence, the ego development, and the general power of the personality.

Every other part of the chart becomes a natural extension of the first house. We carry our physical constitution, personality type and ego into every aspect of life. To a great extent, these factors determine our ability to achieve prosperity, academic and career success, harmonious relationships, and general happiness in life.

It is also from this point that the self begins the journey towards enlightenment. The spiritual self, paramatman, is actually unbounded and unmanifest. The first house, on the other hand, shows the individualized aspect of self, the physically bound, egocentric, personalized self. Over the course of a lifetime, a healthy individuality will expand beyond egocentrism, gradually identifying more and more with unbounded awareness.

This process is naturally seen in the development of a child. The child begins with only body consciousness, spending his first year exploring physical sensations and abilities. Later the child becomes aware of other people and objects, gradually forming a self-oriented attachment to them. People and things are selfishly seen as producers of pleasure or pain, happiness or misery. If the individuality is strong, the child later learns to be aware of other people and objects in a relatively unselfish way. He forms relationships based on compromise, learns to share, and learns to love others when others love or praise him. As awareness expands further in adulthood, he begins to realize that attachments cause suffering and selflessness seems to cure suffering. He begins to develop unconditional love, compassion, true generosity, acceptance, forgiveness, and other virtues which naturally arise as the self gradually de-individualizes, becoming less neurotic, less egocentric, more accepting, and more universal.

This process of gradual expansion of consciousness is signified sequentially in the twelve houses of the horoscope, culminating in the twelfth house, the house of moksha or liberation. From this point of view, the chart shows the evolution of the soul over the course of a lifetime. The foundation of this evolution, however, is the first house. Before one can deindividuate and attain liberation, one must first be an exceedingly strong individual. In fact, in order to accomplish anything in life, whether it is spiritual enlightenment or simply earning a living, it helps to be physically, mentally and emotionally strong. For this reason, the first house should be analyzed thoroughly before delineating any other house in the chart, and constantly referenced when explaining any aspect of life represented in the horoscope.

Significations of the First House Given by Classical Authors of Vedic Astrology:

Self; temperament; personality; manners; diplomacy; peace of mind; general happiness or misery; knowledge; dignity; fame or reputation; general status; prominence; general achievement; victory over enemies; general prosperity; asceticism or worldliness; birthplace.

Physical Significations:

The body; physical constitution; health and illness; appearance; longevity; strength or weakness; complexion; proportions; hair. Depending on whether the first, second or third drekkana rises—head, neck, and pelvis.

The Ruler of the First House Placed in the Twelve Houses

First House

Positive: When the ruler of the first house is placed in the first house, the person will have a strong constitution and sound health. This placement also suggests good longevity, and a strong sense of self. The person will tend to succeed in life. He will have a strong libido due to high vitality, a beautiful or handsome body, and will attract romantic relationships easily. As a result, the classical literature suggests that he will be fickle and will have "two wives" (spouses or lovers). This is also a good position for owning houses, land, and for general success and prosperity. The person will also have a good reputation and will tend to succeed in the place where he was born. If the planet that owns the first house and is placed in the first house is Mars, Mercury, Jupiter, Venus, or Saturn, this placement produces a Mahapurusha Yoga. This strengthens the ego and makes the positive significations of the planet dominate the chart, making the person successful according to the planet's nature.

Negative: If the ruler of the first house is afflicted in the first house, the person could have health problems and a shorter life span. He will have a strong ego that will be influenced in a negative way according to the nature of the affliction. If a malefic Saturn influences the Ascendant, for example, the person might be reserved, shy, demanding, or controlling. The influence of a negative Mars brings aggression and anger.

Second House

Positive: If the ruler of the first house is placed in the second house, the person will identify with second house matters. Consequently he will have a desire for comfort, affluence, and luxury in life. In this respect he will have many qualities that are like the sign of Taurus (see Taurus). This placement gives a tendency towards financial and material success, which is greatly magnified if the first lord is influenced by benefics or by the rulers of the eleventh, second, ninth, or fifth houses. The person will be knowledgeable, honorable, and will have a good self-image. He will also have a good relationship with family members and will be generous.

Negative: If the ruler of the first house is afflicted in the second house, the person will have financial problems, expenses, or debts. He will also have difficulties regulating his diet, resulting in health problems, and a lack of mental peace. He might also speak harshly, swear, or tell lies.

Third House

Positive: When the ruler of the first house is in the third house, the person will be communicative, flexible, passionate, and versatile. In this respect he will have many traits related to the sign of Gemini, the third sign of the zodiac (see Gemini). He will be bright, active, charming and will get bored easily. He will also be highly intelligent and might work in a career that involves communications or information processing. He could also have talent in music, math, or writing. He will have good experiences with his siblings and they will be a source of support to him. He will constantly be involved in errands, projects, phone calls, and short trips. He will also be curious and courageous.

Negative: If the first house ruler is afflicted in the third house, the person will have problems in communication. He will also have difficulties regarding his siblings. Sometimes the siblings will have difficulties in their own lives. In other cases the person has a hard time relating to them. Siblings become a source of anguish or he might simply not have any siblings. This position also brings difficulties during short outings and doing errands. The person could also have difficulty reading, studying, or generally processing information.

Fourth House

Positive: If the ruler of the first house is placed in the fourth house, then the person will have a strong relationship with his mother, who will also be a good influence in his life. He will also experience harmony in the family home while growing up and will have a good relationship with his family in general. He will enjoy being at home and will have a sensitive, caring and nurturing personality. In this respect he will have many personality traits like the sign of Cancer, the fourth sign of the zodiac (see Cancer). He will be good-looking, charming and will have a good deal of material success in life. He will go to a good school. He will own a nice home and might have other real estate as well. He will also own good cars. His life will be happy and secure.

Negative: If the ruler of the first house is afflicted in the fourth house, the person will have a difficult relationship with his mother, or his mother might have a difficult life. He will have problems concerning real estate and cars and might change his residence several times. He will find it hard to achieve peace of mind and will feel insecure. This placement brings problems in the place of education, and makes it difficult to get accepted to preferred educational institutions.

Fifth House

Positive: If the ruler of the first house is placed in the fifth house, the person will be very fortunate, successful and prosperous. He will have many personality traits like the sign of Leo, the fifth sign of the zodiac (see Leo). He will have a strong physique and a robust constitution. As a result, he will be healthy and will live a long time. He will be very intelligent and successful in his educational pursuits. He will like games and sports and might be athletic. This placement also makes the person creative, dramatic, and artistic. The person will be noble, magnanimous and will possess leadership abilities. If the first lord is associated with the rulers of the second, eleventh, ninth, or fifth houses, the person will become prosperous and will do well in the stock market.

Negative: If the ruler of the first house is afflicted in the fifth, the person will have problems with children. In cases of serious affliction, this can mean loss of the first child. On the other hand, it is possible that the first child could simply have a generally difficult life. He will also have fluctuations of luck and should should avoid the stock market. He will have difficulty in school and could have an interrupted education. Since the fifth house indicates the mind and education, the nature of the subjects studied in school will be indicated by the combination of planets influencing the fifth house. Natural malefics sometimes produce a technical or mechanical mind and a similar style of education, so their influence here is not always bad for education.

Sixth House

Positive: When the ruler of the first house is placed in the sixth house, the person will be a hard worker and will accomplish his goals over time. He will obtain good jobs, raises, promotions, and will become prosperous. He will be intelligent, analytical, and critical. In this respect he will have personality traits that are similar to the sign of Virgo, the sixth sign of the zodiac (see Virgo). He will also be competitive and will overcome his competitors. This is also a good position for making money through real estate. The person will have good health and high vitality. He will take an interest in his own health and the health of others. This position is beneficial for healing or service professions. The person will also be courageous.

Negative: If the ruler of the first house is afflicted in the sixth house the person will have health problems. He will also have problems getting good jobs or experience obstacles with jobs. He will be argumentative and will make enemies as a result. He will have financial problems and debts.

Seventh House

Positive: If the ruler of the first house is placed in the seventh house, the person will be intelligent, good-looking, and will have a congenial wife. He will be very diplomatic and charming and will enjoy relationships of all kinds. He will have many personality traits that are like the sign of Libra (see Libra), the seventh sign of the zodiac. He might possibly work in one-to-one relationships with others, such as in partnerships or client-professional relationships. He will also have good health, a good reputation, and success.

Negative: If the ruler of the first house is afflicted in the seventh house, the person will have difficulties in marriage. He will also find it difficult to create harmony in other one-to-one relationships. As a result, he could feel isolated and unloved, even though he feels a deep need to be in relationships. Sometimes this placement suggests problems in marriage stemming from passion or romance difficulties. The person or his spouse could have an affair, or they could simply "fall out of love." Depending on other indications in the chart, the person could get a divorce or go through a period of separation.

Eighth House

Positive: If the ruler of the first house is well-fortified and placed in the eighth house, the person will have a long life and good vitality. He will become wealthy and successful and will have financial gains from outside sources such as inheritances, insurance, contracts, and clients. He will have a knack for business. This placement causes the person to have personality traits that are like the sign of Scorpio (see Scorpio), the eighth sign of the zodiac. He will excel in yoga and be interested in anything that gives him personal empowerment. The lagna lord here also suggests an interest in various types of therapies and self-development regimes. As a result, the person might be interested in psychology, bodywork, and various healing modalities. This position also produces an interest in astrology and other occult sciences.

Negative: If the ruler of the first house is afflicted in the eighth house, the person will have health problems. His life will be filled with many changes and obstacles. He might also be accident-prone. In this placement the lagna lord brings difficulties regarding money from outside sources such as wills, insurance, and clients. Partnership money or joint finances through marriage can also be a source of problems. The person might have personality traits which reflect the negative side of the sign of Scorpio. He might be manipulative or controlling, or he might be mean or cruel.

Ninth House

Positive: When the ruler of the first house is placed in the ninth house, the person will have a strong sense of purpose and high integrity. He will be generous and optimistic and have other personality traits that are like the sign of Sagittarius, the ninth sign of the zodiac (see Sagittarius). He will be interested in spirituality, travel, philosophy and other higher knowledge. He will have a good relationship with his father who will give him plenty of support in life. Generally, this is also a good placement for marriage and it is excellent for prosperity. The person will travel widely, obtain a good education and will be successful in his career.

Negative: If the ruler of the first house is afflicted in the ninth house, the person will have difficulties in his relationship with his father. He will display personality traits that reflect the negative side of the sign of Sagittarius, and might be judgmental, self-righteous, or tactless. His university or college education might be interrupted or simply difficult. He will have problems with teachers, mentors, and gurus. Afflictions to the lagna lord here can also produce financial fluctuations.

Tenth House

Positive: If the ruler of the first house is placed in the tenth house, the person will be self-employed, or in a leadership position in his place of employment. He will be career-oriented and become very successful professionally. He will display character traits that reflect the best side of the sign of Capricorn (see Capricorn), the tenth sign of the zodiac. As a result of his career success, his reputation will grow. He will be thought of as an expert, and become prosperous as well.

Negative: If the ruler of the first house is afflicted in the tenth house, the person will experience many difficulties and changes in his career. The influence of natural malefics on this house, however, increases ambition and professional drive, so care should be taken in assessing the negative results of this placement. Frequently, an afflicted lagna lord here produces a personality which is pushy and assertive, and the person wants to succeed at all costs. The exact nature of the malefic influence will determine the specific results. Serious afflictions to the lagna lord in the tenth sometimes bring professional disgrace or failure.

Eleventh House

Positive: If the ruler of the first house is placed in the eleventh house, the person will become wealthy. He will achieve his goals easily and have constant successes in life. He will be successful professionally and have a good reputation. This is also a good placement for friendships, giving an expansive social circle and a general inclination to be social. The person will have personality traits similar to the sign of Aquarius (see Aquarius), the eleventh sign of the zodiac. He will have a good relationship with his next older sibling and the sibling will give him plenty of support. He will have good children, a good marriage, and will prosper.

Negative: If the ruler of the first house is afflicted in the eleventh house, the person will have failures and interruptions in the process of trying to achieve goals. He will have financial losses or difficulties as well. Natural malefics, however, usually give good results when placed in the eleventh house. So if the lagna lord is with natural malefics, the person might simply be aggressive and ambitious. When the influences on the lagna lord are truly negative, however, it spoils the person's ability to succeed and produces a great deal of frustration. He will have a difficult relationship with his next older sibling and also with friends.

Twelfth House

Positive: If the first house ruler is placed in the twelfth house, the person will be introspective and reflective. He might take an interest in psychology or religion. The best expression of this placement is a healthy desire for solitude orients the person towards spirituality. He will be intuitive, selfless, idealistic, romantic and compassionate. He will display the best traits of the sign Pisces (see Pisces), the twelfth sign of the zodiac. He will enjoy travel and have many positive experiences in foreign countries. He will sleep well and have positive sexual experiences.

Negative: If the ruler of the first house is afflicted in the twelfth house, the person will be shy and self-conscious. This placement strongly challenges the person's self-confidence. In many cases this manifests early in life and leads the person through an anguishing search for self. Saturn's aspect or association with the lagna lord here, for example, can cause the person to struggle to become more self-aware, resulting in spiritual growth. Even in such cases, however, the person will go through inner turmoil or depression. In cases of serious affliction, the person becomes unable to assert himself in any meaningful way whether professionally or in relationships. As a result, this placement gets in the way of professional success and marital bliss. Sometimes this placement indicates ill health and occasionally the person experiences periods of confinement.

Planets in the First House

Sun in the First House

Positive: The Sun in the first house is generally a positive placement. The person will be lucky, intelligent, healthy and successful. This placement gives leadership ability. The person seeks to shine in front of others. He is here to provide an example for others to follow. He has a strong will, fixed opinions and is very determined. He is ambitious and works hard in order to gain success and status in his chosen field. The person may also move to a distant place due to the profession. He is charismatic and outgoing. This Sun placement also favors health. It give the person a strong, vital, energetic body and good recuperative powers.

Negative: A negative Sun in the first house makes the person egotistical, arrogant, selfish, and overbearing. He will have a strong need to be the center of attention. Physically, the Sun raises the level of pitta (fire) dosha in the constitution. This can cause physical problems resulting from excess heat such as fevers and rashes. Sometimes the Sun in the first house also creates difficulty in having children.

Moon in the First House

Positive: The Moon in the first house causes the person to be fortunate, charming, and magnetic. He will love people and have many friends. He will also have a gentle, amiable nature. As a result, he will attract romantic relationships easily and be interested in creating a home and family. He may also be nurturing and supportive to others. This placement brings a deep desire to achieve personal happiness and an ability to do so. The person might also have contact with the public in his career, or become well-known or even famous. He will also benefit through his mother and females in general.

Negative: A negative Moon in the first house will make the person either overly concerned with his personal needs, or in the case of Saturn aspects to the Moon, neglect his personal needs in order to take care of responsibilities. His personality will be changeable and sometimes fickle. He will be influenced easily by other people. His view of the world will be strongly affected by the various ups and downs of his mood. He will take many things personally. His reputation will be questionable and there may be some problems with his vision, hearing, or speech. His relationship with his mother will be difficult and he may have similar difficulty with other females. The Moon is a watery or kapha planet, so this can bring physical problems that are related to the fluids in the body such as bladder, breast, or blood problems.

Mars in the First House

Positive: Mars in the first house will make the person assertive, ambitious, and fiery. It gives great vitality and enthusiasm in life. The person will also be energetic, outgoing, impulsive, hard-working, and constantly active. He will have a rugged appearance and good muscular development. He may have mechanical ability. He will have good stamina and be competitive. Usually this results in a high capacity for productivity. A good Mars in the first house can also give courage, leadership abilities, martial tendencies, and bring great success in life.

Note: Mars in the first house in Aries or Scorpio causes Ruchaka Yoga, a Mahapurusha Yoga, which produces the best attributes of Mars in the personality. As a result, the person gains success, prosperity, and reputation.

Negative: A badly placed Mars in the first house can make the person angry, irritable, and aggressive. As a result, relationships and marriage become difficult. Mars is impulsive, so this placement can sometimes produce impatience and rashness. The person with Mars in the first house doesn't always think before he acts. In some cases, this tendency can lead to accidents and injuries. In any case, a negative Mars in the first can be difficult for physical well-being. Mars is a pitta (fiery) planet, so the ailments related to this placement are usually a result of excess heat in the body. Fevers and rashes are typical symptoms. Conditions requiring surgery are also common. Mars tends to produce acute rather than chronic problems, however.

Mercury in the First House

Positive: Mercury in the first house causes the person to identify with the intellect. He will be intelligent, curious, communicative, charming, and clever. He will analyze, evaluate, and compartmentalize. He will also tend to be quite intelligent. He will be logical and will also be good at imitating others. This placement of Mercury makes the person talkative, witty, and talented. Sometimes it gives musical or literary ability. The person may see himself as an intellectual or at least a very bright person. As a result, other people will be impressed with his multiple abilities. He will gain a good reputation. He will have a great sense of humor and an ability with languages. He may sweat a lot. He will eat sparingly, but he will eat pure food. He will be good at astrology. Yet a good Mercury in the first house sometimes gives problems with a sibling at age 16 (the 17th year of life). A good Mercury here also makes the person precocious and sometimes makes the person a child prodigy. In any case, the person displays his many talents at a young age. He will also be good-looking and have a youthful appearance.

Note: Mercury in the first house in Gemini or Virgo creates Bhadra Yoga, a Mahapurusha Yoga, which makes the personality reflect the best attributes of Mercury and brings achievements, reputation, and success as a result.

Negative: A negative Mercury in the first house will make the person too clever for his own good. He could become dishonest and manipulative. He might have problems with learning or with education. He might also become a compulsive talker, or have other problems with the communication process. This position can produce a sensitive nervous system that gets overloaded easily. The person might have too many irons in the fire, and be excitable and irritable. There might be problems with the skin, nervous system, or lungs. Since Mercury is a eunuch, impotence or lack of sexual interest is also a possibility. Conversely, because sex is primarily a mental experience, the person may be highly sexual. Hence, a negative Mercury can produce an imbalance in the sexual arena.

Jupiter in the First House

Positive: A positive Jupiter in the first house is the greatest blessing in a horoscope. It is said that Jupiter in this position removes a crore of doshas (100,000 blemishes in the chart). It gives self-confidence and leadership abilities. The person becomes an expert or highly educated in some field. There is a tendency to become a professional such as a doctor, lawyer, or teacher. The person loves the truth and would rather be honest and direct than to tell a sweet truth. As a result there can be a tendency to be a little too blunt or even a little tactless at times. But the overall nature is optimistic and generous, so the person is usually popular, jovial, and very sociable. This placement also favors abundance, prosperity and sometimes makes the person wealthy. He will also have an inherent philosophical or spiritual nature. He will have a positive attitude, which will make him see the glass as "half-full." This attitude is based on his purvapunya (positive karmas from past lives) manifesting as a sense that his life is blessed in some way. In fact, he will be protected from many problems in life and spared many of life's more difficult experiences. His body will be healthy and robust and he may be tall or large. He will live a long life.

Note: Jupiter in the first house in Cancer, Sagittarius or Pisces creates Hamsa Yoga, a Mahapurusha Yoga which makes the person's life reflect the positive qualities of Jupiter in a dominant way. He may be a teacher, advisor, or professional. He will also have a strong sense of what is right and true. He will achieve academic credentials and become an expert in his field. He will live a long, prosperous and healthy life.

Negative: A negative Jupiter in the first house sometimes causes the person to be overconfident or arrogant. He might feel that he already knows it all. As a result, he might resist teachers and be difficult to teach. He will have strong beliefs, which can make him dogmatic, self-righteous, and judgmental. He may have problems with money and difficulty succeeding at a profession. He could have a tendency towards secret sexual affairs. He will either have no children or have trouble with his children. Jupiter tends to make the body large, so a negative Jupiter here can give a tendency to become overweight or even obese.

> *Once again, any exalted planet will manifest negatively as well. Jupiter in Cancer is not such a blessing to those who have to live with this person.*

Venus in the First House

Positive: A good Venus in the first house makes the person charming and graceful. It produces a quality of warmth, which is very attractive and results in positive experiences on the social and romantic levels. The person will be friendly and light-hearted. He will be diplomatic, and if the absolute truth is too harsh, he will choose to tell a "sweet truth" rather than offend the other person. He will also be sensual, enjoy the arts, and may have some creative talents. He will tend to live an affluent, prosperous, and comfortable life. He will be happy and enjoy life. He will also be well-educated and cultured. Venus sometimes gives an attraction to gemstones or jewelry. The person will like nice clothing and his general appearance will be one of grace and style. This position of Venus usually produces physical beauty as well, but always makes the person attractive on some level. As a result, the person will be well liked by other people and may become quite popular. The person will also have many positive experiences related to females in general, and his marriage will be happy.

Note: Venus in the first house in its own sign (Libra or Taurus) or in exaltation (Pisces) causes Malavya Yoga, a Mahapurusha Yoga that gives the attributes of Venus, mentioned above, in a strong dose. As a result, the person's work might revolve around art, gems, healing, or other Venusian values. This yoga also increases the potential for success and prosperity.

Negative: When Venus gives negative results in the first house, then the person will become overly sensual and self-indulgent. He will value comfort and luxury above all else and may become unwilling to work hard. He might overindulge in sex, food, spending money, parties, or any other value related to Venus. On the other hand, if Venus is badly afflicted by Saturn, it will be difficult to derive fulfillment from all of Venus' values. The person will not feel truly lovable or attractive. He might be charming and friendly, but at the same time be very afraid of really expressing his truest, most intimate feelings of love. Or he may just feel that love, affection, pleasure, and even material affluence are hard to find. He might also have some problems with animals. He could have eye, kidney or urinary problems. There could also be a tendency towards venereal disease and other diseases related to sensual excess.

Saturn in the First House

Positive: Saturn in the first house, if well placed, can be a great blessing to life. It makes the person hard-working and responsible. He will be slow to start, but thorough and meticulous in completing his work. He will have great integrity and achieve great things in his profession. He will take pride in the fact that people can count on him once he makes a commitment. He will be patient, persevering, and come into his power in his mid-thirties. Since Saturn comes to maturity at the age of 36, even a good Saturn in the first house can give some experience of limitation up until age 36. But the person will have a sense of personal empowerment from age 36 onward, taking on new responsibilities that will be the source of future success. With Saturn in this position, the person makes his own way in life by personally taking responsibility for creating success in his life. He knows that anything worth achieving in life takes effort and hard work and he is willing to take that responsibility. He will have managerial and organizational abilities. He will also be reserved, practical, conservative, and pragmatic. A strong Saturn causes the person to demand much of others, but he also demands more of himself. His strength carries him through life and brings many blessings. He will be introspective, philosophical, and become an expert at the art of detachment. His greatest virtue is his equanimity, which can become the source of his enlightenment. He will probably marry late in life, but will be a committed and responsible partner. Saturn is the indicator of old age, so the person becomes better with age. In fact, a strong Saturn in the first house is a good indicator of a very long, successful life.

Note: Saturn in the first house in its own signs (Capricorn or Aquarius) or in exaltation (Libra) creates Shasha Yoga. This is one of the five Mahapurusha (Great Man) Yogas. It gives the above qualities in a strong dose in the personality and leads to professions that include management, business, and administration. It also gives the person a greater tendency to become successful and prosperous.

Negative: A negative Saturn in the first house can make life quite difficult. The first 36 years of life will be full of delays, obstacles and pressures. It can also be marked by ill health. The person will have a negative self-image, and will be reluctant to accept praise or appreciation. He might see himself as reserved or humble, but this is the ego's way of covering up deeply rooted self-doubts and producing a sense of having the personality under control. In fact, this position of Saturn actually shows a negative egotistical quality. Instead of bragging as a result of pride, the person is proud of being humble. He looks at people who brag or try to get attention as inferior people due to their lack of ability to control their personalities. In spite of deep self-consciousness and personal doubts, the person with Saturn in the first house sees himself as having one great virtue, humility, which ironically, becomes the source of pride and self-esteem. He likes the feeling of being in control of himself. Sometimes this makes the person harsh and demanding. He can be controlling and uncompromising. On the other hand, a weak Saturn in this position can also cause the person to totally avoid taking certain kinds of responsibilities in life. He might have difficulty holding down a steady job, for example, or lack stamina and perseverance in other ways. He will also have some problems with making a good first impression. Due to self-consciousness, he will tend to not look directly at another person while talking. He may seem aloof and detached in an unhealthy way. As a result, he may have problems in marriage or may not marry at all. This position is also problematic for health, usually producing problems which are characteristic of the sign in the first house.

Rahu in the First House

Positive: A good Rahu in the first house will make the person a natural leader, wealthy and successful. Rahu is a revolutionary planet and causes the person to take the lead in everything that is new and progressive.

There will be a natural interest in astrology, psychology, metaphysics and new technology. The person will also be quite independent. He will project a strong persona, which becomes the source of many attractive personality traits. As a result, other people will be drawn to him. In spite of his popularity, however, he will remain somewhat independent and separate from others. In another way, however, he might become involved with groups either personally or professionally. Since Rahu is a non-material graha signifying the astral plane, the person might have vivid dreams and good intuition. He will also be impulsive, restless, and enjoy stimulation. As a result, the person will enjoy traveling to exotic places and will have a variety of exciting experiences. This placement, if favorable, allows the person to place a lot of positive attention on the process of individuation and self-actualization as well. In any case, there will be a sense of urgency to improve the self. He might, for example, become very interested in exercise and physical development. He may also have a great interest in psychological or even spiritual development. At its best, Rahu in this position can give first-rate spiritual experiences and even produce an awakening of the kundalini.

Negative: When Rahu in the first house produces negative results, the person will seem to have a big ego, but actually be plagued with self-doubts. He will be impulsive, impatient and sometimes rash in action. This placement makes the person rebellious as well. There is a strong need for independence that goes with this position of Rahu, and when out of balance, it can cause the person to be stubborn. This can lead to difficulties in relationships. Sometimes it produces out-of-body experiences as well, so the person may appear to be distracted much of the time. In any case, it makes it difficult for him to stay "in the here and now." He might also become too materialistic, preempting any spiritual tendencies with a sense of urgency about having wealth. A difficult Rahu in the first is also bad for health. In Ayurveda, Rahu is one of the chief indicators of vata (wind) issues. This leads to problems related to too much activity. The person might become busy to the point of nervous agitation, for example, producing a variety of vata disorders. Rahu is also a chaya graha (shadow planet) as well, so symptoms that manifest under its influence are often difficult to diagnose or treat.

Ketu in the First House

Positive: When Ketu is favorable, it produces good results in the first house. The person becomes spiritually inclined and idealistic. He has a strong sense of taking life one day at a time and lives life in the moment.

The Vedic texts say that "Ketu is a Buddhist," so a good Ketu will allow the person to enjoy the whole idea of simplicity, detachment, and mindfulness. A great saint from India once said, "Most people suffer because they want what they don't have and they don't want what they do have. It should actually be the other way around. People should want what they have and not want what they don't have!" This is the strength of a good Ketu, to be happy with whatever the present moment brings. Ketu is also a chaya graha (shadow planet). In the first house, it shadows or veils the persona and the body. A good Ketu will manifest this quality by making the person successful "behind the scenes." He will also be humble and will enjoy his anonymity. Yet he will also have a magnetic, attractive quality. Sometimes, for example, the person's eyes will seem to have a mysterious or hypnotic quality. People will be attracted to him, but find him hard to get to know. In any case, the person will be "hard to see." A physically beautiful woman with Ketu on the ascendant, for example, might appear to be ordinary at first glance. Similarly, a person with great talents or abilities might find that he is overlooked or unappreciated at times. The person will have natural intuition and may have healing ability. There will also be an ability to benefit from alternative healing modalities as well.

Negative: If Ketu gives negative results in the first house, then the person will feel invisible and overlooked. He will have many self-doubts and feel disconnected from any clear direction in life. He might be very shy and withdrawn as well. Sometimes this leads to isolation. Like a monk, who is dissatisfied with life and seeks retreat in a cave, the person with a difficult Ketu in the first house will sometimes become alienated. He will also be chronically dissatisfied with many other aspects of life. In some cases this can produce depression. Ketu in the first house can also cause the person to be distracted and uncentered. He might be evasive, manipulative or deceitful. Since Ketu veils what it touches, he might become sneaky or secretive. In extreme cases there can be an unhealthy interest in the occult or the underworld. When Ketu is negative, even its spiritual nature is experienced in a negative form. This placement can also make the person a wanderer, lacking roots and stability. It can also produce health problems that are difficult to diagnose or treat. Therefore, if the person receives a serious diagnosis by a regular doctor, a second or third opinion is important, because misdiagnosis and misprescription are common with this placement.

The Second House (Dhana Bhava)

The second house signifies the material possessions and resourses that are required for the purpose of self-maintenance. Obviously, food is the most important thing for survival. Therefore, food, eating, cooking, the mouth, and the voice are represented by the second house. Similarly, clothing and other possessions become natural extensions of this house.

The second house reflects more than survival-oriented needs, however. In fact, all material attachments, including money and luxury items are included under its rulership. It not only gives an indication of our general financial potentials, but also reveals our attitudes toward spending money and acquiring possessions. In this manner, the second house indicates the level of thriftiness or extravagance with money, a factor that is very important to one's overall financial health.

Wealth is also dependent on learning. In ancient times, learning was mainly an oral process. In this respect, verbal education has been allotted to the second house by some classical authors.

In the past, wealth was also measured by many things other than money, such as jewelry, grain, and even family members like children and wives. For this reason, and even more importantly because parents provide our original sustenance, the second house has been a significator of family members and family events in general. Even though we no longer view our family members as part of our wealth, we do share our possessions and our food with them.

In fact, it is our family members with whom we first learn to share our treasured possessions. So the second house shows how we begin to deal with selfishness and greed in the process of learning to be aware of other people. In short, this house represents the first step of the egocentric self on the path towards enlightenment. Here the individual encounters the material world, gets attached, learns to survive and, as consciousness expands, learns to extend the realm of personal attachment to include other people. In the process, the basic social unit, the family, is formed.

Significations of the Second House Given by Classical Authors of Vedic Astrology:

Wealth; food; drinks; family; cloth; jewels; precious metals; education (acquisition of knowledge through speech); buying and selling; speech; power (money and power go together); truthfulness (related to speech); generosity in giving; attitude towards spending; cheerfulness; happiness; determination; efforts to get wealth; faith in God (that "God will provide").

Physical Significations:

Face; eyes (especially the right); teeth; tongue; mouth; nose; nails. Depending on the drekkana rising—right eye, right shoulder.

The Ruler of the Second House Placed in the Twelve Houses

First House

Positive: If the lord of the second house is placed in the first house, the person will be healthy and prosperous. He will have an ability to benefit from real estate. He will make personal efforts to improve his financial condition. He will also be a passionate person and a good speaker.

Negative: If ruler of the second house is afflicted in the first house, the person will have problems earning money by his own effort. He will also have problems in his relationship with his family of origin, and might be fickle romantically. He might eat an imbalanced diet, poor quality food, or suffer from an eating disorder. He could also have difficulty expressing himself verbally or might speak harshly.

Second House

Positive: If the ruler of the second house is placed in the second house, the person will have financial gains. He will also be capable of benefiting from real estate. He will also get a good education and have many positive character traits. He will value religion and spirituality. As a result, he will have self-respect and a steady life.

Negative: If the ruler of the second house is afflicted in the second house, the person will have financial losses and difficulty earning money. His education might be interrupted or he could simply have problems in school. He will eat poor quality food and find it difficult to regulate his diet. This can have a detrimental effect on his health and mental peace.

Third House

Positive: If the ruler of the second house is placed in the third house, the person will have courage. He will be successful and prosperous. He will earn money through his ability to communicate or through his siblings. His work might require him to spend a great deal of time in his car, going on short errands. He could also earn money from music, writing, or crafts.

Negative: If the ruler of the second house is afflicted in the third house, the person will find it difficult to earn money. The daily errands and chores of his profession will be constantly interrupted or will present him with many obstacles. He will experience communication problems that result in financial loss. He could also have financial problems related to his siblings. This position sometimes produces addictions to food, drink or drugs. It can also cause the person to become a miser.

Fourth House

Positive: If the ruler of the second house is placed in the fourth house, the person will gain or purchase real estate. He will also profit from the sale of real estate. This is also a good placement for financial gains through the mother or the family in general. The person will be good-looking, virtuous, and have a great respect for his mother. He will be frugal and will spend his money in ways that enhance his sense of security and overall happiness. A positive second lord here can also enable the person to purchase nice cars and profit through buying and selling cars. It can bring financial gains through hotels, inns, housecleaning, construction, as well as any other fourth house signification.

Negative: If the ruler of the second house is afflicted in the fourth house, then the person will lose money or have difficulty making money through all fourth house matters. He could find it difficult to find and purchase a house, for example. Or he might lose money on the sale of a house, land or car. He might spend money in a way that promotes worry and insecurity, which will have a general effect on his sense of overall happiness.

Fifth House

Positive: If the ruler of the second house is placed in the fifth house, the person will make money easily and could become wealthy. This is a first rate combination for financial prosperity which manifests in a pronounced way in the period or sub-period of the second lord. He will have a good income from his own earnings and also from stock market investing. He could also profit from creative projects, such as publishing his own books, selling of other people's books, or from art, drama, education, entertainment or any other fifth house matter. In addition to the excellent financial results, this placement makes the person efficient and gives good experiences related to children. The first child might be self-employed, or might have leadership or management abilities.

Negative: If the ruler of the second house is afflicted in the fifth house, the person will have financial problems, and be particularly vulnerable to losses through stock market investing. He will also have financial problems related to children. He might constantly have to give them money to help them solve problems, for example. He could also spend his money impulsively on gambling, sporting events, dating, parties and other fifth house activities.

Sixth House

Positive: If the ruler of the second house is placed in the sixth house, the person will make money through jobs in the employment of other people. A positive second lord here suggests the ability to be hired in a good job, even if the competition for the job is stiff. Similarly, the person will get regular raises and financial benefits through his employer. He could also earn money through a self-employed job that provides a service to others. This placement connects the income to all sixth house significations, so the person could earn money through a health profession. He could also earn money competing with others and beating them, or through business arrangements with his competitors. The person will eat a healthy diet and might take supplements, herbs or medicines to promote vitality.

Negative: If the ruler of the second house is afflicted in the sixth house, the person will have expenses related to health. He will have problems getting raises in his job. He might also spend his own money in order to complete work for his employer. When he is out of work, he could have difficulty finding employment. This placement can also produce health problems related to the diet, mouth, teeth, or eyes. The person might be forced to take prescription drugs. An afflicted second lord here can also suggest food poisoning, drug abuse or alcoholism.

Seventh House

Positive: If the ruler of the second house is placed in the seventh house, the person will gain financial prosperity through marriage or partnership. This is also a good placement for producing financial gains through clients and also through the healing arts. Both the person and the spouse will be sensual, passionate, and will have liberal attitudes towards sex. The spouse will have many Scorpio-like qualities and could be a businessperson or a physical or psychological therapist.

Negative: If the ruler of the second house is afflicted in the seventh house, the person's spouse will be very unstable and will be the source of expenditure or financial losses. Partnerships will also produce losses, expenditure, or even debts. The partner or the spouse could go through constant upheavals and changes, especially during the period of the second lord. The person will have marital problems related to finances.

Eighth House

Positive: If the ruler of the second house is placed in the eighth house, the person will have financial gains through outside sources such as inheritance, insurance, legal matters, tax rebates, contracts or clients. He will be good at borrowing money and paying it back after making a profit. He will also recover money that he has loaned to others. Although his day-to-day financial situation will fluctuate, a fortified second lord here will give wealth through all eighth house matters.

Negative: If the ruler of the second house is afflicted in the eighth house, the person will have many financial losses and obstacles to becoming prosperous. He will have difficulty getting loans or will go into debt. He will be dependent on other people for money. This is not a good placement for inheritances, indicating disputes, obstacles and other problems related to inherited wealth. Joint finances will also be a source of problems, and he might lose money through a divorce. Similarly, partnerships and business agreements will produce financial problems, losses, and misunderstandings. The person could also have tax problems and should be particularly careful to pay his taxes and to keep his dealings with the IRS completely honest.

Ninth House

Positive: If the ruler of the second house is placed in the ninth house the person will be very prosperous. This is a first-rate combination for wealth, linking the house of money to the house of abundance. This position also gives the person the ability to speak and to teach. The person's father will be a source of financial support or inheritance. He will spend his money wisely, especially on ninth house activities such as getting a good education and travel. He will be generous and honest with money.

Negative: If the ruler of the second house is placed in the ninth house, the person will have financial problems related to his father. The father could be miserly or manipulative with money, for example. Afflictions to the second lord here reverse the normally abundant financial results of this placement. The person could incur excessive expenditure related to higher education, the father, long-distance travel or other ninth house significations. He could also have childhood illnesses (or other difficulties), but will tend to recover and become healthy in later life.

Tenth House
Positive: If the ruler of the second house is placed in the tenth house, the person will earn money through his own efforts in his career. He will also pursue a career that involves buying and selling, food, speaking, teaching, finance or other second house matters.

Negative: If the ruler of the second house is afflicted in the tenth house, the person will have money through his profession. He could also have career and reputation problems that are linked to questionable financial practices. Natural malefic influences on the tenth house must be carefully scrutinized, however, because frequently they contribute to financial gain and career success. In these cases, the person usually becomes avaricious or mercenary, or earns money through a technical profession.

Eleventh House
Positive: If the ruler of the second house is placed in the eleventh house the person will become very prosperous. This is a first-rate combination for wealth, linking the house of money to the house of achievements, gains and increase. As a result, the person will set and achieve his financial goals. He will also have many positive and lucrative interactions with his friends. He will derive financial benefit through groups, teams, or organizations. This is a good placement for investing in mutual funds and for setting long-range goals for wealth and prosperity. The person will grow more and more prosperous as he gets older. He will be generous with his resources and will contribute money to organizations, groups and friends in need. The person could have weak health or physical vitality during childhood and will become very strong and vital as an adult.

Negative: If the ruler of the second house is afflicted in the eleventh house, the person will have difficulty setting and achieving financial goals. A seriously afflicted second lord here reverses the normally lucrative indications of this combination, making it difficult or impossible to amass wealth. The person might, for example, lend money to his friends and not get it back, or friends might be the source of financial loss in some other way. This placement also signifies illness, weak vitality or other problems in childhood that tend to improve with age.

Twelfth House

Positive: If the ruler of the second house is strong and influenced by benefics in the twelfth house, the person will gain money from distant places, travel, psychology, intuitive pursuits, spiritual pursuits, hospitals, charities and other twelfth house sources. He will also be generous and will give money to worthy causes. He will spend money on travel and have many positive experiences in distant places and foreign countries. He might also purchase objects while traveling or might simply purchase or collect items imported from foreign countries. He will be skilled in the art of bargaining and will get many discounts and complimentary services.

Negative: If the ruler of the second house is afflicted in the twelfth house, the person will have many debts, expenses, losses and uncertainties with money. He will incur expenses and losses while traveling as well, and should always take extra care of his money and belongings while away from home. He could also lose money through hospital expenses or other twelfth house sources.

Planets in the Second House

Sun in the Second House

Positive: The Sun in the second house causes the person to identify with his material resources. As a result, a positive Sun here can make the person prosperous. He will become successful, learned, and wise. He will live a prosperous and affluent life. He will have a great family and be proud of them. He will also have some distinction in his education. He will be very articulate and put a lot of himself into his speech. This is a common placement for teachers and public speakers. The Sun here can also produce financial gains through successful or influential people. The father can also be a source of income.

Negative: When the Sun's malefic influence predominates in the second house, it causes problems with finances. The person's self-worth is tied to his financial situation, so he feels humiliated and unhappy when his finances decline. He might also speak in an overbearing, conceited or brash way. In some cases, he will not always speak the truth. Since the Sun is the karaka for the father and since the second house is the sixth from the ninth house, an afflicted Sun here can cause health problems for the father. This placement is also said to produce a lack of gratitude and unfaithfulness. He could associate with friends of questionable character. He might have frequent changes of residence and problems with his spouse and children. He will also have problems with education.

Moon in the Second House

Positive: A benefic Moon in the second house will make the person wealthy. He will be friendly, charming, respected and popular. He will have the "gift of gab." His speech will have a gentle, sociable quality and he may have poetic abilities. He might gain a good reputation as a public speaker. He will have a good education and a good family. He will also be close to his family members. He will be good at business and be able to benefit from real estate. He will be deeply attached to having a comfortable life and will be motivated to become materially successful. He will be a good cook and enjoy good food. He will also have a beautiful or handsome face.

Negative: When the Moon is malefic in the second house, the person has many fluctuations with finances. He might lose money through friends, family members or women. He will be unhappy and will be very insecure about money. The Moon here can also cause impulsive spending based on the various fluctuations of a person's moods. His education will be broken or difficult. He will be materialistic and unable to adjust to simple living. This position of the Moon will also give speech problems. He might have a fear of speaking in public, for example, or he might speak in a style that is too personal or too emotional. He will also have inconsistent dietary habits and will probably be allergic to milk products.

Mars in the Second House

Positive: A good Mars in the second house indicates prosperity and financial success due to ambitious efforts. The person has a good desire to become wealthy and backs it up with industrious action. He will also spend a lot of money. With a good Mars, however, the person earns more than he spends and ends up with a net gain. This position also causes the person to have an assertive style in speech. He will speak with passion and energy and have a dynamic speaking style. Even a good Mars in the second, however, can lapse into occasional critical or harsh speech. The person will also tend to be self-employed, and may do well in some form of business. In any case, he will have an assertive, competitive style when it comes to money.

Negative: A negative Mars in the second house creates financial problems and expenditure. The person spends as much or more than he earns. He will have an aggressive speaking style, which may include a liberal use of profanity. He will also be dishonest at times. He will have problems, arguments and disagreements with family members. His education will be interrupted or he will have problems with education in general. There might be a scar on the face or a problem with the right eye. He might also have dental problems requiring surgery and other invasive procedures. He will be a meat-eater and he will eat fast food, so his diet will not be very healthy.

Mercury in the Second House

Positive: A good Mercury in the second house produces an interest in business and finance. The person will earn his fortune by his mental abilities, or his ability to communicate. He might also have a handsome, young-looking face. This position of Mercury will produce a good education. The person will be well-versed in several subjects. He will also be a good speaker with a broad vocabulary and a good sense of humor, which may include the use of puns. The classics say that the person who has a good Mercury in the second house is "like Maha Vishnu in riches, like Brihaspati in intelligence, like Kalpa Vriksha (the celestial boon-giving tree) in granting others' wishes and like Veda Vyasa (the great Vedic sage) in learning." So the person will be wealthy, intelligent, generous, and learned. This position can also produce great respect for the father and a virtuous nature, leading to a happy life. If Jupiter influences Mercury here, the person will become good at mathematics and astrology.

Negative: When Mercury in the second house gives malefic results, the person sometimes becomes shifty and deceitful. He might have a speech problem, such as a speech impediment, or he might simply have problems conveying his ideas. He will have financial losses due to recklessness, extravagance, and wastefulness. He will also have a tendency towards gastritis.

Jupiter in the Second House

Positive: When Jupiter is placed in the second house, it gives prosperity and abundance. The person will have a natural sense of material support and comfort. He will also be lucky with money. He will be generous with his resources and will spend money both on himself and others. He will have a moderate income before marriage, and will become much more prosperous after marriage. He will also have a spouse who is strong, well-educated and possibly a professional of some kind. As a result, the spouse might be the more dominant partner. He will receive a good education, which might include philosophy or astrology, and have teaching ability. He could also be a good writer or even a poet. His speech will be positive and uplifting. He will also have good recuperative ability and good health in general.

Negative: Jupiter in the second house, if malefic, will produce financial problems based on extravagance and excessive optimism with money. The person might exaggerate or simply talk a lot. On the other hand, if Jupiter is influenced by Saturn, he might be very hesitant to speak, and might have a reluctance to speak in public. In some cases the person will lie, or simply speak in critical or judgmental ways about other people. A weak Jupiter, regardless of the house it is in, suggests problems with children, either in having them, or in the relationship with them. In the second house, the classics also indicate that a malefic Jupiter will give female children. This, of course, is simply a reflection of cultural values. In India, where male children are the source of a person's security in old age, a malefic Jupiter will give girls. In any case, a malefic Jupiter in the second can indicate some problems regarding children. It can give health problems related to the diet, such as over-eating, or eating too many rich foods.

Venus in the Second House

Positive: When Venus is well placed in the second house, it will produce an opulent life. The person will have and enjoy positions that are of the finest quality. He will enjoy purchasing things which are designed well and which have aesthetic appeal. For example, he may enjoy purchasing gemstones, art or other beautiful objects. He will be prosperous and have an easy time with money. Money, however, is not seen as an end in itself, but rather a means for creating grace and style in life. He will earn money through females or through sources ruled by Venus. Marriage might also be a source of gain, so this placement also suggests more prosperity after the time of marriage. The person with Venus in the second house will also speak with tact and diplomacy. He will be charming and sensitive and will seek to create harmony in all relationships. He will be handsome or beautiful. He will also be a good cook and will eat food that is very tasty and well-prepared.

Negative: A negative Venus in the second house will produce lavish expenditure and squandering of wealth. The person will be self-indulgent and lose money as a result. There might also be financial problems related to marriage, friendship, or females. The person will also have some problems with diet. He could have a "sweet tooth," for example, and if Jupiter is also afflicted, then this could lead to a sugar problem such as hypoglycemia or even diabetes. Venus here could also give some problems related to the eyes. A negative Venus in the second house suggests that the marriage will be problematic as well.

Saturn in the Second House

Positive: A good Saturn in the second house can bring wealth and prosperity through hard work. The person will be a good speaker, but will have a serious or reserved speaking style. He will also have a strong sense of responsibility for providing a secure material foundation for his family. He will work hard in school and get a good education as a result. He might earn money through organizational or management skills. Because Saturn comes to maturity at the age of 36, he will become more prosperous after that age. If he is disciplined in his eating habits, he will also have excellent health.

Negative: When the second house is occupied by a malefic Saturn, then the person will have a sense of limitation regarding money. In some cases, this means significant financial problems. In other cases, it simply indicates a need to struggle in order to earn. This position of Saturn also obstructs the education, making the whole process tedious and sometimes causing an interruption. The person might also have a monotonous, limited diet, and he will be quite resistant to making changes in his diet. Usually the food is of poor quality. Unfortunately, this pattern leads to negative effects on health. Even the person's face could seem dull. He may have skin problems that can be traced back to what he eats. Saturn here may also give problems with the voice or speech. There could be a fear of public speaking, or the tone of his voice might seem uninspired and lifeless. Family life will also be marked with a sense of heavy responsibility and frustration. Sometimes this indicates divorce or separation.

Rahu in the Second House

Positive: When Rahu is positive in the second house, the person will make a great deal of money. Rahu gives a sense of urgency to achieve financial goals, so this drives the person to achieve prosperity and abundance. There will also be a good deal of expenditure, but if Rahu is benefic, then the person will end up with a net gain. There will also be a good deal of attention placed on the diet. The person will revolutionize it in some way, trying various alternative dietary programs, supplements, and medicines. Rahu here also suggests a non-vegetarian diet. In the second house, Rahu gives a strong impulse to speak. The person will speak with energy and have a lot to say. This will make him a very interesting and innovative speaker, who sometimes surprises his listeners.

Negative: A negative Rahu in the second house will produce financial losses. The person will have a sense of urgency with money that leads to compulsive expenditure and over-expansion. He might take unnecessary financial risks. He can get over-extended or go into debt as well. It is also possible that he will experience outside circumstances that seem beyond his control, which are the source of financial problems. In any case, a bad Rahu in the second house will produce a lot of worry about money. Rahu here can also produce dietary problems. For example, the person might develop an obsessive-compulsive disorder related to food, or he might have allergic reactions to particular foods. Rahu rules poisons, so the person could take drugs, alcohol, or medicinal drugs. Rahu also promotes negative speech patterns when it is in the second house, so the person may use profanity or be prone to sudden outbursts of anger.

Ketu in the Second House

Positive: When a benefic Ketu is placed in the second house, the person will become prosperous through the use of intuitive, creative, or healing abilities. He will have an idealistic approach to money and be quite selfless with his resources. He will be non-materialistic, yet will also prosper. Ketu in the second house will give the voice a hypnotic quality. The person will say things that are prophetic or intuitive. He will be able to heal others with his words or with the quality of his voice. He will understand the value of limiting his speech and will enjoy periods of silence for spiritual reasons. This placement of Ketu will also cause the person to let go of his attachment to food. He will adopt a simple (usually vegetarian) diet, which will be conducive to his spiritual practice or philosophy of life. He might also fast occasionally. This position of Ketu will also allow the person to receive a good education, but in an alternative or idealistic area such as art, religion or philosophy.

Negative: A difficult Ketu in the second house will cause many uncertainties and problems with money. The person may have a hard time making a living and will feel that prosperity is beyond his grasp. Sometimes the person will have a relatively prosperous financial situation, but will be chronically dissatisfied with his financial condition. In either case, a malefic Ketu in this house brings a sense of financial lack. This position of Ketu can also cause the person to have dietary problems. There could be reactions to food which are weird or hard to understand. He could suffer from food poisoning or other negative effects from poisonous substances, including drugs and alcohol. He might adopt a diet that is too restricted and suffer some form of nutritional deficiency as a result. Ketu in the second will also bring problems with speech. The person might be shy or afraid to speak.

The Third House (Sahaja Bhava)

Probably the most prominent signification of the third house is brothers and sisters. It is here that the individual learns to further expand his awareness of others to the realm of co-operation and shared information. In ancient India, work and the resources produced from work were shared with brothers and sisters. Even today, in modern civilizations, brothers and sisters share common chores related to food, clothing and other aspects of sustenance. In this way, the third house is not only the house of brothers and sisters, but also of small tasks and errands.

Furthermore, the third house also shows the qualities of intellect needed to do work. It shows our interests, hobbies, and tendencies related to gaining bits and pieces of information. In this respect, the third house has a relationship to both communication in general, and education. It shows the level of mental stamina, desire and courage necessary to carry out our work in the outer world.

This is a very busy house. Here the errands of the day are carried out. Short distance journeys, letter writing, short distance telephone calls, and all types of activity that convey bits of information are part of its signification.

In addition, the third house is a creative house. It is related to the ears, so it naturally signifies music. Even though the fifth house is the house of creative energy, the third house is related to cleverness with the hands, language, and ideas, so it is usually strong in the charts of artists, musicians, writers and other creative people.

Significations of the Third House Given by Classical Authors of Vedic Astrology:

Brothers and sisters; desires; short journeys; music; courage; curiosity; parent's death; what is heard; stamina; mother's and father's brother; physical and mental prowess; patience; perseverance; fighting; confusion in the mind; friends; walking; foot travels; legacy apportioned between brothers; virtues; education; hobbies; status from birth in a good family; servants.

Physical Significations:

Ears (especially the right ear); throat; neck; windpipe; shoulders. Depending on the drekkana rising—right ear, right arm, and right testicle (male chart) right ovary (female chart).

The Ruler of the Third House Placed in the Twelve Houses

First House

Positive: If the ruler of the third house is placed in the first house, the person will be busy, inquisitive, and versatile. He will be charming, talented, and might have abilities in music, writing, or literature. His daily activities will include plenty of errands, telephone conversations and short tasks. He will be passionate, courageous, ambitious, successful and prosperous. He will tend to be lean and tall. He will have a good relationship with his siblings and his siblings will become successful and prosperous.

Negative: If the ruler of the third house is afflicted in the first house, the person will have a difficult time learning, reading, and communicating. He will find it difficult to process information and might be impatient or disorganized. He could also have a short attention span and tend to be fickle. He will be passionate, but may not be able to channel his desires constructively. This is also a difficult placement for his relationship with his siblings. The person might also be dishonest, deceptive, or manipulative.

Second House

Positive: If the ruler of the third house is placed in the second house, the person will be able to gain money through his siblings. He might also earn through work that involves communication, short journeys or information processing. His next younger sibling could be introspective or spiritually inclined. The sibling might also travel extensively to distant places.

Negative: If the ruler of the third house is afflicted in the second house, the person's next younger sibling (and siblings in general) will be a source of disappointment or loss. The person could have a negative relationship with a sibling, resulting in a rift or separation. The next younger sibling might be self-conscious and have a general lack of confidence. The person could also argue with a brother or sister over money. This placement also suggests procrastination in beginning projects.

It also gives the person a tendency to desire the spouses of other people as well as their material resources. It can also cause the person to oppose his own family and friends.

Third House

Positive: If the ruler of the third house is placed in the third house, the person will have strong, healthy, talented, and successful siblings. The next younger sibling, especially, will have these traits, and will particularly display the qualities of the planet occupying the third house. In addition, the person will be courageous and will be a good communicator. His communication style will also reflect the qualities of the planet in the third house. He will be charming, social and popular. This position also promotes career success and general prosperity.

Negative: If the ruler of third house is afflicted in the third house, the person's next younger sibling will display the negative traits of that planet. He will be very busy and will constantly be doing errands, but will also experience problems during his short journeys that are characteristic of the afflicting planet. If, for example, Saturn afflicts the third lord, the person will have delays and obstacles while doing errands. The same idea applies to the area of communications. The person will experience communication problems characteristic of the afflicting planet. A Mars aspect on the third lord will bring arguments. If the ruler of the third house is seriously afflicted, the person may not have any younger siblings.

Fourth House

Positive: If the ruler of the third house is placed in the fourth house, the person will have comfort, wealth and affluence. He will have a good education and happy life. The spouse will work at a purposeful career, which could require an advanced degree or professional certification, and will be successful. His mother may be spiritually inclined, introspective or might like to travel.

Negative: If the ruler of the third house is afflicted in the fourth house, the person will have difficulty communicating with his mother. His mother may also be self-conscious, shy or have a lack of self-confidence. This position also makes the spouse harsh, cruel or abusive in some way. The person will have uncertainty regarding his place of residence and might have to rent, rather than own a home. He could also experience many changes of residence and a lack of stability, security and happiness.

Fifth House

Positive: If the ruler of the third house is placed in the fifth house, the person will have successful and prosperous children who are also social and popular. This is a generally a good position for longevity as well. The person will be intelligent, virtuous, generous, and committed to helping others. This is also a good placement for writing, publishing, music, art and drama. The person will enjoy going on short journeys or outings that are for the purpose of entertainment, sports, or romance.

Negative: If the ruler of the third house is afflicted in the fifth house, the person will have problems communicating with his children. His children will tend to make friends with people who have questionable characters, or who have difficult lives in some way. This placement can also affect the person's education in some way. If Mercury is also afflicted, he may have difficulty reading, or might have an interruption in his education. He could also have communication problems in his marriage.

Sixth House

Positive: If the ruler of the third house is strong, well aspected, and placed in the sixth house, the person will be very intelligent. He will go many short distance errands and trips that are related to his employment. He might also spend a good deal of time researching information about health, or going on errands related to health or healing. His next younger sibling might have good luck owning or selling real estate and will be happy and successful in his life. This placement also suggests a benign form of sibling rivalry, which helps motivate the person to become successful.

Negative: If the ruler of the third house is afflicted in the sixth house, the person will have a difficult relationship with his next younger sibling and siblings in general. The sibling could be argumentative or simply have ill health. This is also a negative placement for the person's own health, and suggests problems related to the right ear, neck, or shoulders. This is a difficult placement for maternal aunts and uncles, and could indicate that they have difficult lives or that the person has a poor relationship with them. This will be most applicable to the aunt or uncle who is the mother's next younger sibling.

Seventh House

Positive: If the ruler of the third house is strong, well aspected, and placed in the seventh house, the person will have a good wife who is virtuous, well-educated and spiritually inclined. He will also have a good relationship with his next younger sibling, who will be very intelligent, talented, and have a strong, expressive personality. A sibling might also spend some time in a foreign country and will give the person help and support. This placement suggests difficulties in childhood that are overcome later in life.

Negative: If the ruler of the third house is afflicted in the seventh house, the person will have a hard time communicating with his spouse and will have marital problems related to passion and desire. He will also have problems relating to his next younger sibling or siblings in general. The sibling might have interruptions or problems in his education. This placement also suggests that the sibling could move far away, and have difficulties there. The person will have ill health or other problems in childhood that may be overcome with some difficulty later.

Eighth House

Positive: If the ruler of the third house is strong and well-aspected in the eighth house, the person's next younger sibling will be analytical, bright, successful, a hard worker and will be very lucky at getting jobs. This is a good placement for doing research as well. The person will have an intense and profound style of getting information, and will try to get to the bottom of any subject that interests him. As a result, he might have talent conveying information that is transformational or therapeutic.

Negative: If the ruler of the third house is unsupported or afflicted in the eighth house, the person's next younger sibling, and siblings in general, might have a difficult life, filled with struggle, obstructions, or ill health. In cases of serious affliction, a sibling could die or the person's relationship with the sibling could be upset, resulting in alienation and separation. This position also generally undermines the character of the person, suggesting a lack of honesty, cruelty, a manipulative nature, or a tendency to steal.

Ninth House

Positive: If the ruler of the third house is placed in the ninth house, the person will travel widely and will have many good experiences in the process. He will also have financial gains through women, and will have children who are helpful and generous. His material situation will improve significantly after the time of marriage. He will obtain a good education and be interested in a variety of subjects. As a result, he could receive degrees in more than one subject.

Negative: If the ruler of the third house is afflicted in the ninth house, the person will have problems during long distance travel, or might not be able to travel for some reason. He will have difficulties communicating with his father, which could spoil their relationship. He might also have problems in school and could have an interruption in his college education. This is also a difficult placement for the person's relationship with his teachers or his spiritual guru, and may make it difficult for him to find a teacher or guru. An afflicted third lord here makes it difficult for a person to hear and appreciate advice, resulting in a general resistance to teachers, professionals, consultants, gurus and others who have knowledge to share.

Tenth House
Positive: If the ruler of the third house is placed in the tenth house, the person's career will involve a great deal of communicating, short errands and journeys, or information processing. He will be successful and gain recognition. He will also have several talents and might have more than one job, or a job and an avocation. His next younger sibling, and siblings in general, will be successful and will be helpful in promoting his success and prestige. This is also a good placement for success in arts, crafts and music.

Negative: If the ruler of the third house is afflicted in the tenth house, the person will have career problems related to communications. He might have a difficult time understanding or being understood by his boss. He could also experience many delays, problems, interruptions or pressures related to business errands and other short journeys connected with his profession. This placement also suggests that his next younger sibling, and siblings in general, could be the source of business losses, embarrassment, misunderstandings and setbacks.

Eleventh House
Positive: If the ruler of the third house is placed in the eleventh house, the person will be passionate and courageous. His next younger sibling will be strong and well-educated. The person will be social and have many friends. He will also enjoy going on short outings with his friends. He could have financial gains related to his ability to communicate or process information. This placement can be very good for

success in high-tech professions and promotes any aspirations related to the internet.

Negative: If the ruler of the third house is afflicted in the eleventh house, the person will have difficulty regulating his passions and desires. This placement also produces general health problems and suggests a lack of physical beauty. In addition, the person will tend to work for (or be under the control of) other people. He will have problems making and maintaining friends due to an inability to communicate with them effectively. His next older sibling could have problems related to children.

Twelfth House

Positive: If the ruler of the third house is fortified and placed in the twelfth house, the person will travel to distant places and will have good experiences during his trips. He will be intuitive and will have an ability to flow through daily errands with ease, and with what seems to be an unseen, divine support. For example, when he is looking for a parking place in a crowded city, other cars might seem to magically pull out just in time to give him a place. His communication style will be fluid and intuitive. His next younger sibling could be self-employed or self-directed professionally. The sibling will also be very successful and will have a good reputation.

Negative: If the ruler of the third house is afflicted in the twelfth house, the person will have losses and disappointments related to his siblings. He will also repress or withhold information. He could be manipulative as well. In cases of serious affliction, this placement makes the person evasive and even dishonest. As a result, he might have problems in his marriage that are based on poor communication. The person will also waste money and will have difficult experiences while traveling in foreign countries.

Planets in the Third House

Sun in the Third House

Positive: When the Sun is in the third house, it causes the person to identify with providing and receiving information. He will learn a lot, and as a result, he will be an excellent communicator. He will also be busy and very active, constantly going on errands and other short-distance journeys. He will enjoy distant travel as well. He will be proud of his siblings, and may have a brother or sister who has leadership abilities, or who has a very expressive personality. The Sun here also gives courage, a bold style, and will make the person productive and successful in whatever he does. He may also have some dramatic or musical ability. His profession will be communication-oriented.

Negative: A malefic Sun in the third house will give the person an overbearing, egotistical or authoritarian way of communicating. He might also have problems with his brothers or sisters, or may simply not have any siblings. He will have strong desires and will have a hard time fulfilling them. A negative Sun in this position sometimes gives problems with vision as well. The person will also have problems with competitors and enemies, due to either having too little courage or having too much. In other words, his competitors might see him as being too aggressive or not aggressive enough. In either case, he finds himself in conflict with them. The exact results depend on whether the Sun is strong or weak, and whether it is associated with aggressive or inhibiting planets.

Moon in the Third House

Positive: The Moon in the third house causes the person to be physically attractive, charming, magnetic, and fortunate. He will be happy and fond of his siblings. He will also have successful relatives and will have a tendency to have male children. He will be attached to his brothers and sisters, especially the next younger sibling, who might have a charming, sociable, and gentle nature. The person will also be communicative, inquisitive and constantly busy. He will have diverse interests and abilities, and will do well academically. He may also be talented in music, writing, crafts, or other artistic areas.

Negative: When the Moon is malefic in the third house it causes problems in communication. The person might also have difficulties in his relationships with brothers and sisters, or simply not have any siblings. It is also possible that his siblings will go through difficulties in their own lives. A difficult Moon here also suggests financial loss due to governmental penalties or fines. The person could also be inclined towards unwise or illicit romantic involvements.

Mars in the Third House

Positive: A good Mars in the third house confers the ability to accomplish any task. The person will be courageous and will also have good health and energy. He will tend to be successful and prosperous. He will have good judgment and be fortunate. He will be constantly involved in short journeys, errands or telephone conversations. He might have a tendency to be logical and may have some mathematical ability. He will also have an assertive communication style. His next younger sibling will tend to have an assertive, martial nature.

Negative: A negative Mars in the third house will create an argumentative nature. The person will have a brash or overly assertive communication style and might have problems in marriage as a result. He will either have difficulties with his siblings or will not have them. He will have a passionate nature and this could lead to some sort of addiction. He might also have problems with his ears or hands.

Mercury in the Third House

Positive: When Mercury is benefic and placed in the third house, the person can be successful, popular, attractive, and sometimes even famous. This position produces an agile, clever intellect. The person will be articulate and talented. He might have ability with music, writing, or poetry. He will also have a very good mind for business and finances. He will acquire fixed properties and will tend to be happy. After he gets married, he will have children quickly. He could possibly come from a relatively large family. His next-younger sibling will be intelligent, communicative and humorous.

Negative: A challenging Mercury in the third house makes the person manipulative and sometimes even cunning. He will have all kinds of communication problems. He will either not have siblings or he will have many communication problems with his siblings. His next younger sibling might have difficulties in life due to mental imbalance, or due to poor communications skills.

Jupiter in the Third House

Positive: A beneficial Jupiter in the third house will give great results. The person will be very intelligent and will succeed at whatever he undertakes. His family members will look up to him and he might become respected or honored in his community as well. The classics say that he will become "a famous jewel of the earth." He will be a good communicator who will have a positive and uplifting communication style. He will also be spiritually-oriented and philosophical. He will be a good teacher. He will like to travel and will travel extensively. His next younger sibling will have some leadership abilities or might become successful or prosperous. The person will also be able to benefit financially from contact with his siblings. He will have a good relationship with his father. He will tend to be happy, well-educated, and prosperous, and will spend money on good causes.

Negative: When Jupiter in the third house is malefic, the person will have problems with children and money. He might also lose money due to his siblings. His communication style might be judgmental or domineering, or he might be dominated by his wife or siblings. He might also incur problems due to overconfidence or recklessness while traveling. His next younger sibling might have financial problems. This position also suggests that the person might have problems either in finding a good teacher, or in his relationship with the teacher. He might also have digestive problems.

Venus in the Third House

Positive: When Venus is in the third house, the person becomes self-controlled, charming, magnetic, and physically beautiful. He will be kind and compassionate. He will have artistic or musical abilities, and might have a beautiful singing voice. He will have a diplomatic and friendly communication style. As a result, he will be popular and successful. This position favors success in all undertakings, and although it makes the person frugal, it can bring prosperity. The person will be interested in reading poetry and romance novels. He will also be good at communicating affection. His next younger sibling will be charming, talented, magnetic, handsome, and successful, and the person will be particularly fond of him.

Negative: When Venus is malefic and is placed in the third house, the person will have a stingy nature. He will be very sexual and might be promiscuous. He will also be lacking in courage and physical stamina. He will have problems in communication with his spouse. He might have eye problems as well. He will lack tact and diplomacy and have problems in friendships. His next younger sibling might have a divorce or problems in relationships. The sibling could also be self-indulgent or promiscuous.

Saturn in the Third House

Positive: When Saturn is placed in the third house, the person will be a careful, responsible, and deliberate communicator. He will tend to live a long healthy life. He will be meticulous and organized, executing all his tasks and errands. He will also have wisdom born of fortitude and patience. He will work very hard in life and will achieve success in his career, usually later in life. This position of Saturn also causes the person to link business or practical agendas with travel. His next younger brother will be patient, persevering, reserved, and responsible. The sibling will also come into his own in his mid-thirties.

Negative: When a difficult Saturn is placed in the third house, the person will be jealous by nature. He might be the youngest of the family, but could have many problems regarding his siblings. One of the siblings will have a difficult life involving many obstructions and pressures, or might have health problems. The person will also have problems in communications. He will be ungrateful and generally unhappy. He could have a tendency to be selfish and could possibly have a difficult time in old age.

Rahu in the Third House

Positive: Rahu in the third house will bring success, victory and fame. The person will outdo his competitors and will gain wealth and happiness. He will have a happy family. He will also be constantly busy with errands and short journeys. He will read books on esoteric or technical subjects. This position also gives musical ability, and sometimes brings a connection to music that is revolutionary or that makes use of hi-tech or electric instruments. He will be courageous and innovative. Rahu here also produces a good spouse and children. The person will be sociable and will have many friends from diverse backgrounds. He may speak a foreign language as well. His sibling will have a strong and independent personality. He will have a nice car and may tend to have employees.

Negative: A negative Rahu in the third house spoils the person's experience with brothers and sisters. The siblings in general, but especially the next younger sibling, could be a source of anguish or difficulties. The person will experience many communication problems as well. He could become agitated due to too many errands and short journeys. He could also be a compulsive talker or simply have a rebellious communication style. He might also have strong desires and compulsions which he has difficulty fulfilling. This position could also give a tendency towards ear or throat infections.

Ketu in the Third House

Positive: When Ketu is in the third house, the person will have an intuitive nature and this will affect the communication style. He will be spiritually inclined, selfless and helpful to other people. He will also be creative, artistic, or musical. Ketu here tends to make the person prosperous as well. He will take the many tasks and errands of the day as they come, and will accomplish them without making an itinerary. This placement also tends to mysteriously eliminate the person's enemies or competitors. His siblings, especially the next younger one, will be spiritually inclined, intuitive, creative, or may have healing abilities.

Negative: A negative Ketu in the third house can cause the person to be slippery, manipulative or dishonest. He will be evasive and have many difficulties in communication. He might lose a sibling, or experience some disappointment regarding his siblings. A difficult Ketu in the third also tends to produce mysterious ear, throat or shoulder problems that are either difficult to diagnose or treat.

The Fourth House (Sukha Bhava)

The fourth house represents foundations in life. The most obvious of these foundations is the home or house. It also indicates cars, other vehicles, property and fixed aspects of our material wealth. These are the things that we rely on for security and stability.

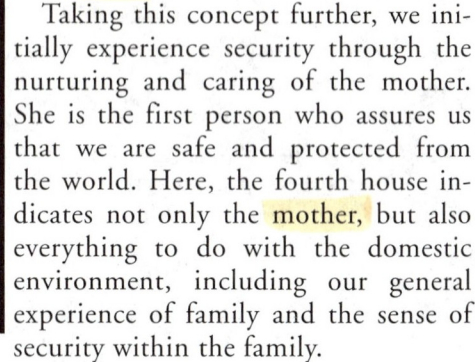

Taking this concept further, we initially experience security through the nurturing and caring of the mother. She is the first person who assures us that we are safe and protected from the world. Here, the fourth house indicates not only the mother, but also everything to do with the domestic environment, including our general experience of family and the sense of security within the family.

This house also reveals our own ability to care for and nurture others. Our early experience of the mother, her support, care and love, all contribute to this nurturing ability. In this way, hospitality and other social virtues contributing to friendship can be seen here. As children, in our own neighborhood (the environment near the family home), we find other children to play with, invite them to visit our house, and learn to extend our hospitality. So the fourth house is also related to friends.

Again extending the ideas of environment and security, this house can also signify environments beyond our home, which later in life, we come to view as home. A classroom, for example, can become a home away from home, providing some of the same fundamental sense of security of the family home. For this reason, many authors look to the fourth house for clues about the education. Other authors say the fifth house, the house of intelligence, is the house of education. This point has been widely debated by various experts in astrology. A point to remember, however, is that education, like any aspect of life, has many sides. In as much as it provides an environment, a surrogate family, and a place of security, the classroom is related to the fourth house. The actual subjects learned in school, and the education you receive is related to the fifth house, the house of intelligence.

The fourth house is very subtle. It is sometimes overlooked, but it is one of the most important houses in the chart. It represents self-awareness, the culmination of the preparation of consciousness begun in the first house. From the security provided here, the individual becomes confident, based on his sense of self, home and family. Yet many of the qualities of this house remain latent, hidden beneath the surface like the foundation of a building.

This house is one of the moksha houses, which means it is related to the spiritual nature. It shows the fundamental underpinnings of the mind. It indicates the hidden foundations of consciousness, the deepest aspect of mental security or insecurity upon which the personality rests. It reveals our capacity for happiness, peace of mind, and inner faith. So a clear understanding of this house gives a giant clue to basic character traits, virtues, emotions and values in life.

Significations of the Fourth House Given by Classical Authors of Vedic Astrology:

Home; mother; mother's happiness; relations through the mother; other relatives in general; education (south India); vehicles for land or water; hereditary house; residential house; the doorway to the house; architecture; property, fields; gardens; gardening; farming; domestic animals; places of religion; temples; shrines; devotion to God; milk; water; tanks; wells; modern plumbing; underground things; buried things; place where stolen property has been hidden; happiness; emotional qualities; confidence; temperament; belief; knowledge of the scriptures; virtues; morals; righteous conduct; reputation; friends; public; diagnosis; herbs for medication; end of life.

Physical Significations:

Chest; lungs; heart; diaphragm. Depending on the drekkana rising—right nostril, right side of the body, and right thigh.

The Ruler of the Fourth House Placed in the Twelve Houses

First House

Positive: If the ruler of the fourth house is placed in the first house, the person will have good luck with real estate. He will own a beautiful home, have a nice car, and will acquire general material security. He will be very close to his mother and will have good relationships with other family members as well. His spouse might work in a partnership, or in a client-based occupation. His mother might be quite successful in her profession. This is also a good placement for the person's education. If the fourth lord is strong and well aspected, he might come from a rich family and could attend exclusive schools. A good fourth lord in the first house brings happiness and security in life.

Negative: An afflicted fourth lord in the first house will produce problems with real estate. The person might also come from a family which is poor or which is dysfunctional in some way. He might have problems in his relationship with his mother or his mother might simply have a difficult life. This placement also produces educational problems, and could make it difficult for the person to get accepted at his school or university of choice. He might have difficulty obtaining a vehicle or he could purchase vehicles that break down or get damaged. This placement can create problems regarding inherited property or money because it suggests that the person will not derive much material benefit from his family.

Second House

Positive: If the ruler of the fourth house is placed in the second house, the person will purchase a nice home, which will be a symbol of affluence and comfort. He will also make money through the sale of homes or land. He will purchase or even collect nice cars as well. This placement usually signifies a larger than average family of origin. It also produces general happiness in life. The person's mother will be prosperous, successful and social. She could also be a good cook.

Negative: If the ruler of the fourth house is afflicted in the second house, the person will have difficulty purchasing a home. He will have many expenses related to his home or residence. He might have a sarcastic nature and will be generally unhappy. This placement suggests problems related to inherited property or wealth. The person will also have other problems related to his family of origin. His mother might resist cooking or simply will not be very good at it. As a result, she might feed him poorly prepared food or fast-food as a child.

Third House

Positive: If the ruler of the fourth house is placed in the third house, the person will be talented, possibly displaying musical or literary ability. He will also have courage and will have a good relationship with his siblings. He will have a generous and giving disposition, and will make money by his own industriousness. His siblings, especially the next younger one, will be prosperous. His mother will be introspective, spiritually inclined, and might like to travel. His spouse will work at a profession that involves certification or a university education, and will have a strong sense of purpose.

Negative: If the ruler of the fourth house is afflicted in the third house, the person's parents will have many uncertainties during their lives. His mother will be self-conscious or shy. She might also experience emotional losses or depression. It is possible that the person will have problems due to a stepmother or stepbrothers or sisters. This placement can produce problems regarding houses, land or cars. The person might disagree with his siblings about family property or about the care of elderly parents.

Fourth House

Positive: If the ruler of the fourth house is placed in the fourth house, the person will have a strong, healthy mother who lives a long time. He will be stable and secure and generally happy in life. This placement allows the person to own land and houses and have general material security. He will also own good cars, which will be well-maintained. He will go to a good school and easily gain admission to the university of his choice. His spouse will be successful at a profession that will be characterized by the planets ruling and occupying the fourth house. If the fourth lord is Mars, Mercury, Jupiter, Venus or Saturn, then this placement produces a Mahapurusha Yoga, causing the positive significations of the planet to dominate the chart. This planet's energy will not only manifest in the personality of the horoscope owner, but also in his mother's personality and the career of his spouse. If the planet is Saturn, for example, then the person will have a strong sense of responsibility. His mother might also have that quality. His spouse, however, could work at a job that requires organizational or management skills, and will be quite successful.

Negative: If the ruler of the fourth house is afflicted in the fourth house, the person will probably still own a house, but will have many problems related to the house. The same is true for vehicles. The person will have a strong mother, but might have problems in his relationship with her. Similarly, his mother could have her own problems that will be characterized by the afflicting planet, the houses it owns and the house in which it is placed. Afflictions to the fourth lord placed in the fourth house also disturb peace of mind and make it more difficult to achieve happiness.

Fifth House

Positive: If the ruler of the fourth house is placed in the fifth house, the person will be very fortunate. This placement constitutes a kind of

Raja Yoga, which promotes general success and prosperity. The person will easily obtain good land, houses, cars and other vehicles. His mother will be a source of comfort and support and will be a particularly good influence on his education. As a result, he will attend good schools and will get a good education. He will be popular and respected by everyone. His mother's family will also be respected and prosperous. He will have a natural sense of faith and will be devoted to Vishnu, or an incarnation of Vishnu, like Krishna or Rama. In the West, this placement can suggest a devotion to Jesus.

Negative: If the ruler of the fourth house is afflicted in the fifth house, the person will have mixed success in life. He may still reap many of the benefits mentioned above, but with more difficulty. For example, he might be intelligent and attend a good school, but have to struggle to achieve his academic goals. He could also have an interruption in his education. He might purchase a house, but have many domestic expenses. His mother could come from a poor family or might have other financial problems.

Sixth House

Positive: If the ruler of the fourth house is strong, fortified, and is placed in the sixth house, the person will have a mother who is a good communicator. She will be clever, talented and will have diverse interests. The person will have a good relationship with his mother's next younger sibling, and with his maternal aunts and uncles. He might be employed in a field related to schools, foundations, hotels, or homes. He will be thoughtful and intelligent. His spouse could travel for work.

Negative: If the ruler of the fourth house is afflicted in the sixth house, the person will have struggles and problems related to land and houses. His mother could be sickly, or he could have a bad relationship with her. This placement suggests that the person will be irritable, impatient or mean. His mind will be restless and he will lack a sense of peace and happiness. He will also have difficulty purchasing houses or land and might live in a rented house. If he owns a house, then it will involve many problems, repairs and expenses. His spouse will have many professional interruptions or uncertainties. The person could also have health problems connected with the diaphragm, chest, heart or breasts.

Seventh House

Positive: If the ruler of the fourth house is placed in the seventh house, the person will be very knowledgeable and possibly an expert in more than one subject. His spouse will have a successful career and will be highly-respected. The person will have an easy time obtaining a good house or land. He might collaborate with his wife in building or buying a house, or may buy real estate in conjunction with a business partner. He will go to good schools and will get a good education. His mother will be a good person, who is devoted to her own mother and family of origin. She will also have a nice home, be well-educated, secure and happy.

Negative: If the ruler of the fourth house is afflicted in the seventh house, the person will have difficulty with contracts or agreements that are related to land, houses, or cars. His relationship with his mother might be problematic, or she could be insecure or generally unhappy. This placement can also cause marital problems, resulting in general unhappiness and an agitated mind.

Eighth House

Positive: When the ruler of the fourth house is strong and fortified in the eighth house, the person might inherit land, money or houses from his parents. He might live in good houses, but will probably change his residence many times. This is also a great placement for remodeling a home. The person's mother will be very intelligent and devoted to her children. She might also be well-educated. This placement also makes the person spiritually inclined or intuitive. His spouse will be successful and prosperous professionally.

Negative: The placement of the ruler of the fourth house in the eighth is generally bad for the person's stability and happiness. He will have many changes of residence and will experience many obstructions to owning property. If the fourth lord is also afflicted here, the person will have a difficult relationship with his mother, or he might lose one of his parents early in life. This is also a negative placement for cars or vehicles generally, indicating expenses, damage, accidents and other mishaps. The person could also suffer from physical problems related to the diaphragm, chest, heart or breasts.

Ninth House

Positive: If the ruler of the fourth house is placed in the ninth house, the person will have good luck with houses and land. He will also own nice cars and other vehicles. This placement creates a type of Raja Yoga, and is generally favorable for success, prosperity and happiness. The person will have a natural sense of faith, and might be religious or devoted to God. He will have a noble character and will be virtuous. His mother could be religious or at least a person of integrity and virtue. Similarly, the person will hail from a respectable family of origin.

Negative: If the ruler of the fourth house is afflicted in the ninth house, the person will have a difficult relationship with his father and might generally avoid him. His father could also go through many upheavals and changes in life. Although the person will be able to own cars, land and houses, he might have many expenses, repairs, disputes, or other problems related to them.

Tenth House

Positive: If the ruler of the fourth house is placed in the tenth house, the person will have an office in his home, or will have an office that is like a home away from home. This placement is also good for a career linked to houses, land, institutions, or the community in general. It also suggests that the person will own good houses, land and vehicles. He will attend a good school and receive a good education. The fourth lord here is also good for political aspirations and suggests a position as a councilperson, congressman, or senator. The person will also have good health, be self-controlled, successful, respected, and might be good at chemistry.

Negative: If the ruler of the fourth house is afflicted in the tenth house, the person will have a loss of reputation. He will have a strong desire to have an office in the home, but will experience problems actualizing his dream. Although he will probably own a house or land, he will experience many problems related to real estate. Similarly, he will own a vehicle, but might have many vehicle expenses or other related problems.

Eleventh House

Positive: If the ruler of the fourth house is placed in the eleventh house, the person will have financial gains through the sale of property. He will be able to own a home, but will have better luck actualizing his real estate goals from middle age on. He could purchase a home that he gradually improves upon over a long period of time. This position also favors socializing, and the person will probably enjoy entertaining friends in his home. His mother will be successful, charming and prosperous.

Negative: If the ruler of the fourth house is afflicted in the eleventh house, the person will experience problems actualizing his dreams, and could be unhappy as a result. For example, he might have a desire to purchase a house and find it hard to achieve this goal. His mother might have ill health, or she might go through many big changes in her life. This placement also suggests that the person could have health problems related to the diaphragm, heart, chest or breasts.

Twelfth House

Positive: If the ruler of the fourth house is strong, fortified, and placed in the twelfth house, the person could spend time living in foreign countries. Similarly, he might live in a place that is distant from his place of birth. This placement also suggests time spent in retreats, ashrams, camping or other places that promote introspection and spiritual awareness. Another variation on this theme would be owning a vacation home in a secluded or distant place. In any case, he will prefer to live in a secluded and spiritually vibrant residence. His mother could be spiritually inclined and might live in a distant place.

Negative: If the ruler of the fourth house is afflicted in the twelfth house, the person will have many uncertainties regarding his residence. This can mean he finds it very difficult to purchase a house. It can also make it difficult to find a house or apartment to rent. The person will have many expenses related to homes, land or apartments as well. Sometimes this placement suggests the loss of property or the loss of money related to the sale of real estate. If the fourth lord is seriously afflicted in this position, the person could be homeless. The same condition can cause the early loss of the mother or father. This position generally makes it hard to achieve peace of mind and happiness.

Planets in the Fourth House

Sun in the Fourth House

Positive: If the Sun is in the fourth house, the person will be physically beautiful and will come from a good family and have a nice home. He will also be proud of his home and family. This position of the Sun can produce a fondness for flashy cars, convertibles or other cars that are also status symbols. The spouse will be a source of happiness and will probably be successful professionally. The Sun in the fourth can create wealth and success. The person might inherit land or a house from his family. He will tend to be a dominant member of his family, and feel that he should be the head of the family. Similarly, he may do well as the leader of institutions, foundations, towns, schools or other fourth house organizations. As a result of the high self-regard, leadership ability, and family pride generated by a good Sun in the fourth house, the person will lead a happy, successful life, that becomes more fruitful as he ages.

Negative: A negative Sun in the fourth house is not good for happiness. The person will have deep insecurities and a low self-image. He could be ashamed of his family or the opposite, subject to arrogance and too much family pride. He might have an overbearing, patronizing nature, seeing himself as the natural leader of his family, whether they agree or not. He could squander his family property as well. This position of the Sun is not good for the person's relationship with the mother, and it tends to produce an interruption in education. In the political arena, the person will also suffer due to his tendency to be overbearing and unwilling to listen to others. He will also have a predisposition to heart problems.

Moon in the Fourth House

Positive: A positive Moon in the fourth house produces happiness and security in life. The person will have a charming and supportive mother and will be very attached to her. He will also be attached to women in general. His spouse will work at a job that will be connected to the public in some way. He will receive a good education and do well in life. The family will be a source of happiness and security. This position causes the person to be sociable, popular, and gives leadership abilities as well. He will have financial gains or inheritance from his family. He will be generous and supportive. The Moon here brings ownership of elegant and comfortable vehicles and nice homes. The person will also enjoy spending time in the home tending to domestic activities. He will also have a desire to live near the water. At the end of his life, he will be happy, settled, well-liked, and will have the comfort of good friends and family.

Negative: A difficult Moon in the fourth house is an indication of problems for the mother, or for the person's relationship with her. This position also causes general unhappiness in life. The person might have fluctuating health. He will have problems with family members and will be generally insecure. He could also have many changes of residence and other problems related to homes and real estate. Vehicles may also be the source of problems. He could also have difficulties in school.

Mars in the Fourth House

Positive: Mars in the fourth house is a great indication of vitality and energy when it is positively placed. The person will be quite active and busy, right up to the end of life. He will also spend much time taking care of the domestic scene, doing projects around the home. He will enjoy the whole idea of "do-it-yourself" home improvement. This idea can extend to the environment in general, causing the person to work for environmental causes. He will be ambitious and enterprising in his profession due to a drive to create a secure material foundation. As a result, he will be successful professionally. His mother will be an assertive, ambitious, or physically-fit person. His spouse will also be quite ambitious and may have leadership abilities. This position of Mars will make the person driven to acquire property, and lucky with real estate.

Negative: An afflicted Mars in the fourth house disturbs happiness and peace of mind. The person will probably have domestic disputes and arguments. He could be defensive or insecure. He will also have problems with land and houses. This position suggests problems in his relationship with his mother and with other women as well. The mother can have a tendency to manifest physical problems involving surgery, accidents, or injuries. The father might also have problems too, especially during the person's eighth year of life. The family of origin might be dysfunctional in some way. This is also a placement, which suggests the need to be careful in automobiles, and if it is seriously afflicted, could produce car accidents.

Mercury in the Fourth House

Positive: When a benefic Mercury occupies the fourth house the person will be very intelligent, well educated and successful. He will have a strong body and good health. He will also have an intelligent, well-educated, or talkative mother and have a good relationship with her. This position favors prosperity, and the person could begin to earn well as early as age 16. He will also do very well with real estate. Mercury here produces good experiences in the domestic sphere, both with the family of origin and with the spouse and children. The spouse will work at a profession that involves communication or analytical ability and will be very successful. The person will also own nice vehicles. He will be popular and respected in his community.

Negative: When an afflicted Mercury occupies the fourth house the person will have communication problems with his mother and other family members. His mother could be nervous, mentally agitated, a poor communicator, or a worrier. The person could experience a break in his education or have difficulty learning. He could be nervous or unable to handle stress well. Real estate issues might be a source of disagreement or misunderstanding. He might also have difficulty communicating with children. At the end of his life, he could suffer from nervousness, lung problems or poor memory.

Jupiter in the Fourth House

Positive: Jupiter in the fourth house is an excellent placement. Here it protects the person's life and gives him a good family. His mother will be optimistic, generous and positive, providing constant support in life. She might be a professional, or have leadership or teaching abilities. Similarly, the spouse will have a successful career and will tend to have a profession requiring expertise, credentials, or certification. The person will also derive material support from his mother and his family, and could receive a good inheritance. This placement of Jupiter will also give the person excellent luck with property. He will have a large spacious home, and will enjoy entertaining his friends there. He may also make his home a center for learning, counseling, or spiritual gatherings. He will enjoy a high degree of respect within his community. Jupiter in the fourth can also suggest that the person prefers to drive a large vehicle, such as a truck. He will also be very intelligent and receive a great education. Physically, Jupiter in the fourth house is a great protector. The person will be healthy, and at the end of his life he will be prosperous and happy.

Negative: An afflicted Jupiter in the fourth will cause difficulties with children and other family members. The mother could be domineering or a bit of a "know-it-all." The person will probably have some financial difficulties related to the family. There could be disputes over inheritances. He could also have expenses related to land or property. An afflicted Jupiter here also suggests lack of peace of mind due to a sense of being treated unfairly, or possibly due to financial worries. The person will probably also have problems with vehicles that cause expenditure.

Venus in the Fourth House

Positive: Venus in the fourth house is an excellent placement for happiness. The person will have a comfortable, artistically designed home, in which he will enjoy entertaining his friends. He will like to drive luxury cars, or at least cars that have a stylish design. This position also produces prosperity and affluence. The person will have a loving supportive mother and a great relationship with her. He will also be very fond of his other family members, and have a happy domestic life. The spouse will have a great love of the chosen profession, and might have artistic or musical abilities. The person will also be friendly, charming, compassionate, artistic and sensual. As a result, he will be popular and might even achieve honors in his school and community. Venus here is said to give good health and immunity from disease, as well as a tendency to live a long life.

Negative: An afflicted Venus in the fourth house can upset marital harmony. The person could experience a divorce and remarriage. He could also have emotional self-esteem problems and not feel that he is truly loved. His mother could be frivolous, materialistic or self-indulgent. He could have problems with houses and cars, or spend his money extravagantly in order to own them. He could live in uncomfortable, poorly designed homes and drive run-down cars. A difficult Venus here obviously disturbs comfort, peace of mind and happiness in life.

Saturn in the Fourth House

Positive: When Saturn is benefic and is in the fourth house the person comes from a solid background. His mother and other family members will be responsible and hard-working. He will also be a stable and responsible person. He will spend a good deal of time organizing his family affairs and tending to other domestic responsibilities. He may demonstrate an ability for property management as well. This position also suggests organizational or management ability for institutions, schools and communities. The person will live in a good, well-built, conservative home, that he will be more likely to obtain after the age of 36. His spouse will have a good job and may have management or organizational abilities. His father could also have a long life.

Negative: When Saturn is afflicted in the fourth house, the person's life will probably be unhappy. His mother will struggle in life and may have low energy, chronic health problems or other pressures and difficulties in life. In case of an extremely afflicted Saturn, the mother could be lost in childhood. The parents and the family will probably be a source of strain, demands, and pressure. Saturn here can also be pressurizing for the person's marriage, and tends to mar domestic peace. The spouse will probably have delays and pressures in the profession. The person may have career and financial problems. A negative Saturn here will sometimes cause problems connected with the person's automobiles. He could have many changes of residence and also experience difficulty purchasing homes. His home will constantly need repair, be dilapidated and uncomfortable. The end of his life will also tend to be difficult.

Rahu in the Fourth House

Positive: Rahu in the fourth house, if positive, produces an independent nature. The person will live in homes that have an alternative design, and contain plenty of technical or electrical appliances. His mother will be independent, or different in some way, and she might even be an immigrant to his place of birth. His mother will also have a long life. The person will experience many exciting trips and adventures. He will be interested in progressive philosophies related to the environment. He might also attend a school that is unorthodox, progressive or geared towards technology or science. Rahu here will also produce professional success for the spouse, who will tend to be physically thin. This position also favors the birth of one son.

Negative: A negative Rahu in the fourth house usually produces an unhappy life. The person will have a constant sense of urgency about getting a home or place to live, yet never will be satisfied with wherever he is living. This position gives an "itch you can't scratch," which means that there is a chronic sense of restlessness that will be projected outwardly into the environment. As a result, many things in the person's environment will be experienced as the source of the restlessness. The point here is that the restlessness comes from deep within, and can't be resolved by changing the outer environment. The person will also have problems with vehicles, and if Rahu is badly afflicted, he should drive carefully in order to avoid accidents. The spouse may be excessively ambitious or compulsive about the career. Rahu placed here is also a negative indication for the mother, either for her physical well-being or for the person's relationship with the mother.

Ketu in the Fourth House

Positive: When a benefic Ketu is placed in the fourth house, the person will be spiritually oriented, creative, or compassionate. He might come from an artistic or spiritual family. His mother will be intuitive, and will have a very uncommon personality. She will not be a public person, but will prefer to stay "behind the scenes." The person will have nice homes that are designed to create a soothing, spiritually uplifting feeling. He might use Feng Shui or Vastu to create a more spiritual environment, or he might live in a place with an oriental motif or a Japanese garden. He will like staying at ashrams and retreats. He will attend an alternative educational institution. The end of life will be spent in solitude or spiritual retreat.

Negative: A negative Ketu in the fourth house does not augur well for happiness in life. The person will probably be chronically dissatisfied. This dissatisfaction will be projected onto the mother, family, home, car and the environment in general. His mother might be undependable, evasive, and manipulative, or she might suffer from hard to diagnose health problems. She might also be depressed or feel like she is unrecognized or invisible. The person will have many changes of residence, and will not have a solid sense of security. He might also quit school before his education is completed. Homes will be the source of losses and disappointments. The person will also have troubles with automobiles and might hitchhike at times. The domestic life will also be colored by emotional loss and sadness. As a result, marriage and family life will be difficult.

The Fifth House (Putra Bhava)

The fifth house is the house of creativity, but here the word "creativity" is being used in the most fundamental sense. In the fourth house, the individual is connected with inner, transcendent consciousness, an infinitely stable aspect of self. Here in the fifth house, that consciousness begins to express itself. What this house signifies, then, is the impulse to create, to put awareness to use or to manifest it in the outer world.

One profound way in which this happens is by having children. The urge to reproduce, or to procreate, is caused by a fundamental play of consciousness that seeks to express its joy and reproduce itself in the outer field of diversity. So the fifth house signifies children and everything to do with children, including the sexual act leading to their creation.

This impulse for consciousness to express itself is also why the fifth house is termed the house of intelligence. Here we find not only the individual's basic intelligence level and memory, but also the particular subjects that engage his intellect. So, the fifth house can be used effectively to determine the type of education the individual receives.

Creative intelligence can be quite playful as well. In fact, that is its nature, pure joyfulness. In the fourth house, consciousness is stable and peaceful. Here it is vibrant and ecstatic. The fifth house is the house of play, recreation and entertainment. In fact, it symbolizes that part of our inner psychology, our "inner child" perhaps, which only wants to overflow with enthusiasm in an endless stream of creative play. This makes the fifth house the natural place of sports, games, drama, art, and all kinds of entertainment.

In this regard, romantic play also becomes an element of the fifth house. While the seventh house is the house of marriage and partnership, signifying the compromise and give and take aspects of relationship or married life, the fifth house is related to the romantic and sexual aspects of life. In Western cultures, it is also related to dating or courtship leading to marriage or a committed partnership.

This house also shows spiritual development. Consciousness, from the point of view of the fourth house, is flat and unmanifest. Here, consciousness becomes lively. From a yogic perspective, the first impulse of creative awareness, called ritam bhara pragya, has great power. By chanting mantras, doing pujas, or other spiritual practices that involve some form of repeated prayer or mantra, the spiritual aspirant refines his awareness to a level where the most subtle impulse of creative awareness can be perceived. At this level, siddhis, or psychic powers can manifest. Here the yogi begins to perceive celestial beings, such as one's Ishta Devata, or personal deity, who can assist him in his spiritual journey and even help him overcome material problems. For this reason, the fifth house signifies mantras, pujas, incantations, repeated prayers, affirmations, and other devices used to refine awareness.

Clearly, the fifth house has an element of magic to it, but it is actually a house of purvapunya, or accumulated merit from past lives. We really only receive what we have earned. This house, nevertheless, plays an important part in what we commonly term as luck in life. It allows us to play, to win, and to celebrate. It also plays a prime role in determining our financial achievements and general affluence in life, all as a result of past karma.

Significations of the Fifth House Given by Classical Authors of Vedic Astrology:

Past life credit (purvapunya); children; conception; yantras; mantras; realization through mantras; devotion to God; Ishta Devata (personal deity); religion; the mind; intelligence; memory; discrimination; mental inclinations; mental depth; seriousness; intensity; cheerfulness; worrying or thinking about the future; good advice; good heart; virtuous acts; giving of grain in charity; education; talent; musical instruments; entertainment; poetry; writing of books; fall in career; ruler; royalty; important invitations; father; disciples; money through the spouse; sex with a prostitute; personal love; mystery; business; affluence.

Physical Significations:

Heart; upper abdomen; stomach; liver; gall bladder; spleen; duodenum; intestines. Depending on the drekkana rising—right cheek, right side of the heart, and right knee.

The Ruler of the Fifth House Placed in the Twelve Houses

First House

Positive: If the ruler of the fifth house is placed in the first house, the person will be very intelligent. He will have one or two good children. This position gives the person a sense of authority and good judgment.

It also suggests that the person could have employees or subordinates. He will also be creative and might be talented in art, drama or writing. He will like sports, games and entertainment in general.

Negative: If the ruler of the fifth house is afflicted in the first house the person might not have children. This placement also causes the person to be susceptible to negative spiritual influences, and produces a tendency to associate with people who lack morals or integrity. In its most afflicted form, the person makes the proverbial "deal with the devil," and the classics say that he becomes the leader of a gang of thieves. If only moderately afflicted, however, the person may simply have political aspirations trading his integrity to some degree.

Second House

Positive: If the ruler of the fifth house is placed in the second house, the person becomes prosperous. This is a very good money combination. Since the fifth house represents the stock market, this placement suggests gains through investments. It can also allow the person to profit through contact with people in positions of authority. The person could be a good singer or simply interested in music. He will be attractive to the opposite sex and will have a good reputation. He will have a physically attractive spouse and great children. The first child will be very successful in his career, and will gain respect and status as a result. The fifth lord here is also a good placement for the study of astrology.

Negative: If the ruler of the fifth house is afflicted in the second house, the person could have financial gains and also financial losses. This placement suggests poor judgment regarding the stock market, so the person should be very careful not to get into risky investments. He might also have problems related to his children and spouse, so his domestic situation can lack harmony.

Third House

Positive: If the ruler of the fifth house is placed in the third house, the person will have more children than average for his culture. His children will become more successful and prosperous as they grow older. This placement is also good for the person's siblings, producing a positive relationship with them, and generally suggesting that they are intelligent and successful people. This placement seems to be quite common in the charts of writers, artists, and musicians, and suggests general creative talent.

Negative: If the ruler of the fifth house is afflicted in the third house, the person will have problems communicating with his children. His children might have difficulty achieving their goals, or will associate with friends of questionable character. Afflictions to the fifth lord here suggest a lack of mental balance for the person, producing communication problems, stinginess, and a tendency to gossip.

Fourth House

Positive: If the ruler of the fifth house is placed in the fourth house, the person will be successful and prosperous. This placement creates a type of Raja Yoga, a combination that promotes success and reputation. The person will have a good relationship with his mother, who will be an intelligent and successful person. He will also have a long life. He might also pursue a profession or business that he learns through his family. He will be intelligent, attend good schools, and receive a good education. He will have a good relationship with his children. One of his children might have an interest in gardening, houses or real estate. The first child might be introspective, spiritually inclined, and might like to travel. His children will tend to live near him, even after they grow up.

Negative: If the ruler of the fifth house is afflicted in the fourth house, the person will have problems with his children that will disturb his happiness and peace of mind. Similarly, he will have a difficult relationship with his mother, and she might have financial problems. This placement suggests that the first child will have many self-doubts and be shy or self-conscious. It is also possible that the person's grown children might live with him, creating financial strain and personal conflicts. (Please note: This is a possible result, peculiar to Western society, where children are expected to make their own living after they become adults. The combination might give completely contrary results in India, where the custom is different).

Fifth House

Positive: If the ruler of the fifth house is placed in the fifth house, the person will be lucky, prosperous, intelligent, and successful. He will do very well in school and could achieve some sort of academic distinction. He will have good children and a good relationship with them. The first child will be healthy, strong, intelligent, and have a powerful personality that is characterized by the qualities of the planet that is the fifth lord. This placement also produces "friends in high places" and knowledge of mantras and rituals. In addition, his mother will do well financially. His wife will be able to easily achieve her goals, have many friends, and become prosperous.

Negative: If the ruler of the fifth house is afflicted in the fifth house, the person will experience mixed results regarding children. For example, he might have children, but find it hard to communicate with them. It is also possible that he might have a good relationship with his children, but the children could have personal problems related to the afflicting planets and the houses they rule. In cases of serious affliction, the person may have no children at all. This placement also suggests problems in the educational process related to the afflicting planet. Although the person might be intelligent, he might interrupt his education for some reason. Similar mixed results might be noticed in the investment area, suggesting the need for caution regarding the stock market. The ruler of the fifth house, placed in the fifth, will usually give some good results even when it is afflicted, unless the affliction is very potent. Afflictions here also suggest a wavering mind, lack of integrity, and negative mental qualities.

Sixth House

Positive: If the ruler of the fifth house is strong, aspected by benefics, and placed in the sixth house, the person's children will be prosperous. The person could have an interest in health and might learn a good deal about various healing modalities. His maternal uncle or aunt could also be successful in some way. The person will have good luck getting employment. He will also get promoted or advance professionally by constantly taking classes and extra professional training. As a result, the person will gain more and more knowledge as he gets older, eventually becoming a real expert in his field.

Negative: The placement of the ruler of fifth house in the sixth house is generally problematic because it tends to spoil the person's luck. The person will have difficulty with finances, and will find it hard to succeed professionally. He might also have problems with authority figures at his place of employment. This placement also produces disagreements with children. If the fifth lord is also afflicted, then the children, especially the first child, could have health problems as well. This placement also spoils the person's mental balance, and can make the mind critical, argumentative, and cruel. As a result, the person could make enemies, or at least experience frequent friction with other people. This placement is also detrimental to the person's general health and vitality.

Seventh House

Positive: If the ruler of the fifth house is placed in the seventh house, the person will be lucky in marriage, and will marry an intelligent, successful, and physically attractive spouse. He will have good children, and it is possible that one of them could move to a foreign country. He will also have a good education and become successful and prosperous. He will be proud, helpful, virtuous, and have a natural faith in God. He will also be quite devoted to his teachers.

Negative: If the ruler of the fifth house is afflicted in the seventh house, the person will have difficult relationships with his children. His children, especially the first, might also experience relationship problems of their own. This placement can also produce various problems for a child living in a foreign country.

Eighth House

Positive: If the ruler of the fifth house is strong, aspected by benefics, and placed in the eighth house, the person will have an interest in the occult, and he might study astrology or related subjects. He might practice mantras and gain spiritual power as a result. He will have a great deal of spiritual progress in his life, based on his intense spiritual practices. Similarly, he might become interested in psychology or other therapeutic modalities. His first child will own nice houses, land, or cars, and will be generally happy in life. This placement can also give sudden, financial gains, and suggests that the person will benefit from inheritance, insurance, clients, or contracts. His mother might also become quite prosperous, and might have a knack for stock market investing.

Negative: Generally, the ruler of the fifth house, placed in the eighth house, is a placement that spoils the person's luck. He will have many losses and mishaps in life. He might also go into debt at times. This placement is also detrimental for any kind of speculation, gambling or stock market investing. The person could lose a child if the fifth lord is seriously afflicted. In most cases, however, the child simply goes through many dynamic changes in life, or becomes rebellious and hard to handle.

Ninth House

Positive: If the ruler of the fifth house is placed in the ninth house, the person will be very intelligent and will receive a good education. If the fifth lord is particularly strong and positive, then he might take his education to a very high level and become an expert in his chosen field of study. His children will also be quite successful and intelligent, and will become highly educated. He will be interested in religion and spiritual philosophies, and fortunate in getting good teachers and a spiritual guru. This position also produces creative potential and is quite good for writing, publishing, art, music, and drama. It also makes a positive contribution to the person's physical appearance. In general, the person will be successful, prosperous, well-educated and very fortunate.

Negative: If the ruler of the fifth house is afflicted in the ninth house, the person could still be intelligent, but might possess some negative mental traits. As a result, he could be irreverent and disrespectful of teachers and religion. He might have problems with teachers, spiritual gurus and even his father. His children could also have educational problems, in spite of being highly intelligent.

Tenth House

Positive: If the ruler of the fifth house is placed in the tenth house, the person will be very creative. For example, his work could involve writing, and his writing could focus on a subject that is characterized by the natural significations of the planet that rules the fifth house. This placement also suggests that the person's career is intimately linked to his education, which requires him to write a thesis in order to obtain a certification or credential. Sometimes the career is linked to education more directly and the person becomes a teacher. The person could also have a position of authority in his work. In any case, the connection of the fifth lord with the tenth house creates a RajaYoga and is extremely favorable for professional success and reputation.

Negative: If the ruler of the fifth house is afflicted in the tenth house, the person will have career problems related to education. He might fail important exams related to professional certification, and have to make several attempts before he passes. He could also find it difficult to write or publish material related to his work, or might simply be criticized for what he writes. If he teaches for a living, then he might find his students hard to handle. An afflicted fifth lord here disrupts the normally positive results of this placement, and makes it harder to achieve success professionally. In cases of serious affliction, the person could experience professional disgrace or scandal related to something that has been written or published, or possibly related to a romantic affair.

Eleventh House

Positive: If the ruler of the fifth house is placed in the eleventh house, the person will be well-educated, successful, prosperous, and will gain more and more success as he gets older. This placement is a very positive combination for financial gains in general. If the fifth lord is strong and supported by other benefic influences, then the person could become a good investor who derives particular benefit from mutual funds. This is also a great placement for writing, allowing the person's publications to reach the masses. His children will also be healthy, intelligent and successful. The first child will be particularly attached to his spouse and will be a very social and easy-going person. This placement also makes the person friendly and social.

Negative: If the ruler of the fifth house is afflicted in the eleventh house, the person will have a combination of financial loss and gain through investments. As a result, he should be cautious regarding stock market investing, and might do better if he sticks with conservative mutual funds and a long-term strategy. If the afflictions are severe, then the person should avoid market investing altogether, because this placement will give poor judgment and produce financial losses related to risk-taking. This placement also suggests that the person's first child could experience marital difficulty.

Twelfth House

Positive: If the ruler of the fifth house is strong, supported, and placed in the twelfth house, the person will be very spiritually inclined. He will be interested in psychology, introspection, reflection and meditation. He could practice a meditation that involves the use of a mantra. He might also be interested in travel, and will have a good deal of luck and positive experiences while in foreign countries or distant places. He will get a good education at a school that is in a distant place. He could spend some time studying in a foreign country.

Negative: If the ruler of the fifth house is afflicted in the twelfth house, the person will have a wavering mind and difficulty focusing. As a result, he might find it difficult to study and even to stay in school. He might fail exams or quit school. This placement also causes difficulties, uncertainties, and losses concerning children. The person will also experience romantic disappointments and losses. This is a common placement in the charts of people who have been separated from their children through divorce.

Planets in the Fifth House

Sun in the Fifth House

Positive: A positive Sun in the fifth house will give the person a strong sense of self-expression. He might have a dramatic flare or be talented in the arts. This position promotes athletic prowess. The person will have a desire to be in charge and may have leadership abilities. He will have a magnanimous and loyal nature. He will also be proud of his children, and the first child will have an outgoing personality, leadership abilities, physical beauty, and might become very successful. The person might also begin to make money at a young age. This position also makes the person very intelligent, and will give him some distinction in his education. The classical literature suggests that he will be skilled in the use of mantras and also with grammar. He will be interested in romance, and will be a very passionate person, with a sense of drama and a playful nature.

Negative: An afflicted Sun in the fifth house spoils the person's luck to some degree. He will have struggles in life as a result. He will experience difficulties regarding children, either in having them or in his relationship with them. If the Sun is severely afflicted, loss of a child can result. The first child might have a patronizing or overbearing personality. The person will also have problems in education. This position of the Sun is also detrimental to the longevity of the father, especially if it also occupies a malefic navamsha. It is also said to make the person pursue various vices, have a bilious constitution and many enemies. He will have an overly dramatic personality, and might be prone to illicit romantic affairs.

Moon in the Fifth House

Positive: When the Moon is in the fifth house, the person will be very intelligent. He will have a strong attachment to his children. The first child will have a gentle, sociable nature and might be special in some way, or could be in the public eye. The person will do well in his education and might even achieve some educational distinction. The classical literature suggests that the person will receive honors from "Brahmans and Gods." He will also have an attractive appearance, a charming nature, and will be appreciated by his superiors. He will be a passionate person and will gain through his relatives and through marriage. He will have a good spouse who has a gentle and sociable nature. He might worship a female deity.

Negative: If the Moon is weak or afflicted in the fifth house, the person will have a moody and changeable mind. He will have an overly dramatic disposition and will be a constant seeker of pleasure and romance. As a result, he will be prone to affairs. He might also become emotionally dependent on a lover, or on the concept of romantic involvement in general. He will have many ups and downs in marriage and may get a divorce as a result. This position of the Moon also produces many difficulties with children. The person will be very attached to his children, but his children will be a source of unhappiness. He will have problems in his education due to the passionate, changeable nature of his mind.

Mars in the Fifth House

Positive: Mars in the fifth house gives vitality, energy and a tendency to become involved in sports and games. The person will be enthusiastic and will have an energetic mind. He might have some skill in mathematics or receive a technical education. His children, especially the first child, will have an ambitious, assertive nature. The person will [Sarah] have good luck through stocks and other investments, and will become successful and prosperous. Mars here can also make him creative in a way that uses the physical body, such as dance or sculpture. He can also express his creativity in a technical way, such as technical writing or programming. He will also be attractive to the opposite sex and will have a strong libido. As a result, he will be romantically assertive. A woman with this position, for example, might be willing to ask the man out on a date, or might take the initiative in making romantic connections in other ways.

Negative: A difficult Mars in the fifth house will make the mind critical and angry. The person will have problems with children. If there are other natural malefics influencing Mars, this could produce a miscarriage, abortion, caesarean section or other complication with childbirth. This position of Mars also gives problems with education. The person might be a busybody. He will also have a passionate nature, and will tend to become involved in illicit romantic affairs. Marriage will also be a source of difficulties. Since an afflicted Mars in the fifth house disrupts the mind, the person's education will probably be disrupted as well. He should stay away from speculation, gambling, and the stock market because these kinds of investments will bring financial loss.

Mercury in the Fifth House

Positive: When Mercury is in the fifth house, the person will be very intelligent. As a result, he will excel in school and receive a great education. He might study language, humanities, communication, economics, accounting or literature. He will enjoy reading. This position of Mercury will tend to make the person successful and prosperous. He will be a good writer or musician. His children will be very intelligent and will be good communicators. His children, especially the first child, will also have a good sense of humor and will be charming and clever. He will also have an intelligent and successful spouse. According to the classics, Mercury in this position also confers skills in "mantra shastra, astrology and mathematics." It is also a fortunate position for having a good relationship with one's mother. The person might develop an interest in art, music, or drama. He could also develop knowledge of investing. A positive Mercury in the fifth can make the person very good at analyzing and investing in the stock market.

Negative: Mercury in the fifth house, if afflicted, can produce problems regarding children. The person might have problems having children or have communications problems with the children. He could adopt a child. In some cases this position suggests that the person will cause problems for his children through constant meddling in their affairs. His education will also be disrupted or difficult. He will have losses through speculation, gambling or the stock market. In general, an afflicted Mercury in the fifth house is unfavorable for success.

Jupiter in the Fifth House

Positive: When Jupiter is in the fifth house the person will be blessed with good luck in life. He will be highly intelligent and will receive an excellent education. His mind will tend to be buoyant and optimistic. He will have good teachers and other types of benefactors. This position of Jupiter sometimes gives good luck in speculation, gambling and stock market investing. It is also a great position for overall success and prosperity, and sometimes gives unexpected financial gains. Finances will tend to be more abundant after the age of 28. Regarding children, however, Jupiter gives limited quantity but high quality. It is very common for this placement to produce one good child. Since Jupiter aspects the Ascendant from the fifth house, it gives good health and increases the longevity. This is also a good placement for teaching and for all activities related to children or students. It can allow the person to benefit from the practice of mantras as well.

Negative: If a malefic Jupiter is placed in the fifth house, the person will have problems with money. He might gain money and then lose it. He could also have losses in any speculative venture, so he should never take risks with money. Children will also be a source of difficulty. Although the person might be intelligent, he will not use his intelligence in the best way. He could also have problems or disagreements with teachers, and his education could be delayed or interrupted. Although Jupiter in the fifth will tend to produce romantic involvements, an afflicted Jupiter can produce problems with lovers.

Venus in the Fifth House

Positive: If Venus is well placed in the fifth house, the person will be very creative. This is a good position for an artist or musician. The person will have a joyful, happy nature and will be very fond of play, recreation and pleasure. He will be romantic and attractive to the opposite sex. His romantic and sexual life will be loving, affectionate, passionate and joyful. This position of Venus is also good for children. The person will have a loving and warm relationship with his children, and will have a special fondness for the first child. Similarly, the children, especially the first child, will be charming, creative, diplomatic or beautiful. The classics say that this position causes the children to have the ability to speak well. The person's education will be enjoyable, and he might study arts, music or humanities. He might also learn astrology. He will be generous and fortunate, and will easily be prosperous. He will be quite lucky with respect to the spouse as well, attracting a loving, knowledgeable or successful mate.

Negative: A negative Venus in the fifth house will make the person overly sensual and prone to have problems related to overindulgence. He might have an excessively strong libido, for example, and channel his sexual energy in directions that aren't in harmony with his health or happiness. On the other hand, if Venus is seriously afflicted, his libido might be very low, or he might have a lack of affection in his life. Needless to say, a negative Venus in the fifth house is not a great placement for marital bliss, and tends to produce problems related to sexuality. This placement also can produce problems with children, who might exhibit these negative Venus traits as well. It is also a negative factor for the financial prospects, bringing the likelihood of financial loss through self-indulgent dissipation of resources.

Saturn in the Fifth House

Positive: If a strong and positive Saturn is placed in the fifth house, the person will have good children. The first child will be patient, persevering, responsible, and successful. This child will also come into his power after his mid-thirties. The person will have children late in life and after much deliberation. There will be a distinct sense that raising children is a serious responsibility, so he will plan it carefully. Contraception is usually an important part of the scheme. Saturn here will also give the person perseverance and patience on the academic level. He might, for example, attend school for a long period of time in order to get an advanced degree. This is also a good position for prudent and conservative management of investments and profiting from the stock market.

Negative: A negative Saturn in the fifth house will spoil the person's luck and make life difficult as a result. He will have problems in school and could struggle academically for a long period of time before completing his education. His finances will also suffer and he will frequently over-extend himself. He will have an inhibited, pressurized mind, find it difficult to be generous and loving, and will find it hard to create a loving relationship. Sexual experience and romantic encounters could occur later in life. His marriage might lapse into a routine, with limited passion and affection. His children will also be a source of pressure and frustration. In many cases, the person senses in advance that raising children will be difficult, and chooses not to have them. In other cases, having children is postponed until it is too late on biologically.

Rahu in the Fifth House

Positive: When Rahu is in the fifth house, the person becomes fascinated by astrology, metaphysics, technology or other revolutionary subjects. He will be a good writer with a spontaneous writing style. He might have a child who is very bright, or who has some revolutionary or innovative qualities. A good Rahu here favors financial prosperity as well, especially investments in stocks that are related to technology. The person will be highly intelligent, and his education will be alternative in some way, or he might study a technological subject. He will be highly creative and innovative. His creative pursuits will also have a Rahu-like quality such as playing an electric or technological musical instrument. If he is a writer, he could write and even publish books on alternative subjects. He might become a technical writer or write computer programs. In all of these areas, he will display a unique and innovative style of thinking. He will also have an interest in mantras and rituals, and may know a variety of spiritual techniques.

Negative: When Rahu is malefic and placed in the fifth house, the person will have a compulsive, driven mind. The mind will be distracted, constantly veering off the subject. The person will find it hard to stay in the present moment. Rahu represents the astral plane, so when it is located in the fifth, the person will get caught up in streams of consciousness such as daydreaming. This is also a difficult placement for children. The first child especially, will be rebellious and overbearing. If Rahu is aspected by other malefics, then there could be a miscarriage or abortion. Rahu here also suggests that the person could have surprising experiences related to children, such as an accidental pregnancy. It can also cause problems in the relationship with the child. The person might give their child up for adoption or place the child in foster care. This is also a difficult placement for stock market investing or any other form of risky investments. The person will lose if he gambles or takes risks with money in any way. He could experience health problems that affect the joints, hips, or neck, or restrict movement in some way. Rahu here can give nervous indigestion or ulcers due to an over-active, compulsive mind and an excess of vata.

Ketu in the Fifth House
Positive: When a positive Ketu occupies the fifth house, the person will be very creative. He will use art as a meditation. He will also enjoy journaling, or writing in a free-flowing intuitive style. Ketu here also gives intuitive, spiritually-oriented, or creative children. The first child will take things a day at a time, and have a very alternative approach to life. The person will allow his children plenty of space to grow and develop, without much interference. He will not be attached to solving their problems for them, but will allow them to find their own solutions. Ketu in the fifth also suggests that the person might study alternative subjects in school, such as religion, philosophy, art or music. Ketu is also a planet of refined technologies, so he could study high-tech subjects. The person may demonstrate an interest in spiritual subjects, especially those that come from ancient traditions. He could also be interested in healing.

Negative: A malefic Ketu in the fifth house is an indication of disappointments regarding children. The person could feel let down by his children, especially the first child, who will fail to meet his expectations. The first child could be evasive, deceptive or irresponsible, or the child might simply move away. In the case of a seriously afflicted Ketu, even loss of a child is possible. The person will also have difficulty with his own education. This is not a good placement for any kind of financial risk-taking, and the person should avoid the stock market and gambling. Unless the chart has other strong yogas for money, an afflicted Ketu in the fifth house will generally spoil the person's financial prospects. Even on the spiritual level, the person will attract difficulties. Any practice of mantras, for example, should be done carefully, in order to avoid negative results due to mispronunciation or improper attitude.

The Sixth House (Roga Bhava)

Traditionally, the sixth house has been thought of as the house of disease, enmity, obstacles, and struggle. While it does signify these things, it is also important to understand this house in the broader context of the evolution of consciousness. In the fifth house, spontaneous self-expression was the rule. In the sixth house, that self-expression is challenged, questioned, analyzed and forced to perfect itself.

In this house the natural fifth house urge to play takes on a new tone. Instead of simple playfulness, the sixth house introduces the element of competition. Here, we are motivated to beat our competitors and vanquish our enemies. As adults, we act out our sixth house energy by competing in academics, business, politics, and sometimes even go to war. It is important to remember, however, that what we are really doing is attempting to overcome obstacles, which we believe are blocking our progress.

The sixth house also symbolizes how disease appears in the body, presenting us with a sense of physical limitation. It reveals not only the nature of diseases or physical problems we may contract during our lifetime, but also the possibility of overcoming those diseases. From this angle, it is important to remember that astrology, in its best application, is an effective tool for helping to identify and prevent potential health problems reflected by the sixth house.

This house also indicates how we deal with negative emotions like anger, fear, resentment and hatred. While the experience of emotion through the fifth house is simple, expansive joy, in the sixth house, the heart shrinks as we become aware of criticism. When criticized, it is a natural reaction to attack or resent our critics in return. This brings conflict, changing the critics into enemies. This is why the sixth house is traditionally used to signify enemies.

When we are attacked or criticized, however, we can choose an alternative reaction, seeking instead to express one of the more positive qualities of the sixth house. This positive sixth house quality is discrimination. While the fifth house shows raw intelligence, educational pursuits and various interests that engage the mind, the sixth house, because of its natural relationship to the sign of Virgo, shows how the mind categorizes, analyzes, and thus limits the subject of interest. In its positive mode, analysis can be a very useful tool in dealing with negativity. In fact, it is an indispensable tool for the purpose of cultivating spiritual awareness. Choosing the higher discriminative power of the sixth house over its more surface, reactive tendencies, allows us to not only understand our critics, but also to diagnose and even cure misunderstanding, which is the root cause of most anger, resentment and other negative emotions. In fact, cultivating the sixth house ability to discriminate and understand is a major key to dealing with, and ultimately transcending, all types of limitation. This doesn't mean that simply understanding our sixth house issues will make us totally free from troubles in life. Karmic law, after all, dictates that whatever we have sewn in the past will inevitably come back. To really understand astrology, in fact, is to accept the polarities of positive and negative karma. Once accepted, however, the idea is to stop interpreting problems as limitations. Instead, the idea is to seek to understand the situation rather than struggle to overcome it.

As a matter of fact, a deeper understanding of karmic theory reveals that there is really only one negative karmic pattern. It is called "the belief that we are limited," and it is in the sixth house that this belief is confronted head-on. For some people, the sense of limitation is very strong. Others hardly notice it. Some people, for example, are born with weak constitutions, suffer congenital diseases, accidents, and are recipients of all sorts of so-called negative karma. Yet they refuse to interpret their experience as limited. Thomas Edison made more than one thousand attempts to invent the light bulb before he eventually succeeded. When a newspaper reporter later asked him, "Mr. Edison, what did it feel like to have failed so many times?" Edison responded, "What do you mean fail? I now know more than a thousand ways not to make a light bulb."

Clearly, the sixth house is more than a house of disease and limitation. It is also a house that holds a key to happiness and even to success in life. It is an arena in which the spirit is tested, in which we learn how not to be overshadowed by the illusion of limitation. Even though we may not be able to change some of the actual karmic situations reflected by this house, we can learn to interpret them, not as problems, but as opportunities for growth. Suffering may be the common reaction to many sixth house issues, but it is, ultimately, an unnecessary one.

Significations of the Sixth House Given by Classical Authors of Vedic Astrology:

Diseases; enemies; job (in the employment of others); competitors;

service to others; employees; tenants; debts; enmity; injury; accidents; obstacles; battles; miserliness; theft; debt; receiving charity; guarding of one's credit; worry; anxiety; fear; reproach; misunderstanding with brothers; insanity; vices; imprisonment; prisons; cruelty; stepmother; maternal uncle; god of death; thieves; injury; handicaps; exertion; wounds; irregular meals; phlegm; poison.

Physical Significations:

Large intestine; kidney; diseases in general. Depending on the drekkana rising—right jaw, right lung, right breast, and right calf.

The Ruler of the Sixth House Placed in the Twelve Houses

First House

Positive: If the ruler of the sixth house is strong, supported, and placed in the first house, the person will have great health and strong vitality. He will have a bright, analytical mind. He will be meticulous, courageous, reliable, and will be a very hard worker. This placement also makes it easy for the person to find employment, and to succeed by his own efforts. He will be competitive and will outperform his competitors. If other factors in the chart agree, the person will have a pet with whom he is deeply bonded.

Negative: If the ruler of the sixth house is weak and afflicted in the first house, the person will have ill health and poor recuperative powers. He will suffer from diseases characteristic of the planet that rules the sixth or first houses. This is also a placement that makes the person argumentative, impatient, and critical. As a result, he will have problems in his relationships with family members, spouse, and friends. He will probably make enemies as well. He will find it difficult to find good employment. Once employed, he will have problems advancing or simply maintaining his job. In cases of serious affliction, this placement can indicate criminal tendencies.

Second House

Positive: If the ruler of the sixth house is strong, supported and placed in the second house, the person will become successful and prosperous through his hard work and personal effort. He will be respected among his family and friends, and will always fulfill his duties in life. He might also spend some time living in a foreign country. He will eat a very healthy diet that will contribute to a high vitality level. If the person has a pet, he will enjoy spending money on him, and will feed the pet high quality food.

Negative: If the ruler of the sixth house is afflicted in the second house, the person will experience financial losses and setbacks. His dietary habits will be inconsistent and he will eat poor quality food. This will detract from his vitality level and weaken his health. It also suggests ailments related to the eyes, teeth or mouth. Similarly, the person might have a speech impediment or fear of public speaking. This placement is also problematic for the person's relationship with his family, suggesting that he could find it difficult to provide for them. The person could also lose money or possessions through theft. This placement can also prompt the person to spend money on pets or animals.

Third House

Positive: If the ruler of the sixth house is strong, supported, and placed in the third house, the person will be very hard working and industrious. His siblings, especially the next younger sibling, will own nice houses, land or cars, and will generally be prosperous and successful. Similarly, a maternal aunt or uncle
will be very successful and highly respected. His spouse will be spiritually inclined and may travel extensively.

Negative: If the ruler of the sixth house is ill placed in the third house, the person will have a negative relationship with siblings, or his siblings might have health problems. If the third lord is afflicted here, the problems related to his siblings will be magnified. The person could be angry or critical, and will alienate other people through his communication style. He could have physical problems related to the ears or shoulders. If he has employees, then they might be unreliable, deceitful, or disagreeable.

Fourth House

Positive: If the ruler of the sixth house is strong, supported, and placed in the fourth house, the person might own rental property. He will be very consistent and thorough regarding maintenance for his home, car, yard, and rental properties. He could find employment working for the school district, the city, or for other foundations or institutions. He will also be quite helpful to his mother. This placement is also good for general prosperity. If the person has a pet, he will probably let the animal stay in the house, or could possibly build a special house for him outside.

Negative: If the ruler of the sixth house is afflicted in the fourth house, the person could have a negative relationship with his mother and other family members. He will live in an uncomfortable house or apartment, and will probably rent, instead of owning his residence. He will lack steadiness, security, peace of mind and happiness. He will drive used cars that are constantly in need of repair. If the person has a pet, the animal could damage the person's furniture or house in some way.

Fifth House

Positive: If the ruler of the sixth house is strong, supported and placed in the fifth house, the person could have an interest in medicine or healing, and study subjects related to the healing arts. His children, especially the first child, will be prosperous. The person will be happy, kind, and always ready to help his children. He will also be very lucky getting jobs, and will easily get promotions and raises. As a result, he will become prosperous and successful through his own work. This placement also promotes good health and vitality. If other factors in the chart agree, then the person could get a pet to please his children.

Negative: If the ruler of the sixth house is afflicted in the fifth house, it can make the person unfortunate. He will find the educational process difficult and tedious, and he could be antagonistic to his teachers. This placement also makes it generally difficult to succeed at the profession. It also creates difficulties in friendships. The person could be negative, selfish, critical, or even unethical. He could also experience negative relationships with his children. If the fifth lord is afflicted here, then these indications will be magnified, and the children could suffer from ill health.

Sixth House

Positive: If the ruler of the sixth house is placed in the sixth house then the person will have good recuperative ability, high vitality and good health. He will get employment easily, work hard, and will become successful. His mother's next younger sibling will be strong, healthy, and successful and will have a personality that is characterized by the qualities of the planet that rules the sixth house. This placement is also good for the general well-being of the person's siblings and suggests that his next younger sibling might own land or houses. The person could have employees in his home or business. If he has a pet, then the pet will be strong, healthy and will have a long life.

Negative: If the ruler of the sixth house is afflicted in the sixth house, the person will have health problems related to the parts of the body represented by the planet that rules the sixth. Although he will probably get employment, he may have problems, delays, or obstacles in the process of getting a job. Similarly, he could be laid off, fired, or criticized by his employer. If he has employees, then they could create problems related to the planets aspecting the sixth lord or the houses they own.

Seventh House

Positive: If the ruler of the sixth house has positive support and is placed in the seventh house, the person will take a service-oriented approach to marriage. He will be willing to help other people as well. His spouse will be introspective, shy, or spiritually inclined. This placement is also generally beneficial for wealth. If the person has a pet, then the pet will be easy-going and mellow, and the person will greatly enjoy the pet's companionship.

Negative: The placement of the ruler of the sixth house in the seventh house is generally difficult for marriage. If it is afflicted, separation or divorce can result. In any case, it suggests arguments and general marital conflict. The spouse could be insecure or self-conscious. The person could be selfish and unwilling to help other people.

Eighth House

Positive: If the ruler of the sixth house is supported and placed in the eighth house, the person will be interested in various healing therapies, either for his own benefit, or for the benefit of others. As a result, he will go through a metamorphosis with his physical body, overcoming physical limitations and building a strong body and high vitality. He could also find employment in a job in which he handles or manages the money of other people.

Negative: The placement of the ruler of the sixth house in the eighth house is a famous combination for overcoming problems. This, however, infers that there will be problems to overcome. The person will suffer from health problems characteristic of the planet that rules the sixth house. He might also be irreverent or even hostile towards good people. This placement can make the person covet the wealth or spouses of others. If the person has a pet, the pet might have a negative disposition, become sick, or die suddenly. This placement is also seen in the charts of people who are afraid of animals, or who have negative experiences related to animals.

Ninth House

Positive: If the ruler of the sixth house has positive support and is placed in the ninth house, the person's father will be successful and highly respected in his career. Similarly, he might have a maternal aunt or uncle who is prosperous, happy, stable, and owns a good house or property. This placement is also good for a service approach to spiritual development, and sometimes gives the person the opportunity to be of service to his teachers, or even a spiritual guru. It is also suggests a link between the person's physical health and his spiritual development. In the West, for example, the person with this combination is often involved in healing modalities that have spiritual roots such as Ayurveda, oriental medicine, or spiritual healing. If other factors in the chart agree, this is also a good position for people who work or deal with wood. It is also favorable for owning pets, suggesting that the person will have a sense of purpose stemming from his relationship with animals.

Negative: If the ruler of the sixth house is afflicted in the ninth house, the person could have a difficult relationship with his father. He may have an antagonistic attitude towards religion. This placement suggests financial problems, as well as problems with higher education. The person might be critical of his teachers, professors, or gurus. In cases of serious affliction, this placement can suggest problems to the hips, and has been associated with lameness.

Tenth House

Positive: If the ruler of the sixth house is strong, supported, and placed in the tenth house, the person will be successful in his profession, and will be respected in his family. He will obtain employment, as well as raises and promotions easily. This placement suggests service-oriented work (if self-employed), or work dealing with the employment of other people. It is also a common placement in the charts of people who work in health-related professions. Sometimes this position also gives the ability to speak well in front of others. A maternal aunt or uncle could be very intelligent, successful, and respected. The person could also live comfortably for a time in a foreign country. If he owns a pet, the pet will be active, playful and intelligent, and the person will include the animal in many of his activities.

Negative: If the ruler of the sixth house is afflicted and placed in the tenth house, the person will have a negative relationship with his boss or his coworkers. He might be criticized at work and could experience many professional uncertainties, such as being laid off or fired. This placement is also detrimental to the person's relationship with his mother. He will have powerful competitors or enemies.

Eleventh House

Positive: If the ruler of the sixth house is strong, supported and placed in the eleventh house, the person will achieve his goals through hard work, perseverance and patience. He will be proud, and courageous and will be able to overcome any competitor or opponent. He will even be able to profit from his opponents or competitors. This placement can also be good for owning pets, and the person will consider his pet to be his friend.

Negative: If the ruler of the sixth house is weak, afflicted and placed in the eleventh house, the person will have physical problems related to the planet that is the sixth lord. The person will have to struggle very hard in order to achieve his goals, and will face many obstacles in the process. He will also experience various financial hardships, and could be overworked and underpaid. His next older sibling may experience many upheavals and changes in his life, and could have ill health. He could also have an antagonistic relationship with his older sibling. His opponents or enemies could get in the way of his achievement and success. This is also a position that suggests financial losses through theft. If the person has a pet, the animal could have health problems related to the planet that is the sixth lord.

Twelfth House

Positive: If the ruler of the sixth house is strong, positive, and placed in the twelfth house, the person will adopt service as a form of sadhana or spiritual practice. He will also have a strong sense of the connection between the state of his health and his spiritual development. He could also enjoy going to health spas and other retreat centers where healing is the focus. He might have an intuitive relationship with his pets, and even be able to communicate with animals.

Negative: If the ruler of the sixth house is afflicted and placed in the twelfth house, the person could have a negative attitude towards psychology, introspection, and meditation. He will also be antagonistic towards spirituality in general. He may have a tendency to become physically ill while traveling in foreign countries or distant places. His pets could die, run away, or get lost, or he might simply choose not to have a pet. This is also a negative placement for finances, suggesting wasteful expenditure and general losses. If the sixth lord is seriously afflicted, the person could be forced to spend his money in the process of overcoming a health problem.

Planets in the Sixth House

Sun in the Sixth House

Positive: When a beneficial Sun is placed in the sixth house, the person will be very intelligent and will have an analytical mind. He will be a hard worker who will take pride in his work and will become progressively more successful in his career as time goes on. He might be interested in doing service-oriented work or healing work. This is a good placement for getting jobs under the employment of other people. If the person is self-employed, then he could hire loyal, capable employees. The Sun here also suggests that the person's reputation will grow as he gets older. He will be competitive and ambitious. As a result he could become powerful and influential. He will also have good digestion and good vitality. This position favors wealth, success, power, and fame. If the Sun, Moon or the Ascendant falls in a chatushpad drekkana, then the person will have a love of pets, and might have a dog or a cat.

Negative: When the Sun is afflicted and is placed in the sixth house, the person will struggle in life. He could have health problems related to the digestion, bones, teeth, or heart. He could also have problems that are produced by an excess of pitta (fire), such as inflammations or rashes. The Sun here also produces problems with animals and fire. The father will go through health problems or career problems, or the person might have a difficult relationship with the father. In cases of a seriously afflicted Sun, the father might die when the person is young. The Sun here also produces problems with employment. The person may not be recognized or appreciated at his place of employment, or he could have problems finding or holding a job. These problems will cause the person to feel like a failure, because his self-esteem is wrapped up in his ability to shine in his work. If the person is an employer, then he might have problems with his employees, or he might be domineering in his attitude towards his employees.

Moon in the Sixth House

Positive: If the Moon is beneficial and is placed in the sixth house, the person will have a bright, analytical mind and a helpful nature. He will enjoy his job and make friends at his place of employment. His career will rise in the middle part of life. The person will become successful as an employee and will get promotions and the praise of his employers. He will also have an interest in either his own health, or in the healing arts. He will recognize the importance of good dietary habits in maintaining sound health and will regulate his diet accordingly. He could also become a good cook or even work in the food industry. As a result, a beneficial and well-aspected Moon in the sixth house can suggest good health. The person may also be attached to his maternal aunts and uncles. If the Moon, Sun or Ascendant falls in chatushpad drekkanas or in nakshatras related to animals, the person will be very attached to a pet.

Negative: A negative Moon in the sixth house suggests fluctuating health. The person might have digestive problems, rheumatism, arthritis, or problems related to the bladder or breasts. His health will also be influenced by the state of his mind and his moods. This position of the Moon suggests physical or emotional difficulties in childhood. In extreme cases, this position could indicate death in childhood. The person will either have a difficult relationship with his mother or the mother will have a hard life in some way. He will experience losses and difficulties through other females as well. Some classical texts suggest that the person will have a sexual relationship with a widowed female after the age of 36. An afflicted Moon in the sixth suggests unreliable employees, as well as bad relations with them.

Mars in the Sixth House

Positive: Mars in the sixth house makes the person hardworking and competitive. He will have abundant energy and ambition, and will become successful and prosperous. He will be a fighter, both literally and figuratively. If he has setbacks, Mars here will allow him to recover his losses quickly. Similarly, Mars in the sixth house gives the ability to fight back and recuperate from health problems. This overall fighting attitude will allow him to overcome his enemies or competitors. He will also have a strong libido and will be passionate. His digestion will be good, and he will have good health and strong vitality. He will have leadership abilities and one of his sons could become famous. If other factors in the chart suggest a love of animals, then he might have a dog.

Negative: A negative Mars in the sixth house is bad for health. If it is seriously afflicted, the person might have surgeries, injuries, blood problems or other physical problems related to Mars. In charts of doctors, however, this placement sometimes relates more to the surgeries or health problems of their patients. He might experience problems from animals or might mistreat animals. The person will have many disputes and difficulties with competitors or enemies. This is also a bad placement for his mother, his mother's siblings, and his own siblings, or his relationship with them.

Mercury in the Sixth House

Positive: When Mercury is in the sixth house, the person will have a very analytical mind and might show an interest in the healing arts. He will also be interested in learning about his own health, and in reading books on diet, exercise and other subjects which contribute to maintaining personal health. As a result, he will tend to have good health and vitality. He will be a good writer and also have some ability in astrology. His employer might provide advanced education or job training for him, which will enable him to advance in his job situation. He will always be interested in gaining the most advanced training available in his field. He will be an intelligent and good worker who is very capable of achieving any task. He will also be very methodical and meticulous in work. If the Sun, Moon, or Ascendant falls in chatushpad drekkanas or in nakshatras signifying animals, then the person may be interested in animals, and could have a cat as a pet.

Negative: A negative Mercury in the sixth house can produce negative thinking. The person will tend to be critical and argumentative. As a result, this is not a very good placement for relationships in general, and can spoil domestic harmony. The person will also have difficulty in his job, either in becoming proficient at the necessary job skills, or in his relationship with coworkers. He will also make enemies, and may have to deal with lawsuits and other disputes. If he is an employer, this placement of Mercury could suggest problems with employees. An afflicted Mercury here can also bring health problems. The person might have problems with the lungs, thyroid, nervous system, or skin. He could also experience problems that are caused or magnified by worry. In some cases, the person will be a hypochondriac. This placement is also challenging for education. The person struggles in order to learn, or his education could be interrupted.

Jupiter in the Sixth House

Positive: Jupiter in the sixth house is a good placement for getting jobs. The person gets good, well-paying jobs, even when there is stiff competition for the job. He will be very successful in his job and will be highly respected. He will have good relations with coworkers and employers. If self-employed, he might do service-oriented work. He will become prosperous slowly, through hard work and perseverance. This is also a good placement for working in a health-related field. Similarly, Jupiter in the sixth house gives good recuperative ability, and suggests general freedom from disease. This placement is also good for the study of astrology. If the focal point, such as the Sun, Moon or Ascendant, falls in chatushpad drekkanas or in nakshatras related to animals, then the person will enjoy pets and may like riding horses. He might even have a horse or a large dog as a pet.

Negative: When Jupiter is afflicted and placed in the sixth house, the person will struggle in order to become prosperous. This could take the form of interruptions in employment. He might be lazy or could try to get other people to do his work. He might also adopt a know-it-all attitude at work. There could be health problems related to the digestive system, the liver, gall bladder or with allergies.

Venus in the Sixth House
Positive: Venus in the sixth house is a good position for enjoying work. The person makes friends at work and might even meet the spouse in the place of employment. In general, marriage will be more likely and more enjoyable later in life. The person's job could involve the arts, creativity, beauty, gems, clothing, food, or social values. This position generally suggests love of animals. The person's health will also tend to be good. Normally, a positive Venus would be thought of as an unafflicted Venus. In the case of Venus in combustion or in an enemy's sign, however, the person will get a good education and will become highly skilled in some field. (The same condition will not be good for marriage, however).

Negative: An afflicted Venus in the sixth house suggests arguments and disagreements in marriage. In many cases the result will be divorce. The person will find it difficult to give or receive love and affection. He will also have to struggle for comfort and affluence in life. A malefic Venus here can also produce health problems that are related to the kidneys, eyes or sexual organs.

Saturn in the Sixth House
Positive: A positive Saturn in the sixth house will produce a person who

is disciplined in the area of health. He will set formal routines of diet and exercise and will stick to them. As a result, his health will improve. A good Saturn here also promotes the area of employment, making the person work hard and succeed at his various ambitious projects.

Negative: A negative Saturn in the sixth house can be challenging for health. This may produce health problems, including low vitality and general fatigue. If other malefics, the Sun or the Moon are also placed in the sixth house, then this Saturn placement may produce more pronounced negative effects including more serious diseases. The person could work very hard at his job, neglecting health routines because of a lack of time and energy. This results in a weakened and depleted immune system. A typical expression of this placement is that the person tends to get colds, infections and other saturnine ailments, which result from a compromised immune system.

Rahu in the Sixth House

Positive: A positive Rahu in the sixth house is very good for productivity and innovation in work. The person could change his place of employment, getting a new and better job. This is also a great placement for health, allowing the person to benefit from alternative healing modalities and a variety of beneficial natural medicines.

Negative: A negative Rahu in the sixth house may produce detrimental effects on the health. Sometimes this takes the form of a strange illness or symptom that traditional doctors have difficulty diagnosing or treating. Rahu is the ruler of the nakshatra, Shatabhisha, which means "a hundred medicines" or "a hundred physicians." Sometimes health problems that manifest under this placement cause the person to obsess about a cure, consulting with a variety of doctors and medicines from various healing modalities. This placement can also produce various kinds of addictions. It can cause problems with employment or employees. It stimulates arguments and contention. Rahu in the sixth also increases enmity from competitors or enemies.

Ketu in the Sixth House

Positive: Ketu in the sixth produces healing ability in its positive mode. This placement gives the person an inclination to channel subtle healing energy as well as an interest in natural healing. Ketu rules herbs and roots, so various forms of herbalism are under its domain. Ketu is the planet of Moksha and subtle awareness, so it also enables the person to benefit from spiritual healing. This is also a very good placement for spiritual development, giving the person a growing interest in spirituality as his life progresses. He may also become interested in spiritually-oriented healing practices such as Ayurveda, yoga, or Reiki.

Negative: A negative Ketu in the sixth house produces health problems that are difficult to diagnose. The person might be misdiagnosed or may receive the wrong prescription, so it is important that he get a second opinion if any serious diagnosis is given. The most typical outcome of this position is the vague symptom rather than a serious disease. This placement also can be problematic for employment, causing the person to feel chronically dissatisfied with his job. This might make him want to quit the job or he might be laid-off or fired.

The Seventh House (Kalatra Bhava)

The seventh house is about partnership. Here the process of expansion of consciousness moves to a new level. In the second, third and fourth houses, the individual learns to share resources, to live with family members, and even learns the art of hospitality. In the fifth house, awareness expands to include sharing pleasure, sports, and play with others. In the sixth house the lesson is to learn to deal with criticism by cultivating deeper understanding. Here in the seventh house, we are finally ready to take on a partner.

The most obvious form of partnership is marriage. In societies where orthodox traditions dominate, marriage is the main signification of the seventh house. In most western countries, however, the seventh house signifies alternative types of relationships as well. The main distinction here is commitment. Unlike the fifth house, where relationships are based on mutual enjoyment and entertainment, the seventh house is a house of responsible, committed partnership.

The seventh is also a house of desire, so it is naturally related to sexual desire in relationships. But sexual relationships, from the seventh-house point of view, are still commitment and trust-oriented. It is here that we are able to bond with a life partner sexually, forming a relationship of mutual support. It is also possible to violate the trust of a marriage or committed relationship. For this reason, the seventh house can indicate affairs and infidelity.

Marriage isn't the only type of partnership signified by the seventh house. Business partners are also part of its repertoire. Again, the idea is of trust, commitment and mutual support. We are agreeing to cooperate with another person for mutual profit or accomplishment. From this vantage point, we can even extend the umbrella of the seventh house to include the client-professional relationship, which is also a type of partnership or agreement. In fact, all sorts of contracts and agreements are defined in the seventh house.

Obviously, the seventh house includes much more than just marriage. It actually shows how we perceive and interact with others in general. Since the seventh house is naturally related to Libra, the sign of harmony and balance, it shows how we either support or disturb the harmony of relationships. This house indicates our ability to be diplomatic and tactful, desiring to blend and adjust to others. It shows political influence, arbitration skill, and even persuasive power. On the other hand, under the influence of malefic planets, the seventh house can cause us to view life as a battlefield, and see others as potential enemies. It can cause us to be argumentative, defensive, or tactless. It also shows how we either succeed or fail to live up to our commitments to others, which is an aspect of integrity and trustworthiness. In this respect, even legal matters are related to the seventh house.

In the context of spiritual evolution, the seventh house plays an important role. In Vedanta philosophy, enlightenment is described as a state of consciousness in which the individual ceases to feel separate, and begins to perceive that he is one with everything and everyone around him. In the seventh house, we make our first attempt at trying "to unite" with another person.

From the typical western perspective, marriage means falling in love and "becoming one" with another person. Westerners are programmed by their families, television and social environment to find a "soul mate," a perfect partner. According to this romantic notion, marriage, or union with one's romantic partner, is the cure for the loneliness and self-doubt that seems to plague the spiritually impoverished western cultures. Through the seventh house, however, this romantic ideal is tested and sometimes shattered. After marriage we are rudely awakened to the fact that we still feel alone. No matter how inspiring the partnership, we still have to deal with our own emotional, psychological and physical baggage. Driven by a desperate desire to escape from psychological turmoil and suffering, many people chase the romantic illusion, and enter into marriage or relationships only to find themselves thrown back to confront their inner demons in an even more upsetting way.

The resolution of this dilemma not only depends on the seventh house ability to blend with others, but also on the strength of the individuality reflected in the first house. Without a strong body, a clear sense of self, and a healthy psychology, a healthy relationship becomes difficult or even impossible to attain.

The seventh house, then, shows how we harmonize ourselves with others, holding up a mirror in the process. Through this "mirror" of relationship, we begin to see the flaw in the romantic illusion. We begin to realize that our relationships are only as healthy as we are. We start to see that real unity is expression (rather than a loss) of self, and we come one step closer to removing the veil of ignorance.

Significations of the Seventh House Given by Classical Authors of Vedic Astrology:

Wife; husband; sexual desire; sexual relations; extra-marital affairs; prostitution; eating good food; nice scents; sweet drinks; cloths; sons; adopted sons; journeys; getting lost while traveling; interruption in travel; foreign places; battlefield; victory over enemies; litigation; controversies; memory loss; misplaced money; business; trade; charity; theft; expenditure at night; death.

Physical Significations:

Lower urinary tract; uterus; ovaries; testes; prostate gland; seminal vesicles; anus; groin; semen. Depending on the drekkana rising—mouth, navel, legs and feet.

The Ruler of the Seventh House Placed in the Twelve Houses

First House

Positive: If the ruler of the seventh house is placed in the first house, the person will marry someone who will be an attractive, intelligent, charming and healthy person. His spouse will also be very supportive and devoted. It is possible that he will marry a person whom he has known since childhood. The person will also be diplomatic, charming, passionate, and generally interested in relationships and partnerships. He will have good health and lead a successful life. This placement also produces aesthetic sensitivity and sometimes indicates artistic ability. It is also good for the marriage of the second child.

Negative: If the ruler of the seventh house is afflicted in the first house, the person will probably still get married, but will have marital problems related to the afflicting planets and the houses they rule. The same results could also be true concerning the marriage of the second child. If Venus is also afflicted, then the person could have affairs, a divorce or separation. This position also suggests health problems that are caused by excessive vata.

Second House

Positive: If the ruler of the seventh house is strong, supported and placed in the second house, the person will have financial gain through marriage or partnership. In general, the person's financial condition will improve from the start of the marriage. The spouse will be interested in creating a comfortable and affluent life. It is also possible that the spouse will be a good cook. This placement is frequently found in the charts of people who earn income through clients.

Negative: If the ruler of the seventh house is weak or afflicted in the second house, the person will experience financial losses through partnership or marriage. The marriage will be troubled by financial problems, which could be a source of argument or general discontent. If Venus is also afflicted, there could be a divorce. The spouse will go through many dynamic life changes in career, residence or health. He will eat poor quality food, and will occasionally eat food served at funeral receptions and wakes. He will be very sensual and his mind will be unsteady. This placement makes the seventh lord a first-rate maraka (death-inflicting planet). The seventh lord's dasha or bhukti should be watched carefully for negative results. (Please note: This period will only produce death if the person has reached their allotted span of life. In most cases, it simply produces difficulties such as ill health.)

Third House

Positive: If the ruler of the seventh house is strong, supported and placed in the third house, the person will be passionate, loving, and will have internal fortitude. He could have a sibling who is intelligent, well-educated or prosperous. He could also have a sibling who lives in a foreign country and becomes successful. This placement also produces good communication between husband and wife, and supports marital happiness as a result. The spouse will be a well-educated person who has a strong sense of purpose.

Negative: If the ruler of the seventh house is afflicted in the third house, the person will have marital problems stemming from a lack of good communications. If Jupiter is also afflicted, then a child could be lost by miscarriage or abortion. If Venus is afflicted, there could be affairs or divorce. This placement also creates difficulties for the siblings, or the person's relationship with them.

Fourth House:

Positive: If the ruler of the seventh house is strong, supported and placed in the fourth house, the person will have a happy marriage to someone who is very successful professionally. The spouse could be self-employed, or simply be a leader in his profession. The person will build or buy a house in conjunction with a partner or a spouse, and will become materially secure and prosperous. This placement is also good for the success and general well-being of the second child. The person's mother will own land, houses and nice cars.

Negative: If the ruler of the seventh house is weak, afflicted and placed in the fourth house, the person will experience marital difficulties that will affect his peace of mind and happiness. The spouse could have problems succeeding in the profession. The spouse might have a detrimental influence on his car or house. If Venus and the seventh lord are both badly afflicted, the person could get divorced, and lose his house or car in the divorce settlement. In other cases it suggests marital instability related to frequent changes of residence. This placement also undermines the happiness and stability of the mother.

Fifth House

Positive: If the ruler of the seventh house is placed in the fifth house, the person will marry someone who is intelligent, strong, successful or prosperous. The spouse will be a person of integrity and virtue, and the marriage will be successful. This placement also gives a tendency to fall in love and to marry early, relative to the person's cultural norm. The spouse will have many friends and will be very devoted to them. This is also a good position for success through partnerships. It also suggests that the mother could profit through the sale of houses or land.

Negative: If the ruler of the seventh house is afflicted in the fifth house, the person will have marital problems related to sex, passion and romance. He or the spouse could have an affair, or they may simply "fall out of love" and drift apart. This placement also suggests marital problems related to children such as disagreeing on how to raise them. If Venus and Jupiter are also afflicted, then the person could divorce and go through a custody battle. An afflicted fifth lord here can also produce financial losses or expenses related to property for the mother.

Sixth House

Positive: If the ruler of the seventh house is strong, supported and placed in the sixth house, the person will marry someone who will be introspective, reflective or spiritually inclined. The spouse will also enjoy retreats, vacations and travel. The person will be helpful, supportive and generous with his spouse, adopting an attitude of service in marriage.

Negative: This placement of the seventh lord is generally detrimental to marital harmony. The spouse might be self-conscious, shy, introverted, or could have ill health. The person will be antagonistic towards the spouse and vice-versa. If the seventh lord or Venus is also afflicted, then divorce or separation is possible. This placement also undermines the person's relationships with partners and other people in general, making him disagreeable and short-tempered. It also suggests lawsuits, legal problems and challenges regarding contracts or agreements.

Seventh House

Positive: If the ruler of the seventh house is placed in the seventh house, the person will be sexually attractive and will have plenty of opportunities for sex, romance or marriage. He will marry a person who is strong, successful, and has the characteristics of the planet that owns the seventh house. This placement is also very good for contracts, legal matters and partnerships. The person's second child will also be a strong person, with a general tendency towards success and prosperity. The seventh lord here also allows the person to have good judgment selecting various professionals to consult, such as lawyers, dentists, doctors, and contractors. If the seventh lord happens to be Saturn, Jupiter, Venus, Mercury or Mars, then this combination constitutes a Mahapurusha Yoga, which causes the qualities of that planet to dominate the horoscope. When it occurs in the seventh house, then in addition to expressing the planet's best qualities himself, the person chooses a partner who reflects those qualities in a pronounced way.

Negative: If the ruler of the seventh house is afflicted in the seventh house, the person will probably get married, but will experience marital discord related to the afflicting planets and the houses they rule. Similarly, the spouse could be a strong person, with some annoying personality traits. Usually this placement gives mixed results, but if Venus is afflicted and the seventh lord is seriously challenged, then the person could experience divorce, affairs, separation, loss of spouse, or the denial of marriage altogether.

Eighth House

Positive: If the ruler of the seventh house is strong, supported and placed in the eighth house, the person will marry a wealthy spouse or will become prosperous after marriage. The marriage will go through a metamorphosis, allowing the couple to overcome their differences and renew their marriage. This placement suggests that the person and his wife might gain positive results from marriage counseling or psychological therapy. This placement also generally favors financial gains through wills, lawsuits, clients, contracts, insurance, or other outside sources.

Negative: The placement of the ruler of the seventh house in the eighth house usually brings marital difficulties. The person could marry someone who is personally or physically weak. The partner could experience financial problems, or money could simply be a bone of contention between the person and his spouse. His marriage will be a vehicle for revealing his deepest psychological complexes and hang-ups. As a result, marriage will challenge him to work on his own psychology. In many cases, this placement allows the person to push through marital problems and emerge in a more empowered condition. Quite frequently, this means some form of marriage counseling or therapy will occur. If Venus and the eighth lord are too seriously afflicted, however, this placement can also bring divorce, separation, or even the death of the partner.

Ninth House

Positive: If the ruler of the seventh house is placed in the ninth house, the person will marry a spouse who is good-looking, virtuous, knowledgeable, and successful. This placement causes the person to have a strong sense of purpose and commitment in marriage. It also suggests that the spouse, and marriage in general, will be supportive of his spiritual path. The person and his spouse will also enjoy traveling together. The person's father will be prosperous, successful and will have many friends.

Negative: If the ruler of the seventh house is weak or afflicted in the ninth house, the person will have disagreements and other communication problems with his spouse. The partner or the person could be self-righteous, patronizing or judgmental. This placement also disturbs the person's relationship with his father.

Tenth House

Positive: If the ruler of the seventh house is placed in the tenth house, the person will work at a profession that involves clients or partnership. He could also work with his spouse. The spouse will own good houses, land, or cars, and will be an intelligent, and happy person. His relationship with his spouse will center on mutually shared activities and projects. This position is also good for the person's general character, prosperity and success.

Negative: If the ruler of the seventh house is weak or afflicted in the tenth house, the person could experience problems in collaborating with others at work. He might, for example, be uncooperative and unable to compromise. On the other hand, his business partner could be unreliable, dishonest, or a difficult person. The person and his spouse may find it difficult to agree on the way to complete various domestic tasks. His spouse could also be obstinate or uncompromising.

Eleventh House

Positive: If the ruler of the seventh house is placed in the eleventh house, the person will have a spouse who is both his lover and his friend. He could meet the spouse in a group setting or through a friend. Similarly, it is possible that he will marry someone who has first been his friend for some time. His marriage will grow stronger over time, and the relationship will center on both friendship, and the setting of mutual goals. The spouse will be intelligent, well-educated, social, popular, physically attractive and financially successful. It is also possible that the spouse will come from a wealthy family. This is also a good placement for having children.

Negative: If the ruler of the seventh house is afflicted in the eleventh house, the person could have more than one marriage. Unless Venus is also seriously afflicted, the person will probably have many sexual relationships before marriage. After marriage there could be a tendency toward casual affairs with opposite-sex friends or the spouses of friends. If Venus is afflicted, this placement suggests marital problems related to a difference in mutual goals. In some cases it will produce divorce. The person's spouse could become involved in an affair with one of the person's friends, or a friend could interfere in the person's marriage in some way.

Twelfth House

Positive: If the ruler of the seventh house is strong, supported and placed in the twelfth house, the person will have a spiritually-oriented marriage, characterized by selflessness, compassion and unconditional love. The spouse will have high vitality and good health. It is also possible that the spouse will travel a good deal. This placement also makes it possible for the spouse to easily get employment. The person could marry someone from a distant place or a foreign country. It is also possible that the person will marry someone he meets while traveling, and the couple will enjoy traveling together.

Negative: If the ruler of the seventh house is weak or afflicted in the twelfth house, the person will experience difficulties, uncertainties, disappointments or losses through marriage. The spouse could be a source of expenditure or financial loss. If Venus is also afflicted, then this placement can sometimes produce divorce or separation. It also suggests that the spouse might do many things in private, or at least be somewhat evasive. As a result, it is sometimes seen in the charts of people whose spouses have affairs.

Planets in the Seventh House

Sun in the Seventh House

Positive: If a benefic Sun is in the seventh, the person will be diplomatic and congenial. He will have a desire to create peace and harmony in his interpersonal relationships. He will also have a love of aesthetics, art, and music. The Sun here can produce a partner who is a leader or who has a strong personality. The partner will like attention and might have a career that involves being in front of people. The person will also be able to benefit from business partnerships, clients, or other one-to-one relationships. He will use relationships as a vehicle for his self-actualization process.

Negative: If a malefic Sun is placed in the seventh house, the person will have problems with marriage. The spouse will probably have a need to dominate or rule the roost. The person may have a deep need for passion and romance, and could tend to identify too much with relationship, losing his sense of self as a result. Power struggles, arguments and other fiery encounters sometimes result from this placement. In some cases, however, the spouse simply dominates, and the person gives in for the sake of preserving peace. In any case, this placement of the Sun produces an individuality vs. mutuality dilemma. The person learns the hard way that a healthy relationship requires a strong personality as well as an ability to harmonize.

Moon in the Seventh House

Positive: When a benefic Moon is placed in the seventh house, the person will have a deep and powerful attachment with his spouse. The spouse will be sociable, gentle, nurturing and supportive. A good Moon here allows the person to derive a sense of security from his marriage. He will also be passionate and romantic. He will value harmony and be willing to share and compromise. As a result, he will have harmonious experiences in all one-to-one relationships. This placement also suggests that the person will have many friends, and be quite social and popular. His family members will be intelligent, successful, and highly regarded by others. He will also have a strong sense of justice. He will like to travel as well.

Negative: An afflicted or malefic Moon in the seventh house is a difficult placement for marriage. The marriage will have many ups and downs. The person may be overly dependent on the spouse for security and support, or could feel that these things are lacking in the relationship. The spouse could be defensive or emotionally unstable. The Moon here suggests that the person will have difficulties in friendships, and may feel that he is not well liked by others. He will constantly compare himself with others and may be insecure. He will probably be very passionate, and possibly jealous. As a result, in spite of having a good-looking spouse, the person could have affairs.

Mars in the Seventh House

Positive: When a benefic Mars is placed in the seventh house, the person will be energetic, passionate, and physically active. He will be ambitious, and will like working in partnerships. His partners and his spouse will be assertive, physically active, ambitious and successful. Mars here also gives good health and high energy. The person might work in a client-professional career, or a career that involves contracts, negotiation, legal matters or disputes. He will also be quite competitive in his work, and enjoy competitive games as well.

Negative: A negative Mars in the seventh house suggests difficulties in marriage. The person may be tactless and undiplomatic. The spouse might be argumentative also. The person at the very least, projects that the spouse is the source of conflict. In many cases, however, the person creates the conflict himself, by constantly challenging, criticizing or simply disagreeing with his spouse, yet he feels like he is the victim. In any case, an afflicted or malefic Mars in the seventh brings arguments or disagreements in marriage. In some cases, this will bring divorce or separation. In extreme cases, the partner or spouse dies. Sometimes an afflicted Mars here causes addictive tendencies. It can also signify that the person lives far away from his birthplace.

Mercury in the Seventh House

Positive: When Mercury is benefic and placed in the seventh house, the person will marry a bright, successful, prosperous, and charming spouse. The spouse will be communicative, well-educated, beautiful and young looking. The person will be diplomatic, tactful and generally good at public relations and communications. He could be concerned about the opinions of others, and will avoid disagreements and disputes by trying to create peace and harmony in his relationships. This placement generally makes the person good at business, and may even denote some mathematical ability. He will have many friends who are bright or intellectual. He will be well dressed, will have a good reputation and will be popular. This placement also gives a good sense of humor, writing and language ability, and may indicate artistic or musical abilities.

Negative: A negative Mercury in the seventh will bring communications problems in marriage. The person will either marry a spouse who is argumentative, deceptive, or manipulative, or he will have these traits himself. He will also have problems communicating in other kinds of relationships such as partnerships and friendships. As a result, his reputation may suffer. This placement also suggests problems with agreements or contracts. The person should be especially careful when signing contracts, making sure to read every detail carefully. Mercury here can bring broken contracts, misunderstandings, and unfulfilled commitments, either on the part of the person or the people with whom he deals. Another idiosyncrasy of this placement is that it sometimes causes the person to be attracted to his employees, and occasionally this leads to an affair or even marriage. An afflicted Mercury suggests problems as a result of such attractions.

Jupiter in the Seventh House

Positive: A good Jupiter in the seventh house brings luck, prosperity and abundance through marriage. The person will have an open, friendly, and generous disposition. As a result, people will naturally be attracted to him. This position gives plenty of romantic opportunities and plenty of friends. The person will have a good reputation and will be popular. He will be well-educated and like to travel. The spouse will have a proud, confident, positive nature and have a good education. It is likely that the spouse will have some sort of professional certification. It is also possible that the spouse will be physically large or tall. This is also a good position for having and raising children. The person could also benefit from partnership or from a client-professional business.

Negative: A negative Jupiter in the seventh house will give difficulties in marriage. The spouse may be opinionated, judgmental, a "know it all," or might simply have a need to dominate. An afflicted Jupiter here can also cause financial problems through the marriage or partnership. It can give problems in business and in legal matters. Normally, Jupiter in the seventh protects the marriage, but if it is afflicted or retrograde it fails to do so. It can cause differences of opinion stemming from opposing philosophical outlooks on the part of the person and his spouse.

Venus in the Seventh House

Positive: A positive Venus in the seventh house makes the person sensuous, loving and romantic. As a result, he will attract beautiful, refined, artistic and charming sexual partners. He will have a deep love of art, music, or literature. He will possess a love of truth and a strong sense of justice. Sometimes all these great qualities are actually reflected more in the partner. The person will tend to marry early. A good Venus here can also give abundance and affluence through marriage. It can give much happiness, prosperity and comfort in life. The person will be sociable and popular. This position of Venus usually gives positive results regarding legal matters. If legal problems arise, they are usually settled out of court and to the person's benefit. One idiosyncrasy of Venus in this position is that it is the karaka or significator of the seventh house, and is placed in its own house. Even a good Venus in the seventh can cause the person to emphasize passion and romance in his relationships too much. This emphasis on passion, however, either by the person or by his spouse, usually becomes the source of problems in the marriage, even in the cases of benefic Venus in the seventh house.

Negative: A negative Venus in the seventh house will make the person sensual and passionate in a harmful way. An emphasis on passion and romance could disrupt relationships, or in some cases, the person or the spouse will have affairs. Needless to say, this position does not bode well for marital harmony, and can lead to divorce or separation. Afflictions to Venus here also create difficulties in expressing and receiving feelings of love and affection. The person may not feel like he is truly lovable, or could seek out illicit relationships in order to fill an emotional void, using sexuality and sensuality to produce a sense of emotional well-being.

Saturn in the Seventh House

Positive: A good Saturn in the seventh house will bring stability and longevity to the marriage. The spouse will be steady, stable, hard-working, persevering and patient. The person will look at the marriage as a practical arrangement and a valuable commitment. This placement sometimes gives a good marriage to someone who is older, or who displays Saturn's best traits, such as organizational or management ability and a sense of responsibility. Even a good Saturn in the seventh tends to delay marriage, however. This has a different meaning in different cultures. In the United States, it frequently means that the person marries after his mid-thirties when Saturn comes to maturity.

Negative: A malefic Saturn in the seventh is a difficult placement for marriage. The person will look at marriage and all committed relationships as a source of tedious pressure and too much struggle. He will project that the source of his relationship problems is the partner, and will feel that he is relatively blameless. Frequently the person experiences a sense of resistance from the spouse, who may not be so demonstrative with affection and warmth, or might simply work too hard, making it difficult to share time together. Sometimes an afflicted Saturn here can produce a partner who is a controller or who demands too much from the person. In any case, the person feels the spouse blocks him. What is difficult to understand about this placement is that, like any placement of Saturn, the person is being challenged to quit blaming the problem on his spouse and start taking personal responsibility for making his relationship work. This frequently means setting clear boundaries and expectations, and being willing to ask for more respect, love, consideration, and attention. It also means not letting the spouse get away with being overbearing, controlling or demanding. The person needs to make a clear, deliberate plan to improve the quality of the marriage. Sometimes the only way to do this is through divorce, and a second attempt with someone new. In the case of truly committed people, however, Saturn has a way of rewarding those who persevere. This placement also shows difficulties through partnerships, legal matters, and contracts. The person will generally feel that his interaction with others on a one-to-one basis is frustrating and full of resistance.

Rahu in the Seventh House

Positive: A benefic Rahu in the seventh house will bring marriage to someone who represents the best side of Rahu. This can mean the spouse will be a very unique and innovative person, someone from a foreign country, or someone from an ethnic group with dark skin. Sometimes the spouse is simply from a different religious background or has an unconventional belief system. The point is that Rahu is unconventional, and the spouse will probably reflect this in some way. One exception to this rule is that because Rahu also signifies technology, it sometimes gives marriage to someone who is involved in technology or science, which by today's standards is rather conventional. Regardless, the spouse will be interested in cutting-edge concepts. Rahu is also an independent planet that causes separation from the spouse when placed in the seventh house, but when it is well placed, then the separation can be benign. For example, the spouse might travel for a living. There are even cases of people with Rahu in the seventh house who marry happily, yet live in a separate house from their spouse. The key point here is that Rahu in the seventh allows the person to become more self-actualized through relationships. Instead of getting married and becoming more bonded to their mate, the person gets married and becomes happily separate. He learns that the key to balance and harmony in marriage is to have time and space away from the spouse. In short, when benefic Rahu is placed in the seventh house, the person redefines the whole concept of marriage in some way, coming up with a rather unconventional approach that matches his or her emotional wiring. Marriage will also be a source of prosperity and wealth.

Negative: A malefic or afflicted Rahu in the seventh house is not a good sign for marital harmony. The person will have a sense of urgency to be married or to be in a relationship, yet will also experience alienation and separation when relationships take place. He will have a restless itch that makes him dissatisfied with the spouse, and makes him desire to separate. The partner might be compulsive or rebellious in some way. There may be arguments, power struggles and other communication problems. This placement can also give unexpected and upsetting relationship events such as affairs, scandals, misunderstandings, accidents or health problems to the spouse. Usually the karmas dispensed by a negative Rahu feel like they are unavoidable. Indeed, if several factors indicate that Rahu is negative, it can reflect an affair, divorce, or other marital disaster that is relatively unavoidable. The classics suggest that the first spouse may die prematurely and the second could have liver problems. Even in the case of an intensely difficult Rahu, however, the person can do a great deal to mitigate suffering through meditation, prayer and the use of appropriate remedial measures.

Ketu in the Seventh House

Positive: A good Ketu in the seventh house indicates a happy marriage or relationship with a partner who is creative, has healing ability or is spiritually inclined. The primary emphasis of the relationship will be a mutually shared inspirational or spiritual theme. A person who is a musician, for example, could get together with an artist or musician and bond over their similar inspirational commitment to the arts. Since Ketu is the planet of detachment, this is also a placement that demands a "day at a time" attitude towards relationships. For this reason, a beneficial Ketu in the seventh sometimes suggests that the person chooses not to get married. He has a natural sense of the impermanence of relationships, and prefers to experience his partnership as it is in the present moment. He does not strive to make love permanent. He has an instinctive sense that relationships change, so he does not depend on his partner for ultimate happiness. Instead, he commits to a higher, more lasting ideal. In some cases, however, a good Ketu in the seventh does create happy marriages, but in these cases the husband and wife are mutually devoted to a spiritual or creative principle. The person learns to drop expectations and conditions, and loves the spouse unconditionally. Sometimes this placement gives marriage to a person from an exotic foreign country. Because the classics say, "Ketu is a Buddhist," the partner could be from an Asian country or of Asian descent. (Note: Ketu is particularly well placed in Scorpio or Sagittarius in the seventh house.)

Negative: A malefic Ketu in the seventh house gives the person a chronic sense of dissatisfaction in relationship. Usually the person has an underlying conviction that the soul mate must be out there somewhere, and that somehow he has temporarily been given the wrong partner. As a result, he finds it hard to really commit to the spouse or partner, and always finds the relationship lacking. In this case, no matter how hard the spouse tries to please him, the person remains a little disappointed. He projects that spouses, lovers, and even business partners are the source of his disappointment. In fact, this placement of Ketu will probably give him many experiences that prove his conviction. This, however, reinforces his feeling that other people fall short of his ideal, and ultimately keeps him accepting the challenge of letting go of his expectations, conditions and dependency on relationships as a source of happiness. In cases of serious afflictions to Ketu in the seventh, relationships will be a source of unexpected emotional loss or trauma. In other cases the spouse or partner will be abusive, addictive, uncommitted, deceptive, or lacking direction. Sometimes divorce is the only alternative. In any case, Ketu asks the person to let go, either of the partner or of conditions and expectations of the partner.

The Eighth House (Mrityu Bhava)

The eighth house is the house of life, so it has been traditionally used to determine the vitality and the lifespan. The flip-side of life is death, so it also gives clues about the nature of one's death. Understanding this house literally means understanding the nature of life and death.

On the deepest level, the eighth house is the house of metamorphosis, reflecting an ongoing process of life and death. Here we are asked to shed our old skins and move on to new states of living. The old state dies, giving birth to a new and more empowered one. Like a butterfly coming out of a cocoon, we let go of the lower way of being in order to live with greater freedom and vitality.

One level on which this metamorphosis takes place is the psychological level. Being one of the moksha or spiritual liberation houses, the eighth house shows how we confront our deepest, darkest psychological and spiritual demons. For this reason, it is a house that can give insight into some of our hidden or repressed psychological complexes. This doesn't mean the house itself is complex. On the contrary, the energy found here is actually quite simple and even primal by nature. It represents the life force, the kundalini energy residing at the base of the spine. Planets that become associated with this house, however, are broken down or reduced to their primal condition. If we have psychological complexes related to these planets, these are also broken down and revealed to us so that we can experience the fundamental spiritual quality of the planet's energy. If we go through this process consciously and willingly, our demons are released, liberating unlimited energy and vitality. But if we fight the process of reduction, the experience will only be suffering.

This is the reason that, for most people, the eighth house is a difficult house. In classical Vedic astrology, the eighth house destroys or ruins the planets that occupy or are associated with it. Even the houses owned by such a planet are said to be ruined. It is important, however, to understand this process in its deeper, spiritual context. What is really happening is the eighth house is giving life to these planets. In fact, that's all it can give. Its name is "ayu," meaning life. But the nature of its energy, being primal life force, is transformative, and unfortunately, most of us deeply resist real transformation. Most of us want to cling to business as usual. The result is that we are broken down, without realizing that real empowerment through deep spiritual insight is even possible.

On the outer level, the eighth house signifies dynamic, transformative conditions as well. Accidents, traumatic experiences and chronic diseases, are part of its repertoire. These significations and many others, listed by the classical authors, are related to the process of breaking down, which is the negative side of the eighth house. On the other hand, this is also a house where diseases and physical traumas can be overcome. By involving ourselves in transformational therapies, intense programs of physical, emotional or psychological healing, we can "tune in" to our eighth house challenges and frequently transcend them altogether. This is the reason that many psychologists, physical therapists and physicians have one or more key planets in the eighth house, showing that they have not only learned to transform themselves, but have also become a catalyst for the transformation process in others.

The key is to first accept and then transcend the pain and trauma of life. The perfect metaphor for this process is that of Christ dying on the cross. He willingly and consciously accepts his human vulnerability. Though he has his moment of doubt, in the end he transcends the suffering and is transfigured. He rises from the dead in a new and more empowered form.

In real life this translates into being willing to accept and grow beyond the pain of living. The karma presented by the eighth house may be difficult at times, but it can also be very liberating. Every day, we hear about people who experience miraculous changes in the face of devastation. Dennis Byrd, the famous football star for the New York Jets, for example, recovered from a serious spinal injury, even though the doctors had given up hope. As he lay on his hospital bed, in traction, with his teammates crying at his bedside, he calmly told them not to be afraid. He said he was determined to be happy in his life and he refused to let his injury cripple his spirit. He not only transcended his pain, but he miraculously regained his ability to walk.

Clearly, the eighth house is one of the deepest and most dynamic houses in the birth chart. It represents the primal life force that has the capacity to illumine the entire nervous system, giving vitality and awareness to life. That life force is relentless, however, breaking down anything that blocks its flow and creating upheavals and changes in life. In this way, the eighth house is the house of evolution. Through its many changes and permutations, it moves us slowly, over the course of many lifetimes, from a state of limited consciousness to that of unbounded awareness. Evolution is a ceaseless process, where change is inevitable, so there is no question that the eighth house will produce evolutionary changes in life. The only question is whether we will go with the flow of those changes or keep swimming upstream.

Significations of the Eighth House Given by Classical Authors of Vedic Astrology:

Longevity; death; calamity; destruction; mutilation; agony; mental distress; bad news; getting lost; dangerous paths; arduous journeys across mountains; forests or oceans; boats; bad reputation; battle; fort; fear from enemies; brother's enemy; arrest; detention; punishment; defeat; loans to others; debts; repayment of debts; loss of money; theft; inheritance; money kept permanently (deposited in banks); money coming through others; separation between partners; separation between friends; difficulties in marriage; the ability to discern what is not openly stated (shrewdness, intuition).

Physical Significations:

External genitals; chronic disease; longevity. Depending on the drekkana rising—left jaw, left lung, left breast, and left calf.

The Ruler of the Eighth House Placed in the Twelve Houses

First House

Positive: If the ruler of the eighth house is supported by benefic influences and placed in the first house, the person will be intense, passionate and interested in creating positive changes in his own life and in the lives of others. He could be interested in hidden things, alternative subjects, astrology or other occult subjects. Although he will go through many changes in his life, he will constantly evolve and improve. This placement can be good for gaining financial prosperity through clients, contracts, legal matters, or inheritance. It is seen in the charts of various kinds of therapists and business people.

Negative: Without support, the ruler of the eighth house is usually detrimental to the significations of the first house. This placement can be an indication of ill health and many upheavals and changes in life, particularly if the eighth lord is afflicted. Changes of residence, changes of job, and financial fluctuations seem to characterize this placement as well. As a result, it sometimes creates difficulty for the person to succeed financially. He could also be irreverent, a rebel, an iconoclast or even exhibit criminal tendencies. In cases of serious affliction, the person could suffer from accidents or injuries.

Second House

Positive: If the eighth lord is strong and supported in the second house, the person will have financial gains through wills, partnerships, insurance, or clients. If this placement is supported by other financial combinations, it can indicate overall prosperity. The person can loan money to other people and have no problem being repaid. Similarly, he might borrow money occasionally, or at least benefit from the use of credit cards.

Negative: If the ruler of the eighth house is placed in the second house without support, then it usually causes problems with second house matters. The person will experience financial fluctuations, losses and many expenses. He could be forced to take out loans and might experience difficulty either getting loans or paying them back. This placement also suggests that the person will not eat a balanced diet, and could have a tendency to binge or to eat poor quality food. If the eighth lord is afflicted here, then it could produce physical problems related to the eyes or the mouth, and may indicate dental problems.

Third House

Positive: If the ruler of the eighth house is strong, supported and placed in the third house, the person could have financial gains through siblings. He might experience sudden gains through writing or music. This placement also suggests an intense and profound style of communication, and is seen in the charts of therapists and people who go to therapists. It also brings a strong interest in hidden knowledge. The person reads books on astrology, metaphysics or other occult subjects. He could also be interested in science and might have an ability to do research.

Negative: If the ruler of the eighth house is placed in the third house without support, then the person will have difficulty in his relationships with his siblings. In some cases, the sibling relationship is fine, but the sibling simply has a difficult life. In cases of serious affliction, the sibling could have health problems and even die. Sometimes an afflicted eighth lord simply means that the person does not have siblings, or at least a younger sibling. This placement is also detrimental to the person's communication style, coloring it with a tendency to manipulate, control, evoke guilt, or create jealousy. It can also produce physical problems related to the ears or shoulders.

Fourth House

Positive: If the ruler of the eighth house is strong, supported and placed in the fourth house, the person will be spiritually inclined and will constantly strive to gain peace of mind. He will live in good houses and will be particularly good at remodeling or landscaping. He will find it easy to get loans for purchasing property and will profit through the sale of homes or land. This placement is also good for receiving grants or scholarships for educational purposes. It suggests that the person will inherit land, houses or money from his parents.

Negative: If the ruler of the eighth house is placed in the fourth house without support, the person will find it difficult to achieve security and stability in life. He will have many changes of residence, and will find it difficult to purchase property or houses. If the eighth lord is also afflicted here, he can incur many expenses related to his home or car. It is also possible that his home or car could be damaged in some way. If he inherits property or money, he might lose it. This placement also suggests domestic problems, and a general lack of happiness in life. The person will find it very hard to achieve peace of mind. Similarly, he can experience a lack of harmony in his relationship with his mother. The eighth lord afflicted in the fourth house can make it difficult to receive financing for educational purposes, and sometimes produces several changes of schools.

Fifth House

Positive: If the ruler of the eighth house is supported and placed in the fifth house, the person will have sudden financial gains from outside sources. His partner or spouse will become wealthy and successful. If other elements of the chart agree, then the person could have talent in stock market investing. This placement is generally excellent for wealth and general prosperity. It also promotes longevity. His first child will live in a nice home, drive a nice car and will live a peaceful, happy life. The second child could become wealthy or prosperous. The person could study a subject that requires deep research or which is alternative in some way. This is also a good placement for the study of astrology and other occult subjects.

Negative: If the ruler of the eighth house is placed in the fifth house without support, the person will have financial losses due to risk-taking, and he should be very conservative regarding the stock market. He will have a troubled and complex mind. As a result, he may have a difficult time learning. He could have breaks, interruptions, or obstructions in his education. This placement also produces problems regarding children.

For example, the first child could be restless and unsettled, and will probably have several changes of residence in life. If the eighth lord is seriously afflicted in the fifth house, then there could be a loss of a child, or one of the children could have health problems. Due to an excess of negative karma coming from past lives, the person feels unlucky and generally unfortunate. This placement also makes it difficult for the person to benefit from good advice.

Sixth House

Positive: If the ruler of the eighth house is supported and placed in the sixth house, the person could have an interest in various healing therapies. The partner or spouse could spend money on travel or on spiritual activities. The person will have a natural ability to overcome his competitors. If the eighth lord is placed in the sixth with the ruler of the sixth house, the person could become successful and prosperous.

Negative: If the ruler of the eighth house is placed in the sixth house without support, or it is afflicted, the person will have chronic health problems. He will have difficulty getting and keeping jobs, and could go through many changes in employment. This placement also makes it difficult to get or repay loans, and suggests indebtedness. It is important to keep in mind however, that the eighth lord placed in the sixth house creates Vipareeta Raja Yoga, which essentially enables the person to overcome obstacles.

Seventh House

Positive: If the ruler of the eighth house is supported and placed in the seventh house, the person will marry someone who is prosperous, or who becomes prosperous after marriage takes place. This placement also produces financial gains through partnerships, legal matters and clients. It suggests that the person will go through a natural metamorphosis in relationships or marriage, working out marital problems, usually through psychological counseling or other kinds of relationship therapy. Similarly, this placement denotes a person who has a transformational effect on other people, and is seen in the charts of professionals who help their clients resolve various types of issues.

Negative: If the ruler of the eighth house is placed in the seventh house without support, the person will experience upheavals and changes in relationship or marriage. If the eighth lord is badly afflicted, or if Venus is afflicted, the result could be divorce, separation, and in extreme cases, the death of the spouse. This placement makes it difficult to profit through partnerships or business, and sometimes produces losses from these sources.

Eighth House

Positive: If the ruler of the eighth house is placed in the eighth house, the person will have financial gains from outside sources such as wills, loans, insurance, legal matters, contracts, and clients. This placement elevates the level of the person's vitality and suggests long life and good health as a result. The person will marry a spouse who is prosperous. He will also benefit through partnerships, clients, legal matters and business contracts.

Negative: If the ruler of the eighth house is afflicted in the eighth house, the person will experience various problems related to money from outside sources. His spouse will also experience financial fluctuations. The person will have good vitality; yet can also experience intermittent health problems. In cases of serious affliction to the eighth lord, the vitality level could be low and various health problems could manifest. The length of life will correspondingly tend to be shorter than when the eighth lord is not afflicted.

Ninth House

Positive: If the ruler of the eighth house is supported and placed in the ninth house, the person will adopt an alternative philosophy of life. He will probably have an interest in astrology, metaphysics or the occult. He could also be attracted to spiritual paths that include deep psychological work, or which focus on activating the kundalini. Regardless, he will reject the orthodox religions or belief system of his family. Yet he will not experience undue resistance from his family members as a result. This placement also produces an attraction to teachers who are powerful or charismatic, and who have unconventional methods of teaching. It can also suggest inheritance from the father.

Negative: If the ruler of the eighth house is placed in the ninth house without support, the person will have problems in the relationship with his father. He will be antagonistic toward organized religion and could become an atheist or an agnostic. This placement makes it more difficult for the person to develop a belief system and tends to obstruct his sense of purpose in life. Similarly, he will find it difficult to benefit from teachers, spiritual gurus, and professionals such as doctors and lawyers. In some cases, this placement gives an interest in the occult that is not healthy or balanced. An afflicted eighth lord makes it difficult for the person to see the future. As a result, his various predictions may not be accurate.

Tenth House

Positive: If the ruler of the eighth house is supported and placed in the tenth house, the person will work at a profession that involves many dynamic changes. This is also a placement commonly found in the charts of therapists of different kinds. The person will probably go through a fairly significant metamorphosis in the career at least once in his life, rising to a more connected and empowered situation as a result.

Negative: If the ruler of the eighth house is placed in the tenth house without support or is afflicted, the person will experience many changes and problems related to the career. He will have a problematic relationship with his boss, and will find it hard to get promotions and achieve in his profession. He could use unscrupulous means to attain his career goals. An afflicted eighth lord in the tenth interferes with status, recognition and overall career success. In cases of intense affliction, the person could have a professional fall, or experience disgrace or scandal.

Eleventh House

Positive: If the ruler of the eighth house is supported and placed in the eleventh house, the person will have financial gains and prosperity from outside sources such as wills, insurance, contracts, legal matters or clients. This placement also produces financial gains later in life. The person's spouse will be prosperous and successful. He will have friends who are leaders in their professions, are self-employed, or simply are successful professionally. Also, his next older sibling will become professionally successful.

Negative: If the ruler of the eighth house is placed in the eleventh house, unsupported or afflicted, the person could have problems related to friends. He could loan money to a friend and not be repaid. In cases of serious affliction, he could become friends with people who go through many hardships and upheavals in life. Occasionally this placement can suggest the death of a friend. It also makes financial prosperity harder to achieve. The person will experience many delays, obstacles and problems in the process of trying to achieve goals.

Twelfth House

Positive: If the ruler of the eighth house is supported and placed in the twelfth house, the person will be spiritually inclined. He could have a strong interest in psychology and the development of consciousness. He may practice a form of meditation that focuses on the chakras or on the activation of the kundalini energy. This is also a good placement for the practice of yoga.

Negative: If the ruler of the eighth house is placed in the twelfth house without support or is afflicted, the person might have difficulty meditating. This placement is sometimes associated with uncomfortable experiences related to the kundalini. The person could develop insomnia, for example, as a result of too much meditation. Even without the practice of meditation, he could find it hard to sleep. The person will face many obstacles and inner demons in the process of psychological therapy. This placement can also suggest a lack of sexual fulfillment. The person could waste money and experience financial losses in various ways. If other factors agree, the eighth lord here can indicate a tendency to steal money. It is important to remember, however, that this placement produces Vipareeta Raja Yoga, which can allow the person to overcome problems as well.

Planets in the Eighth House

Sun in the Eighth House

Positive: When a benefic Sun is in the eighth house, the person will have an intense, penetrating, transformational personality. He could be interested in psychology or other therapeutic or self- improvement modalities. The Sun in the eighth house suggests that life will be full of dynamic changes, but a benefic Sun causes the person to consciously instigate and benefit from most of them. He will have a constant desire to improve himself in every way. He will be interested in life's deepest mysteries and will enjoy confronting his own "dark side" as part of his psychological and spiritual process. He could also have an interest in astrology. He will have no fear of death and may be able to support others who are dying. This position also suggests involvement with other people's money on the professional level. It is a typical placement in the charts of bankers, brokers, and people who work with clients, for example. The Sun here also suggests that the person will have a good inheritance and will be prosperous and successful. He might also derive pride and self-confidence from marrying a prosperous spouse. A good Sun in the eighth house also gives the person power and authority. It is a good placement for business, and sometimes gives sudden financial gains through speculation. The person likes to travel. He will have good vitality and a long life.

Negative: A malefic Sun in the eighth house brings all kinds of changes and upheavals in life. Many of these dynamic changes produce a sense of struggle or obstruction. Because this position of the Sun also suggests a strong need to be in control, the person can experience change and transformation as undesirable, and yet sometimes unavoidable. He could be fearful and subject to dark moods. The key to handling this placement well is to be on good terms with the evolutionary process. By taking a proactive approach to creating positive change and evolution in his life and the lives of other people, the person can sometimes offset much of the suffering usually associated with this placement. Therapists, either psychological or physical, who first experience their own inner transformation, and then guide their clients through the process of metamorphosis, often have this placement. Nevertheless, this placement does make a certain amount of struggle mandatory. How much suffering the placement produces is simply a matter of attitude and intention. On the physical level, an afflicted Sun in the eighth can produce difficulties with the heart, the spine, or the digestion. It is usually a rather difficult placement for health in general.

Moon in the Eighth House

Positive: When a positive Moon is placed in the eighth house the person will have a deep and intense emotional nature. He will go through a constant, yet positive, process of transformation and change in life. Even though some of his transformational lessons will be intense, he will emerge from all of them renewed and revitalized. Like a butterfly coming out of a cocoon, life will be a constant process of metamorphosis. The person will have a deep interest in psychology, the occult, astrology, symbols, myths or other hidden knowledge of life. He will also have an ability to be a transformational agent in the lives of other people and might make a good therapist or counselor. This placement is also good for financial gains through inheritance, insurance, clients, or other sources other than the person's own salary.

Negative: When the Moon is malefic or afflicted in the eighth house the person will have a hard time achieving happiness. This does not mean that happiness is impossible, rather the person will have to work through the many dynamic fluctuations of the mind that the placement suggests. The person will have emotional losses and disappointments.

The mother will have a difficult life or will be the source of loss or disappointment. Women in general will also be a source of problems. Early childhood will be full of difficulties, traumas and insecurity. As a result, the person is constantly challenged to deal with mental unrest. Meditation, psychological therapy, introspection and other mental exercises are all ways to settle down the mental turmoil suggested by this aspect. A malefic Moon in the eighth is also a negative factor for health. The person could suffer from problems related to the stomach, bladder, fluids in the body or the breasts.

Mars in the Eighth House

Positive: When a positive Mars is placed in the eighth house, the person will be courageous and powerful. He will have an ability to wield power and authority. This position suggests physical strength, vitality and an ability to constantly renew one's energy. For example, the person can work long hours, missing sleep for many days, and show no evidence of his fatigue. The eighth house is the house of ayu (life force), and a positive Mars (energy) here increases health and vitality in a good way. The person will have a strong will and be able to accomplish any goal. He will be able to benefit from inheritance, partnership and business in general. He will become successful and prosperous.

Negative: Mars in the eighth house is not an easy placement and is generally difficult for marriage. It makes the person controlling and resistant to the assertive advances of others. Since conventional sexual programming produces women that are passive and men that are aggressive, Mars here is obviously more difficult for marriage in the chart of a woman. The woman feels that she needs to be in control, and sometimes the sexual advances of the man are interpreted as an intrusion. Similarly, men having this aspect will also want other people to respect their space, and will feel a need to be in control. This expression is also true for benefic Mars in the eighth. In the case of a malefic or afflicted Mars, however, the experiences of intrusion become more pronounced. If Mars is heavily afflicted by Rahu and other malefic influences, it can sometimes suggest sexual abuse or rape. Other times, however, the person is just unable to control his temper. A heavily afflicted Mars in the eighth house also suggests a tendency towards injuries, surgeries and accidents. It is a negative factor for health, and can produce problems related to the blood, the head, or the muscles. The practice of yoga, as well as meditation and astrological remedial techniques, can offset the challenges of this placement to a great extent.

Mercury in the Eighth House

Positive: When a benefic Mercury is placed in the eighth house the person will have a deep interest in psychology, astrology, or the occult. He will be very intelligent and have a desire to go deeply into any field of study. As a result, he could be interested in science or in doing research of some kind. He will gain a good education and become an expert in his chosen field. A well-placed Mercury also promotes wealth and abundance, especially through other people. The person benefits through business, contracts, clients or inheritance. He will have a good reputation. He will be passionate and very sexual, but will channel his sexual energy into areas that are life-supportive. He will also have an intellectual interest in taboo subjects, and will enjoy discussing such topics as sexuality, death, and bowel movements. His spouse will have an interest in finances and could be good at business or accounting. The person can also excel at analyzing finances and giving advice to others on investing.

Negative: A malefic Mercury in the eighth house is a difficult placement for mental balance. There can be mental challenges or problems processing and expressing information that could make learning difficult. As a result, his education could be interrupted or involve struggle. This placement also suggests communication problems. The person's communication style might be manipulative or controlling. He might also have disagreements regarding money, especially concerning joint marital finances, money related to business, lawsuits or inheritance. His spouse could be a source of financial loss, mismanaging or squandering the joint resources. The person will also be quite passionate and indiscriminate with the expression of sexual energy. As a result, this is not a great placement for marital fidelity or marital harmony. An afflicted Mercury in the eighth house also suggests health problems related to the lungs, nervous system, hands, thyroid or skin.

Jupiter in the Eighth House

Positive: When Jupiter is in eighth house, the person will acquire wealth through marriage. Sometimes this means that he marries someone who is wealthy or who earns a high income. Or, it can mean that from the time of marriage, the person himself does better financially, either because of an increase in his earnings, or because of the combined earnings of husband and wife. In any case, Jupiter in the eighth is good for marital abundance. This placement also suggests financial gains from outside sources, such as inheritance, insurance, legal matters, and benefactors.

Sudden gains are also within the scope of the eighth house Jupiter. The person could earn through clients, contracts or business partnerships. A good Jupiter in the eighth house can be a sign of an alternative or unconventional philosophy of life. The person will have an interest in astrology, metaphysics, tantra, kundalini, and similar subjects. He will possess the ability to make accurate predictions. He will be attracted to yoga, meditation and other spiritual practices. He will have a powerful guru or teacher who may be known for his psychic powers (siddhis). Since the eighth is the house of ayu (life force), he will have high vitality, good health and a long life. He will experience an easy death.

Negative: A malefic or afflicted Jupiter in the eighth house can produce financial fluctuations and setbacks. The person will lose money through the spouse, business partners, inheritance or legal matters. This is not a good placement for business. The person might be irreverent and resistant to spiritual philosophies, religions and teachers. As a result, he will have difficulties either in finding a guru (teacher) or problems with the guru once he has one. The guru could turn out to be a scoundrel (in the person's opinion), leading to a break or separation from the teacher. This placement of Jupiter is also difficult for having and raising children. It can suggest an unscrupulous use of sexual energy that may include extramarital affairs. In spite of his occasional misbehavior, the person will put on an air of nobility and virtue. Physically, this placement suggests problems of the hips, liver, gall bladder and digestion. The person might have a tendency towards colitis, problems related to childbirth, or jaundice. The age of 15 will probably be difficult for matters related to the houses Jupiter rules in the person's chart.

Venus in the Eighth House

Positive: A benefic Venus in the eighth house will promote prosperity and comfort through marriage. The person will benefit through wills, the spouse, business partners, and other outside sources of income. The spouse will spend money on well-designed, high quality items. The person may become wealthy, affluent, and lead a luxurious life. He will have a passionate, yet profound emotional nature. Marriage will go through a constant metamorphosis. With a few supportive aspects from benefic planets, marriage can become the source of passion, happiness and prosperity. The person will be interested in the relationship between sexual energy and kundalini. As a result, he might take classes or seminars on how to deepen sexual pleasure and ecstasy through the use of tantric practices. He will always be interested in deepening his ability to experience intimacy, affection and sexual pleasure. He will be very compassionate and could have healing abilities. He will have a long life and will die peacefully.

Negative: A malefic or afflicted Venus in the eighth house will bring problems through marriage. The person will have a deep need for affection and warmth, but will not feel emotionally or sexually fulfilled. He will be very passionate and sexual, but sexual attachments could be filled with jealousy, power struggles and control issues. Marriage or relationships will go through gut-wrenching upheavals and changes that will give the person strong motivation to practice meditation or get psychological help. If he does this, then there is a potential to rebuild and empower a troubled relationship or marriage. In cases of serious afflictions, however, the spouse or partner could resist the whole process of metamorphosis that is demanded by Venus in the eighth. If so, then divorce or separation is likely. In cases of very serious affliction, the spouse could become ill or even die. This position of Venus also indicates health problems related to the sexual organs, kidneys, or eyes.

Saturn in the Eighth House
Positive: A benefic Saturn in the eighth house is a classical placement for long life. The person will also prosper due to partnership and business, and will be good at organizing joint finances. He will also be good at managing the finances of other people. This placement suggests that the partner will work very hard for a living and earn a good income. After the age of 36, the person will have greater financial benefits through partnership, marriage, and inheritances. Saturn placed here will also give the person the discipline necessary to study and practice spiritual techniques that will bear fruit in later life. He might also use psychological therapy as a means for spiritual growth. In either case, a good Saturn in the eighth gives the person a willingness to confront and work on his inner complexes and fears, resulting in good spiritual progress.

Negative: If a malefic Saturn is placed in the eighth house, the person will go through many ups and downs in life. The spouse or partner will work very hard, but earn very little. The person has a tendency to go into debt, so he should avoid using credit cards. This position also shows problems with creditors, and can produce tax problems. He will either have no inheritance or will experience difficulties, delays and obstacles regarding it. The age of 35 could be difficult for the career, health or finances. An inimical Saturn in the eighth also suggests difficulties with psychological or physical therapies. The person either resists taking responsibility for making needed changes, or in spite of making the effort he experiences little progress. As always with Saturn, the key to this dilemma is patience, perseverance and more patience. Saturn rewards those who work hard and persevere. An afflicted Saturn in the eighth house also suggests chronic health problems. The person could have problems related to the bones, teeth, immune system, colon or sexual organs. The eighth house is the house of sins from the past life. Obviously, an afflicted Saturn placed here suggests a larger than average karmic debt. Establishing a regular routine of spiritual practices can help to mitigate the negative karma and will diminish many of the problems due to this placement.

Rahu in the Eighth House

Positive: A benefic Rahu in the eighth house will produce a profound interest in the occult. The person will be interested in metaphysics and other revolutionary philosophies. If other astrological factors agree, he might become a good astrologer. He will also be interested in science and technology. He will benefit from wills, insurance, clients, or partnerships. Rahu here also suggests that the person will find the idea of change and transformation exciting, and he will be interested in various aspects of personal growth. He may have an interest in spiritual practices that focus on the development of the kundalini. The person could also marry someone who is interested in making money and who becomes prosperous.

Negative: A negative Rahu in the eighth house produces many unwanted or problematic changes in life. The person may experience frequent changes of residence, profession, and relationships. He will have financial fluctuations and losses. He might have a compulsion to spend money, running up large balances on credit cards. For this reason it is generally advisable not to borrow money when a malefic or afflicted Rahu occupies the eighth house. The person might also refuse to pay (or cheat) on his taxes. This is a bad idea since Rahu in this position can also produce tax penalties. This position also gives the person very unusual sexual experiences, and can indicate impulsive affairs. As a result, this is a negative placement for any kind of lasting relationship. In cases of intense affliction, Rahu in the eighth house can result in sexual abuse. It can also indicate accidents or injuries. The person might have chronic health problems such as venereal diseases, hard to diagnose diseases, viruses, candida and colon ailments. These problems can usually be offset to a great extent through the practice of appropriate techniques of meditation and astrological remediation.

Ketu in the Eighth House

Positive: A good Ketu in the eighth house suggests prosperity and abundance. The person will have good intuition in business and investing. He will have no attachment to the wealth of other people, yet will have unexpected gains from wills, joint finances and other outside sources. He will marry someone whose interest is not focused on money, but on a spiritual, creative or healing pursuit. The person will have good ability to adapt to changes in life, and will always "land on his feet." He could also have an interest in astrology, metaphysics and the occult.

Negative: A malefic or afflicted Ketu in the eighth house will produce financial problems related to marriage and partnership. The person will either not have an inheritance, or he will lose or squander inherited money. His spouse will have many unexpected financial losses and poor judgment with money. This is also a bad placement for dealing with banks, suggesting difficulty in getting important loans, as well as a general tendency towards indebtedness. The person with a malefic Ketu in the eighth should avoid borrowing money if possible. He will be a passionate, seductive person and tend to have affairs, so this is not the best placement for a happy, stable marriage. He will also tend to have health problems, such as hard to diagnose ailments, sexually transmitted diseases and colon problems. Because Ketu is the planet of moksha, however, most of these problems can usually be mitigated through the practice of meditation and other spiritual techniques.

Path of Light – Introduction to Vedic Astrology

The Ninth House (Dharma Bhava)

The ninth house is a house of dharma, the inner perception of truth and purpose in life. Here we are motivated to gain deep knowledge and wisdom. In the fifth house, another dharma house, we express our intelligence and engage in the learning process. In the ninth house, we are motivated to expand our knowledge to a deeper, more profound level.

In ancient times, students who wanted to learn more about life went to a guru, an enlightened teacher who, in many cases, turned out to be one's father. This may be the reason the ninth house has been used by some classical authors to represent the father. He would help them go beyond simple academic knowledge to a more abstract understanding of philosophy. In this way, the student learned that all subjects could be understood in terms of deep, harmonizing spiritual principles.

Today, motivated by the same desire to get to the roots of knowledge, we go to universities where teachers help us probe the abstract depths of physics, music, mathematics, philosophy and many other subjects. The more deeply we learn about these subjects, the more we find that they are all interrelated by fundamental, unifying principles.

In no area is this more apparent than in the field of quantum physics. Modern physicists are now theorizing models of the universe based on a unified field, a vacuum state, from which all matter is constantly being created and destroyed. The more progressive of these scientists are even postulating that this underlying and unifying field is also a field of consciousness. Science is discerning what the Upanishads have taught for thousands of years, that life is a wholeness, one being, that is called Brahman. Everything around us is just an expression of pure consciousness. This is what happens when we take physics, or any subject for that matter, to its subtlest and most abstract level. We eventually discover the deepest truths of life.

On a simpler level, the ninth house can represent a search for knowledge in universities and other institutions that allow us to freely explore abstract thought. As awareness develops, however, we are quickly motivated to look beyond the academic level to spiritual teachers or teachings that can provide us with a more profound sense of truth. This is why one's religion, belief system and spiritual teacher are represented by the ninth house.

The ninth house also signifies long distance travel. But even here, we can define travel as a way of expanding knowledge. When we take a long trip to a distant place, we broaden our perspective, become more philosophical, and come back with a new outlook on life. In the United States and in other western countries, for example, it is common for a person to take a year off from work or school and travel around the world. This is seen as a form of education, a first-hand experience that no university can supply. It is actually motivated by an unconscious desire to expand beyond limitations.

This ninth house desire to expand can be seen on a material level as well. The ninth house is a house of wealth and prosperity. Like every aspect of life, wealth can be understood from the point of view of several houses. The eleventh, the second and the fifth houses all signify important and various aspects of wealth. The ninth house, however, represents our prosperity in general terms. Here we develop a more expansive relationship to money. As this relationship becomes more refined, we may even become philosophical about wealth. Through the expansive nature of the ninth house, a philosophy of abundance evolves. We become aware that giving, as a natural expression of having more than enough, is not only a good, virtuous thing to do, but is actually the key to prosperity.

Ultimately, the deep feeling that there is an unbounded and absolute truth drives this house. People who have key planets associated with the ninth house frequently have a clear sense of purpose, deep faith, and strong ideas about right and wrong. They are motivated to live good, pure, virtuous lives, seeking truth and justice above all else. They can also be self-righteous and judgmental, which are the negative, or possibly the naive expressions of the house. For example, a freshman university student begins to think he has the world figured out after taking just a few courses in philosophy or psychology. On another level, the religious or spiritual fundamentalist, in an effort to be right and good, often becomes intolerant of the beliefs of others. Instead of realizing that most of us only perceive a relative and highly programmed version of truth, one feels that his belief is the ultimate truth.

Even though the ninth house is traditionally connected to positive values such as knowledge, religion, and wealth, it clearly has its dilemmas. On one hand, it allows us to sense the truth and adopt beliefs in an attempt to express or explain that truth. On the other hand, it sometimes perpetuates the illusion that our beliefs are actually "the truth." As a result, the world has split into countless religious and political factions, each righteously and sometimes violently, convinced that they have the real truth.

In resolving this ninth house dilemma, American folk wisdom offers the simplistic solution to "never discuss religion or politics." Although this might keep people from fighting, it hardly resolves the problems of the ninth house. The real key to understanding this house involves two elements. The first lies in our ability to continue to expand and refine what we believe. The second, however, is more important and usually more difficult to accept. In order to really get in touch with the essence of this house, it is necessary to recognize that our beliefs are only beliefs and not reality. Although certain beliefs can be useful, they ultimately keep us from experiencing the truth. Even the Vedas, the ancient teachings that form the basis of Hinduism, clearly state that truth is transcendent. No belief, sacred book or religion can truly describe it. The ninth house, then, motivates us to search for the truth, by developing and evolving our beliefs, and ultimately challenging us to let go of them altogether.

It is at this point that the real meaning of the ninth house becomes clear. This is the house of dharma, purposeful and conscious living. The fulfillment of the ninth house is expressed in the message of Lord Krishna to Arjuna in the Bhagavad Gita. Confused by conflicting beliefs about right and wrong, Arjuna asks Lord Krishna what to do. Instead of making the decision for him, Krishna tells Arjuna, "Yogasthah Kuru Karmani," meaning "Established in Being, perform action." Being is defined as pure consciousness and absolute truth, beyond the realm of belief. Once Arjuna drops his past programming and directs his attention inward, directly experiencing his inner reality, his doubts disappear and he simply acts in accordance with his nature as a warrior. In this way, he realizes the highest expression of the ninth house, life in accordance with dharma.

Significations of the Ninth House Given by Classical Authors of Vedic Astrology:

Dharma; good morals; goodness of heart; righteous conduct; devotion to God; worshiping in temples or shrines; the next world; religion; religious preceptors; religious austerities; religious properties; counselor; teacher; efforts to learn; father; wife's brothers; brother's wife; grandchildren; children; the people with whom one dines; general prosperity; wealth; investments; generosity; charity; residential house; conveyances; travel; medicines.

Physical Significations:

Hips; thighs. Depending on the drekkana rising—left cheek, left side of the heart, and left knee.

The Ruler of the Ninth House Placed in the Twelve Houses

First House

Positive: If the ruler of the ninth house is placed in the first house the person will be healthy, well-educated, prosperous, successful and virtuous. This placement produces a good relationship with teachers, gurus and the father. His father will be very bright, well-educated, and interested in sports, drama, art or music. This placement also produces a strong sense of purpose in life. The person will have strong beliefs, and a natural sense of what is true and real. He will be devoted to gaining knowledge and will do well in all educational pursuits. He will travel extensively and have many positive experiences in distant places. This placement is also said to produce a small appetite.

Negative: If the ruler of the ninth house is afflicted in the first house, the person will experience difficulties in his relationship with his father. His father could be intelligent, but may have experienced a break in his education. The person could also have educational problems or problems in his relationship with teachers. He could also encounter difficulties during long-distance travel. These problems, however, will only manifest according to the degree of intensity of the particular afflictions to the ninth lord. In cases of serious afflictions, the person could experience loss of the father, teacher, and educational pursuits. In cases of mild affliction, he will have a good father and education, but will have minor problems related to them.

Second House

Positive: If the ruler of the ninth house is placed in the second house, the person will be wealthy. This is a classical combination for financial increase and prosperity, especially if the ninth lord combines with the ruler of the eleventh or fifth houses or with Jupiter. This placement is also good for teaching, enabling the person to speak with a sense of purpose and expertise. It is also good for marriage and domestic life in general. A strong and supported ninth lord in the second also suggests that the person will have a wealthy father, who will be a source of financial support. The person's first child could have writing abilities, or may work at a career that involves children, education, or creativity.

Negative: If the ruler of the ninth house is afflicted in the second house, the person could have various problems regarding money that originates from the father. This placement can also give fluctuations in the general financial situation, creating periods of financial gain, alternating with periods of loss. The first child could experience problems passing tests for professional certification. This placement could produce financial strain related to higher education. The person's guru could also be a source of financial losses.

Third House

Positive: If the ruler of the ninth house is placed in the third house, the person will travel. The travel will be more frequent and dramatic if the location of the ninth lord, lagna, or the Moon is in a movable sign. This placement is also good for education, giving a strong desire to read and to acquire knowledge. The person will be physically attractive, prosperous, and will possess writing abilities. His siblings will be fortunate and prosperous, and his relationship with them will also be good. He will have a positive relationship with his father, staying in touch via the telephone, the internet, or by writing letters. The next younger sibling may have a spouse who is very devoted and attractive.

Negative: If the ruler of the ninth house is afflicted in the third house, the person will experience difficulties while traveling. If the ninth lord or lagna lord is located in a fixed sign, then the person may resist traveling, or will not be able to travel. This placement also suggests a tendency to disagree about what is right, fair, or just. As a result, it can cause communication problems in the person's marriage and also create issues with his father, teachers, and spiritual guru. It suggests marital difficulties for the next younger sibling.

Fourth House

Positive: If the ruler of the ninth house is placed in the fourth house, the person will be lucky and prosperous. He will come from a good family and could inherit family property. He will have excellent luck with real estate and will live in a beautiful home. He will also own a nice car. This placement favors education, and suggests that the person will attend a first-rate college or university. His mother will be a strong, virtuous person with a pronounced sense of purpose in life, who will provide him with a solid upbringing and high values. His father could be instrumental in helping him purchase a home, land or a car. Similarly, his father will probably pay his university tuition.

Negative: If the ruler of the ninth house is afflicted in the fourth house, the person could have problems regarding property inherited from his father. His father could also be the source of domestic disharmony when the person is growing up. If the person approaches his father for money to purchase homes, cars, land or college tuition, he might meet with resistance or disagreement. It is also possible that the father could have several job changes that make it necessary for the person's family of origin to move frequently. This is also a negative placement for the health of the mother, producing physical problems signified by the afflicting planets and the planet that is the ninth lord.

Fifth House

Positive: If the ruler of the ninth house is placed in the fifth house, the person will be highly intelligent, successful and prosperous. He will be very loyal and devoted to his teachers and spiritual gurus. As a result, he will receive a good education, which may include advanced university degrees. This placement also suggests that the father will be a strong, virtuous, prosperous, and successful person. The first child will be very intelligent, creative, charming and successful. The person will have a natural sense of faith, and will be devoted to his religion or spiritual path. The ninth lord indicates that the person comes into life with a strong dose of purvapunya (merit from past lives), and will lead a fortunate life.

Negative: If the ruler of the ninth house is afflicted in the fifth house, the person will experience problems related to education. Unless the afflictions to the ninth lord are very serious, he will probably still receive a good education, but with some obstructions and difficulties. Similarly, the first child will still be intelligent, but could have a disruption in his education. The person may have disagreements with his teachers or spiritual gurus. It is important to note, however, that the influence of malefics on the fifth house, often signify an education which focuses on science, math or technology, so the entire horoscope should be scrutinized before predicting educational problems. In any case, afflictions here can diminish the effect of the positive karma that results from this combination.

Sixth House

Positive: If the ruler of the ninth house is supported and placed in the sixth house, the person will have good health. His father will be a successful person and could be self-employed or a leader in his field. The person will be quite willing to help his father, and he may work for his father at some point in his life. This placement is also good for service to the guru and suggests that seva (spiritual service) is an important part of the person's spiritual path. Also, the person could take a positive and active interest in developing sound health, as a support to his spiritual development.

Negative: If the ruler of the ninth house is afflicted in the sixth house, the person could experience enmity with his father, teacher or guru. The father, teacher, or spiritual guru could have weak health or intermittent health problems. Because the sixth is the tenth from the ninth house, this placement can cause problems to the career and general status of the father. The person will resist serving or helping his father. He will also experience problems while helping teachers or his spiritual guru. If the ninth lord is seriously afflicted here, the person could have physical problems related to the hips.

Seventh House

Positive: If the ruler of the ninth house is placed in the seventh house, the person will marry a spouse who is intelligent, attractive, well-educated, purposeful and virtuous. The marriage will be happy and the couple will prosper. This is also a good placement for a harmonious relationship with the father. It indicates that the father could be prosperous, successful and popular. The person will travel to foreign countries and could receive an education or find a guru there. This placement is also good for the marriage of the next younger sibling, indicating an attractive intelligent spouse. It suggests that the second child will have a clever, versatile mind, and will be a good communicator.

Negative: If the ruler of the ninth house is afflicted in the seventh house, the person will have philosophical differences and communication problems with the spouse. It is also possible that the spouse will not get along with the person's father, or that the father (or guru) may interfere in the person's marriage in some way. Unless the ninth lord is seriously afflicted, this placement will probably still produce marriage to a good person, but the marriage will have less harmony than when the ninth lord is strong and supported.

Eighth House

Positive: If the ruler of the ninth house is strong, supported and placed in the eighth house, the person could inherit money or property from his father. He will be spiritually inclined, will reject the religions of his parents, and will be interested in alternative philosophies and religions. This placement also suggests an interest in astrology and other occult sciences. The person will have a teacher or a spiritual guru who is powerful and charismatic. If the ninth lord and Jupiter are both strong and supported, then he could receive shaktipat (awakening of the kundalini) from his guru, or his guru might have siddhis (miraculous spiritual powers).

Negative: If the ruler of the ninth house is afflicted in the eighth house, then the person could lose his father early in life, or the father could be a source of consternation to him in some way. If he decides to have psychological counseling, he will spend much time working through issues related to his father. If he receives an inheritance from his father, then it will be subject to dispute, litigation, loss, or other obstructions. This placement also makes it difficult to find a good spiritual teacher. In fact, it also makes it difficult to attract any kind of teacher, or to benefit from the good advice of counselors or consultants like doctors, lawyers or even astrologers.

Ninth House

Positive: If the ruler of the ninth house is placed in the ninth house, the person's father will be healthy intelligent, successful and prosperous. The father will have personality traits that strongly resemble the planet that is lord of the ninth and sign of the ninth house. The person will become prosperous as well. He will receive a good education, and will have excellent teachers. It is also an excellent placement for having a spiritual teacher, especially if Jupiter is strong. A good relationship with siblings is also possible. The person will be virtuous and will have a strong sense of purpose.

Negative: If the ruler of the ninth house is afflicted in the ninth house, the person will probably still have a strong successful father, but could have problems and complications in his relationship with him. Unless the ninth lord is intensely afflicted here, all ninth house matters will thrive, yet will be obstructed according to the intensity of the affliction.

Tenth House

Positive: If the ruler of the ninth house is placed in the tenth house, it forms a special kind of Raja Yoga that gives the person a strong sense of purpose in his career. This fortunate combination enables the person to follow a career path that gives him a feeling of making an important contribution. It is also seen in the charts of experts, professionals, and consultants whose careers are dependent on the development of expertise, and require credentials, academic degrees or professional certification. This placement also suggests that the person could benefit professionally from contact with a mentor, patron, or teacher. He could follow the same career line as his father, and receive his father's guidance.

Negative: If the ruler of the ninth house is afflicted in the tenth house, the person will have a desire to do important and purposeful work, but could find it difficult to actualize such a profession. If the ninth lord is not too intensely afflicted, he could still get a mentor or patron, but could experience problems in his relationship with him. It is also important to note that the influence of natural malefics on the tenth house sometimes suggests technical, scientific, or mechanical work, and is not always detrimental to professional success. As in all other cases, it is important to consider the entire chart before predicting negative results.

Eleventh House

Positive: If the ruler of the ninth house is placed in the eleventh house, the person will become prosperous. If it is associated with the rulers of the second or fifth houses, he could become very wealthy. This is a first rate combination for material prosperity. This placement also suggests a spiritual path that connects the person to a spiritual community, or at least to friends who share a similar spiritual philosophy. The person will also be virtuous and will have a strong social consciousness. He will believe in human rights, and generally be interested in moral and ethical principles that are related to large groups of people, the community, society, and humanity at large. The ninth lord placed here also suggests that the person will have friends who are successful and prosperous.

Negative: If the ruler of the ninth house is afflicted in the eleventh house, the person will probably have financial gains, but they will be mixed with losses or difficulties. If the afflictions are powerful, he could experience serious resistance to achieving his financial goals. This placement also suggests that the person could have problems in his relationship with friends, groups, organizations, or his spiritual community, due to philosophical, moral or ethical reasons. It is also possible that unreliable friends could be the source of financial loss or contribute to failure in achieving other goals.

Twelfth House

Positive: If the ruler of the ninth house is strong, supported and placed in the twelfth house, the person will be very spiritually inclined. He will practice meditation and may receive diksha (spiritual initiation) from a spiritual guru. He will travel to foreign countries and distant places and will have many positive experiences while traveling. In fact, if other factors in the chart agree, it is possible that the person could be more successful in distant places than he is in his own city or country. This placement also suggests that the person could go to a university that is located in a distant place or even spend some time studying abroad. It is also an excellent placement for spending time in ashrams or retreat centers. He could have a teacher or spiritual guru who lives in a distant place or who is from a foreign country.

Negative: If the ruler of the ninth house is afflicted in the twelfth house, the person could lose his father, or the father could move to a distant place. This placement disturbs general prosperity and makes it difficult to accumulate wealth. He will have difficulties while traveling in distant places and foreign countries that are defined by the nature of the afflictions on the ninth lord. If the afflictions are severe, the person's father could die, he may not be financially able to travel and he could be poor. He could lose his guru or simply find it hard to get a good teacher.

Planets in the Ninth House

Sun in the Ninth House

Positive: When the Sun is in the ninth house the person will have a strong sense of right and wrong. He will be honest and honorable. He will value knowledge and will derive a great deal of his self-esteem from getting a good education. As a result, he will probably be well-educated, and could develop expertise in a profession. He will also enjoy traveling, especially to sunny destinations. This position of the Sun suggests a religious or philosophical nature. The person will be orthodox in his beliefs and will be devoted to God and righteous living. He will also be generous, optimistic and will tend to be prosperous. He will be proud of his father and will be like him in some ways. He will also honor his teachers and will identify closely with a teacher. This is a good placement for deriving a great deal of benefit from a spiritual guru. He will like to travel.

Negative: When a negative Sun is placed in the ninth house it brings problems with his father, or the father will have a difficult life in some way. The person will have problems with teachers and other authority figures. He will feel that he is right, but sometimes this can take the form of self-righteousness. In some cases the person becomes authoritative and dominating. He will rebel from the religion or belief system of origin and will adopt a new spiritual philosophy. He may also have difficulties during long distance journeys or want to travel, but not be able for some reason. The Sun placed here might also produce communication problems with the spouse and can disrupt marital relations.

Moon in the Ninth House

Positive: When the Moon is in the ninth house, the person becomes prosperous and well-educated. He may have a strong interest in foreign countries and foreign languages. As a result, he will like to travel, especially to destinations near the water. He will be generous and open. He will also be very interested in having children and will be a nurturing, supportive parent. His third child could be special or gifted, possibly being in the public eye in some way. He will be particularly attached to his father, who will be a gentle and caring person. This position of the Moon makes the person spiritually inclined. He will base his belief system on his personal experiences, feelings and perceptions, which will be rooted in a strong sense of what is true and real. He will derive great benefit from spiritual teachers, especially female gurus. His teacher will give him support and nurturance. He may also be attracted to a teacher who is popular or famous.

Negative: If a weak, malefic or afflicted Moon is placed in the ninth house, the person will have financial losses and difficulty becoming wealthy or prosperous. Although he will see himself as firmly rooted in "dharma," his sense of right and wrong and his sense of purpose will change according to his moods. This position also shows a very subjective belief system in which personal feelings and personal experiences play a great part, but his perceptions may be skewed by personal needs and desires. As a result, he might lack one-pointedness and could frequently change his spiritual path. He might also become a "guru hopper," moving from one spiritual teacher to another, depending on who is trendy at the moment. This position of the Moon, especially when afflicted by malefics, is detrimental to the health of the mother. It also suggests a difficult relationship with the father.

Mars in the Ninth House

Positive: When Mars is in the ninth house, the person will be a spiritual warrior. He will have a strong sense of right and wrong, and will always be ready to stand up for what is right. He will apply his ambitious energy to undertakings that give him a sense of purpose, and which contribute something positive to others. He will be confident, successful, prosperous and courageous. His father will have an ambitious nature, and could have a military or athletic background. His mother will be competitive and hardworking. The person will be successful with real estate. He may also come from a large family. This placement of Mars also suggests that the person enjoys traveling to places where he can participate in physical activities outdoors. He will be ambitious to gain knowledge, and will become well-educated as a result. He will tend to have male teachers who are assertive, ambitious and bold.

Negative: When Mars is malefic, and is placed in the ninth house, the person could be argumentative and self-righteous. He will have problems in his relationship with his father, or the father might have a difficult life, poor health, or even pass away when the person is young. It is possible that the father could have some negative experiences in the military, such as being in a war. A negative Mars here is problematic for the health of the mother as well, suggesting problems related to blood, surgeries, accidents or injuries. This placement disrupts the person's education and his relationships with teachers, producing arguments and disagreements. If he does manage to find a guru, the person could be very critical of him or vice-versa. A malefic Mars in the ninth is also an indication of problems occurring during travel, so the person should be careful in foreign countries, and generally avoid places that are politically unstable.

Mercury in the Ninth House

Positive: If a benefic Mercury is in the ninth house the person will be very intelligent and articulate. He will receive a good education and may become an expert in his chosen field. His father will be intelligent, charming and have a good sense of humor, possibly specializing in the art of puns. The same qualities will generally be true of teachers, and Mercury here suggests that the person will gain a great deal of knowledge from his teachers. He will also possess an intellectual approach to knowledge, using logic and discrimination to discern the truth. He may read religious or philosophical books, and could become well-versed in spiritual literature. He will also be interested in mathematics, languages and music. He will be a good writer and could even write and publish books.

Negative: If Mercury is malefic or afflicted in the ninth house, the person will find it difficult to receive a good education. Afflictions to Mercury here disrupt the relationship between the person and his teachers, violating the flow of knowledge in some way. Also, the person may find it hard to communicate with his father. The person could adopt an unorthodox belief system. In cases of severe affliction, the person might be an atheist. The mother might suffer from physical problems related to the skin, nervous system, lungs or thyroid.

Jupiter in the Ninth House

Positive: When Jupiter is in the ninth house the person will be healthy, prosperous and wise. He will have a noble, successful father, who is virtuous and confident. His father might be a professional and could be physically tall or big. In any case, the father will be large in spirit and a generous person. The person could receive money or financial help from his father as well. He will have healthy, bright, cheerful, and virtuous children. Jupiter placed here creates self-confidence and purpose, giving a strong sense of right and wrong. It insures that the person will have good teachers and a great education. As a result, he will become very successful. It also suggests good fortune in finding a spiritual teacher or guru. The more benefic the Jupiter, the more wisdom and spiritual benefit are derived from the guru. A good Jupiter here also protects the health of the mother, giving her good recuperative ability.

Negative: When Jupiter is afflicted in the ninth house, the person has a difficult time becoming prosperous or successful. He will experience financial fluctuation, expenses and losses. His university education can be difficult or interrupted. He will experience challenges related to children, either in having them or in his relationship with them. He will also have problems with teachers and gurus. He might reject his family religion in favor of an alternative belief system. If Saturn aspects Jupiter, the person could pursue a spiritual path characterized by austerities, simplicity or effort. In any case, a malefic influence on Jupiter suggests struggles, interruptions, or in cases of severe affliction, even the negation of spiritual progress. It can also suggest health problems for the mother related to the liver or gall bladder.

Venus in the Ninth House

Positive: When Venus is benefic and placed in the ninth house, the person becomes wealthy. He will be very fortunate in his choice of a spouse, and could meet his spouse either while traveling or attending college. The spouse will be well-educated and possess high integrity and intelligence. In general, his marriage will be a source of support and will promote his prosperity. This position indicates that the person will have a loving relationship with his father, who will be charming and sociable. The person will be extremely devoted to his teachers and could even develop a social relationship with a teacher. In any case, he will enjoy his education, especially his university years and will receive a well-rounded liberal arts education. He will have a devotional nature and be very attached to his spiritual teacher or guru. This position also acts to support and balance the health of the mother.

Negative: A negative Venus in the ninth house can cause self-indulgence. The person feels he should be wealthy and could spend money extravagantly. Or he simply has trouble saving money and developing a nest egg. His father could be a passionate person, with a tendency towards affairs, addiction, or emotional abuse. As a result, the person can suffer from a lack of emotional self-esteem or a lack of emotional balance and prudence. A negative Venus placed here suggests that the person can waste his time while attending a university, indulging himself excessively in fun, games, parties, and romance. As a result, his education could suffer. This position produces difficulties in marriage. It can suggest health problems for the mother related to the eyes, kidneys or sexual organs.

Saturn in the Ninth House

Positive: When a positive Saturn is placed in the ninth house, the person works hard in school, receives a good education and becomes very successful. In some cases, the person stays in school a long time, taking his education to a very high level. In other cases, he returns to school in mid-life and gets an advanced degree. Saturn causes the person to work hard and achieve a high academic standing. This hard-working, responsible quality will also be reflected in the person's father, who may have management or organizational qualities. From his father, the person learns that hard work and a sense of responsibility are the cornerstones of character. His father will also live a long time. This position also presents the individual with no-nonsense teachers who make the person work very hard. The same will be true for the guru, who will ask him to establish a discipline of meditation or perform other formal spiritual practices. He could also meet his guru or become more serious about his spiritual path around the age of 35. A good Saturn in the ninth house can also suggest that the mother is a hard worker, and that she has a disciplined attitude about her body, involving a healthy diet and regular exercise.

Negative: A malefic or afflicted Saturn in the ninth house will obstruct prosperity. The person can have financial responsibilities that seem overwhelming. He will fear his teachers, who will seem to place impossible demands on him. He will find it hard to be accepted at the university or college of his choice. He may also experience his university studies as being tedious and pressurizing, and he will have difficulty learning and benefiting from his education. As a result, he may quit school before receiving a degree, or he may experience many obstructions and delays before he graduates. This position of Saturn suggests that the father will be a source of pressure and negativity. In some cases, the father is absent during the person's childhood, leaving a gap in his emotional psyche. In cases of serious affliction, the father could have ill health or even die. Saturn here is also detrimental to the mother's health, and may create a tendency towards overwork, stress, colds, chronic diseases, dental problems, or simply a general depletion of energy. *[handwritten: All true, and Rahu/ Ketu on the Ascendant means that the native has justification for the grudge (See page 113)]*

Rahu in the Ninth House

Positive: When a benefic Rahu is placed in the ninth house, the person becomes wealthy and successful. He might study science or technology and receive an advanced degree. In any case, he will be driven by a strong desire to gain advanced or cutting edge knowledge. He will be interested in an alternative philosophy and will be spiritually inclined. He will attract teachers who have revolutionary approaches to their subjects. The same will be true of his guru, who will depart from conventional methods of teaching, or his guru might separate from his own spiritual tradition. This position of Rahu creates an independent and highly intelligent father. The person will enjoy traveling to exotic countries, having many surprising and exciting experiences enroute.

Negative: When a malefic or afflicted Rahu is in the ninth house, the person's father becomes the source of problems. The father might have had a difficult life and the person will feel alienated from him. Sometimes this manifests simply as a matter of physical separation. In other cases, the father is strange or rebellious in some way. In the case of a serious affliction, the person experiences physical, mental or emotional abuse from the father, or the father can have an accident or hard to treat illness. This placement of Rahu is also detrimental to the mother's health. She may suffer from a hard to diagnose disease or from viruses or chronic diseases. Rahu placed here also suggests that the person will be rebellious regarding religion and spirituality. In extreme cases he will be an atheist, but most of the time he simply adopts a very "out of the mainstream" belief system. He will rebel from the conventional codes of conduct and virtue, creating his own code of ethics. The sense of urgency that accompanies Rahu sometimes makes the person a religious or spiritual fanatic.

Ketu in the Ninth House

Positive: When a beneficial Ketu is placed in the ninth house, the person adopts a minimalist approach to spirituality. For example, he will like religions such as Buddhism, which center on a philosophy of detachment, involving only a few simple principles. He will be very spiritually inclined, and will prefer meditation and inner experience to intellectual study and discussion. He will combine travel with spirituality and prefer pilgrimage to pleasure travel. When traveling for pleasure, though, he will enjoy going to exotic places and Asian countries. His father will be artistically, medically, or spiritually inclined, and will not be a disciplinarian. His mother could have an interest in natural methods of healing. He will have teachers who are intuitive and inspirational, but he will not become dependent on them, and will always follow his heart.

Negative: When Ketu is malefic or afflicted in the ninth house, the person experiences losses and disappointments regarding his father. In some cases, this simply means that he is constantly dissatisfied with his father. In cases of serious affliction, this indicates loss of the father, either emotionally or physically. This position also suggests problems and disappointment related to teachers, and the person could quit school before getting a degree. On a spiritual level, he will lack direction and have trouble finding a teacher or a spiritual path. If he does find a guru, then the guru can become a source of disappointment to him. The person will have difficulty amassing a nest egg and will have other financial problems as well. This placement produces problems during long-distance travel, such as theft, accident, illness, lost tickets and lost luggage.

The Tenth House (Karma Bhava)

The tenth house is the house of karma or action. This is the area of the chart where we play out our desire to have an impact on the world. Just as the ninth house gives us an internal sense of purpose, the tenth house motivates us to express that purpose in the field of action. Just as the fifth and ninth houses allow us to express our intelligence in the process of learning, the tenth house provides us with an arena in which we can actualize our knowledge and put it to good use.

One's career is the most obvious expression of this house. Even though several houses play a part in determining career prospects, the tenth house is one of the most important indicators of both one's choice of career and level of professional success. As a result, this house also shows our reputation, status and level of authority.

In ancient India, one learned his profession from his father. This is probably why some classical writers have used the tenth house to indicate the father. In this respect, there seems to be a contradiction between the significations of the ninth and tenth houses. Both are claimed as the house of the father by different classical authors. In practice, however, it should be remembered that astrology is not really as compartmentalized as it seems. Each signification in astrology is actually multifaceted. One's father, for example, can be a teacher, preceptor, guru, or the person from whom we learn our belief system. In this case, he may be signified by the ninth house. On the other hand, the father can also be defined as a role model for the person's career. He exemplifies how to impact the world through action. In this respect, the father is clearly a tenth house concern.

The tenth house also indicates authority figures. It represents bosses, superiors, people of reputation, and governmental authorities. Even the person's father, from the tenth house point of view, is seen as a person of authority and power in the world.

The tenth house, like the sign of Capricorn, its counterpart in the natural zodiac, is a sign of practical results through action. For this reason, people who have key planets in this house usually display pragmatism, organizational ability, and are motivated by a desire for status or prominence. They live in a practical world where actions speak louder than words and where abstract concepts have little value unless they can be made concrete and put to some good use.

In another respect, the tenth house actually has quite a spiritual role to play in the chart. In spite of the fact that on the surface it seems to be a mundane house, the tenth is also the place where one actualizes one's spirituality and fulfills one's spiritual purpose in the world. Again, using the example from the Bhagavad Gita, Lord Krishna's advice to Arjuna actually had two parts. First, go within. By directing the attention inward (through meditation) to the source of his sense of purpose, Arjuna could realize his dharma, or inner purpose, in the abstract form of pure consciousness. This is usually what is defined as spirituality, and can be related to the ninth and twelfth houses. Surprisingly, however, Krishna then advises Arjuna to go out into the battlefield and take action according to this intuitive sense of purpose, even if that meant killing his relatives. This action was required because remaining constantly in the abstract, whether that means meditating, philosophizing, or moralizing, will only cause spiritual stagnation. Action is an essential part of the spiritual journey. Enlightenment is more than simple awareness of the self. It also includes the expression of pure consciousness in the outside world through action.

It is the tenth house that allows us the opportunity to express our sense of purpose, "to walk our talk" so to speak. Whatever we are, academically, philosophically, morally, or spiritually, is demonstrated through this house. Practically speaking, the tenth house allows us to take our knowledge, talents and abilities and put them to good use through a career. From the spiritual point of view, however, the tenth house represents the natural and spontaneous expression of self in the field of action.

It is at this point that the deepest understanding of the tenth house can be understood. The tenth is commonly viewed as the house of desire for power, authority and prestige; values which have driven the western world into a sort of madness in the past few centuries. This house, however, actually has a much higher potential. In fact, classical authors have allotted pilgrimage and spiritual renunciation to its repertoire. When we really tune in to this house, it becomes an action house, where the fruits of actions can be renounced. In other words, as a person's consciousness develops, he begins to realize how to do work as a simple expression of self, for the sake of the work rather than the prestige or status at the end of the work. Power, fame and prestige may still come if they are indicated in the chart, but the desire for these things ceases to grip the mind, no longer binding him in compulsive behaviors, worry and frustration. In this way, the tenth house truly becomes a house of pilgrimage, where each action becomes a natural expression of karmic purpose and a joyous step towards deeper fulfillment and greater self-awareness.

Significations of the Tenth House Given by Classical Authors of Vedic Astrology:

Profession; kingdom; rank; honor; status; position; authority; respect; rulers; business; debts; athletics; teaching; agriculture; renouncing the world; temples; city; government councils; lodgings for pilgrims; the road of a journey; living abroad; father; adopted son; elders; mother; sky; talismans; sleep.

Physical Significations:

Knees; knee caps. Depending on the drekkana rising - left nostril, left side of the body, and left thigh.

The Ruler of the Tenth House Placed in the Twelve Houses

First House

Positive: If the ruler of the tenth house is placed in the first house, the person will be independent in work. Frequently this indicates that he will be self-employed, but it can also mean that his career will allow him a great deal of independence or authority. This placement also suggests professional fame and recognition, especially if the tenth lord combines with the lagna lord, or the rulers of the fifth or ninth houses. The person will become progressively more successful and prosperous.

Negative: If the ruler of the tenth house is weak, or afflicted in the first house, the person will have professional problems related to a tendency to be too independent. He may find it difficult to harmonize with his boss or coworkers, or he could have professional setbacks and reputation problems. This placement can also produce ill health in childhood, usually followed by improvement and better health later in life.

Second House

Positive: If the ruler of the tenth house is placed in the second house, the person will have many good qualities and virtues. He will pursue a profession related to money, trade, food, speaking, or teaching. He will have a commercial approach to his work. As a result, he will become prosperous and successful through his profession or business. It is possible that he could become involved in a family business or trade.

Negative: If the ruler of the tenth house is afflicted in the second house, the person will have a hard time earning money at his profession. For example, he could make bad business decisions, resulting in financial losses. It is also possible that he may simply find it hard to be "commercial," and could even hesitate to charge people for his work. This placement gives the person some definite money issues related to work. He could feel overworked and underpaid, but usually this will be (at least partially) his own doing.

Third House

Positive: If the ruler of the tenth house is placed in the third house, the person will pursue a career that is communication-oriented. His work might involve many short-distance trips or errands, or cause him to be on the telephone or internet constantly. This placement is also found in the charts of people who process information for a living, and is common in the charts of people who work with computers. The person will have diverse interests and abilities and could even have two professions. He could collaborate with a sibling in his work. This is also a good placement for music or writing as a profession or avocation.

Negative: If the ruler of the tenth house is afflicted in the third house, the person will experience communication problems in his work. He will experience many interruptions, delays, obstacles or pressures related to the various errands and tasks of his daily work. He will have to struggle hard to succeed in his career. If he does succeed, it will be only after much time and effort.

Fourth House

Positive: If the ruler of the tenth house is placed in the fourth house, the person could have a home business or an office in the home. It is also possible that he will simply have an office that is like a home away from home. This placement produces a link between the house of action and the house of the home, so it is common in the charts of realtors, builders, and architects. It produces professional success as a rule. The person could also work for foundations, institutions, or schools. In addition, he will own property and nice vehicles. He will have a good relationship with his parents and other family members.

Negative: If the ruler of the tenth house is afflicted in the fourth house, the person will have a desire to have an office in the home, but might have a hard time actualizing this desire. He may have an office outside of the home that is not comfortable, or he could have to move his office frequently. He will experience various problems with real estate. If he is able to purchase a home, he will have to do many unpleasant tasks related to repairs and upkeep.

Fifth House

Positive: If the ruler of the tenth house is placed in the fifth house, the person will be very successful and prosperous. He will be very creative and could pursue a career or avocation related to the arts. The nature of the creative work, however, will be determined by the planet that rules the tenth house. When malefic planets are involved, the work can include technical creativity, such as technical writing or computer programming. In any case, this is a common placement in the charts of writers, musicians, artists, movie producers, actors, programmers, and even manufacturers. This placement is also common in the charts of schoolteachers and others who work with children. It is found in the charts of stockbrokers and investors as well. The person may become an expert in his chosen field, and take advanced professional training periodically. This placement is seen in the charts of people who occupy positions of authority, and is common in the charts of politicians.

Negative: If the ruler of the tenth house is weak or afflicted in the fifth house, the person could work in a school for problem children. He will have problems in either receiving or continuing with professional training. In his creative pursuits, he could have problems being recognized, or may simply have a problem completing his creative projects. However, it is important to note that the influence of malefic planets can sometimes promote technical creativity, and could suggest success in computer programming or technical writing. This placement suggests financial losses and setbacks if the person invests in the stock market, or pursues an investment-oriented career.

Sixth House

Positive: If the ruler of the tenth house is strong, supported, and placed in the sixth house, the person will obtain good employment easily. He will become more and more successful over time with hard work. As a result he will gain recognition and status in his place of employment. He will tend to be employed by others rather than be self-employed. In some cases this placement produces a service-oriented, type of self-employment. It is also good for work in health-related occupations, and is common in the charts of doctors, nurses, massage therapists, chiropractors and other health professionals.

Negative: If the ruler of the tenth house is afflicted in the sixth house, the person will constantly struggle to succeed professionally. He will have many professional competitors and enemies. He could also have an argumentative nature, and might argue or disagree with his boss or coworkers frequently. He will experience many obstacles to professional advancement, and find it difficult to get raises or promotions. He could become unable to work due to ill health, accident or injury. On the other hand, in the charts of health professionals who work with seriously injured or troubled people, afflictions to the tenth lord in the sixth house sometimes simply reflect the intense problems of their patients.

Seventh House

Positive: If the ruler of the tenth house is placed in the seventh house the person will seek the collaboration of others in his profession. It is also a common placement in the charts of people who work with clients. It can link the career to the law, contracts, business, banking, mediation or politics. The tenth lord here also produces a responsible, hardworking spouse, who supports the person professionally and could even work with him. The spouse will also be interested in acquiring houses, land, or vehicles, and will be happy and successful.

Negative: If the ruler of the tenth house is debilitated or afflicted in the seventh house, the person will experience disagreements and other problems related to professional partners. Similarly, this placement causes broken contracts and legal problems. In the charts of consultants who help their clients overcome problems, a debilitated or afflicted tenth lord here frequently allows the person to benefit by fixing the problems of other people, especially if the tenth lord is neecha bhanga. Needless to say, this is not a good position for working with one's spouse.

Eighth House

Positive: If the ruler of the tenth house is supported and placed in the eighth house, the person will go through at least one powerful metamorphosis in the career. His career could connect this metamorphosis process for other people, so this placement is common in the charts of therapists who work with various healing modalities. Since the eighth house is also a house of the occult, this placement is also seen in the charts of astrologers. It can also propel the person to pursue an alternative career. It is a placement frequently seen in the charts of people who work in insurance, banking, money management, mortuaries, research, and other eighth house occupations. Also, the spouse will have the ability to profit through real estate.

Negative: If the ruler of the tenth house is afflicted in the eighth house, the person will tend to talk negatively about others behind their backs. This placement produces many professional obstacles and challenges and is seen in the charts of people who change their jobs frequently. However, in the charts of therapists, malefic influences to the tenth lord in the eighth house sometimes reflect the intense problems of the patient. In the charts of people with more dubious characters, this placement can suggest a tendency to manipulate, break the law, or become involved in various negative activities.

Ninth House

Positive: If the ruler of the tenth house is placed in the ninth house, it produces a Raja Yoga that gives the person a strong sense of purpose in his career, and also produces success, a good reputation and prosperity. The person will also have good children and good friends. He will pursue a profession in which expertise, credentials, or certification is required. It is also likely that he will get advanced education in his field, usually in a university. He could become a teacher, doctor, lawyer, spiritual counselor, healer or other kind of expert. This placement also suggests the possibility of having a teacher who becomes very instrumental in the person's career. Even his spiritual guru will give him plenty of support and encouragement in his profession. This is because the ninth lord represents dharma, the sense of purpose. Linked to the tenth house, the person fulfills his dharma through the profession. With a little support, this placement allows him to find a career that will be an integral part of his spiritual development.

Negative: If the ruler of the tenth house is weak, afflicted, and placed in the ninth house, the person will have a strong sense that he should do purposeful work, but will have a hard time actualizing it. His father could be critical, resistant, or negative about his career choices. The person might have arguments, disagreements or separations from his professional teachers or mentors. His professional training and education will be filled with struggle or interruptions. He will probably still become successful, but with more difficulty.

Tenth House

Positive: If the ruler of the tenth house is placed in the tenth house, the person will be successful, prosperous, and famous in his professional field. He will be very efficient in all his activities. He will also have a strong sense of responsibility and good organizational skills. If the tenth lord happens to be Mars, Mercury, Jupiter, Venus, or Saturn, this placement causes a Mahapurusha Yoga, which produces the qualities of that particular planet in a very dominant way. This planet's energy will manifest in the personality, but it will also produce specific results in terms of a career that is signified by that planet. For example, Mercury in the tenth house in Gemini produces Bhadra Yoga, which is common in the charts of writers, poets and musicians. In any case, the ruler of the tenth, strong and unafflicted in the tenth house is a great placement for professional success.

Negative: If the ruler of the tenth house is afflicted in the tenth house, the person will probably have career success, but with more problems, interruptions, and obstacles. It is important to note, however, that malefic influences on the tenth house frequently suggest technical careers. In such cases malefics promote success rather than hinder it.

Eleventh House

Positive: If the ruler of the tenth house is placed in the eleventh house, the person will become successful and prosperous through his career. He will work with groups of people. He could have humanitarian instincts and work to improve the condition of his community, society or even humanity at large. This placement is also seen in the charts of people who make big plans with far-reaching impact. It is common in the charts of people who affect the masses, through jobs such as advertising or public relations. With this placement the person derives professional benefit through friends, and is common in the charts of people who "network," by joining clubs and organizations in order to promote their careers.

Negative: If the ruler of the tenth house is afflicted in the eleventh house, then the person will have a more difficult time achieving his professional goals. His friends could have a negative impact on his career. He could associate with people who give him bad advice, or who are not socially popular. It is also possible that the person could have negative experiences when doing business with friends or in group situations.

Twelfth House

Positive: If the ruler of the tenth house is supported and placed in the twelfth house, the person could pursue an occupation that involves the use of intuition or the unconscious. This is a common placement in the charts of therapists, psychics, healers, and artists. It is also possible that he will work at a job that involves travel, or at least puts him in contact with distant places. This placement normally produces many interruptions in the stream of activity. When the tenth lord is supported, it suggests that the person will have an occupation in which interruptions are integral to the nature of the work.

Negative: If the ruler of the tenth house is afflicted in the twelfth house, the person will have many professional losses, uncertainties and interruptions. For example, he could periodically lose or quit his job. He might also be disorganized. If he travels for a living, then he will probably experience many difficulties in the process. If other psychological factors agree, this placement can cause secret activities, fraud, deceit or even criminal tendencies. It is generally a difficult placement for professional success.

Planets in the Tenth House

Sun in the Tenth House

Positive: When the Sun is placed in the tenth house the person will be very successful in his career. This placement causes him to identify with his career. He takes pride in doing a good job, and strives to achieve recognition. He may become successful and well-known. This position of the Sun gives leadership ability as well. Sometimes the person will work at a job connected to the government. He will be pragmatic and practical, and will believe in the axiom "actions speak louder than words." He may also have talent in art, music, dance or drama. The Sun in the tenth also makes the person an industrious and ambitious student. He will have good organizational skills. He will also be popular and have good friends. This position is also said to make the person "wise, well-mannered and devoted to gods and preceptors."

Negative: When the Sun is afflicted and in the tenth house, the person will experience career problems. In some cases this means intermittent fluctuations in career success. In cases of severe affliction, it can mean that the person will have failures and humiliations. The Sun here is also a difficult placement for peace of mind. Even a benefic and unafflicted Sun placed in the tenth, while good for the career, causes the person to become so involved and consumed with his glorious achievements in the world that his mind becomes somewhat unsettled and agitated. When the Sun is afflicted, this tendency is greatly magnified and compounded with anguish, due to damaged pride. This placement also suggests that the person will be separated from his family and it can be detrimental to the health of his mother.

Moon in the Tenth House

Positive: When the Moon is in the tenth house, the person will do work connected with the public, women, water travel and other significations of the Moon. This placement gives the person a good reputation in his profession and sometimes even brings fame. It generally produces success and prosperity as a result. The person will have many friends and contacts through his profession. He will have organizational ability and he could even manage institutions or foundations. This is also a good placement for writing and publishing. In some cases, the Moon in the tenth gives the person an interest in ancient subjects such as astrology. The person's mother will be ambitious for him to succeed in life, and she will be a dominant influence in his family of origin. She may play an important role in his choice of career, or in promoting his success. Similarly, women in general will be influential in making the person successful and recognized in his profession.

Negative: When the Moon is afflicted and malefic in the tenth house it causes loss of reputation and negative publicity in the career. In cases of severe affliction, the person could rise to a high status in the profession only to have his reputation destroyed by scandal or failure. In some cases this placement gives many fluctuations and changes in the career. The person could change his mind frequently, acting on impulse and constantly uprooting his career. He might also have reputation problems that are due to the influence of women. The Moon afflicted here can indicate a dominant mother who tries too hard to organize the person's affairs and promote his success.

Mars in the Tenth House

Positive: When a benefic Mars is placed in the tenth house the person will be very ambitious and will become very successful as a result. He will have a competitive nature in his profession. If Mars happens to be in the sign of Capricorn, Aries or Scorpio, then Ruchaka Yoga is formed, and the person will have leadership abilities and great professional success. In any case, a good Mars in the tenth makes the person a hard worker and a motivated professional. This position is also said to give financial gains and increased success after the age of 28. Because of the industrious nature and the enthusiasm for work generated by this placement, the person tends to become increasingly prosperous over time. Successful action breeds respect and admiration from others as well, so the person gains friends and social standing.

Negative: A malefic or badly aspected Mars in the tenth will cause many problems in the career. The person could have an avaricious nature, pushing aside his competitors or even his friends in order to succeed. As a result, he could make many enemies instead of friends in his profession. This placement can sometimes cause the person to act in dishonest or unethical ways in order achieve his desires. When Mars is weak or aspected by Saturn, however, it sometimes causes the person to simply feel frustrated, blocked and generally unable to achieve his goals. Aspects by natural malefics on Mars in the tenth can be tricky, however, because they can also indicate a career in a mechanical or technical field.

Mercury in the Tenth House

Positive: When Mercury is placed in the tenth house the person will be successful and well known in his profession. He will work at a job that requires intellectual, communication, mathematical, musical or analytical ability. He will be a conscientious student, and will receive a good education. If Mercury is in Gemini or Virgo, then Bhadra Yoga is formed, so the person will be dominated by Mercury's influence. In this case, he expresses Mercury's best side in the form of eloquence, charm, intelligence, musical ability and academic achievement. He becomes successful and even famous. Even without Bhadra Yoga, benefic Mercury in the tenth is a great placement for career success, prosperity and reputation.

Negative: When a weak or afflicted Mercury is placed in the tenth house, the person will make many mistakes in his profession. Mercury shows how we process and convey information. The person with this placement will have difficulty getting the details right. As a result, he will get a reputation for inaccuracy and unreliability. In some cases, he deliberately misrepresents himself on a professional level, altering facts and details to enhance his reputation. Saturn's aspect on a malefic Mercury sometimes suggests a tendency to be stressed easily or to worry excessively about work. In cases of serious affliction this placement can be associated with a nervous breakdown due to professional stress. It can produce arguments and disagreements with coworkers or bosses, as well as other communication failures. In other words, the person experiences professional strife resulting from the inability to process and express information.

Jupiter in the Tenth House

Positive: When Jupiter is placed in the tenth house, the person becomes successful and prosperous through the profession. He may work at a profession requiring advanced training, certification or credentials such as teaching, law, or medicine. Other people will seek out his advice and see him as an expert. He will have great confidence in taking action and will convey an air of authority. As a result, he will be a leader, with a good reputation. People with this placement make good executives, government leaders and business managers. If Jupiter is in Sagittarius, Pisces or Cancer, Hamsa Yoga is formed. This magnifies the above qualities and makes Jupiter dominate the chart. In this case he will also have a sterling character, a deep sense of truth and high integrity. The classics suggest that he will also have a ravenous sexual appetite. Even without Hamsa Yoga, however, Jupiter in the tenth produces excellent career success. If employed, the person will have fair, generous bosses and will have good luck getting jobs, promotions and raises. He will also have excellent rapport with colleagues and coworkers. His actions and projects will get immediate support and bear fruit quickly. A good Jupiter placed here also gives the person spiritual knowledge through the study of philosophical or religious literature.

Negative: A malefic and afflicted Jupiter in the tenth house causes failure in the career due to overconfidence, exaggeration, or poor judgment. The person will have many financial fluctuations. He will also have problems related to his children. This position of Jupiter causes the person to be attracted to the spouses of others as well, so it is not conducive to marital harmony. The person could have a poor sense of justice, or be treated unfairly by others. An afflicted Jupiter here can indicate that the person is a hypocrite.

Venus in the Tenth House

Positive: When Venus is in the tenth house, the person will enjoy his work. He will have very positive and fulfilling social experiences through his profession, and could even meet his spouse through work. His spouse might work with him or support his career in other ways. The person will be highly creative, and may be artistic or musical. He will also use his creative energy in his career in some way. This position of Venus also allows the person to benefit through professional contacts with women. For example, he might have women employees, or simply have mostly women customers. He could also deal in articles related to Venus, such as gemstones, clothing, and food. If Venus is in Libra, Taurus or Pisces, then Malavya Yoga is formed and the person's career will be dominated by Venus. He could become an artist, musician, craftsperson, or diplomat. He will have a compassionate heart and could become a healer of some kind. Even without Malavya Yoga, the person can have healing ability, due to a caring and compassionate nature. This placement is also good for making money through real estate. It gives the person great respect for the Divine and for spiritual teachers.

Negative: When Venus is weak and afflicted in the tenth house, the person will be inconsistent in his work due to self-indulgence. His romantic misadventures could get in the way of professional success, for example. In cases of intense affliction, the person's professional reputation could be harmed by sexual scandal or simply through the destructive actions of female business associates. This placement can also cause the person to put a great deal of emphasis on enjoying his work, in a way that is not grounded or practical. His jovial nature, desire to have fun, and self-indulgent attitudes could be the cause for being fired. He could also have broken love affairs with partners he meets in the work place. He will have similar problems in school, and may drop out of college before completing a degree. This placement also creates an interest in getting ahead in life through romantic and social relationships. It can indicate that he uses other people in friendship and romance in order to advance his career.

Saturn in the Tenth House

Positive: If a benefic Saturn occupies the tenth house, the person becomes very successful in his profession. He will have strong organizational and management skills and will be capable of running his own business or that of others. This placement of Saturn gives a person a strong sense of responsibility and an ability to work hard. The person will succeed in his career through patience and perseverance. Often, he makes a serious commitment to becoming successful around the age of 35. If Saturn is placed in the signs of Capricorn, Aquarius or Libra, then Sasa Yoga is formed. This creates a person who is dominated by the best qualities of Saturn that will primarily manifest in his career. He will become a manager, leader, or might even gain political prominence. Even without Sasa Yoga present, a benefic Saturn will allow the person to make steady progress towards the achievement and actualization of professional goals, leading to prosperity and affluence in life.

Negative: If Saturn is malefic or badly aspected in the tenth house, the person will have delays, obstacles and pressures in his career. Often this placement signifies a rise to professional success and status followed by a reversal or fall from power. Sometimes this is rather benign, as in the case of a person who willingly changes professions and starts over, after having achieved success in a particular field. In cases of intense affliction, however, the person could experience failure, humiliation or disgrace in his professional field. Saturn is also a technical planet, however, so malefic influences can also indicate mechanical or technical professions. If Saturn is weak, however, then the person will avoid taking responsibility in his work. He will have a negative reputation among his coworkers as someone who sloughs off, and will not get along with them. He will look at his work as a tedious and monotonous experience. He will also have problems with his bosses and many obstructions to getting jobs, raises and promotions. It is important to remember, that Saturn aspects the twelfth, the fourth and the seventh houses from its placement in the tenth. As a result, it will also create problems related to the significations of these houses as well.

Rahu in the Tenth House

Positive: Rahu in the tenth house is good for professional success. The person will have a sense of urgency and excitement about achieving his professional goals. He will be somewhat driven and compulsive, but when Rahu is favorable, this takes the form of total fascination with his work. He becomes consumed with ambitious drive and finds great pleasure in working hard. He will be an innovator in his profession, taking a revolutionary approach to his work. Since he prefers to stay on the cutting edge of his field, he may achieve breakthroughs that advance his profession. This placement also suggests that the person could work at a profession that is unconventional. Rahu in the tenth is seen in the charts of computer programmers, electricians, chemists, scientists, chiropractors, engineers, and astrologers. With Rahu placed here the person will be driven to succeed and will achieve both professional and financial success. Because of the strong desires that are always associated with Rahu, however, even a positive Rahu in the tenth house tends to make the mind restless.

Negative: If Rahu is malefic and placed in the tenth house, the person will have many changes in his profession. He will be compulsive in a negative way, possibly becoming a workaholic or a fanatic. He might be very eccentric, alienating his mainstream coworkers. In any case, this is not a good placement for positive relations with bosses, professional peers, or coworkers, and it causes the person to be a loner in his work. If Rahu is seriously afflicted here, the person may have sudden reversals or disasters in his work. For example, his boss could suddenly fire him, or he could accidentally make a fatal mistake in his work that causes him to lose status or to lose his job. Because this placement gives a rebellious nature, the person will try to avoid having a boss. If he does have a boss, then the boss might be strange, aggressive, driven, or obnoxious in some way.

Ketu in the Tenth House

Positive: When a good Ketu is in the tenth house the person will always follow his heart when it comes to the profession. He will have a sense that he wants to do something that has an inspirational, intuitive, spiritual, creative, or healing quality. He will have many uncertainties built into his career, which add to the magic of the profession. For example, an artist might not know exactly where he will sell his painting, yet he enjoys the process of finding out. A musician could go from job to job, taking a "hitchhiker's approach," yet he will make a good living in spite of the uncertainty. In fact, the spiritual passion for the career that is represented by this placement is based on the person's willingness to follow his intuition. Even a good Ketu in the tenth, gives a mild dissatisfaction with the mundane qualities that are a part of any successful profession. With a good Ketu, however, this dissatisfaction acts as a fuel to motivate the person to constantly seek higher and more refined experiences through his career. Ultimately, he is looking for God through his profession. At its best, Ketu placed here teaches the person how work and meditation go together. In fact, because the tenth house is the house of karma, which includes all actions, this position can allow the person to cultivate self-awareness or even become self-realized through the practice of mindfulness in each action.

Negative: When a malefic or afflicted Ketu is placed in the tenth house, the person will have a chronic sense of dissatisfaction in his profession. Even a good Ketu gives some dissatisfaction, but a malefic Ketu makes the dissatisfaction more problematic. For example, the person can develop a pattern of becoming frustrated and constantly quitting jobs. As a result, this is not a good placement for consistency in the profession, and the person will have a hard time putting down professional roots and persevering long enough to succeed at anything. In some cases the person works at a job and does not quit, but simply feels mildly depressed by his work. In cases of serious affliction, however, he could experience unexpected upsets and strange disappointments in his work. His company might go bankrupt, for example. The boss could be a dishonest person and refuse to pay him, or the boss might fire him unexpectedly. The person may simply find it difficult to get work, promotions, or raises. Needless to say, this is not a good placement for relationships with coworkers or peers. Of course, like Rahu, Ketu is also a technical planet, indicating refined technologies, so aspects on Ketu by other malefics can sometimes suggest careers in technical fields.

The Eleventh House (Labha Bhava)

The eleventh house signifies increase, gains and achievements. It multiplies anything it touches and brings it to its culmination. It is here that the fruits of labors are accomplished.

On the most obvious level, the eleventh house is the house of income through one's profession. Along with the second, fifth and ninth houses, it can be used effectively to judge both the level of financial prosperity, and the probable times of material increase. But the definition of eleventh house income is different from that of the other financial houses. The second house, for example, views income as a survival need, a source of food and sustenance. In the case of the fifth house, money is related to luck, actually due to positive karmas. In the ninth house, finances extend from our natural sense of abundance. The eleventh house, on the other hand, has a specific relationship to one's earnings through profession. Similar to the ninth house, it also brings abundance, but financial rewards here are usually the direct outcome of actions performed through the tenth house.

The eleventh house also delivers more intangible rewards, such as the successful completion of projects, achievements, important connections, and opportunities of all kinds. It usually works in tandem with the tenth house to magnify and enhance, or if the eleventh house is weak, to inhibit the outcomes of work. In this respect, it is highly beneficial for both the tenth and eleventh houses to be strong, but it isn't mandatory. In fact, if the eleventh house is strong and the tenth is weak, it often signifies financial gains and achievement with minimum effort. In this respect the eleventh house shows a more subtle aspect of accomplishment. It shows how we manifest what we desire. All of our aspirations, goals and wishes are reflected here. If the house is strong, our wish comes true. If not, more effort is needed to accomplish desired results.

The ability of the eleventh house to bring achievements and rewards can have its down side as well. Key planets, especially malefics placed here, may indicate a tendency to become goal-oriented, focusing on outcomes rather than the work itself. This can lead to unhappiness if goals are not achieved. It can also lead to a willingness to resort to any means to achieve the ends. This can be especially problematic in the charts of Westerners, who are already culturally programmed to be consumed by the pursuit of material goals. Subsequntly, the eleventh house can show us how we constructively fulfill our desires as well. The planetary influences on this house indicate the direction in which we channel our energy. The goals, hopes and aspirations that shape our lives are all revealed here.

This house also indicates our relationship to other people. Classically, it is the house of the older sibling, but it also represents friends. Even today in India, one refers to his friend as bhai, which means "brother", and this brings another aspect of the eleventh house to light. From this house, we learn to view not only our friends, but also our society and even all of humanity as our brothers. Even though classical Vedic astrology does not relate this house to groups of people, in a modern context it seems to function that way. The eleventh house brings increase to whatever it touches, and this seems to include relationships with people. This is different from the seventh house, where we relate to others in one-to-one relationships, using a partner to reflect ourselves, in a type of narcissistic self-discovery process. In the eleventh house, however, relationships are multiplied. One's group or society can be viewed as an extended family. The reflection of self takes on a more detached, expansive, and impersonal quality, extending to larger groups and potentially to all humankind.

In the overall spiritual scheme, the eleventh house teaches us to direct our energy along clear channels towards life-supportive goals. Through the cultivation of equanimity, which is the whole purpose of astrology, we learn a self-sufficient and detached approach to our goals, rewards and friendships. Fulfillment is viewed as intrinsic to the self rather than as a function of accomplishment. This brings a natural climax to life in which achievement, prosperity, and even a magnification of social contact are only the natural result of enlightened consciousness, expressing itself in the world.

Significations of the Eleventh House Given by Classical Authors of Vedic Astrology:

Financial income; achievement of knowledge; objectives; possessions; hopes; aspirations; gain from father-in-law; prosperity; lost wealth; master's wealth; ministership; older siblings; children's spouse; mother's longevity; paternal uncle; enemies.

Physical Significations:

Legs; left ear; recovery from disease. Depending on the drekkana rising—left ear, left arm, and left testicle (male chart) left ovary (female chart).

The Ruler of the Eleventh House Placed in the Twelve Houses

First House

Positive: If the ruler of the eleventh house is placed in the first house the person will be wealthy. He will be able to succeed at whatever he chooses and will be very successful as a result. He will have close friends and will treat all people equally. He will have humanitarian instincts and could become involved with clubs, groups, or community organizations. This placement also suggests that the person could come from a wealthy family. He will also be close to his next older sibling, who might be a very clever, charming and versatile person. The eleventh lord here also contributes to writing ability.

Negative: If the ruler of the eleventh house is weak or afflicted in the first house, the person will experience difficulties related to friends and/or the next-older sibling. If it is seriously afflicted, he could lose a friend or a sibling when he is young. This placement also makes it more difficult to achieve goals, and can diminish the person's ability to earn, making prosperity harder to realize.

Second House

Positive: If the ruler of the eleventh house is placed in the second house, the person will be wealthy. This is a classical placement for wealth, linking the house of gains to the house of money. If the eleventh lord is supported by Jupiter or the rulers of the fifth, ninth, or second houses, then these results will be magnified considerably. The person will also be charitable, virtuous and spiritual. This placement also suggests that the next older sibling will have a happy, prosperous life and will be able to own nice cars and homes. Friends will be a source of prosperity, or the person could do business with a friend or an older sibling. It is also possible that he could live with his next-older sibling for some time.

Negative: If the ruler of the eleventh house is weak or afflicted in the second house, the person will experience a mixture of financial gain and loss. His friends or his next-older sibling could be a source of financial loss as well. If the affliction to the eleventh lord is very severe, then losses will predominate and the person will experience great difficulty achieving prosperity. He will also experience domestic problems, arguments, and disputes.

Third House

Positive: If the ruler of the eleventh house is placed in the third house, the person will have many friends and will be popular. It is possible that he will have musical ability and could perform in front of groups. This placement is also good for public speaking. The person will be courageous and virtuous. His next older sibling could be creative, playful, intelligent, or occupy a position of authority. The next younger sibling will be well-educated, successful, purposeful, virtuous, and prosperous.

Negative: If the ruler of the eleventh house is afflicted in the third house, the person will have arguments and disagreements with friends. He will also have communication problems with his next older sibling. This placement suggests financial losses born of misunderstandings or poor communications. The next older sibling could have an interrupted education, and possibly have various problems regarding children. The next younger sibling may have problems related to his teachers.

Fourth House

Positive: If the ruler of the eleventh house is placed in the fourth house, the person will be wealthy and prosperous. He could receive financial support from his mother, or through real estate. His mother will also be his friend, and will provide him with good social skills that will attract many friends. He will enjoy inviting his friends to his home, and might give parties or host social events. This placement is also good for participation in social institutions. His spouse will be creative, charming, virtuous, and could have writing ability. The spouse will also be a good teacher. His mother could be particularly attached to his next older sibling.

Negative: If the ruler of the eleventh house is afflicted in the fourth house, the person will experience financial losses through real estate, cars, or the mother. His friends or older sibling could be the source of real estate losses or damage to his home or car. This placement is also detrimental to the health of the next older sibling, and could produce physical problems signified by the planet that rules the eleventh house.

Fifth House

Positive: If the ruler of the eleventh house is placed in the fifth house, the person will be wealthy. This is a classical placement for wealth, especially if the eleventh lord is supported by Jupiter, or the second, ninth or fifth lords. The person will also be able to profit through investing in stocks or mutual funds. This placement also gives the ability to make money through ventures that involve risk, and can give the person a love of gambling. He will also enjoy entertainment or sporting events that involve groups of people or teams. The eleventh lord placed here also produces and promotes good experiences with children.

Negative: If the ruler of the eleventh house is afflicted in the fifth house, the person could have financial losses through the stock market or other risky investments. His children could be the source of financial loss as well. This placement is also found in the charts of people who lose money through gambling. The first child could have marital difficulties. The person's relationship with his children could be strained or difficult.

Sixth House

Positive: If the ruler of the eleventh house is supported and placed in the sixth house, the person will succeed through hard work and effort. He will also become prosperous by working hard, usually in the employment of other people. This placement is good for financial gains through healing or service-oriented occupations. The person will enjoy being of service to his group, club, organization, community or society.

Negative: If the ruler of the eleventh house is placed in the sixth house, the person will have to struggle hard to achieve goals and to become prosperous. If it is afflicted here, then the process of achievement of desires and goals becomes very difficult. This placement also suggests enmity with friends. Friends can become enemies through disagreement and misunderstandings. The eleventh lord here can also cause the person to be a rabble-rouser, criticizing his friends and generally stirring up negativity among his group or social circle. His next older sibling could have health problems signified by the planet that rules the eleventh house. The person may have problems in his relationship with the next older sibling. This combination is not good for the person's health. It makes him susceptible to theft and the negative actions of enemies.

Seventh House

Positive: If the ruler of the eleventh house is placed in the seventh house, the person will be passionate and could have many love affairs. He might marry a person who is already his friend, or who he meets through a friend. Even if he does not already know his spouse, they will become best friends after marriage. This placement is also good for earning money through partnerships or clients. The person will have good social skills, and will be equally as good one-on-one as in a group of people. If the eleventh lord is under the influence of Jupiter, or the lords of the ninth, fifth, or second houses, then the person could marry a wealthy successful spouse. The spouse will tend to become successful and will promote the person's social standing and success.

Negative: If the ruler of the eleventh house is afflicted in the seventh house, the person could be romantic and passionate, yet frequently disappointed in love. If other factors agree, this placement can suggest more than one marriage. It can also suggest involvement with prostitution. The person's spouse could be a source of expenditure or financial loss. Similarly, the business partner can cause financial losses.

Eighth House

Positive: If the ruler of the eleventh house is supported and placed in the eighth house, the person could have financial gains through inheritance, insurance, clients, loans, or other eighth house sources. His next older sibling could be self-employed or independent in his profession, and will be very successful. This placement also suggests that the person will have successful friends.

Negative: If the ruler of the eleventh house is placed in the eighth house, the person will have financial problems and could go into debt. If it is afflicted, he will find it very difficult to achieve his goals. This placement also suggests losses through groups, friends or older siblings. If the eighth lord is very seriously afflicted, then the older sibling or a friend could die unexpectedly. In any case, he should avoid doing business with his friends or his next-older sibling. An afflicted eleventh lord placed here will make success and prosperity very difficult to attain. The person could also have physical problems related to the left ear or shoulder.

Ninth House

Positive: If the ruler of the eleventh house is placed in the ninth house, the person will become prosperous and successful. He will be virtuous and will have a strong sense of social ethics. He will also be generous and charitable. His spiritual path will center on his relationships with friends and communities that share similar beliefs. His teachers and spiritual guru will treat him with special care and attention. He will become well-educated and could achieve a high academic status. This placement allows the person to achieve any goal easily and suggests an affluent, luxurious life.

Negative: If the ruler of the eleventh house is afflicted in the ninth house, the person might experience financial losses through his teacher, father, or spiritual guru. He might be spiritually inclined, but could experience social or political problems in his spiritual community. His strong sense of social conscience may lead him to work with the underprivileged or downtrodden, in order to better society.

Tenth House

Positive: If the ruler of the eleventh house is placed in the tenth house, the person can be very successful in his profession. He will also become prosperous through his business. He could become very wealthy if the eleventh lord is supported by other money planets such as Jupiter, and the lords of the second, fifth, and the ninth houses. This placement also allows the person to achieve some distinction in his profession, and can produce fame if other factors in the chart agree. This placement is also good for networking, allowing the person to make many contacts and friends who support him professionally. In some cases the person works with a friend or older sibling.

Negative: If the ruler of the eleventh house is afflicted in the tenth house, the person could have friends who interfere with his success. This placement makes it generally difficult to succeed by conventional means, and can cause the person to resort to illegal or dishonest ways to achieve his career goals. In some cases, this means disregarding the feelings and rights of friends in order to get ahead. In other cases, it can be a friend who is overly aggressive. Hence, malefic influences on the tenth and eleventh houses can also promote success, but the means are usually more aggressive.

Eleventh House

Positive: If the ruler of the eleventh house is placed in the eleventh house, the person will be prosperous and successful. He will be able to achieve any goal easily, and will also have many good friends. His style of achieving his goals will be typified by the planet that owns the eleventh house. Saturn, for example, will give him success through hard work and over a long period of time. The Moon, on the other hand, will give success through friends, family, the public, and females. This placement also suggests that the next older sibling will be a strong, successful person, who will have psychological traits reflected by the planet that rules the eleventh house. Similarly, the person will tend to choose friends who are strong, successful, and characterized by the eleventh lord.

Negative: If the ruler of the eleventh house is afflicted in the eleventh house, the person will probably still be successful, but with more struggle and difficulty. This placement also produces problems for friends and also the older sibling, which will be reflected by the natural significations and house rulership of the afflicting planet.

Twelfth House

Positive: If the ruler of the eleventh house is supported and placed in the twelfth house, the person will have financial gains in distant places and foreign countries. He will also be spiritually inclined and will enjoy meditating in groups. If other factors in the chart agree, this placement can allow the person to achieve his goals through subtle psychic means. The practice of meditation will increase the person's ability to achieve both spiritual and material goals. He will choose spiritually inclined friends and could also have friends from distant or foreign places. Also, his next older sibling might live in a distant place or foreign country.

Negative: If the ruler of the eleventh house is afflicted in the twelfth house, the person will spend, lose, or waste his money. He will find it difficult to achieve his goals. His friends could move away, or he could lose them for various reasons. This placement makes it generally difficult to attain material success and prosperity.

Planets in the Eleventh House

Sun in the Eleventh House

Positive: When the Sun is in the eleventh house, the person will become prosperous, successful and will achieve his goals easily. He will be friendly and will enjoy cultivating friendships with creative and successful people. As a result, he will have some friends who have strong personalities and leadership abilities. The person will also be attractive and will have an attractive or beautiful spouse. This position of the Sun will cause him to "think big" and to set expansive, long-range goals. He could have leadership abilities and could take a leading role in his community. In any case, he will become involved in clubs, organizations, and other groups. In its best mode, the Sun placed here produces humanitarian instincts, and the person is open to a variety of people from all walks of life. He will subscribe to universal ethical and moral codes and will enjoy setting an example for others in this regard. His next older sibling will have an expressive and attractive personality and will gain some kind of recognition. This position is also favorable for health and longevity.

Negative: If the Sun is malefic or afflicted in the eleventh house, the person will have difficulty achieving his goals in life. As a result, he will have many humiliating experiences of failure. He will have financial problems as well. In some cases of affliction, the person accomplishes his goals, but at a price. For example, he might take a "success at any cost attitude," disregarding the feelings of his friends and business associates. On the other hand, he may become so involved with friends that he allows them to interfere with his goals. He could have a loss of reputation or money through a friend. In any case, a negative Sun in the eleventh house suggests that the person will generally have difficulties in his relationships with friends and groups of people. It also indicates problems in the person's relationship with his next older sibling.

Moon in the Eleventh House

Positive: When the Moon is in the eleventh house, the person will be social, popular, and very attached to his friends. He will be prosperous or wealthy, and will have good luck with real estate. He will be sensitive, introspective and will have many women friends. He will also have friends who are in the public eye in some way. In any case, he will have many charming and supportive friends. This position also motivates the person to become involved with groups, and to be interested in improving the condition of his organization, community, or even society at large. The Moon placed here is also good for general reputation and popularity, giving increasing prestige and reputation as life advances. After the age of 50, the person could experience a sudden rise in reputation or become famous in some way. This is also a good placement for the person's relationship with his next older sibling, who will be sensitive, social, charming and supportive. Also, the spouse of the first child will be charming, social, and a source of great support to that child.

Negative: When the Moon is malefic or afflicted in the eleventh house, the person will be inconsistent in his ability to achieve his goals. His mind will be subject to many fluctuations, which will cause him to change or give up his goals frequently. He will let his personal problems affect his decision-making process, leading to career and financial problems. Although he will have a deep need for friends, he will feel that he does not get the kind of support he needs from friends. His relationship with females, especially, could be a source of occasional anguish. Sometimes the social problems suggested by a negative Moon here are due to the person being overly needy or dependent on his friends. Other times, it is the friends who are fickle, unsupportive, and unreliable. In any case, this position of the Moon makes it difficult to find fulfillment through friendships. The same is true for the next older sibling, who will be a source of challenge and disappointment.

Mars in the Eleventh House

Positive: When Mars is placed in the eleventh house, the person will be ambitious and will achieve his goals easily. He will become prosperous and successful in his profession. He will gain more and more success and prosperity as he grows older. This position also gives the person fame or recognition related to his ability to achieve or succeed in his ambitious pursuits. He will also be a good speaker, with an assertive and dynamic speaking style. He will own land and houses, and will profit through real estate. If Mars happens to be with two benefic planets, then it creates a Maha Raja Yoga, which will give recognition, fame and wealth, and will also yield great results for siblings.

Negative: If a malefic or afflicted Mars occupies the eleventh house, the person will have arguments and disagreements with siblings and friends. He will have difficulty, or at least possess a harsh approach, in achieving his ambitious goals. Malefics are generally well placed in the eleventh house, giving the assertive push necessary to accomplish goals. For friendships and other personal relationships, however, this position causes friction. There could also be financial losses through friends with a negative Mars placed here. The person could cultivate friendships with ambitious or aggressive people. Also, the older sibling could have an aggressive or argumentative nature. This position of Mars is also detrimental for the marriage of the first child, signifying arguments and general disharmony.

Mercury in the Eleventh House

Positive: When a benefic Mercury is placed in the eleventh house, the person will have many bright, well-educated and articulate friends. He will be a good speaker and writer, and could speak or write for large audiences, or simply gain a reputation as an articulate person. This position of Mercury also suggests that the person will also be very intelligent and will achieve his educational goals easily. He will have a versatile mind and diverse interests and abilities. As a result, his education will be well-rounded, including subjects such as music, languages, writing, mathematics, and engineering. He will be open-minded and interested in new concepts, progressive ideas and esoteric philosophies. He will also be good in business and will become prosperous as a result. Mercury here also gives the person the ability to communicate with all types of people, and can give him the ability to lead or organize large groups. The first child will marry a person who will be good-looking, intelligent and charming.

Negative: A negative Mercury in the eleventh house signifies financial losses and communication problems. The person could receive bad advice from friends, or might have friends who can't be counted on to give accurate information. Mercury placed here suggests that the person will have various problems in groups. For example, he might think in an offbeat way, have an interest in unconventional topics, and feel misunderstood by his group. It is also possible that he could have difficulty speaking or reading in front of a group. An afflicted Mercury placed here is not good for the person's education, producing various problems with reading, writing, and expressing ideas.

Jupiter in the Eleventh House

Positive: When a benefic Jupiter occupies the eleventh house, the person becomes wealthy. This is one of the best placements for financial gains. It also allows the person to achieve whatever goals he sets. He will tend to aim high because he expects to succeed at whatever he does. He will have many friends who will be the source of constant benefit. His friends could help him to succeed financially, offering good suggestions and dependable advice. As a result, this is a good position for networking. In any case, the person will develop a large social circle and a generous, open relationship with his friends. He will be a team player. He will have many successful, prosperous, well-educated and spiritually-oriented friends as well. His reputation will be great, and he could even achieve fame in some area. Although the person will have few children, he will have good experiences related to children, and they will be healthy, intelligent and successful. His first child will become more prosperous and successful after the time of marriage, and will attract a successful and knowledgeable spouse. This is also a protective and beneficial placement for the person's own marriage, bringing an intelligent, generous, successful spouse.

Negative: When Jupiter is afflicted or malefic in the eleventh house, the person will have financial problems. He may have financial losses due to friends, children or older siblings. His older sibling could be dominant, bossy, or moralistic. The same could be true for his friends, who could seek to reform his character with unwanted advice and preaching. Sometimes an afflicted Jupiter placed here causes the person to develop friendships simply for the possibility of financial gain. Conversely, he could be the object of solicitous friends, who are only interested in his friendship for their personal or monetary gain. If Jupiter is badly afflicted in the eleventh house, the person could have health problems related to Jupiter's significations.

Venus in the Eleventh House

Positive: When Venus is placed in the eleventh house the person will be charming. He will have well-developed social skills. He will have close friends and will be very attached to them. He will also receive a great deal of love and appreciation from his friends. This placement also produces many friends of the opposite sex. The person will enjoy various social gatherings and participate in organizations and clubs. Venus placed here is also good for material prosperity, suggesting financial gains, accumulation and affluence. The person will lead an increasingly comfortable and luxurious life as time goes on. He will meet his spouse through his friends or while participating in a group activity, and his spouse will be his friend as well as his lover. This can work the other way around as well, causing a long time friend to become a lover or spouse. The person will be attracted to religious or spiritual groups that have a strong social orientation. He will be successful as a student, and could study art, music, or literature. Venus in the eleventh house also suggests that the person will be very fond of his older sibling, who will be very attractive, charming and magnetic. The spouse of the first child will also possess some of these qualities.

Negative: When Venus is malefic or afflicted in the eleventh house, the person will have problems with friends. He may have friends who are self-indulgent and unreliable, or he might have these qualities himself. With an afflicted Venus, the person can use his charm and personality purely for social advancement, or to seduce potential sexual partners. He will be a very passionate person. In cases of serious afflictions to Venus, this can create a tendency to experience marital infidelity. In other situations, it simply produces an inability to find romantic fulfillment. Nevertheless, an afflicted Venus in the eleventh house will cause marital and relational problems related to passion and romance. The marriage of the first child is also likely to have problems related to romantic passion.

Saturn in the Eleventh House

Positive: When a benefic and well-aspected Saturn is placed in the eleventh house, the person will set long-term goals and fulfill them through hard work and determination. As a result, he will become prosperous and successful, especially from middle age onward. He will also do well with real estate. He will have a reputation for being a responsible and dependable person, and will cultivate friendships with other people with similar qualities. He will also have many important and influential friends who will contribute to his prestige and success. Saturn here produces friendships with older people and generally gives loyal, long-lasting friends. The person will have the ability to manage and organize groups, and will work hard for the social good. The marriage of the first child will probably be stable, and the spouse of that child will be down-to-earth, responsible and reserved.

Negative: A malefic or afflicted Saturn in the eleventh house can block the person's ability to achieve goals. Sometimes this indicates that the person will be reluctant to set long-range goals, since he feels overwhelmed by the amount of effort necessary to achieve the goal. Or, the person simply expects to fail, so he refuses to try. In any case, he feels frustrated and limited in his ability to achieve. As a result, this placement limits the potential for material and professional success. The person will also have many problems and limitations related to friends. He may feel unpopular, for example. He could also be fearful of being in front of groups of people, as a result of his failure to gain social approval. Sometimes an afflicted Saturn here simply shows a tendency to either use friends (or be used by them) for material or professional advancement. Since malefics are welcome in the eleventh house, even an afflicted Saturn placed here can sometimes give some material achievement. It is a less beneficial placement, however, for the social and emotional aspects of life. This placement is also challenging for the marriage of the first child.

Rahu in the Eleventh House

Positive: When Rahu is placed in the eleventh house, the person becomes driven to achieve goals. As a result, he will become successful in his career and very prosperous. This is an excellent position for all kinds of material gains and achievements. The person will attract a diverse array of friends from all walks of life and from different ethnic backgrounds. His next older sibling will have a strong personality and be independent. This position of Rahu also suggests involvement in social causes and other revolutionary mass movements. The person could, for example, become intensely involved in the internet, or use other technologies to influence the masses. He will set unconventional, revolutionary or cutting-edge goals, rapidly accomplishing them with great passion and intensity.

Negative: When Rahu is malefic or afflicted in the eleventh house, the person will have a compulsive desire to succeed, which will be his downfall. He will live in the future, constantly thinking about tomorrow's projects and plans, and will have difficulty staying in the present moment. An afflicted Rahu placed here will give financial problems. The person's friends will be strange and undependable. Some friends could even be addicts, or at least be compulsive in some way. This placement is also detrimental to the next older sibling, as well as to the person's relationship with the sibling. It can produce ear or shoulder problems.

Ketu in the Eleventh House

Positive: When Ketu is in the eleventh house, the person will have spiritually-inclined or creative friends. He could become involved in spiritual groups, but will not seek recognition or prestige within the group. He will try to stay behind the scenes in all group activities. He will have an unattached, yet healthy attitude towards friends and will not depend on them for his happiness. He will achieve his goals through intuitive means, letting each intermediate step lead him to the next. In other words, he will be process-oriented rather than goal-oriented. This is also a good placement for unexpected gains and providential help. As a result, it is sometimes a good position for speculative gains through the stock market. Prayer, meditation and surrender will be the keys to his success, manifesting his desires through a natural process of letting them go. Yet he will not focus on material goals. Instead, he will set life goals that are profound and spiritually elevating.

Negative: A negative Ketu in the eleventh house signifies financial losses. The person could lose money through deception or theft. Friends can be a source of financial loss, and the person should generally avoid financial dealings with them. He will be chronically disappointed in his friends, who will constantly fall short of his expectations. His next older sibling will feel unnoticed and unappreciated, and could be a source of disappointment to the person. In cases of serious affliction to Ketu in the eleventh, the older sibling can have health or emotional problems. Sometimes this placement produces an unexpected loss of the older sibling. Afflicted Ketu placed here can also produce health problems, related to the left shoulder or left ear, that are hard to diagnose or treat. It is also detrimental to the relationship or marriage of the first child.

The Twelfth House (Vyaya Bhava)

The twelfth house is the house of moksha, liberation from karmic bondage. It is here that the true spiritual goal of life is achieved. More commonly, this house is used to signify all types of loss.

In order to understand why a house with such a positive connotation can also be defined in such a negative way, it is important to understand that the quality of consciousness that gives spiritual liberation is not concrete, but completely abstract and dissolute. In a purely material context, this means that anything that is connected with the twelfth house becomes more diffuse and less defined. Placed here, a personal planet such as the ruler of the first house can indicate personal uncertainties or a lack of self-confidence. A financial planet, like Jupiter, placed here, can indicate expenses or other uncertainties regarding money. In this way, the twelfth house dissolves whatever it touches and is known as the house of loss.

On the positive side, the twelfth is also the house of travel. In foreign countries we naturally feel more uncertain. We rely less on structured routines and rely more on intuition, naturally flowing with life and taking things as they come. In ancient times, wandering in a foreign country was considered bad fortune, presumably because of the great risks involved. Today, travel seems to be more desirable. It is the underlying "traveler's attitude" of taking things as they come, that actually gets to the heart of the twelfth house experience. From this perspective, travel becomes a mechanism through which life works to break down rigid aspects of the ego, making us more flexible, intuitive and open to life.

This house also represents the bedroom, the quality of our sleep and everything else that takes place in the bedroom. In fact, since sexual relations commonly occur in the bedroom, the twelfth house can also give clues to the level of sexual fulfillment or frustration we experience. From this point of view, the twelfth house can be an important house to scrutinize when considering romantic relationships. A disturbed twelfth house can contribute to disharmony in marriage, while a strong one can help support and cement a relationship. The point is that the twelfth house is where the ego retreats, dissolves and ultimately finds bliss. The bedroom is simply the first and the most obvious place in which we begin this process.

There are many ways in which this house can make a positive contribution to material life. Even though a planet like the Sun or the ruler of the first house placed here can give self doubts, it can also motivate one to confront those self-doubts through an introspective process, leading to greater self-awareness and, ultimately, to a more profound level of self-confidence. Similarly, a career planet placed in the twelfth, which can bring uncertainties or interruptions to one's career, can alternatively indicate a successful career that involves travel or, in some other way, has built-in interruptions. In sum, this house, like the other dusthanas, is not an intrinsically "bad" house. It is true that negative results are more commonly associated with this house, but this is more a function of limited human awareness. In the spiritually inclined chart, however, this house can be a place of incredibly positive results, ranging from the enjoyment of peace and quiet, to the experience of ecstatic meditative bliss.

In fact, on the highest level, the twelfth house represents meditation, the most profound kind of internal process. It is here that the ego actually dissolves into pure consciousness, experiencing itself as formless, transcendent bliss. At first this experience is only momentary, constantly being interrupted as karmas from the past are burned off, causing the emergence of thoughts and desires. Through repeated meditation, however, the karmas that bind awareness are released, allowing the mind to maintain a state of constant self-absorption. When all karma has been shed, the soul becomes free. No longer requiring a body, the soul attains moksha, liberation from the cycle of birth and death, and the goal of life is achieved.

Significations of the Twelfth House Given by Classical Authors of Vedic Astrology:

Expenses; loss; charity; paying of debts; paternal wealth; sleep; bed pleasures; sexual dysfunction; adultery; loss of wife; confinement; arrest; imprisonment; punishment; mental distress; enemies; fear of enemies; travel in foreign countries; sins; acceptance; fall; humility; heaven or hell after death.

Physical Significations:

Feet; left eye; insomnia; mental imbalance; hospitalization; death. Depending on the drekkana rising - left eye, left shoulder, and anus.

The Ruler of the Twelfth House Placed in the Twelve Houses

First House

Positive: If the ruler of the twelfth house is placed in the first house, the person will be introspective, reflective, or spiritually inclined. He will be idealistic and intuitive. He will love travel and could live in foreign countries. He will be very liberal and generous. He will also be charitable, kind and compassionate. This placement can also make the person handsome or beautiful.

Negative: If the ruler of the twelfth house is afflicted in the first house, the person will be very self-conscious and shy. His constitution could be weak and he may be prone to physical problems related to the planet that rules the twelfth house. He could also suffer from problems that are due to excess kapha, such as gaining weight. This placement also suggests problems during long distance trips or while in foreign countries. It is also detrimental to the financial situation due to heavy expenditure or financial loss.

Second House

Positive: If the ruler of the twelfth house is supported and placed in the second house, the person will be very generous and charitable. He will spend money on travel and could gain money from distant places or foreign countries. This result will be more pronounced if the twelfth lord is combined with two or more money planets, such as Jupiter, or the rulers of the second, fifth, eleventh, or ninth houses. This placement is also good for chanting mantras. It suggests that the person's intuition could channel through his speech, and he could unconsciously say things that come true. Similarly, he could develop the ability to intuitively sense what he should eat, promoting a balanced diet and good health as a result. He will be sensitive to what he eats and will adjust his diet to promote higher awareness.

Negative: If the ruler of the twelfth house is afflicted in the second house, the person will have many expenses and financial losses. His financial activities could be unscrupulous or he could have losses due to the unscrupulous dealings of others. He could have financial losses in distant places or while traveling in foreign countries. This position also suggests that the person eats at irregular intervals or eats foods of poor quality. An afflicted twelfth lord here can also produce eye problems.

Third House:

Positive: If the ruler of the twelfth house is strong, supported and placed in the third house, the person will be soft spoken and intuitive. His communication style will be inspirational and idealistic. He will also be capable of expressing compassion and kindness. This placement also produces travel, and suggests that the person enjoys going on outings, errands and other short trips while visiting foreign countries. The next younger sibling could be self-employed or independent in work, and will probably be successful professionally.

Negative: If the ruler of the twelfth house is afflicted in the third house, the person will have trouble communicating. He could be evasive, slippery and deceptive. If other factors in the chart agree, then the person could be dishonest. This placement also suggests financial or emotional losses, and various disappointments connected with the siblings. The next younger sibling could move to a distant place or a foreign country. Sometimes with this placement the person does not have a younger sibling. An afflicted twelfth lord placed here can also cause physical problems related to the ears or the shoulders.

Fourth House

Positive: If the ruler of the twelfth house is supported and placed in the fourth house, the person could have a secluded home that is located in a forest, the mountains or near the water. He may commute a long distance to work. Sometimes the person will have two homes, with one of them being a cabin, retreat, or vacation home. He could attend a good school in a distant place. This placement also suggests long distance travel by car. The person's mother will be very spiritually inclined, purposeful, and well-educated.

Negative: If the ruler of the twelfth house is afflicted in the fourth house, the person will have a very difficult time purchasing or owning homes, land, or vehicles. He will have many changes of residence and will not be stable. This placement also makes it difficult to achieve peace of mind and overall happiness. The person's mother could be a source of financial or emotional loss or disappointment. His experience of living or traveling in foreign countries will be surrounded by discomfort and hardship.

Fifth House

Positive: If the ruler of the twelfth house is supported and placed in the fifth house, the person will be very intuitive and spiritually inclined. He will benefit from practicing a meditation technique that involves the use of a mantra. He will be very generous and kind to his children. This position can also motivate the person to get an education in a distant place. He could profit from investments or work in distant places or foreign countries, especially if the twelfth lord is influenced by a combination of money planets. If the twelfth lord is associated with Raja Yoga planets (the rulers of angle and trine houses) then the person could develop a good reputation or even become famous in a distant place. If the twelfth lord combines with benefics and the Rahu-Ketu axis, then the person could adopt a child from a distant place or foreign country.

Negative: If the ruler of the twelfth house is afflicted in the fifth house, the person will experience losses or disappointments related to his children. The first child could move away, or he may have a difficult time understanding that child. If the twelfth lord is afflicted by at least two natural malefics, then abortion or miscarriage is a possibility. In cases of intense afflictions to both Jupiter and the twelfth lord, a child could die or go through serious hardships in life. This placement also fills the person's romantic life with loss and disappointment.

Sixth House

Positive: If the ruler of the twelfth house is supported and placed in the sixth house, the person will have an ability to overcome problems. He will progress spiritually through compassionate service to others. This is also a good placement for using the physical body as a vehicle for meditation. It is seen in the charts of people who become involved with spiritual paths that encourage the use of massage, Ayurveda, acupuncture and other alternative healing modalities. This placement also produces a Raja Yoga that supports general success in life, and makes the person virtuous, prosperous and happy.

Negative: If the ruler of the twelfth house is afflicted in the sixth house, the person could have many problems to overcome in life. It suggests a lack of scruples, a critical and argumentative nature, and other negative personality traits. As a result, the person tends to undermine his own well-being, prosperity and success. This combination can be detrimental to the person's health, indicating physical problems related to the feet, and also to the parts of the body signified by the planet that rules the twelfth house.

Seventh House

Positive: If the ruler of the twelfth house is supported and placed in the seventh house, the person could meet their spouse in a foreign country or distant place. This is also a common placement in the charts of people who have long-distance romantic relationships. It is also possible that the spouse will travel frequently. The spouse could be creative, intuitive, or spiritually inclined. In its best form, the person has a happy marriage, which is based on unconditional love, compassion, and acceptance.

Negative: If the ruler of the twelfth house is afflicted and placed in the seventh house, the person will have marital difficulties. Sometimes this means that he simply finds it difficult to find a suitable romantic partner. Frequently, this is partially due to having high or unrealistic expectations. As a result, he either remains single, or feels chronically dissatisfied with his partners. In cases of serious afflictions to the twelfth lord, this placement can produce emotional or financial upsets and losses due to the actions of the romantic partner or spouse. Similarly, the business partner could be a source of financial loss or expenditure. If Venus is also afflicted, then divorce or separation becomes a strong possibility.

Eighth House

Positive: If the ruler of the twelfth house is supported and placed in the eighth house, the person will be able to overcome problems. This placement forms a Raja Yoga that supports success, prosperity, and a comfortable life. It is also good for practicing a meditation which focuses on awakening the kundalini, or which uses the chakra system as a focus. It is a common placement in the charts of psychologists. This placement is also seen frequently in the charts of those who practice hatha yoga. It produces an interest in mystical, hidden, and occult subjects.

Negative: If the ruler of the twelfth house is afflicted in the eighth house, the person will have many expenditures and financial losses. If the afflictions are not too intense, then he will overcome his problems and recoup his losses. He could have an interest in occult practices and meditations which seek to awaken the kundalini, but he could also experience problems resulting from improper or excessive practice. In such cases, the practice of hatha yoga is sometimes more beneficial that intense meditation techniques, and should at least be done in conjunction with meditation.

Ninth House

Positive: If the ruler of the twelfth house is supported and placed in the ninth house, the person will travel to distant places and have many good experiences. He will be spiritually intuitive, and spiritually inclined. He could spend time in retreats and ashrams. If Jupiter is strong, he will have good luck finding a spiritual teacher, who might come from a distant place or foreign country. This placement is also good for living in foreign countries.

Negative: If the ruler of the twelfth house is afflicted in the ninth house, the person will have interruptions, discomfort, losses, and other problems while traveling. It will be difficult to find a good teacher or to relate to teachers. If the afflictions are intense, he could lose his father by death or separation at an early age. Similarly, his spiritual guru could be a source of disappointment or loss.

Tenth House

Positive: If the ruler of the twelfth house is supported and placed in the tenth house, the person could travel for a living. If the twelfth lord is involved with a Raja Yoga combination, then the person will develop a good professional reputation in distant places or foreign countries. He could even become famous in a foreign country. This placement is also good for intuitive careers, and is seen in the charts of artists, musicians, healers, psychics, astrologers, and psychologists.

Negative: If the ruler of the twelfth house is afflicted and placed in the tenth house, the person will have many uncertainties and changes professionally. In some cases, this means that he has difficulty focusing on a single profession. This placement is also associated with occasional loss to the person's reputation. He will not get along with his superiors, and find it difficult to receive promotions as a result.

Eleventh House

Positive: If the ruler of the twelfth house is supported and placed in the eleventh house, the person will have financial gains in distant places or foreign countries. This result will be magnified if the twelfth lord combines with money planets, such as Jupiter, or the rulers of the second, eleventh, ninth or fifth. This placement is also good for practicing meditation in groups, and is seen in the charts of people who belong to spiritual communities or who frequent ashrams and retreat centers. The person will choose friends who are creative, intuitive or spiritually oriented. His next older sibling may love to travel or could live in a distant place. That sibling could also be prosperous and successful.

Negative: If the ruler of the twelfth house is afflicted in the eleventh house, the person will have financial losses and difficulty achieving goals. His friends and older siblings could be the source of financial or emotional loss and disappointment. He may also choose friends of dubious character, or who have unstable lives. His next older sibling could be unstable financially, emotionally, or even physically. In cases of serious affliction, the person could lose his next older sibling at an early age, or the sibling could move away under negative circumstances.

Twelfth House

Positive: If the ruler of the twelfth house is placed in the twelfth house, the person will have many good experiences in distant places and foreign countries. If the Moon and Venus are also strong, he will sleep well and also have many pleasant sexual experiences in the bedroom. His next younger sibling will be successful in his profession and his next older sibling could be prosperous. He will be intuitive, inspirational, and spiritually inclined. He may also be good at finding bargains, and could give money to good causes. The spouse will find employment easily and will have good health and vitality.

Negative: If the ruler of the twelfth house is afflicted in the twelfth house, the person will have many expenses and financial losses due to the natural significations of the afflicting planet or the houses that planet rules. This placement can also produce health problems for the spouse that are characteristic of the planet that rules the twelfth house or the sign of the seventh house. He will be very restless, and will have some negative experiences in distant places or foreign countries.

Planets In the Twelfth House

Sun in the Twelfth House

Positive: When the Sun is benefic, well-aspected, and is in the twelfth house, the person will be introspective and spiritually inclined. He will enjoy travel and could travel as part of his work. He will also travel for pleasure to places that are sunny and warm. He will have a desire to live in a place that is secluded and peaceful. He could spend some time in ashrams, or he may simply enjoy camping or other get-away vacations. He will have a strong libido and will have many opportunities to express it. This position of the Sun suggests a liberal, generous nature, so the person can spend his money freely, sometimes on good causes. The next younger sibling will be very successful at a career that might involve leadership.

Negative: When a malefic Sun is in the twelfth house, the person will be self-conscious and shy. This placement undermines self-confidence and makes the person experience many self-doubts. As a result, he has a hard time finding a satisfying career and could change jobs frequently. He will avoid the company of other people, feeling isolated or lonely. He will have many expenses and financial problems. This is also a difficult placement for the person's relationship with his father. The Sun here also suggests that the person will have problems in the bedroom. This means that he may have an unfulfilling sex life, which has obvious ramifications for marriage. On the other hand, sometimes this placement produces an excessive sexual appetite, giving the person a tendency for infidelity and extramarital affairs. If the Sun is afflicted here, it also produces health problems. It can produce digestive problems, especially around the age of 35. This will be more pronounced if the Sun is aspected by Saturn.

Moon in the Twelfth House

Positive: When a benefic Moon is placed in the twelfth house, the person will be spiritually inclined and will enjoy introspection and meditation. He will love travel, especially to places near water. He will also enjoy solitude and will spend time in ashrams, retreats or other places conducive to reflection and contemplation. Since the twelfth house represents the bedroom, a good Moon here will give peaceful sleep and many positive sexual experiences. The person will be selfless, willing to give generously to support other people. This placement also gives the person profound spiritual experiences and much spiritual growth. The person's next younger sibling will be very successful in his work, which could include contact with the public, or he could work for a company that is publicly owned.

Negative: When the Moon is malefic and afflicted in the twelfth house, the person will have difficulties during childhood. In cases of serious affliction, this can produce traumas or even death. Such extreme results are not common, however, and must be supported by other factors in the horoscope. More commonly, the person goes through other difficulties during childhood such as changes of residence, disruption of family harmony, emotional upsets or health problems. Later in life he may feel lonely, isolated and withdrawn. In any case, the person will be shy and self-conscious. He will have difficulties in foreign countries or while traveling. He could travel for work, for example, but not enjoy it. This is also a position that can produce sleep disorders, especially if the Moon is conjunct Rahu or Ketu, or influenced by other malefics. It is also not a good placement for marriage because it brings difficulties in the bedroom. The person will have problems related to the mother or other family members. He will also have financial problems, debts, expenses, and general difficulty achieving material security.

Mars in the Twelfth House

Positive: When a benefic and well-aspected Mars is placed in the twelfth house, the person's ambitious energy will be inspirational. He will focus his energy on idealistic, creative, selfless, or imaginative ventures. He will enjoy travel and vacation experiences that include physical activity, such as camping and hiking. His work could include travel. His younger brother will be highly ambitious and successful in his profession. One of his siblings may move to a distant place and become successful there. The person will be sexually attractive and assertive in the bedroom. He will enjoy working in privacy or seclusion. He will practice hatha yoga, tai chi, chi kung or some other physical form of meditation.

Negative: When a malefic Mars is placed in the twelfth house, the person will be secretive and deceptive about his actions. He will hide his anger and will suffer psychologically as a result. He will have a desire to express his ambitious energies in an idealist direction, but will not find an appropriate channel in which to direct them. Sometimes this causes the person to float for long periods, without any real focus in life. The unfulfilled desire for a mission or higher purpose in life becomes the source of chronic dissatisfaction in life. In cases of extreme affliction to Mars in the twelfth house, the person could be confined or restricted in his movement. This could mean imprisonment or it could suggest a physical disability. These results, of course, are only seen when the rest of the chart also agrees. In general, an afflicted Mars in the twelfth makes career and financial success more difficult. The person will have a desire to spend money and will have many expenses and debts. His marriage will also suffer due to problems related to sexual passion. The person could even have extramarital affairs. This position causes arguments and disagreements in the marriage, and is generally considered a difficult placement for marriage. The spouse can be critical and argumentative. In some cases it harms the health of the spouse, creating problems due to excess heat, or through injuries and surgeries.

Mercury in the Twelfth House

Positive: When a benefic Mercury is placed in the twelfth house, the person will be very intuitive. He may be interested in meditation and spirituality. He will be very introspective and will enjoy analyzing his own mind. He might adopt a self-inquiry method of spiritual development where inner analysis plays an important part of the spiritual process. As a result, this is a good placement for a psychologist, especially if Mercury is assisted by an aspect from Saturn. Contrary to many classical interpretations, the person will be fairly prosperous and will be good at getting bargains. A good Mercury in the twelfth house also indicates that the next younger sibling could work at a profession that involves mental analysis, communication abilities, or the ability to process information. The spouse will have a highly analytical nature and take an interest in various healing modalities.

Negative: When a negative Mercury is placed in the twelfth house, the person will be secretive, evasive and will experience difficulties in communication. In some cases this means that the person will be deceitful and manipulative. In other cases, he will simply avoid direct communications in a more benign way. An afflicted Mercury placed here causes the person's intellect to be complex and difficult to manage. When heavily afflicted, the person becomes neurotic or mentally unbalanced. In many cases, this placement of Mercury brings learning disabilities such as dyslexia, reading problems, and a general difficulty processing information. As a result, the person can have difficulty in school, especially as a child. Mercury placed here can create an unfocused mind. The person can be forgetful or spaced out. He may have problems sleeping. The next younger sibling will have communication problems related to work. The spouse could have health problems related to the lungs, thyroid, skin or nervous system.

Jupiter in the Twelfth House

Positive: When a benefic Jupiter is placed in the twelfth house, the person will be very spiritually inclined. He will have good intuition and be drawn to the practice of meditation. In fact, the more he meditates, the more he will contact his inner sense of abundance, represented by Jupiter. He will also be interested in astrology and could study the subject or even become an astrologer. This is also a great placement for travel, producing many positive experiences in distant places or foreign countries. In many cases, this suggests that the person will be able to profit financially from contact with distant places. It gives the person an intuitive relationship with money and he spends it freely. He will be very generous, selflessly giving money to friends, charities, and others in need. Jupiter here is a great placement for the employment of the spouse, giving the spouse a knack for attracting good jobs and promotions in spite of competition. It is also a beneficial placement for the spouse's health that produces good recuperative ability. It also suggests that the next younger sibling will be very successful at a profession that requires expertise, credentials or some form of certification.

Negative: When a malefic or afflicted Jupiter is placed in the twelfth house, the person will have many expenses. This placement suggests financial difficulties and makes it difficult to amass wealth. The person should especially be careful with money in foreign countries or distant places where there is an increased possibility of theft or financial loss. He will also have a tendency to spend money freely and to incur debt, so he should try to develop restraint with spending. In general, this position causes a great deal of uncertainty and mental anguish with money. It also suggests some difficulties in the profession of the next younger sibling, who might be successful, but could simply have difficulties in obtaining required certification for his profession. An afflicted Jupiter placed here can also produce difficulties and disappointments regarding children and teachers.

Venus in the Twelfth House

Positive: When a benefic Venus is placed in the twelfth house, the person will enjoy sex and will have many fulfilling sexual experiences. He will have a love of travel for pleasure and attract many positive experiences in foreign countries. While traveling he will stay in luxury hotels and comfortable surroundings. He will have many friends in foreign countries and could even marry someone who is from a distant place, or who he meets while in a distant place or while traveling. Venus in the twelfth also links love, marriage and emotional fulfillment with the house of moksha, spiritual liberation. This means that the person will find a spiritual approach to relationships in which acceptance and unconditional love are the keys to happiness. In any case, he will be an idealist, a romantic, and will seek to find a spiritual element in his relationship or marriage. This placement also creates a compassionate and sympathetic nature. The person will enjoy spending money on fine things that enhance his feeling of affluence, beauty or comfort. This is generally a good placement for wealth, in spite of the twelfth house's relationship to expenses. The person will simply have money and enjoy spending it. It brings a tendency for the next younger sibling to be artistic and creative in some way. The sibling will enjoy his work and will have positive interactions with coworkers and bosses.

Negative: When Venus is malefic and afflicted in the twelfth house, the person will have difficulty finding a life partner or spouse. He will have emotional self-esteem issues and find it difficult to express and receive love and affection. Sometimes this takes the form of an out-of-balance sexual energy, which manifests in affairs and sensuality. In other cases, the person simply feels unloved and unable to express love. He will spend money freely on clothing, food, gems, travel, and other things which give comfort and pleasure that are associated with Venus. Women (or the spouse) may be a source of expenditure and loss as well. The person could have many uncomfortable experiences while traveling in foreign countries. An afflicted Venus in the twelfth house often causes eye problems. It can produce venereal disease or other ailments related to the sexual organs. This is also true for the spouse. Some authors feel that this placement gives health problems in childhood, and makes the person thin as an adult.

Saturn in the Twelfth House

Positive: When a benefic and well-aspected Saturn is placed in the twelfth house, the person will work and be successful in foreign countries. He could also work in institutions or simply work behind the scenes. He will also have a disciplined and structured approach to meditation, which may develop after his mid-thirties. In his mid-thirties, he may also become interested in making efforts to improve his subjective experience through psychology, introspection or meditation. The person will marry a spouse who will work hard in the service of others. The spouse could also establish regular routines of diet and exercise. If Saturn is associated with natural benefics, then the person will become quite prosperous and happy. This placement suggests that the next younger sibling will have management or organizational skills and will be very successful professionally.

Negative: When a malefic or afflicted Saturn is placed in the twelfth house, the person will have many expenses and debts. He will resist the practice of meditation as well as receiving psychological therapy. He could also experience frustration in the bedroom, so this is not a good placement for sex or marriage. Saturn placed here can be problematic for the health of the person as well as the spouse, bringing problems stemming from overwork, stress, and a depleted immune system. An afflicted Saturn in the twelfth house can also produce problems to the left eye. Professionally, Saturn placed here brings challenges to the person's reputation and sometimes signifies disgrace or failure. It can create difficulty understanding the concept of hard work and responsibility in general, producing an aversion to work and resulting in obvious professional problems. An afflicted Saturn in the twelfth house makes it more difficult to achieve professional success.

Rahu in the Twelfth House

Positive: When a benefic and well-aspected Rahu is placed in the twelfth house, the person will be very interested in meditation, introspection and spirituality. He will have an eclectic approach to meditation, and be willing to try many alternative techniques. Techniques of meditation that use the chakra system which focus on awakening the kundalini may also attract him. This placement is good for travel and will give the person a restless itch to travel to exotic places. During his travels he will have unexpected experiences and surprising events. A good Rahu placed here will also give many romantic encounters, which tend to be impulsive or spontaneous. In the context of a solid marriage, this could keep the sexual aspect of the marriage interesting. In any case, Rahu here tends to strengthen the libido. It can also be a good placement for the professional success of the next younger brother.

Negative: If Rahu is afflicted in the twelfth house, then the person will have many unavoidable expenses and unexpected financial losses. He may have a compulsion to spend, which will result in debt and financial uncertainty. He should also be careful while he is traveling, because this placement can produce theft, hotel problems, lost baggage and other unfortunate surprises. An afflicted Rahu in the twelfth gives problems in the bedroom and is seen frequently in the charts of insomniacs. It also produces a sense of urgency regarding romantic or sexual gratification and sometimes indicates compulsive or unconventional sexual habits, affairs, or association with prostitutes. The next younger sibling could be a workaholic. A bad Rahu in this position is also problematic for the health of the person and of the spouse, possibly signifying accidents, infections, viruses or chronic illness. (Note: With an afflicted Rahu in the twelfth, the person should be cautious about avoiding eye infections due to overuse or lack of cleaning of contact lenses.)

Ketu in the Twelfth House

Positive: When Ketu is in the twelfth house, the person will be spiritually inclined. He may have an interest in a spiritual path that emphasizes detachment, and might practice a meditation technique that has minimal structure, such as Vipassana. They say, "Ketu is a Buddhist," so sometimes the person practices a Buddhist meditation when Ketu is located here. It also gives the person an inclination to travel to Buddhist or Asian countries. In any case, he will enjoy traveling without an itinerary, and will prefer exotic destinations. A good Ketu in the twelfth house also suggests that the spouse will be interested in alternative medicine and could take herbs, homeopathic remedies or other subtle medicines. The next younger sibling may work at a creative, selfless, intuitive, or healing profession, or simply a profession that is unconventional in some way.

Negative: When Ketu is afflicted in the twelfth house, the person will have expenses and losses. He will also have many unfortunate disappointments in foreign countries and distant places. If he has inherited property from his family, he could lose it. He will also have a chronic sense of disappointment regarding sex. As a result, this is not a good placement for romantic partnerships and tends to undermine marital bliss. Afflicted Ketu here can also produce insomnia, especially if it is associated with the Moon. The next younger sibling will float from job to job or will feel constantly unhappy with work. The spouse will have hard-to-diagnose medical problems, which require the use of alternative medicine. The spouse should always get a second opinion when diagnosed or given medicine by traditional doctors, because this placement can produce misdiagnosis and wrong medication, resulting in obvious complications.

Judging the Strength of Houses

The key to determining whether a house will produce positive or negative results is by determining whether the house is strong or weak. A house that is strong will express the positive side of its significations, while a weak house will produce the negative aspect of the things it represents. The following three components are used to judge the strength of a house: the house occupant, the house ruler, and the aspects on the house.

The Three-Part House Analysis

1. House Occupants

House Occupied by Natural Benefics or Malefics

The natural benefic planets, Jupiter, Venus, Mercury and a waxing Moon, usually produce good results in the houses they occupy according to their natures. Jupiter expands the quality of the house and may mark the house as a potential source of prosperity or knowledge. Venus gives pleasurable experiences related to the house it occupies and may suggest the house as a source of romantic relationship or creative expression. Mercury promotes interest and allows knowledge and information to grow within the house significations. A waxing Moon promotes contacts with people and generally promotes the welfare of the house.

Natural malefics, on the other hand, tend to weaken the significations of a house. Saturn, Mars, Rahu, Ketu and the waning Moon are the natural malefics, and each can produce problems according to its nature. Saturn brings delays, obstacles and pressures to the house it occupies. Mars can produce enmity, accidents, and arguments. Rahu can contribute unexpected and unavoidable problems. Ketu can bring disappointments, losses and depression or confusion.

It is very important to remember that all malefic planets have a flip side. Saturn can give patience and perseverance. Mars can give energy and motivation. Rahu can give unexpected opportunities and produce spontaneous insights. Ketu can bring intuition and spirituality. The simple presence of a malefic in a house does not necessarily mean the house will produce big problems. Whether a malefic planet is experienced as positive or negative, to a great extent, depends on one's attitude and awareness.

House Occupied by a Temporal Benefic or Malefic

Planets can also be benefic or malefic by virtue of their house rulership. Saturn, for example, rules the fourth and the fifth houses for a Libra Ascendant. This makes Saturn a first-rate benefic for the Libra lagna. In other words, for Libra lagna, any house occupied by Saturn will benefit in some way. The mode of this improvement will be according to Saturn's nature, which is hard work, responsibility, structure, effort, concentration, patience, and perseverance. It is important to remember, however, that natural malefic planets like Saturn and Mars will always retain their inherent natures, even when they are temporal benefics. In the Libra chart, for example, Saturn placed in the second house may give good prospects with money, being a temporal benefic. As a natural malefic, it may still make the person work very hard and force him to wait to achieve prosperity.

By the same token, a natural benefic can also be a temporal malefic. In the chart of a Sagittarius Ascendant, for example, Venus is a very malefic planet. It rules the sixth house, the house of disease and struggle. Placed in the fifth house, it might indicate problems or disagreements with children. But it will never relinquish its basic nature. This Venus placement will also symbolize love for one's children and may produce a beautiful or creative child.

If a natural benefic also happens to be a temporal benefic, as in the case of Jupiter for a Cancer Ascendant, then it becomes more likely to create positive results in the house it occupies. Likewise, if a natural malefic is also a temporal malefic, as in the case of Mars for a Virgo Ascendant, then its negative influence is increased.

House Occupied by the Yogakaraka

Six of the lagnas have one planet that rules an angle and a trine at the same time. This planet is called the Yogakaraka and is not only a temporal benefic, but a very powerful one. The Yogakaraka usually improves the house in which it is placed. Saturn, in the previous example, is actually the Yogakaraka for Libra ascendant. As such, it gives good results to any house it occupies.

The rules, which differentiate the temporal benefics from malefics, are rather complex. Without going into this explanation in detail, the following table will list these planets for each Ascendant.

Table of Temporal Benefics, Malefics, and Yogakarakas for Each Ascendant

Lagna	Benefics	Malefics	Yogakaraka
Aries	Sun, Jupiter	Mercury, Venus, Saturn	None
Taurus	Mercury, Saturn	Moon, Jupiter, Venus	Saturn
Gemini	Venus	Sun, Mars, Jupiter	None
Cancer	Moon, Mars, Jupiter	Mercury, Venus	Mars
Leo	Sun, Mars, Jupiter	Mercury, Venus, Saturn	Mars
Virgo	Mercury, Venus	Moon, Mars, Jupiter	None
Libra	Mercury, Saturn	Sun, Mars, Jupiter	Saturn
Scorpio	Moon, Jupiter	Mercury, Venus, Saturn	None
Sagittarius	Sun, Mars	Venus	None
Capricorn	Venus, Mercury	Moon, Jupiter, Mars	Venus
Aquarius	Venus, Saturn	Moon, Mars, Jupiter	Venus
Pisces	Moon, Mars, Jupiter	Sun, Mercury, Venus, Saturn	None

2. House Ruler

A house can either thrive or lack strength because the house ruler is strong or weak. This is a very important point in determining the strength or weakness of a house. The conditions for determining if a planet is strong or weak were discussed earlier. If the ruler of a house is strong, it allows the things symbolized by the house to manifest easily and beneficially. If it is weak, then the house significations will manifest with difficulty, if at all. If a house ruler is strong, this is like a house owned by a person who is alive and well. As long as he is in good health and prospering, his house will also do well. If he is sick, poor and otherwise at risk, he will not have the energy to tend to his house properly.

House Ruler Placed in Its Own House

If the house ruler is placed in its own house, then the house will be particularly strong and produce its significations in positive ways. For example, Venus owns the second house for a Virgo Ascendant because Libra is the sign of the second house. If Venus is placed in the second house in Libra, then the person will be prosperous, (the second house symbolizes money and possessions), and will enjoy purchasing beautiful or high quality items that promote comfort or luxury. (Notice how the qualities of Venus, such as enjoyment, pleasure, and beautiful things, were also blended into the interpretation.)

3. Planetary Influences on a House

Aspects

Aside from influencing the house in which it is placed, each planet also influences other houses in the chart. Jupiter, for example, always casts an aspect on the fifth, seventh and ninth houses from itself. For example, if Jupiter is located in the eleventh house, it will also influence the third (five houses from Jupiter), fifth (seven houses from Jupiter), and seventh houses (nine houses from Jupiter) in the chart. This influence is called an aspect. Sometimes astrologers express the concept of a planetary aspect by calling it a glance or a look. In the case of Jupiter, placed in the eleventh house, the astrologer might say "Jupiter is looking (or glancing) at the third house." This means that, even though it is placed in the eleventh house, Jupiter's aspect is influencing the third house. Classical Jyotish recognizes that planets cast full and also partial aspects in different places in a horoscope relative to their placement. In practice, most jyotishis only pay attention to full aspects of planets. The following table shows the full aspects of each planet. These aspects should be plotted from the placement of the planet itself, counting the house in which the planet is located as the first house.

Table of Aspects of the Planets

Planet	Aspect
Sun	7th
Moon	7th
Mars	4th, 7th, 8th
Mercury	7th
Jupiter	5th, 7th, 9th
Venus	7th
Saturn	3rd, 7th, 10th

House Ruler Aspecting Its Own House

Sometimes the planet ruling a particular house is placed elsewhere, but throws its aspect back to its own house. (Remember, the house ruler refers to the planet that owns the sign in a particular house.) This occurs for all planets when they are located in the opposite house, seven houses away from their own house. For Saturn, Mars and Jupiter, special aspects also apply. (See the Table of Aspects of the Planets.) When a house receives the aspect of its ruler it produces good results. This is like a person who owns a house, but who is living across the street at a neighbor's house, keeping his eye on his own property. His glance carries his protective influence. From here he can take special care of his house. Similarly, the attention or aspect of the ruler of a house on it's own house is a very protective and strengthening condition. For example, Jupiter placed in Gemini, for a Virgo Ascendant, is located in the tenth house, seven houses away from Sagittarius (fourth house). Since every planet aspects the seventh house from its placement, Jupiter aspects Sagittarius. Since Jupiter is also the owner of Sagittarius, the fourth house will thrive. The person might do well in real estate, or own property or vehicles.

Benefic and Malefic Aspects on a House

A house also thrives due to the aspect of natural benefic planets. As mentioned earlier, a planet like Jupiter, which is a natural benefic, can also be a temporal malefic, as in the case of a Libra Ascendant. For Libra Ascendants, if Jupiter is placed in the seventh house, then its aspect on the eleventh house will be mostly positive, but also partly negative. In this particular case, it will mainly confer positive results because it is a natural benefic. For example, the person might have many good friends. As a temporal malefic for Libra Ascendant, however, Jupiter's rulership over the sixth house will also be conferred through its aspect, so the person may also occasionally argue with his friends.

At this point, it is also important to note that Jupiter is the "King of the Benefics." Whether it is a temporal benefic or malefic, its aspect on a house almost always produces good results and helps to solve the problems of that house. This is also true for Venus, especially when it comes to producing worldly pleasures and attachments connected with the significations of the house it aspects. If, on the other hand, Jupiter, Venus, or Mercury happen to also be temporal benefics, then they will give exclusively positive results to the houses they aspect. An example of this concept is Venus, placed in the fourth house, aspecting the tenth house in the case of a Virgo Ascendant. As a temporal and natural benefic for a Virgo lagna, Venus might bring professional success to the person, possibly making him an interior decorator.

Natural malefic planets aspecting a house, create problems for the house. Saturn, the "King of the Malefics," aspecting the fifth house, for example, creates delays, obstacles and pressures regarding having children. The person might delay having a child until her thirties or forties. Or she may have children early in life, but go through much struggle in attending to the various responsibilities connected with parenting. In some cases, the aspect of Saturn might prohibit having children completely. If, on the other hand, Saturn is also a temporal benefic, its aspect on the sign might create a very responsible and patient child. But Saturn will always retain its challenging nature. Its aspect on a house invariably produces work, effort, responsibilities, delays, and struggle. One difference between Saturn being a temporal benefic or malefic is simply that as a temporal benefic, its aspect tends to produce efforts, delays or limitations that ultimately culminate in positive outcomes. If a malefic planet such as Saturn or Mars is also a temporal malefic, then it creates a more consistently problematic influence on the house it aspects.

When evaluating the positive or negative influence of the aspect of a benefic or malefic, it is very important to also consider the natural domain of the planet. A planet's aspect tends to have a positive effect on the significations of houses which fall within its domain. For example, in the case of a Libra Ascendant, Saturn is the Yogakaraka and is therefore a temporal benefic. If Saturn is placed in the tenth house, it may be good for the person's career. Its aspect on the seventh house may be good for business partnerships as well, since business is also a value related to Saturn. Saturn's aspect on the seventh house may not be good for romantic partnership, however, and may make the partner detached, unhappy, overworked, or unavailable. This is because Saturn's natural significations are contrary to romance. If another malefic also occupies the seventh house, then Saturn's aspect on the seventh will act to amplify the malefic influences on the seventh house. The same principle can be applied to an exalted Saturn. Generally malefics that are exalted are said to bring out the planet's positive side. The aspect of an exalted malefic, however, can be powerfully negative, especially for significations which fall outside its domain. For example, an exalted Mars, placed in the first house, may make the person physically strong, assertive and bold. But it's aspect on the seventh house can also create arguments in marriage or partnerships. This is because harmonious relationship is a signification that is contrary to the natural significations of Mars. If another natural malefic is also placed in the seventh house, the aspect of Mars can produce aggravated results for the marriage or spouse. In this case, the exaltation of Mars only serves to amplify its capacity to harm the seventh house. If, on the other hand, an exalted Mars is placed in the fourth house, its aspect on the tenth house will produce good results for career. Even if another malefic is placed in the tenth house, the Mars aspect will usually promote industrious action. This is because the domain of the tenth house (career) and the domain of Mars (ambition) are sympathetic to each other.

Unoccupied Houses

When a house is not occupied by a planet, the interpretation should be given on the basis of the ruler of the house, as well as the planets aspecting the house. Generally, the aspects of strong natural or temporal benefics help the house. The aspects of natural or temporal malefics generally bring problems.

Kartari Yoga (House Hemmed In)

If there is a malefic planet in the sign before and the sign after a particular house, then the house is said to be hemmed in by malefics in a combination called Papa Kartari Yoga. In this case the house is weakened. If the planets hemming in the house are benefics, then the condition is called Shubha Kartari Yoga and the house becomes strong, producing good results. For example, in the chart of a Leo Ascendant, if Venus is in Scorpio and Mercury is in Capricorn, then Sagittarius (the fifth house) is hemmed in by benefics. This might produce creative, intelligent, charming or prosperous children.

Author's Journal:

"Do You Want to Fly?"

India constantly draws me back. On one occasion, while visiting Delhi, I had a flying dream. Okay, I admit it. I'm a flapper. I know it's common for people to fly in their dreams, but I have a recurring flying dream in which I begin to float. The floating goes along with an inner realization that I have the ability to fly, which leads me to start flapping my arms. I don't soar through the air like other people, directing every movement like some astral jet-pilot. Instead, I flap, float a little, and then flap some more. Pitiful, isn't it? On this particular night, I was flapping and floating, apparently quite pleased with my progress, because I was also repeating to myself, "I'm getting lighter and lighter and lighter, I'm getting lighter and lighter and lighter!"

The next morning I woke up feeling refreshed and energized. Flying dreams always leave me with an expansive feeling that I can do anything. I had heard through the grapevine that Hans Baba was in Delhi. I had met Hans Baba the previous year for the first time. At that time I was suffering from a bad case of food poisoning. Hans Baba had me stand under his hut while he put his foot over the side of his porch, resting it on my head. He then channeled energy through his foot, telling me that I would begin to feel warm. It was January, and Delhi was cold. I was wearing a down parka. After two minutes of standing under Hans Baba's foot, however, I began to feel very hot and started sweating profusely. I took off my parka and sweater, and stood there in my t-shirt feeling like I was burning up. The whole time, Hans Baba was laughing. He finally said, "Go now, you will feel better." I did feel better. In fact, I felt great for the rest of the month-long trip in India.

On this occasion, however, I had no health problems for Hans Baba to cure. In fact, I was just going to say hello and to receive darshan. As I entered the compound, I could see his manch (the hut on stilts) from a distance. I could see Hans Baba sitting there singing to himself. I was in luck. There was no one else there. I walked up and stood in front of the manch. Hans Baba's smiling eyes looked down at me. His eyes danced and twinkled like the eyes of some great cosmic prankster, "Do you want to fly?" he asked. I paused, "What is he talking about?" I thought. "Uhhh. . . ," I said, a little confused. "Do you want to fly?" he asked again, laughing. "What the heck," I thought to myself, and then blurted out, "Yes! I'd like to fly." For the second time, I found myself standing beneath Hans Baba's manch, with his foot on my head. I was remembering the miraculous healing that he gave me the previous year, thinking, "What now? Is he going to levitate me into the air in front of his hut?" I could feel the energy coming through his foot, through my crown chakra, down through my neck and spine and down to my feet. It felt exhilarating. "I'm ready for anything," I was thinking. Then, out of the blue, Hans Baba began saying, "Are you getting lighter and lighter and lighter? Are you getting lighter and lighter and lighter and lighter?" He laughed and continued to channel energy, repeating the exact words from my previous night's dream to me for the next fifteen minutes.

The next day, I caught a flight to Udaipur. As I looked out the window of the plane, I noticed how barren this part of India looked from the air. "Looks can be deceiving," I thought, as I reflected on the previous day's meeting with Hans Baba. India is a country of stark contrasts, incredible poverty, side by side with incredible wisdom, the most barren deserts and the highest mountains in the world, all in one country. I was thinking about the experience of standing under his foot, and how he asked me if I wanted to fly. "But I didn't actually fly. Well, never mind," I thought, " it was a great experience anyway, and besides, he seemed to know the contents of my dream!"

Whenever I travel to India, I always visit any good astrologer I hear about. Over the years this has taken me into remote villages, big cities and various nooks and crannies throughout India. In the process I have experienced a variety of different types of astrology and other divination systems. Just as each area of India has its own cuisine, so too each area has its own unique style of Jyotish. My trip to Udaipur was for the purpose of getting a Brighu reading. Brighu astrology is a unique style of astrology which works in the following way. Thousands of years ago, there was a lineage of great jyotishis who were followers of a great sage named Brighu. These astrologers wrote down the horoscopes of hundreds of thousands of people. But the horoscopes they calculated were not the charts of people of their own time, but rather people from the future. The Brighus also interpreted these charts, giving great detail about the lives of the people who owned the horoscopes.

These charts were kept in families, passed down through the centuries. The idea is that you go to visit a Brighu astrologer, he looks up your chart, and reads to you what the ancient jyotishis predicted about you.

Good Brighu astrologers are not easy to find in India. There are, understandably, many charlatans. But the recommendation for this particular Brighu astrologer had come from a reliable source and I was very curious to finally meet someone who actually practiced this ancient form of Jyotish. At the airport in Udaipur we hired a taxi and set out for Karoi, a small village, three hours outside of Udaipur on the Jaipur-Udaipur Road. The road to Karoi is not particularly beautiful, but it does have character. It is a mix of rolling hills covered with scrubby-looking trees. We passed through small villages along the way and stopped at one so the driver could get some tea.

When we finally arrived at the Brighu astrologer's place, he already had a line of people waiting at his door. His place was a simple adobe-like house, with a side room for an office. The pundit used to sit there each day and see clients on a first come, first serve basis, no appointments. The pundit was busy with some clients when we arrived so we sat outside with the villagers and waited for a couple of hours for our turn.

The reading itself started in a very unique way. The pundit spoke Hindi, and although I speak Hindi, I am not fluent, so I had taken a translator with me. The pundit asked to see my horoscope. I gave him my chart. "Show me your palms," he said. Even though I had come for an astrology reading, it did not surprise me that he had asked to see my palms. In India, it is very common for astrology and palmistry to be practiced together. What did surprise me, however, was the way he used the palms to verify the horoscope. He did not read my palms as a means of prediction. Instead, as he looked at my palms, he busily wrote with a piece of chalk on a small blackboard on his lap. He filled one side of the blackboard with different numbers. Then he wrote something on the other side. After examining my palms, he showed me the side with the numbers and said, "Point to a number." I pointed to 55. Then the pundit turned over the blackboard where he had already written, "He will point to 55." Apparently, I had passed the test. He accepted the chart I had brought as the correct chart.

Next the pundit used a dial of some sort to locate my chart, apparently keying on planetary positions in the chart I had brought. He then went to one of the many trunks that surrounded him on the floor and started searching for the Brighu version of my chart. Finally, he came up with a chart and matched the positions on the chart with those on the chart I had brought. My translator, who was also an expert jyotishi, also got in on this process, verifying for me that the two charts were the same. When both of us were satisfied that he had chosen the correct chart, the pundit began his reading.

"Your chart is one in a million!" he exclaimed. "Right," I thought cynically, "Every person's chart is one in a million!" I had a sinking feeling, as if all of the time, effort and money I had already spent on this trip was about to be wasted. He went on, "You are an astrologer and you also read palms." My ears perked up. "Okay, I'm listening," I thought. He went on. "On the day you came here, it is a Tuesday, and you came with one other man. Your father is dead. Your mother is sick. You have three brothers and two sisters . . . etc., etc." He continued like this for about a half an hour giving intricate details of my life, which were all extremely accurate, and making predictions on my future, many of which have already come true. I was really amazed. And then, amidst all of the details, he said, "At the age of forty-eight you will purchase an airplane!" My immediate reaction was, "Okay, he's allowed one mistake." An airplane is an extravagance, which would be too great a stretch for my frugal nature. It was an obvious mistake, but he was batting 99 percent and I was very impressed.

On the drive back to Udaipur, as I looked out the car window at the scruffy-looking hills, I reflected on the pundit's reading. "India is a place of mysteries," I thought. First Hans Baba, now the Brighu pundit. How an astrologer from ancient times could calculate and interpret my chart, giving the accurate details of my life, a life taking place many centuries after his time, is a great mystery. I was filled with wonder. In fact, it didn't even matter to me whether any of his predictions came true, much less the one about the airplane. The mere fact that some ancient astrologer had described my life so accurately simply inspired a great sense of wonder. As a practicing jyotishi, I am used to having clients go away with a sense of wonder. It is one of the great side-effects of getting a good astrology reading. It reminds you of the divine mystery of life. But after doing thousands of readings, I am used to how mainstream Jyotish works, so it no longer seems mysterious to me. It just seems beautiful and natural when something that I say in a reading for a client actually comes true. Mainstream astrology has become like a close friend whom I know intimately and love dearly. It is part of daily life, part of my family. The Brighu reading, however, seemed a little mysterious and made me wonder. And I was grateful for that feeling.

One last comment:. A couple of years later, a number of events led my wife and I to buy a house in Nevada City, in the foothills of the Sierra Mountains in northern California. We also have a residence in Los Gatos, and for the time being were intending to maintain our offices in the San Jose area and to commute to Nevada City on the weekends. We are intending to retire there eventually. In the meantime, we were faced with a three-hour commute, once a week, which on a Friday afternoon can turn into a six-hour commute. Without even thinking about the Brighu reading, I got a wild idea. Why not learn to fly and buy a plane? I researched the idea and it seemed a practical solution to our commuting problem. I immediately started taking flying lessons, intending to get my license and plane at age forty-seven. The process was delayed when my flight instructor was unexpectedly fired, setting back my training by several months. I finally got my private pilot's license a year later and, two weeks before my forty-eighth birthday, I purchased an airplane. The pundit's words came back to me. Amazingly, however, so did Hans Baba's, "Do you want to fly?" Now, I am getting "lighter and lighter and lighter," but the only flapping I do is when I put down the flaps on the plane as I make my final approach for a landing!

Chapter Six

Nakshatras

One of the features of Vedic astrology that distinguishes it from other forms of astrology is its use of the twenty-seven nakshatras or constellations. In the West, the zodiac is usually divided into twelve signs. In India, besides dividing the zodiac into twelve signs, the zodiac is also divided into twenty-seven constellations or nakshatras. Each of these nakshatras is related to a particular deity from the Hindu pantheon and shares in that deity's symbolism and mythology. These symbols provide the astrologer with a rich background from which to draw intricate detail and deeper meaning from the chart.

The following is an interpretation of the twenty-seven nakshatras. The meanings in general are taken from classical literature and applied to modern life. In some cases, however, liberal use has been made of the mythology of the ruling deity. In most cases, stories or myths related to the deity for the nakshatra are given. Learning the stories about these Vedic deities can provide additional symbolism, which can be helpful in deepening one's understanding of the nakshatra. In some cases, actual events related to the myths of the deity will take place in the person's life, even though these events may not be listed in the classical astrological literature. An Ashwini person, for example, may become a beekeeper (brings honey to the gods), or drive a "Mustang" (a car with the name of a fast horse), or become an ambulance driver (rescues heroes). The point is that the symbolism of the nakshatra is linked to the deity. The more an astrologer knows about the deity, the more symbolism he has to apply to his understanding of the nakshatra. Most of the mythology has been taken from various English translations of the

Puranas. The general traits of the deities, listed at the beginning of each nakshatra are based on the Sanskrit translations of the deities' names, as well as descriptions of the deities given by Alain Danielou in his book, *The Myths and Gods of India*.

Each nakshatra also has a shakti, a basis, and a desire. The shakti and the basis describe the fundamental energy of the nakshatra, and express the nakshatra's essence. The desire describes the basic aspiration of the nakshatra, and can be applied to those who have focal planets placed within the nakshatra. The shakti, basis and desire are described in an ancient Sanskrit text called the *Taittiriya Brahmana*, and are based on a translation by Dr. David Frawley.

	C	F	M
F		♀	♃
A	♂ ♆ MC		
E	☊ AC	☽	
W	⚷		☉ ☿ ♄

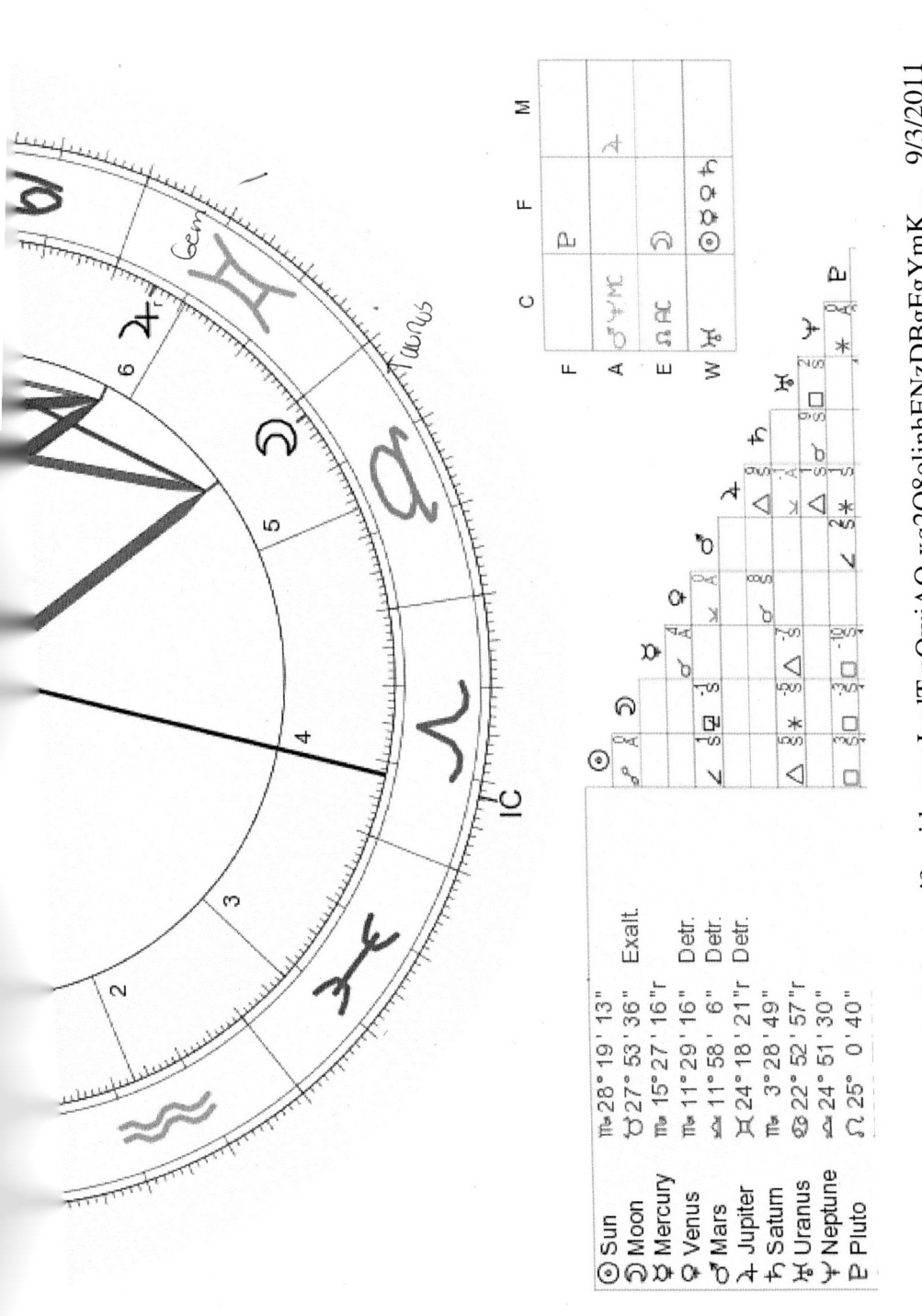

	☉	☽	☿	♀	♂	♃	♄	♅	♆	♇
☉										
☽	☌									
☿	☌	△								
♀	□ 1°	⚹ 3°	□							
♂	⚹ 3°	△ 5°	⚹	☌						
♃	△ 7°	□ 9°	△	⚹ 5°	⚹					
♄	☌	△	☌	□ 3°	⚹ 7°	△ 10°				
♅	△	⚹	△	☌	☌	⚹	△ 7°			
♆	⚹	□ 2°	⚹	△	△	□	⚹	□		
♇	☍	☌	☍	⚹	⚹	△	☍	△	*	

☉ Sun	♍ 28° 19' 13"		
☽ Moon	♉ 27° 53' 36"	Exalt.	
☿ Mercury	♍ 15° 27' 16" r		
♀ Venus	♍ 11° 29' 16"	Detr.	
♂ Mars	♋ 11° 58' 6"		
♃ Jupiter	♈ 24° 18' 21" r	Detr.	
♄ Saturn	♎ 3° 28' 49"		
♅ Uranus	♈ 22° 52' 57" r	Detr.	
♆ Neptune	♎ 24° 51' 30"		
♇ Pluto	♑ 25° 0' 40"		

9/3/2011

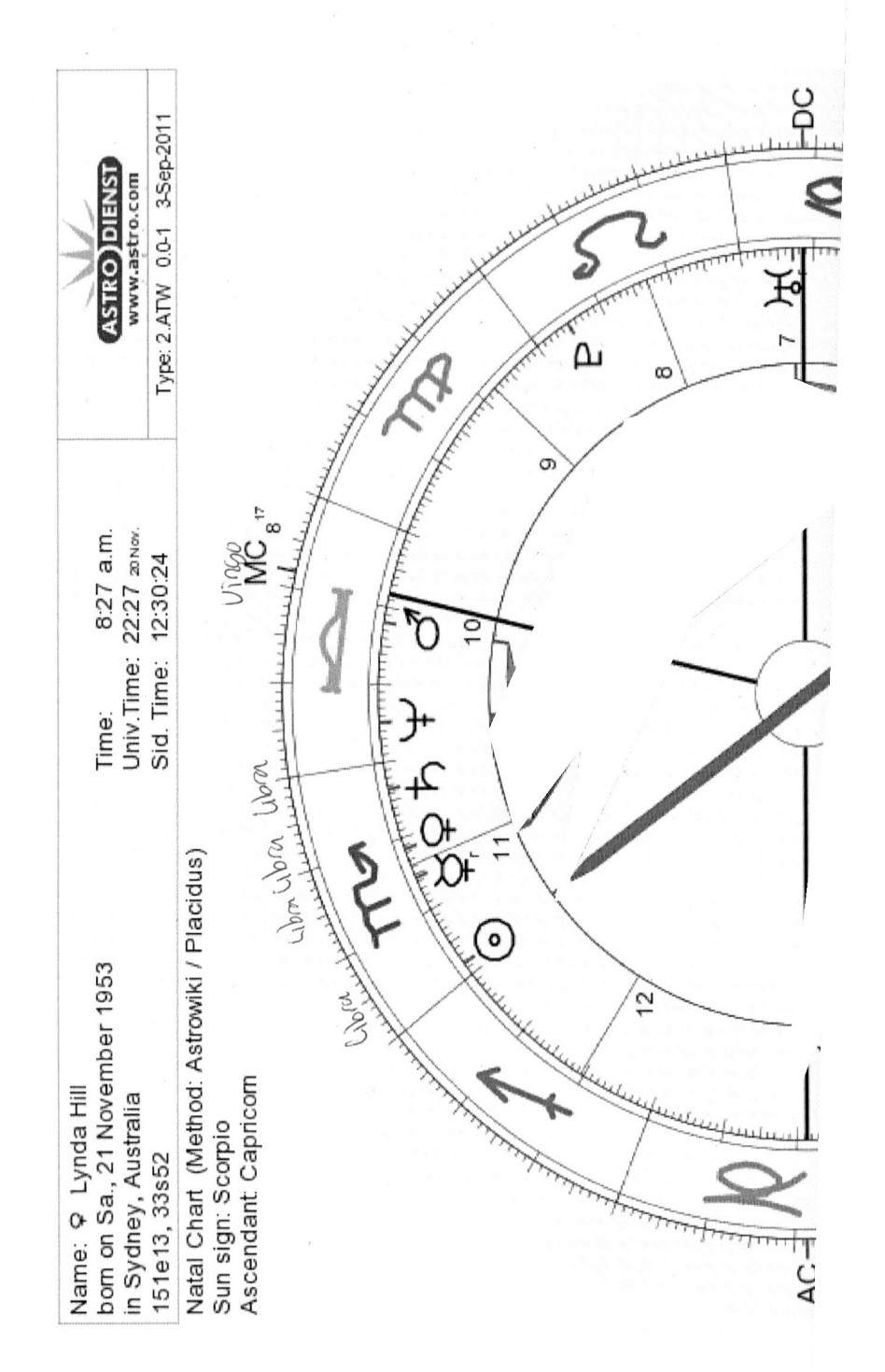

Astro-Databank chart of Lynda Hill born on 21 November 1953 - Astrodienst

Name: ♀ Lynda Hill
born on Sa., 21 November 1953
in Sydney, Australia
151e13, 33s52

Time: 8:27 a.m.
Univ.Time: 22:27 20Nov.
Sid. Time: 12:30:24

Natal Chart (Method: Astrowiki / Placidus)
Sun sign: Scorpio
Ascendant: Capricorn

Nakshatras

Ashwini
The Ashwini Kumaras replace Dadhyan's head after removing the horse's head.

BHARANI

Yama visits Rama for the purpose of carrying his soul away at the end of his life.

Krittika
Sita is purified in the fire after being rescued by Rama.

ROHINI
Rohini dances for Chandra.

Mrigashira
Brahma, in the form of a stag, chases his daughter, in the form of a doe.

Ardra
Rudra cries to his father, "I don't have a name."

Punarvasu
Aditi prays to Vishnu that her sons be restored to their place in heaven.

PUSHYA

Tara nurses Mercury while Brihaspati mistakenly believes Mercury to be his son.

Ashlesha
A yogi performs a yagya in Patala Loka, the abode of the serpents.

Magha
The Pitris drink the last drops of soma on amavasya,
the last day of the waning phase of the Moon.

Purva Phalguni

Lovers embrace in their conjugal bed, the symbol of procreativity.

Uttara Phalguni

Aryaman, the matchmaker, blesses a bride and groom.

Hasta
The demon, Ravana, challenges the Sun to a fight.

CHITRA
Vishvakarma sits on his swan and surveys his heavenly creation.

SWATI
Narada sits under the conceited silk-cotton tree.

Vishakha
Indra does offerings to Agni in front of an archway.

Anuradha
Radha and Krishna play together on their swing.

Jyeshtha
Indra receives a protective talisman from his teacher, Brihaspati.

MULA
Lakshmi visits Niritti on a Saturday.

Purva Ashadha
Apa, the god of the water, brings life into the world.

Uttara Ashadha
Ganesha, the remover of obstacles blesses a devotee.

SHRAVANA

Vamana stands before Mahabali, the noble demon king, and asks for three paces of his territory.

DHANISHTA
The Vasudevas gather and listen to the sound of a drum.

Shatabhisha
Varuna comes to collect King Harischandra's son.

PURVA BHADRAPADA
A yogi meditates on impermanence next to a funeral bed.

UTTARA BHADRAPADA
Bhima is healed by the poison of a water serpent.

Revati
Pushan takes care of the animals.

1. Ashwini (0° Aries - 13° 20' Aries)

Meaning: "owning horses"
Symbol: the horse's head
Shakti: the power to reach things quickly (shidhra vyapani shakti)
Basis above: creatures to be healed
Basis below: healing therapies
Desire: the ability to hear well and not be deaf

Deity: The Ashwini Kumaras. These gods are twins who had the heads of horses. They are the physicians of the gods and they also rule over agriculture. The Ashwini Kumaras appear as young handsome men who have golden skin. They are able to move very fast. They share one wife who is the daughter of the Sun. They are experts in the use of herbs and magical techniques of healing. They are herdsmen and gardeners. They rescue and heal heroes. They bring honey to the gods. They bring the dawn each morning, appearing in the sky just before sunrise.

Interpretation: Ashwini rules healing, especially Ayurveda and other natural-healing systems which make use of herbs. Whether he uses it directly or not, the Ashwini person usually has a natural ability to heal.

This nakshatra can also bring a connection to gardening and animals, especially horses. A focal planet like the Moon, Sun or ruler of the Ascendant placed here may occasionally make the person a twin. Alternatively, the person might have a best friend who is sometimes mistaken by others to be his sibling. This constellation stimulates activity and promotes a youthful appearance. Sometimes it creates a love of cars or other vehicles. Ashwini people may incur initial resistance or even prejudice in the process of attaining the status, position or acceptance they desire. This resistance can be overcome through selflessly serving, helping or healing others, rather than focusing on recognition and status directly. Ashwini people tend to gain elite status in their chosen profession or social circle. They can be good listeners, and often become counselors or therapists. They can possess the ability to listen internally as well, making them naturally inclined to be introspective.

Stories Related to Ashwini:

Indra Acknowledges the Ashwini Kumaras

Indra, the king of the gods, would not admit that the Ashwins were divine because they were part of a lower worker cast (herdsmen-agriculturists). The Ashwins, however, gave eternal youth to the great sage, Cyavana (which means activity). Cyavana, in turn, compelled Indra to acknowledge their divinity and their right to the soma offering.

The Ashwini Kumaras Learn the Knowledge of Immortality

Once there was a hermit named Dadhyan, who had learned the secret knowledge of immortality from Indra. The Ashwini Kumaras, who were the physicians of the gods, found out and wanted to learn this from Dadhyan. Dadhyan, however, was afraid to teach them because Indra had stipulated that if he taught anyone, Indra would cut off Dadhyan's head. The Ashwini Kumaras went to Dadhyan and said, "This is not a problem, we know the art of healing. We will simply cut off your head and replace it with a horse's head. Then you can teach us what you know, and when Indra cuts off your new head, we will replace it with your own head." Dadhyan agreed and this is how the Ashwini twins attained the knowledge of immortality. This is also how the Ashwini nakshatra came to be have such healing power.

The Ashwini Kumaras Test Sukanya

Once there was a rishi named Cyavana. He sat near a lake and meditated so long that shrubs and bushes grew all around his body so that only his eyes could be seen. One day, King Saryati visited the lake where he was staying. Saryati had four thousand wives, but he had only one daughter, Sukanya, an incredibly beautiful girl who he loved very much. Sukanya was playing in the bushes where Cyavana was meditating with his eyes open. She saw two gleaming points in the bushes. Out of curiosity she poked at them with a sharp stick, putting out the eyes of the sage.

Although the sage was blinded, he did not curse Sukanya. Nevertheless, the violent deed did have the effect of bringing misery to the people of that area. When the King found out that his daughter had blinded Cyavana, he pleaded for forgiveness. Cyavana gave his forgiveness, but only on the condition that the King give Sukanya to him as his wife. The king was reluctant, but his daughter was quite willing and became the rishi's wife.

Although Cyavana was old and blind, Sukanya served him day and night with the greatest devotion. One day the Ashwini Kumaras saw her tending to the old sage with such care and tenderness that they decided to test her. They approached her saying, " Sweet girl, you are very beautiful and could have a much better husband than this old, blind rishi. Why don't you choose one of us to be your husband?" At this, Sukanya became indignant and threatened to curse the Ashwini Kumaras if they continued talking like this.

The Ashwini Kumaras did not like the prospects of being cursed, but they were impressed by Sukanya's virtue. As a boon, they promised to restore the youth, vigor, good looks and even the eyesight of Cyavana. But they still continued to test Sukanya. They told the sage to submerge himself in the lake. At the same time, the Ashwini Kumaras also dipped themselves in the lake. When all three of them rose from the lake, they were all handsome, virile and able to see perfectly, but they also looked exactly alike. They told Sukanya that she would now have to choose one of them, and that whoever she chose would be her husband. Sukanya closed her eyes, used her intuition, and was able to choose Cyavana.

The Ashwinis Pray For a Boon

Once the Sun told his two twin sons, the Ashwini Kumaras, "Pray to Brahma with devotion so that he will give you a boon." Taking his advice, the Aswinis began reciting the Brahmapara hymn. They continued this for many years, with great intensity and devotion. Brahma was pleased and said, "Ask for a boon which is rare, even to the gods, and by which you can go everywhere in the heavens." The Ashwinis said, "Oh great Creator, please give us our share among the gods. Please give us the position of gods who drink soma juice and an eternal place in the assembly of the gods." Brahma said, "You will get all of the following gifts - beauty, luster, uniqueness, the position as the physician for all beings, and a place among the gods entitled to drink the soma juice in the worlds." All this happened on the second lunar day, Dwitiya.

2. Bharani (13° 20' Aries - 26° 40' Aries)

Meaning: "she who bears"
Symbol: the vulva
Shakti: the power to carry things away (apabharani shakti)
Basis above: to remove the life from the body
Basis below: to carry the soul to the world of the ancestors
Desire: to be the lord of the ancestors

Deity: Yama (the binder), the god of death and the king of justice. He is also the king of the ancestors. He appears to the virtuous, riding on a giant bird, Garuda (the wings of speech), wearing a crown, earrings and a garland of wild flowers. To sinners he is fierce and roars like an ocean of destruction. He has long teeth and a frowning brow. He is known as "he who controls all beings." He is a judge and a restrainer of men. He is also called the twin, the finisher, time, the noose carrier, and the settler. He represents and upholds the codes of social morality. He also owned two four-eyed dogs. His direction is the South.

Interpretation: The shakti of this nakshatra is the power to carry things away, which is what Yama does when he collects the souls at the end of life. This gives the Bharani person the ability to clear away and dispose of things or conditions that have come to a conclusion. The idea of carrying may also link this nakshatra to the concept of carrying or bearing, as in bearing a child. This may lead the Bharani person to gradually develop his ideas and plans internally before "giving birth" to them through the field of action. Also, they can "carry or bear" by allowing a project, plan, business, or career to develop first for a period of time, before letting it to move to the desired level of fruition.

The deity, Yama, prompts the Bharani person to be a fighter in the cause of social justice. Bharani people sometimes subscribe to revolutionary social philosophies. They have the ability to make good judgments. On the negative side, they can also become judgmental. They tend to be self-controlled, persevering and they have a strong sense of duty. They can sometimes be moralistic. They may have a twin or a sibling that is very attached to them or visa versa. They can sometimes be controlling or jealous. They can also be quite fierce when they perceive injustice. They are, however, amenable to pity and forgiveness. Yama was also the lord of the ancestors, so Bharani people have a natural desire to rule or lead their peers.

Taking the dual symbols of Yama (death) and the vulva (pregnancy and birth) together, Bharani becomes a constellation of death, transformation and rebirth. This allows the significations of planets placed in Bharani to go through a metamorphosis process, sloughing off the old (as in menstruation), and giving birth to the new.

Stories Related to Bharani:

Yama's Twin Sister

Yama had a twin sister named Yami, who loved him passionately. He resisted having sexual relations with her, but after his death she was so upset and depressed that the gods created the night in order to make her forget.

Yama and Shiva

Yama came to take the life of Markandaya, who was a great Shiva devotee. Markandaya hid behind a statue of Shiva. Yama tried to throw his noose around him, but it accidentally went around Shiva's neck instead. At this, Shiva opened his third eye and glared at Yama who was burned to ashes in its fire.

Yama is Cursed by His Mother

Once Yama was not being treated fairly by Chhaya, the shadow substitute of his mother. As a result he became very angry and even raised his foot as if to kick her. Chhaya reacted by putting a curse on Yama that would make his foot fall off. Yama was really upset so he complained to his father, the Sun, saying that Chhaya could not be his real mother because a real mother would never curse her own son. After talking to his father and mitigating the effects of the curse, Yama went to a special place of pilgrimage and meditated there for a hundred thousand years. Then Lord Shiva appeared to him and told him to ask for any wish. Yama asked for the power to protect both the worlds of men and the ancestors (pitris). He also asked for the ability to judge between virtue and vice, good and evil. After granting his wish, Shiva disappeared. (Also see Hasta nakshatra for more of this story.)

Yama Visits Rama

After Rama spent his years in the forest, he returned to Ayodha, where he ruled for 11,000 years. When it was time for his life on earth to end, Brahma (the Creator) sent Yama to bring him back to Vaikuntha. Yama disguised himself as a young sage and went to Ayodha to meet Rama. He told Rama that he was a disciple of sage Atibala and had come to tell him a secret. So Laksmana was posted to guard the door and keep anyone from entering. He announced that anyone who tried to enter would be slaughtered.

Rama and Yama talked secretly for a while and then Durvasas, a great sage who had been fasting for a thousand years, arrived at the door. He wanted to break his fast and he was very hungry. When Laksmana told him that he could not enter, he became very angry and was about to curse the entire race of Kings. So Laksmana entered the room and told Rama. Vasistha suggested that it should be enough if Laksmana was banished from the palace. So Laksmana was expelled and he went to the river and drowned himself. Rama was heartbroken, so he also went to the river and drowned himself. Yama took their souls to Vaikuntha.

Yama and Crows

Yama was once frightened at the sight of Ravana and escaped in the form of a crow.

3. Krittika (26° 40' Aries - 10° 00' Taurus)

Meaning: "the cutters"
Symbol: a razor or sharp cutting blade
Shakti: the power to burn or purify (dahana shakti)
Basis above: heat
Basis below: light
Desire: to be the eater of food for the gods

Deity: Agni, the god of fire. He is the purifier. He is usually depicted with two heads. He lives both in heaven and on earth and is the mediator between men and the gods. He presides over all great events in life. He eats flesh. He can eat anything, whether pure or impure and it will be purified. He rides on a ram and sometimes in a chariot. He represents intelligence, health, strength and beauty. He is called the all-pervader, the proud, the burning, the purifier, the resplendent, the gold-maker, the flickering, the seven-tongued, and the giver of wealth. He signifies knowledge and rules the Southeast.

Interpretation: Krittika people are bold, courageous, and fiery. Karttikeya, Shiva's son, was the god of war, so this constellation rules warfare and battle on various levels. Krittika people have the ability to cut through resistance and accomplish great things. They are proud, confident, ambitious, leader-types. They tend to set high goals and sometimes take risks in the process of accomplishing them. They sometimes use sharp objects or instruments in their work. They thrive in occupations that require precision and skill. Planets placed in this nakshatra may become refined, purified, or tested as if by fire.

This constellation also rules over the fire of digestion and the fire of the mind. Krittikas tend to have a strong digestive fire, powerful appetites, and even the ability to digest things that might not be good for them. They also tend to be very bright, with a natural ability to absorb and utilize knowledge.

Krittika also rules over gold, so those born with focal planets placed here tend to be prosperous. Physical beauty, or a tendency to be attracted to others who are physically beautiful also goes along with this constellation.

The myths related to Krittika suggest that one of the idiosyncrasies of this constellation is the tendency toward affairs, especially with the spouse of another person. In one of the stories, however, illicit sexual relations are averted by the quality of "offering" or sublimation. In either case, strong sexual passions are a natural part of the energy of Krittika.

Stories Related to Krittika:

Agni Seduces the Wives of Six Rishis

Once there were seven wives of seven great sages. Agni was sexually attracted to all seven of them. In order to seduce them he took on the form of their husbands. He was successful in seducing the six wives but not the seventh, who retained her virtue. The Krittikas (the six wives together) later gave birth to Agni's child who is named Karttikeya, the god of war.

In another version of the story, Agni does not actually unite with the wives of the rishis, but with Svaha (meaning offering) who is the daughter of Daksha (ritual skill). Having a strong desire for Agni, she tricks him by taking the form of the wives of the rishis.

According to yet another version, at a time when the demons were destroying the world, the gods obtained the seed of Lord Shiva and asked the Krittikas to nourish it in their collective womb. They gave birth to Subrahmanya, who is supposed to be the son of Lord Shiva. When

Subrahmanya was born he had six heads, so that he could be breast-fed by his six mothers, the Krittikas. His name then became Karttikeya. After feeding him, the Krittikas entered into the heavens, becoming the constellation of Krittika.

Narada's Advice

Narada once said that if one feeds Brahmins with ghee and pudding when the Moon is in Krittika, one may ascend into Devaloka, the abode of the gods.

Agni and the Phantom Sita

Sri Rama and his brother Lakshman were living in the forest. One day Agni disguised himself as a Brahmin and approached them saying "Oh Sri Rama, the time is soon coming when you will save the world by killing the demon, Ravana. You will be motivated by the love of your wife, Sita. Ravana will soon come and kidnap Sita. If you don't mind, I would like to play a trick on Ravana. Let me take the real Sita to a safe place and replace her with a Phantom Sita, which will be an exact living duplicate of your real wife. After you kill Ravana and save Sita, you are going to have to throw your wife into the fire to test her chastity. At that moment, I will take back the replica and give you back your real wife." Sri Rama agreed, so Agni used his yogic powers to manifest a phantom Sita. Rama kept this as a secret and didn't even tell Lakshmana. Later, when he fought with Ravana, Rama killed Ravana and saved Sita. In order to demonstrate the purity of Sita in public, Rama put her into the fire. At that moment, Agni took back the replica and gave the real Sita to Rama.

Agni Gets Indigestion

Once the great Sage, Durvasas, was doing a twelve-year yajna in which he poured food continuously into the mouth of Agni. As a result, Agni got indigestion. When the indigestion would not stop, Agni went to Brahma and asked him for a cure. Brahma told him that he would only cure him on the condition that he would burn a huge forest where the demons lived. Agni agreed and immediately started burning the forest. Then Indra sent down heavy rain and put out the fire because he had a friend who lived in the forest. So Agni went to Krishna and Arjuna and asked them to help him burn the forest. As an incentive, Agni gave Arjuna an arrow-case that would never be empty, and a chariot bearing a monkey flag. He also gave him four white horses adorned with gold chains and the Gandiva bow. He gave Sri Krishna the Cakrayudha, which was a divine wheel-weapon. When these gifts were given to Krishna and Arjuna, they helped him to burn the forest. Once again, Indra tried to stop Agni by pouring down rain, but Arjuna created a canopy of arrows over the forest. Agni succeeded in burning the forest and was cured of his indigestion.

4. Rohini (10° 00' Taurus - 23° 20' Taurus)

Meaning: "the growing" or "the red"
Symbol: an ox cart
Shakti: the power of growth (rohana shakti)
Basis above: the plants
Basis below: the waters
Desire: to attract a lover and unite with her/him

Deity: Brahma, (Prajapati) the Creator, is the source of the universe who provides the conditions for the manifestation and development of the world. He gives the first impulse of individual existence. He is called the Immense-Being. He is also called the Golden Egg (Hiranya-Garba) of the universe. He is the Lord of Progeny as well as the inventor of theatrical art, music, and dancing. He rides on a swan, the symbol of knowledge. This nakshatra is also related to Lakshmi (Brahma's consort), the goddess of wealth.

Interpretation: Rohini is a constellation that produces creativity. Those with focal planets in this nakshatra usually love to dance and also love music and art. They are frequently the objects of envy and jealousy. This seems to be truer in the case of Rohini women. Occasionally, they can also be jealous of others.

This is also a sensual and passionate constellation. One of the alternative interpretations of the name Rohini is "red," which symbolizes sexual passion and desire. Rohini people are usually charming, charismatic, and physically attractive. They emanate sexuality and have a natural ability to attract the love, affection, and sexual interest of others.

The symbol of the nakshatra is an ox cart, so Rohini also signifies vehicles, especially trucks and other utility vehicles. In keeping with the translation of the name (the growing one), Rohini people have the capacity to create and develop ideas and projects. They give their creative impulses the space and time necessary to develop and fructify. In the process they often gain great skill and knowledge.

Stories Related to Rohini:

Rohini and the Moon

Rohini was the favorite wife of Chandra (the Moon). She was one of twenty-seven daughters of Daksha, who had given them in marriage to Chandra. Rohini was incredibly beautiful, artistic, a great dancer and also quite skilled in the conjugal arts. As a result, the Moon fell totally in love with her and did not pay any attention to his other wives. Naturally, the other wives became very jealous and complained to their father. Daksha told Chandra to treat his wives equally, but Chandra disregarded his advice. Again the twenty-six wives complained to their father, and again Daksha chided Chandra. But Chandra continued to stay only with Rohini. It is said that in those days, the Moon only stayed in one place in the sky (the constellation of Rohini). When his daughters complained to him a third time, Daksha got angry and cursed Chandra that he should get tuberculosis. So Chandra was afflicted by consumption and he constantly waned. Chandra tried to cure himself by doing many yajnas, but they did not help. On earth, as well, many living beings also contracted consumption, and even the medicinal plants stopped growing. As all of the people were becoming very thin, the Devas interceded. They asked Daksha to lift his curse. Daksha did this, but only partially. He told Chandra that if he dived into the Sarasvati Tirtha in the western sea he would be free from consumption for half of every month. Chandra did this and that is the reason that the Moon waxes for half of the month and wanes for half of the month. It is also the reason that the Moon now resides in each nakshatra for an equal amount of time.

Brahma and Valmiki

Once a hunter shot down one of a pair of birds that were making love on the banks of the Tamasa River. The Sage Valmiki saw the hunter do this, and cursed him. This curse, according to folklore, was the world's first piece of poetry. Brahma heard this poem and was attracted to the Hermitage of Valmiki. He encouraged Valmiki to compose the story of Rama in verse. This is how the Valmiki Ramayana was written.

Brahma Loses His Head

In ancient times, Vishnu and Brahma were doing rigorous austerities in order to suppress their passions. After a while, they decided to take a break, and went for a walk. They happened to meet each other on the way. Each asked the other, "Who are you?" This began as a conversation and ended in a debate as to who was the greatest. Each claimed himself to be the supreme power of the world. Neither would recognize the other. In the middle of the debate, a huge phallus appeared. Then a celestial voice from the sky said, "You don't have to argue about who is the greatest. The one who reaches the end of this phallus is the superior person." So both set out to find the end of the phallus. Vishnu went downwards to find the bottom and Brahma, upwards to find the top. Vishnu continued downward for a long time and ultimately gave up because he could not find the base of the phallus. Brahma went upward and also could not find the top of the phallus, but on his way upward, he saw a petal of a pandanus flower floating down. So he caught the petal and went back to meet Vishnu. He said, "See, I have taken this flower from the head of the phallus. It is evidence that I reached the top. I beat you and you should admit that I am greater than you." Vishnu did not believe him, so he asked the pandanus flower to tell him the truth. But Brahma had already spoken to the pandanus flower and convinced it to lie for him. The flower took a false oath and swore that Brahma had reached the top. But Mahavishnu was still not convinced. So he said, "Let Shiva be witness to this flower." At these words, Shiva appeared before them and revealed the trick of Brahma and the flower and cursed the pandanus flower that it could never again be used as an offering to Shiva. Then Shiva cut off the head of Brahma.

Brahma Loses His Seed

Once Rudra took the form of Varuna and did a sacrifice. All the sages and gods were invited. It was a grand affair, with all sorts of celestial beings and even celestial nymphs. Brahma saw the beautiful nymphs and became aroused. As a result, he had an orgasm and his semen fell on the ground. The Sun scooped up the dirt on which the semen had fallen and threw it into the fire, which caused the fire to rise up in a giant blaze. Out of this blazing semen three sons and many other beings, including the Ashwini twins were born. All the gods got together and praised Brahma as the source of all creation.

5. Mrigashira (23° 20' Taurus - 6° 40' Gemini)

Meaning: "the deer's head" "to hunt" "a well-trodden path" or "to ask"
Symbol: the head of a deer
Shakti: the power to give fulfillment (prinana shakti)
Basis above: to extend
Basis below: to weave or produce clothing
Desire: to gain lordship over plants

Deity: Soma (Chandra the Moon), healer of all diseases, bestower of riches, lord of the other gods, pictured as a priestly sage. He was brought to earth by a large hawk or a thunderbolt. The number three becomes important in all the symbolism describing him. He is the opposite of Agni. Agni is digestion, Soma is the food. Agni is expansion and Soma is contraction. He is the divine nectar. Together they symbolize the ritual sacrifice, the offering of the seed into the sacred fire. Along with Pushan, he is the guardian of animals. Soma is the lord of the Northeast.

According to the Puranas, Soma is the jiva, the experiencer who is in the body. He has an invisible form, which sustains men, trees, plants, as well as sixteen deities. He also has a visible form, (the Moon), which Rudra wears on his head. Water is also his form, so he is considered universal. Brahma gave him Purnima, full moon day as his tithi. If a person fasts and makes offerings to Soma on that day, he bestows food, knowledge, effulgence, health and wealth.

Interpretation: Like the Moon, its deity, Mrigashira is a changeable, timid, charming, sensitive, quick moving, impulsive constellation. Mrigashira people are constantly searching (or hunting) for something. The house in which Mrigashira falls usually symbolizes the object of their search. If the Moon is placed in the fourth house in Mrigashira, for example, the person might constantly search for peace of mind, security, or a perfect home or house.

Mrigashira people are sensual and sometimes fickle. They are also prone to marital problems stemming from their passionate nature. When a focal planet, Venus or the ruler of the seventh house is placed in this constellation, there can be a tendency towards infidelity, either on the part of the Mrigashira person or their partner. This does not mean, however, that all Mrigashira people experience infidelity. The nakshatra's shakti is the power of fulfillment, which means that Mrigashira's basic energy acts to produce fulfillment for the significations of any planet placed within it. The means to this end is desire. It is strong desire that propels the Mrigashira person towards fulfillment. It is the same strong desire that motivates them to occasionally get off the track and follow a desire which is forbidden. Like a deer looking for food, the Mrigashira person follows his desires, curiously checking out all attractions and usually fulfilling his desires. When the desire is healthy, balance and well-being result. If the desire is not appropriate, then sometimes the person gets his "head cut off."

Mrigashira people can also doubt, challenge, and judge prematurely. This, of course, is more the case if malefic influences are involved. This tendency can be related symbolically to Daksha's premature judgment of Shiva. The same myth alludes to the method of overcoming the inevitable karmic repercussions by seeking refuge in Brahma, the creative principle, and shedding blood as rain for mankind. This possibly symbolizes the ability to use insight born of suffering for the purpose of helping others.

This constellation is also associated with wandering, traveling, speaking ability, a tendency to challenge the views or credibility of others, a tendency to become prosperous, love of gems, love of pleasure, weaving ability, love of animals, love of plants, and healing ability.

Stories Related to Mrigashira:

Chandra and Tara

Brihaspati (Jupiter), the preceptor of the gods, had a very beautiful wife named Tara. One day when she was out walking, she came by Chandra's (the Moon's) house. When Chandra saw her, he fell in love with her immediately, and she also fell in love with him. After some time passed, Brihaspati started to miss Tara and started to ask about her. When he found out that she was with Chandra, he sent his disciple to bring Tara back. But Tara would not come. So he sent back his disciples several times and each time they returned without Tara. Finally, Brihaspati decided to go himself. But he could not persuade Tara to come back to him.

This caused Brihaspati to become very angry and he called Chandra, "The Brahman killer, gold thief, drunkard, he who marries another's wife." He also told Chandra that he was not fit to reside in Devaloka. "Unless you return my wife," Brihaspati said, " I will curse you!" Chandra was not impressed and did not give in. He told Brihaspati that Tara had come to him on her own and would leave him when she was no longer satisfied. This made Brihaspati furious, so he went to Indra and asked him to help. Indra agreed and went to Chandra's house and told him to send Tara back to Brihaspati or else be prepared for battle. Again Chandra refused to give in, so Indra started preparing to go to war with Chandra.

News of the possiblity of war came to Shukra, (Venus) who was the guru of the Asuras and also a long-time enemy of Brihaspati. Shukra went to Chandra and promised to help him if war broke out between Chandra and Indra. He also advised Chandra not to give in. Eventually, Indra and Chandra did go to war, causing the whole world to go into turmoil. At the end, Brahma came on his swan and broke up the battle. He scolded Chandra and Shukra and got them to stop fighting. He also made Chandra return Tara to Brihaspati.

How Mrigashira Became a Constellation

Brahama (the Creator) had a daughter who was very beautiful and to whom he was sexually attracted. His daughter sensed his attraction so she took the form of a deer and ran away. Brahma then took the form of a stag and chased her across the heavens. When Indra (the king of the gods) found out what was happening he cut off the head of the stag in order to prevent the incestuous relationship from taking place. The stag's head became the nakshatra of Mrigashira.

Another Version of How Mrigashira Became a Constellation

Daksha was the father of Lord Shiva's consort, Sati. Once Daksha held a great ritual sacrifice called a yagya, to which he invited everyone except Lord Shiva. Sati wanted to go to the yagya, and encouraged Shiva to go with her. When they arrived, Daksha made it clear that Shiva was not welcome. He even said to Sati, "Your husband does many evil things. He wanders around naked in the cremation grounds wearing skulls on his body. He rubs ashes all over himself. He even wraps himself with a serpent instead of a sacred thread. These things are not worthy of my son-in-law, so he doesn't deserve to be invited to the yagya." At this, Sati became very angry and jumped into the sacrificial fire pit. This astonished everyone attending the yagya, and it made Shiva furious. As a result, he started destroying the whole place and was intent on destroying Daksha as well. While this was happening, the yagya took the form of a stag and ran away. Shiva shot an arrow at it and pierced the stag, which jumped into the heavens and tried to gain the protection of Brahma, the Creator. Brahma told the stag, "Great yagya, you have been shot by Shiva's arrow. May you remain in the heavens in the form of a deer from this time onward. You will be known as Mrigashira (the deer's head) and will be close to Rudra (another name for Shiva, who rules the next nakshatra, Ardra). You will always be in the company of Soma, the Moon god. The blood which spills out from your body signifies the rains during the rainy season."

Chandra (Soma) and Rohini

Soma (the Moon) was the son of Atri, who was born out of mind of Brahma. He had twenty-seven wives (the twenty-seven nakshatras). Rohini was his favorite (see the constellation of Rohini for the story of Rohini). Because he was not paying enough attention to his other wives, Rohini's father, Daksha, cursed him. As a result of the curse his light diminished and he eventually disappeared from the world. When this happened, nothing would grow. All the plants shriveled up and the gods got worried. So they approached Vishnu and asked for help. Vishnu listened to their problem and then mentally called Brahma, Rudra, and Visuki (the serpent god) to help. They used Visuki's body as a churning rope and stirred the ocean. Eventually Soma reappeared.

6. Ardra (6° 40' Gemini - 20° 00' Gemini)

Meaning: "the moist one"
Symbol: a teardrop
Shakti: the power of effort (yatna shakti)
Basis above: to hunt or search
Basis below: to reach the goal
Desire: to gain lordship over the animals

Deity: Rudra, the lord of tears. He is a form of Lord Shiva and is the howling god of storms. He is also called "the Lord of Songs, the Lord of Sacrifices, the Healer, He Who Removes Pain, the Wrathful, the Fury, and Brilliant as the Sun." He is considered the best and most bountiful of the gods who grants prosperity and welfare. He wields a thunderbolt. He is called the first Divine Physician. Yet he represents the destructive principle, anger deified, and is called the god that kills and "The Torturer of Men." He is called "the Great Fear" and is thought of as the personification of anger. He is also linked to fire. Agni (the god of fire) is said to be a manifestation of Rudra. Rudra is the hunter and the bowman. He rules over ghosts and graveyards. He wears serpents around his neck. He sometimes drinks and dances around madly, amidst groups of drunken attendants. He is said to carry away everything at the end of the universe. He is the ruler of sleep.

Interpretation: Ardra is a constellation of emotion and feeling. Weeping can be an outcome of both negative and positive emotion. Ardra people are usually emotional and are easily moved to tears. As some of the myths about Rudra suggest, the tears that come through Ardra can be due to personal disappointment. On the other hand, many Ardra people are moved to tears by more inspirational emotions. Rudra, however, is a deity who is connected to suffering and disappointment, so planets occupying this nakshatra are sometimes linked to suffering. In other situations, it is not the owner of the horoscope who experiences the tears and emotional upset. The Sun or the ruler of the tenth house in Ardra, for example, can indicate that the person deals with people who are emotionally upset as part of his profession. Similarly, the Moon or the ruler of the fourth house placed in Ardra can indicate that the mother might be emotional, easily moved to tears, or that she has a difficult life.

Shiva is a god of healing and Ardra people make compassionate healers. They are very sympathetic and usually willing to give help to others in need. They like to remove the pain of others. Also like Shiva, they can be unconventional or even heretical in their lifestyle or philosophy of life.

Ardra is also a constellation that is linked to anger and other negative emotions. Sometimes anger can be expressed as righteous indignation, and at other times it can manifest as cruel and selfish tendencies. This anger may also be expressed by "howling" or shouting.

Tears are cleansing and purifying. Many Ardra people find great release and emotional expansion after crying. Similarly, disappointment and tears often lead to renewal. Like the "fresh and moist" (words which are also used to describe Ardra) dawn after a storm, Ardra people often find relief and new beginnings at the end of their emotional journeys. In this way, Ardra symbolizes the exploration of emotions as a vehicle for deep spiritual metamorphosis.

Ardra also promotes mental genius, fascination with alternative concepts, abstract thinking, intuition, interest in astrology, psychology, science, and technology.

Stories Related to Ardra:

Rudra Cries

When Rudra was born he cried. When his father, Prajapati, asked the reason, Rudra said it was because he had no name. So Prajapati decided to call him Rudra, which means, "to weep."

Shiva Is Easy to Please

Once a demon named Vrka asked Narada which god from the trinity of Brahma, Vishnu and Shiva was the easiest to please. Narada said, "If you want to get your prayers answered quickly, pray to Shiva." When Ravana and Bana prayed to him in the form of a song, he gave them unlimited prosperity and sovereignty.

After hearing this, Vrka went to Kedara in the Himalayas, and started cutting off parts of his body and offering them to Shiva in a sacrificial fire. After seven days of this, when all his efforts had failed to produce a vision of Shiva, Vrka started cutting his head as well as his wet, matted hair. As a result, Shiva came out of the sacrificial fire and appeared to Vrka. He grabbed Vrka's arms to stop him, and as soon as Shiva touched Vrka, all of his wounds were instantly healed and his body became perfect. Shiva said, "My Dear Vrka, that is enough! You do not need to torture yourself. I am pleased even if water is offered to me with reverence. Ask me for one wish and I will give you whatever you ask."

Vrka thought for a minute and said, "Let me have the power that causes anyone I touch with my hand to instantly die."

Shiva was saddened for a minute and then laughed and said, "So be it!"

At this point Vrka decided to test his boon by trying to touch Shiva, himself. Fearing for his own life, Shiva ran away, crossing the whole universe, and finally entered the realm of Vishnu, which is beyond everything. This is the realm where Lord Narayana (Vishnu), resides. Because of his supreme equanimity and ultimate transcendence, Vishnu is the ultimate refuge of all beings who seek to renounce everything for God.

Seeing that Shiva was in a predicament, Lord Narayana took the form of a small boy and approached Vrka. He bowed to Vrka and said, "Oh Vrka, you look tired. You must have come from a long distance. Why don't you sit down, and rest a while. You are such a great and mighty demon! You deserve a rest. What brings you here? Tell me and maybe I can help you."

Unable to resist the little boy's flattery, Vrka told Narayana everything that had happened, including his plan to touch Shiva.

The little boy (Narayana) said, "I don't believe Shiva's words because I know that he has been cursed by Daksha and his powers have been reduced. Now he is only the king of the evil spirits. But if you still think he has the power to give you such a boon, you can easily test the truth of his words right now by simply putting your hand on your own head. You will quickly find out that nothing will happen to you and that Shiva is a fake. Then I suggest that you go kill that rascal Shiva so that he never will tell another lie again."

Lulled into a stupor by the sweet voice of the Narayana in the form of the little boy, Vrka put his hand on his own head and immediately fell dead. Out of the heavens, the gods, the ancestors, and all the heavenly beings showered flowers on the earth in gratitude.

Speaking to Vishnu, Shiva said, "Vrka was killed by his own sins. How can a person be safe when he commits a sin against a great being, not to mention when that great being is the controller of the universe." In the *Puranas* it is said, "Whoever hears this story and tells it to others will become liberated from the cycle of birth and death and will become free from any danger from enemies as well!"

Why Shiva is Easily Pleased

Once King Pariksit asked Sri Suka, "Of all the Gods, Lord Shiva seems to be the easiest to please. Why is it that even though Shiva himself is the embodiment of renunciation of worldly pleasures, those who worship him are blessed with wealth and pleasure? Yet, even though Vishnu is the consort of the goddess of wealth, Lakshmi, those who worship him do not get wealth."

Sri Suka said, "Shiva is associated with Shakti. He is invested with three gunas and rules over the three types of cosmic ego. Out of these three types of ego come sixteen potencies. He who adores one of these potencies is blessed with all types of earthly prosperity. Lord Vishnu, on the other hand is beyond all attributes. Those who worship him become bereft of the three gunas as well."

Vishnu, himself, liked this question and explained further. "I gradually relieve the person of his wealth, on whom I wish to bestow my grace. Then, finding him penniless, his friends and relatives desert him."

7. Punarvasu (20° 00' Gemini - 3° 20' Cancer)

Meaning: "good again" "prosperous again" or "light again"
Symbol: a quiver of arrows
Shakti: the power of wealth or substance (vasutva prapana shakti)
Basis above: air or wind
Basis below: moisture or rain
Desire: to produce herbs and trees

Deity: Aditi (primordial vastness). Aditi is the mother of all the gods, the primary mother-goddess. She is unboundedness, the sky, and space. She is also the earth-goddess. She had twelve sons called the Adityas. These Adityas are related to the twelve months of the year and represent the twelve sovereign principles. These sovereign principles are the fundamental laws of men and gods and are the foundation of the different areas of knowledge. Aditi is worshiped for blessings on children, for forgiveness, and protection.

Interpretation: Like its ruling deity, Aditi, Punarvasu represents freedom, expansion, and unboundedness. It also is associated with things becoming good again. It can promote a return to prosperity, and general well being. Punarvasu means "good again, light again, prosperous again," so

Punarvasu people bring a renewing influence to whatever they touch. They are particularly good at giving birth to ideas that bring renewal. The implementation of their ideas, though, is sometimes carried out by someone else. In any case, the Punarvasu person has the natural ability to restore an old condition, rebuild a career after a loss, or renew a marriage or relationship after a loss or separation.

This nakshatra also brings the development of virtues and blessings as represented by the twelve sovereign principles described below. As a result, Punarvasu people tend to become interested in philosophy and religion and develop deep insight into the meaning of life. They are usually good with language, and tend to become successful, well educated and prosperous. They have a strong sense of right and wrong, valuing virtue and truth above all else. On the negative side, they can also become self-righteous and indignant if they perceive injustice or other transgressions to the basic rules of human behavior. Nevertheless, they are able to allow others the space to be themselves and can learn to be tolerant.

The quiver of arrows suggests the quality of potential or stored up energy, rather than expressed energy. Punarvasu people frequently find themselves storing up energy more than spending it. They usually like to stay at home, or even work at home. They like to save money and they have the natural ability to create prosperity. Occasionally, however, they can spend their energy or resources in a more dynamic way. The arrows in a quiver are there to be used by the archer. Like an arrow, occasionally being sent out from the bow, the occasional utilization of resources seems to keep the energy circulating, contributing to the overall capacity to create energy and prosperity.

Stories Related to Punarvasu:

Aditi Cuts her Unborn Fetus into Twelve Pieces

Aditi was married to Kasyapa (vision). She wasn't able to bear the radiance of her own child, so Kasyapa divided the fetus into twelve parts (the twelve sovereign principles) corresponding to the months of the year. These sons were named, Mitra (friendship), Varuna (fate), Aryaman (chivalry), Daksha (ritual skill), Bhaga (the inherited share), Amsa (the gods' given share), Tvastr (craftsmanship), Savitr (the magic power of words), Puhsan (prosperity), Sakra (courage), Vivasvat (social laws) and Vishnu (cosmic law).

Aditi Prays to Vishnu

Once Aditi was worried about her sons, the gods, who had been kicked out of heaven in a great war. She prayed to Vishnu to restore them to their rightful place in heaven. As a result, Vishnu incarnated as the Avatar Vamana, with Aditi as his mother. Note: Here Aditi represents the power to bring renewal and to make things "good again" through the power of prayer or even through the power of thought. (See the "Myth of Vamana" under Shravana nakshatra for a more detailed version of this story.)

8. Pushya (3° 20' Cancer - 16° 40' Cancer)

Meaning: "nourishing" also "flower"

Symbol: a cow's udder

Shakti: the power to create spiritual energy (brahmavarchasa shakti)

Basis above: sacrificial worship

Basis below: the worshipper

Desire: to possess the splendor of spiritual knowledge

Deity: Brihaspati (the Great Master), the teacher of the gods who rules over mental energy. He was turned into the planet Jupiter by Shiva. He is the teacher of Jyotish, Vedic astrology and astronomy. The movements of all the planets are under his domain. He is the priest, the ruler of assemblies, and the ruler of the elders. He intuited and wrote part of the *Rig Veda*. He also wrote a book of law and a book of politics.

Interpretation: Pushya is probably the most auspicious constellation in the zodiac. It nourishes and promotes growth. Before it was called "the nourishing" it was called "the prosperous" and "the auspicious." Pushya people are also nurturers. They are willing to help, support, care for, and give sustenance to those around them. They tend to become prosperous, well educated, and successful.

Brihaspati (Jupiter), the deity associated with Pushya, was a great teacher, so Pushya people have a natural command of language and the ability to teach. They also develop wisdom and other virtues. They can become very philosophical or religious, and have the capacity to gain great spiritual knowledge as well as the ability to create spiritual energy.

They tend to be rather orthodox in their beliefs. They make good professionals, developing expertise in some field of knowledge. They also make good leaders and have a natural understanding of the subtleties of politics and diplomacy. Pushya people are naturally lucky. This tendency to find nourishment, growth, abundance and success also seems to extend to other planets placed in this constellation. In general, the significations of planets located in Pushya tend to thrive.

Stories Related to Pushya:

Brihaspati's Birth

Once there was a great seer named Angiras, whose wife became pregnant. Due to some bad karma from the past, the baby was born dead. She went to Brahma and he told her to practice some austerities for the purpose of having another child. She did this with great devotion and got pregnant again. This time she gave birth to Brihaspati, The Great Master.

Shiva Makes Brihaspati into the Planet Jupiter

Once Brihaspati entered into a field made of light and prayed to Shiva for a thousand years. After he was finished, Shiva gave him a blessing, making him the planet Jupiter.

How Brihaspati Lost his Wife, Tara, to the Moon

(See the story under Mrigashira nakshatra.)

Brihaspati Is Insulted by Indra

Once Indra insulted Brihaspati, his own guru, who was also the guru of the other gods. There was a great celebration going on and all of the gods were there. Indra was seated on a throne with a white umbrella, looking completely royal and magnificent. As he sat there, sharing his throne with his beautiful wife Sachi, Brihaspati came to visit. Because Indra had become caught up in his own magnificence and prosperity, he forgot to even acknowledge his guru's presence. Brihaspati understood that this was not appropriate behavior on the part of Indra, so he quietly got up and started to walk out of Indra's palace.

Immediately, Indra understood what he had done. He apologized publicly, saying to the members of his audience, "I have done a totally bad thing. I was drunk with the arrogance of wealth and power and have completely disrespected my guru. Now I will go to Brihaspati, humbly bow at his feet and beg his forgiveness."

While Indra was giving this speech, Brihaspati magically disappeared into thin air.

When the demons found out that the guru, protector and advisor to the gods had vanished, they immediately began to attack them. The gods were getting beaten badly, so they went to the great sage, Visvarupa, and begged him to help. Visvarupa agreed to help them. He had done many years of intense spiritual practices in the past and had built up tremendous spiritual power. Using his power, he immediately snatched the treasure of the demons, robbing them of their wealth. Then he gave Indra a protective coat of armor, the Narayana Kavaca. From that time onward, Indra defeated the demons.

9. Ashlesha (16° 40' Cancer - 30° 00' Cancer)

Meaning:	"the clinging" "the embracing" or " the entwiner"
Symbol:	a coiled snake
Shakti:	the power to poison (visasleshana shakti)
Basis above:	the approach of the serpent
Basis below:	agitation or trembling
Desire:	to overcome enemies

Deity: The Nagas (the deified serpents). The Nagas are part human and part serpent. They are quick, violent, poisonous, and courageous. They live in the underworld, Naga-Loka. They also live on earth, under the sea, and in mountain caves. They intermarry with men but are enemies to the gods. The Nagas were the children of Kasyapa (vision) and Kadru (chalice of immortality). They symbolize the cycles of time. They are also symbols of the kundalini energy, which is represented as a coiled snake at the base of the spine. Because they slough their skin, they symbolize metamorphosis and spiritual transformation. They also have the ability to mesmerize, and can be masters of deception, manipulation, and cunning.

Interpretation: Ashlesha is a constellation of deep mystical power. Completely at home in the underworld, those born with focal planets here have a deep connection to both the dark and light sides of their nature. As a result, they usually have a natural interest in the areas of psychology, astrology, and other subjects that explore the hidden aspects of consciousness. They have a transformational nature and are usually deeply interested in spiritual pursuits, especially those that unleash the power of the kundalini. This ability for metamorphosis also gives them a profound ability to heal and transform the world around them.

In keeping with their serpent nature, Ashleshas like to live and work in seclusion. Sometimes they do things in secret. They can also be charismatic. They have a natural ability with language, and use it to mesmerize, bite, poison, or transform those around them. They can be blunt, venomous and lethal if threatened or humiliated. They sometimes become arrogant. They make formidable opponents and have a powerful ability to overcome their enemies. They can become dynamic public speakers and spiritual leaders.

Ashlesha people can also be slippery and seductive, sometimes using their hypnotic power for selfish reasons. As a result, they have a tendency towards infidelity and can sometimes be untrustworthy in other ways. They also frequently have important lessons to learn about gratitude and appreciation. They usually feel unappreciated, especially by their spouses. Often, however, it is the Ashlesha person who needs to learn how to appreciate others.

When planets are placed in Ashlesha, their significations are sometimes "poisoned." On the other hand, sometimes the effect of this nakshatra is to produce change, transformation and ultimate healing.

Stories Related to Ashlesha:

The King of the Serpents, Leaves his Unethical Mother

Once Adisesa's mother and another serpent lady got into an argument as to whether there were a few black hairs on the tail of a particular serpent. They made a bet and decided that the loser would become the slave of the winner. To win the bet, Adisesa's mother asked her sons to help her cheat. Some of her serpent sons agreed, but Adisesa refused saying that it was unethical. His mother cursed him saying that he would die at a serpent yagya.

This made Adisesa very depressed, so he left his Mother and went to various pilgrimage sites, where he practiced deep meditation. After some time, Brahma appeared to him and said, "Don't worry, go to the underworld and support the world on your hoods." Brahma also told him that Garuda would give him help in his new mission. With the blessing of Brahma, Adisesa took on the role of supporting the world on his head.

A Description of Adisesa from the *Vishnu Purana*

The *Visnu Purana* says that at the bottom of the Patala (the abode of the serpents) is the home of a tamasic form of Vishnu called Adisesa. He is awesome and indescribable. Both the gods and rishis worshiped him. Adisesa has 1,000 heads, and 1,000 gems in his heads illuminate all regions. He makes the asuras powerless. He is so powerful that his power overflows, making his eyes constantly rotate. He always wears blue apparel and garlands made from white gemstones. He shines like Mount Kailasa, adorned with garlands made of white clouds. He is served by Sri Devi and by the flow of the Ganges River. He holds in one hand the lamgala and in the other a mace. As the deluge at the end of the yuga approaches, Rudra emanates from the faces of Adisesa and consumes the three worlds. Adisesa lives in the underworld and wears the whole earth as a crown. When he yawns, the earth and seas shake. Even the gods have no idea of his nature, power, or the extent of his attributes. That is why he is also called Ananta (endless).

Adisesa's (and Ashlesha's) Relationship to Astrology

It was by worshipping Adisesa and by his grace that sage Garga was able to master the sciences of astrology and omens (Nimitta).

Adisesa as the Churning Rope

When the gods and the demons churned the ocean of primordial matter with a rope, the rope they used was actually Adisesa.

Naga (Serpent) Chiefs

The chiefs of the Nagas are very long and powerful snakes who are highly poisonous and have extremely bad tempers. They usually have between 5 and 100 hoods. They all worship Adisesa, the king of the serpents. Adisesa has toenails that are like diamonds and reflect like mirrors. As the Naga chiefs bow before him, they see their reflections in his mirror-like nails. They enjoy looking at their own faces, adorned with brilliant earrings that throw reflected light on their cheeks, mirrored in the nails of Adisesa. Note: If Adisesa is taken to represent the awakened kundalini, this story could suggest a tendency for the Aslesha person to become fascinated, with their own powers and abilities, which are only egocentric expressions of the mother of all powers, the kundalini.

Adisesa Surrounded by Serpent Nymphs

The daughters of the Naga chiefs are all very beautiful. They put fragrant pastes on their bodies, which are made from aloe, sandalwood and saffron. They stand around Adisesa and move in erotic undulations revealing their sexual passion. He sits in complete detachment while his eyes roll around in his head in blissful intoxication. He smiles at them mercifully as he holds the world on one of his thousand heads. Note: Mahatma Gandhi, whose Moon was in the constellation of Aslesha, was said to sleep with young girls around him in order to test his celibacy and detachment.

Further Description of Adisesa

Although Adisesa is impulsive and wrathful, he restrains his anger for the well being of the entire world. He entertains his attendants and gods with his powerful and hypnotic speech. He wears blue clothing, one earring, and he has a plough in his hand. He wears a wreath of forest flowers, around which bees are buzzing.

Adisesa and Arrogance

Adisesa is also called Sankarsana "one who arrogantly pulls at everything seen and unseen."

Serpents and the Underworld (the Symbol of the Unconscious)

Daksha had a daughter, Kadru who gave birth to many serpent sons who were all crooked. As their population grew, they started biting and killing the people on earth with their poisonous fangs. The people of the earth went to Brahma and asked him for protection. Brahma agreed. He called all the serpents together and said, " Since you are killing my children, in another age, the Swayambhuva Manvantara, you will decline."

The serpents said, "Oh Brahma, you made us crooked, gave us venom, made us cruel, and gave us the ability to use our eyes as a weapons."

Brahma said, "You are right, but what right do you have to eat men every day?"

The serpents said, "Give us a limit and give us a separate region, in order to prevent us from doing harm."

Brahma said, "Alright, then I will make an agreement between you and men. Listen carefully. You may live in the underworlds. From now on you may only eat or bite a person if it is his destiny, and in order to retaliate when somebody injures you. You should move away in fear from persons who recite mantras, or who take medicine or wear the Garudamandala. Otherwise you will bring about your own disaster." After that, the serpents went to the underworld and remained in Patala Loka.

Panchami Tithi and the Nagas

The lunar day on which the serpents were sent to the underworld was Panchami tithi. This tithi is auspicious and capable of removing sins. It is said that if a person refrains from eating any sour food and bathes statues of Nagas (serpents) in milk on Panchami, then the serpents become friendly to him.

Meditating on Adisesa's Words

It is said in the Puranas that "When one listens to Adisesa and meditates upon his words, the knots of ignorance are cut."

10. Magha (0° 00' Leo - 13° 20' Leo)

Meaning: "the great one"
Symbol: a throne room
Shakti: the power to leave the body (tyage kshepani shakti)
Basis above: mourning
Basis below: leaving the body
Desire: to flourish in the world of the ancestors

Deity: The Pitris (the deified ancestors). Yama is their ruler. Tradition states that they are maintained in their heavenly abode by the offerings of their descendants. Having a child insures that a person will have offerings made on their behalf after death. They are viewed as equal to the gods.

Interpretation: Magha is the constellation of the ancestors, so those born under its influence usually have a natural respect for traditions of various kinds. A Magha person could become involved in a traditional spiritual path, or he might become interested in his own family's genealogy. Sometimes the Magha person becomes attached to a grandparent or simply has great respect for older people. In any case, the area in which this "tradition" theme plays itself out is usually suggested by the house in which Magha resides. The planet occupying Magha, as well as the houses it rules, also gives a clue. The Sun placed here, for example, can suggest a patriarchal tradition, great respect for the father or grandfather, or a career that is linked to a tradition. Like the ancestors, Magha people also like children and sometimes look to their own children for support in their old age, or even after their death through prayer. Self-aware Magha-types also have the ability to renew their energy in the waning phase of the Moon. Amavasya, the last day of the waning phase of the Moon, is particularly important to the Magha person for this purpose.

Symbolized by a throne room, Magha produces a royal demeanor in those who have focal planets there. The Magha person usually has high expectations in life. If the rest of the horoscope supports those expectations, then this constellation really allows the person to live like a king or a queen. Not everyone can be a king, a boss, a movie star, a star athlete, or famous, however. So if the rest of the horoscope shows rather average results in various aspects of life, the Magha person sometimes feels rather disappointed with life. Regardless of their station in life, however, Magha people are powerful. They are the mighty rulers of their domain. They also possess a magnanimous and generous spirit. Perhaps because they really understand the principle of giving, they tend to attract wealth as well. They frequently have servants or employees, and they also love to interact with the wealthy, the famous and the elite. They love their homes and offices, and sometimes even get involved in real estate.

The basic shakti of this constellation is the power to leave the body and its desire is to thrive in the realm of the ancestors. The Pitris are the ancestral spirits who have left the body and gone to the other side. Magha people are naturally intuitive and have a natural sensitivity to subtle energies. On the positive side, many Magha-types become aware of spiritual beings on subtle planes and sometimes become spiritual guides for other people. They are also naturally drawn to the practice of yoga, which is helpful for staying grounded. On the other hand, if this constellation is afflicted it can suggest problems or fears regarding astral beings, ghosts, and other entities. The person can also have difficulty staying grounded and centered. A simple version of this occurs when the ruler of the Ascendant, the Sun or the Moon is afflicted in Magha. This sometimes causes the person to have difficulty "staying in his body," causing symptoms such as distraction and inability to focus.

Stories Related to Magha:

Pitris and the Moon

The Pitris love the Moon. Along with the other devas, they drink the

Moon's nectar and Chandra (the Moon) wanes as a result. On New Moon day, a huge gathering of Pitris collects around the Moon to drink his amrita (divine nectar). In this way all the three classes of Pitris, (Barhisadas, Saumyas and Agnisvattas), receive their nourishment for the entire month. So it is in Krishna Paksha (the waning phase of the Moon) that the Pitris drink in the Moon's nectar and become satiated. (Making this period an important one for Magha people.)

The Pitris and Amavasya Tithi

Once there was a celestial maiden named Achchhoda who practiced meditation for a thousand years. As a result, a young, handsome, and fragrant Pitri named Amavasu appeared before her and told her that he would grant a wish. Overwhelmed by his many attractive qualities, Achchhoda immediately fell in love with Amavasu and told him that she wanted to marry him. As a result of expressing her passionate desire for him, she immediately lost all the power she had accumulated through her spiritual practices and fell to earth. Amavasu Pitri remained detached and did not give in to passion. The day on which this took place came to be known as Amavasya Tithi, the last day of the dark phase of the Moon. Since that time, this day has been cherished by the Pitris.

Pitris and Yoga

Once a daughter of one of the Pitris practiced yoga and meditation for a long time. Finally Vishnu appeared to her and told her to make a wish. She said, "Give me a husband who is very handsome and also give me the power to curb his passions." Vishnu granted her wish by making her the wife of Suka, the great teacher of Yoga. He also blessed her with a daughter who also became a great yoga adept.

Pitris, Past Lives, and Siddhis

In the Matsya Purana it is said that a certain class of the Pitris are reborn at the end of each day of Brahma. As a result of their past practices of yoga, they are born with the memory of their past lives and knowledge of Sankya Yoga. This gives them siddhis (spiritual powers) and the ability to attain enlightenment.

11. Purva Phalguni (13° 20' Leo - 26° 40' Leo)

[Handwritten margin note: "Allen has my Ascendent and he never got his "fair share" with regard to his business partnership with Charlie"]

Meaning: "the former red one"
Symbol: a hammock or a bed
Shakti: the power of procreation (prajanana shakti)
Basis above: the female sexual partner
Basis below: the male sexual partner
Desire: to have the best share amongst the gods

Deity: Bhaga, "the inherited share," the god of wealth, especially wealth that is passed down or shared within families or communities. In ancient times, receiving one's share represented acceptance into the community as an adult. Bhaga does not see differences between individuals and treats everyone equally; this is why he is said to be blind. He brings conjugal bliss and protects the happiness of marriage, especially for women. He bestows sexual pleasure, good luck and prosperity. The name, Bhaga, also means the female sex organ.

Interpretation: Purva Phalguni is a constellation of prosperity, especially prosperity that represents one's inherited share of communal wealth. Purva Phalguni people tend to be lucky with money. They sometimes prosper through inheritance. They have a desire to receive the best share among their peers. If this constellation is occupied by a malefic, however, they may have problems with giving or receiving a fair share, whether in earnings, inheritance, or community property. On the other hand, Jupiter or other money planets located here may indicate a strong tendency to prosper and benefit from family or communal wealth.

This nakshatra is also one of impartiality. In mythology, Bhaga's eyes were poked out and he became blind. Purva Phalguni people can easily cultivate impartial judgment, turning a blind eye to individual differences and treating everyone equally. Afflictions to this nakshatra can also bring negative forms of "blindness" such as being blind to the talents or virtues of other people, or simply not being able to judge character or see people clearly. This is also a constellation that, if afflicted, can contribute to eye or vision problems. For this result, the Sun, Moon, Venus, the second and twelfth houses must also point in this direction.

Purva Phalguni is a nakshatra of sexuality and passion. Those with focal planets placed here are sensual, attractive and playful. They tend to be lucky in relationship and can easily attract a good partner in marriage. Sometimes their fascination with sensuality and excitement can bring problems in marriage resulting from the channeling of sexual desires or sexual attention in inappropriate directions. They may pursue extramarital affairs or they may simply like to flirt. When they allow their passions to run unchecked, they experience suffering and marital problems. On the other hand, in the chart of someone who is interested in commitment and fidelity, the positive Purva Phalguni influence is a welcome support to marital harmony grounded in conjugal bliss. Malefic planets placed in this constellation can give problems related to sexual energy and/or sexual relationship. Rahu located here, for example, may give compulsive or addictive tendencies in relationships or sexuality.

The shakti of this nakshatra is the power of procreativity. This makes it an important nakshatra for judging matters connected with children. Afflictions to Purva Phalguni, along with afflictions to the fifth house and Jupiter, can indicate reproductive problems or problems regarding children. Similarly, benefics in this constellation may suggest procreative powers and easy birthing of children.

Sexual energy is the basis of creative energy, so Purva Phalguni people frequently develop their talents and abilities in art, music, drama, or dance. Like most creative people, they are highly independent and usually do not care what others think of them. Conversely, Saturn in Purva Phalguni may indicate inhibition or blockage of creative energy and a general reticence to freely express oneself.

Stories Related to Purva Phalguni:

Bhaga Loses His Eyes

Prajapati, the lord of progeny, wanted to have sex with his own daughter. Rudra became aware of this and fought with him in order to prevent the incestuous relationship. Some of Prajapati's semen was dropped on the ground so the other gods took the semen and used it as a ritual offering. Bhaga was standing south of the altar and looked at the offering. Rudra got angry and plucked out his eyes, blinding him.

Another Version of How Bhaga Lost His Eyes

At the end of the age of the Devas, Bhaga and the rest of the Devas got together and divided up the shares of the yagyas that they felt were due to them. Unfortunately, they left out Rudra. Rudra got very angry, so he made a bow and started a battle with the Devas. During the battle, Rudra used the point of his bow to poke out the eyes of Bhaga, cut off the hands of Savita, and to extract the teeth of Pusa. In the end, the Devas gave Rudra what he wanted and Rudra returned the Deva's body parts.

12. Uttara Phalguni (26° 40' Leo - 10° 00' Virgo)

Meaning: "the latter red one"
Symbol: a cot or a bed
Shakti: the power of wealth and accumulation through partnerships or marriage (chayani shakti)
Basis above: wealth obtained from one's family
Basis below: wealth obtained from the partner or the partner's family
Desire: to become lord of the animals

Deity: Aryaman (chivalry), one of the Adityas. He is called the god of patronage. He symbolizes help, hospitality, and kindness. He is associated with honor, ethics, and high standards of behavior. He rules over marriage agreements, traditions, customs, and religious rituals. He is the protector of family and community wealth. He is sometimes called the King of the Ancestors (the Pitris, which rule Magha). He also is a protector of paths and roads, insuring the freedom of travelers. It is said that the Milky Way is his "royal path."

Interpretation: Uttara Phalguni people like to practice the art of patronage. They like to help those in need, giving them a boost or a foothold that changes and transforms their lives. They also benefit from the patronage of others. They are devoted to the idea that noble living requires selflessness and service to those in need. The cot, in this regard, can be taken as a symbol of healing, so the Uttara Phalguni person can become a healer of the sick or the weak. So those with focal planets in this constellation are natural helpers, healers, benefactors, and patrons for the less fortunate. They are also sympathetic to animals and frequently express their supportive nature by caring for a pet.

Like the deity, Aryaman, Uttara Phalguni people also have a strong sense of maintaining a proper code of behavior amongst their family and professional communities. They see themselves as standing for nobility, and seek to exemplify and promote ethics, generosity and high values within their various social and professional groups. Those who have focal planets in this nakshatra sometimes become involved in rituals.

The cot or bed is also a symbol related to sexuality. Uttara Phalguni, as well as Purva Phalguni, are both represented by a bed. Their deities, Bhaga and Aryaman are also frequently worshiped together. They are both related to conjugal pleasure, passion and marriage. Like Purva Phalguni, Uttara Phalguni can sometimes be associated with sensuality, infidelity and sexual indiscretion. This, of course, only takes place when other aspects of the chart agree. In fact, this is actually a very good constellation for marriage, ruled over by the deity that blesses and protects marital contracts.

The shakti of this nakshatra is "the power of wealth and accumulation through marriage," so Uttara Phalguni people tend to benefit financially through their associations with others. This signification need not be realized literally through the spouse, however, and is frequently seen in the charts of people who make money through clients, partnerships, contracts, or collaborative ventures. If the rest of the chart agrees, then the Sun, Moon, Ascendant, Jupiter or the Yogi placed in this nakshatra, may be one of several factors indicating a rich spouse. Similarly, afflictions to this nakshatra can hinder joint finances or finances derived from partnerships.

Stories Related to Uttara Phalguni:

There is very little mythology about Aryaman still in existence. See the Story of Aditi (the Mother of Aryaman given under Punarvasu nakshatra). He represents one of the twelve sovereign principles. Being the King of the Pitris, mythology about the Pitris in general under Magha nakshatra may also be relevant.

13. Hasta (10° 00' Virgo - 23° 20' Virgo)

Meaning: "the hand"
Symbol: a hand or fist
Shakti: the power to gain what we are seeking and place it in our hand (hasta sthapaniya agama shakti)
Basis above: seeking to gain
Basis below: obtaining one's desire
Desire: to have the gods place their faith in me

Deity: Savitar, (also called Surya, the Sun), "giver of life," and one of the sovereign principles. He rules over mantras, divine words used for creating change within our world and ourselves. Divine words lead to divine awareness. Savitar rules the mental control and illuminated awareness that is the foundation necessary for the attainment of siddhis or miraculous powers. Savitar also signifies procreation and in later times has been identified also as the Sun, the source of procreative energy. He is worshiped in the Gayatri Mantra, the greatest of all Vedic mantras. Savitar is also connected to divine weapons used by the gods in battle.

Interpretation: Hasta rules the hands. Those born under its influence usually have talents and abilities with their hands. Sometimes this takes obvious forms such as handicrafts, carpentry, manual labor, typing, or hands-on healing. Other times it simply becomes a symbol for action, work, productivity and accomplishment. The hands also symbolize the shakti of this constellation, giving the Hasta person the ability to gain what he is seeking and place it in his hand.

The "divine weapons" which are related to Hasta's deity suggest the ability to conquer ones enemies, both external and internal. As a result, Hasta people may have a subtle advantage when it comes to succeeding in life's battles. The constellation may be linked to warriors of all kinds. As in the myth about Shiva and Surya, Hasta people sometimes become indignant when they perceive injustices done by the strong against the weak. They sometimes react by confronting or challenging even the most powerful opponents. Sometimes they find themselves at odds with opponents who greatly outmatch them. In such cases they are capable of fighting heroically against all odds.

When focal planets occupy Hasta, the person may also be a good writer or an articulate speaker. This nakshatra also suggests the ability to use words in order to create mental power. Affirmations and mantras are both tools that the Hasta person can easily use.

Possibly due to a relationship to the root word "has" which means "to laugh," Hasta also brings humor, laughter, and wit. The Hasta sense of humor can also be directed at others in a negative way, using the "magic power of their words" as "magic weapons" in the form of ridicule, sarcasm or other negative humor.

Hasta people also value the opinion of others. They particularly like to gain the trust and respect of their friends and peers. This desire to become trustworthy, combined with natural language ability and sense of humor, makes the Hasta person likely to become popular and well respected.

Stories Related to Hasta:

Creation

At the time of creation, after the world's egg had divided into two parts, the Sun appeared and "there was a great cry from which all the beings and all their pleasures were born. Hence, at his rising and setting, cries and songs are heard; all beings and desires rise toward it. Those who worship the Sun as the absolute ever hear bountiful sounds and are filled with joy." (*Chandogya Upanishad* 3.19. 1-4 [137] Alain Danielou, *Myths and Gods of India*)

The Sun, Moon and Rahu

Once the Sun and the Moon revealed the identity of Rahu who had come disguised as a god to drink the amrita (nectar of the gods). Mahavishnu cut off his head. As a result, Rahu and Ketu are enemies to the Sun and the Moon. (For the complete story see Rahu).

The Ravana Challenges the Sun to a Fight

Once Ravana traveled to the Solar Region and stopped to rest on Mount Meru. Then he got into his plane, Puspaka, in preparation for the morning battle. When he saw the sunrise, Ravana called his minister and said to him, "Go and tell the Sun that Ravana has come to fight. Tell him to either get down and fight me or admit defeat." The minister walked towards the Sun and told him what Ravana had said. The Sun said, "I don't mind whether I defeat or am defeated by Ravana. The reality is, I have no time." When the minister conveyed this message to Ravana, he left boasting that he had conquered the Sun.

The Sun Fights Shiva

Once Shiva cut off Brahma's head and Brahma cursed him that he would have to beg for food with his skull in his hands. At this, Shiva became very angry and started beating up anyone he met, resulting in the destruction of thousands of gods. Surya (the Sun) saw Shiva's rampage, became indignant, and decided to confront Shiva. Surya put up his fists to fight Shiva, but Shiva took both of Surya's hands in one of his own hands and squeezed so hard that Surya's hands began to bleed. Then Shiva turned Surya around and around causing Surya's hands to shorten. Surya became completely drenched in blood. Finally Shiva let him go, but Surya laughed and challenged Shiva to fight again. This made Shiva so angry that he hit Surya in the face with his fist, and knocked out all his teeth. Bhaga who was watching this gave Shiva a very fierce look, but Shiva plucked out both of Bhaga's eyes. After a while Shiva's temper settled down and Surya was restored to his old form.

The Sun and His Shadow Wife

Once Vishvakarma gave his daughter, Samjna, to the Sun God. He and Samjna had three children, two sons, Yama and Manu, and a daughter, Yamuna. The Sun, however, was so hot and fiery that Samjna found it hard to stay around him, so she concocted a plan. She spoke to her shadow (Chaya). She said, "I am going to my father's house for a while, so I would like you to stay here and take care of my husband. I want you to raise my three children and take care of them without letting my husband, the Sun, know that you are only my shadow. This is a secret between you and me." "Alright," Chaya said. "Don't worry about a thing. I will take care of everything. Unless I am cursed, I will never tell your secret. You can go wherever you like."

Feeling confident that her secret would be safe, Samjna went to her father's house where she stayed for the next thousand years. After a while, Visvakarma became a little concerned that she was not with her husband so he suggested that she at least go to visit him. To give the appearance of following her father's wishes, Samjna assumed the form of a mare and went to the north for a while.

While Samjna was gone, the Sun thought Chaya was his wife and made love to her. As a result, she had three children. Because these were her natural children, Chaya loved them more than Samjna's children and gave them more attention. This favoritism was no problem for Manu, but Yama thought that it was extremely unfair. He became very depressed and then in a fit of childish indignation he raised his foot as if to kick his stepmother. Chaya immediately cursed him saying, "Since you have threatened your mother like this, your foot will undoubtedly fall off."

The fact that he had been cursed, caused Yama to worry, so he and Manu went to their father, the Sun, and told him what had happened. He also told his father, "Because she has cursed me in this way, I really doubt that she is actually my mother." His father said, "My son, there are remedies for almost every kind of curse, but there is no remedy for the curse of a mother. I can, however, diminish the effects of the curse. Let some worms eat at your flesh until some of the flesh falls off onto the earth. This will satisfy the conditions of the curse and you will be saved."

Then the Sun went to Chaya and said, "Why have you played favorites with your sons? If all of these children were really yours you would have treated them equally. You must not be Samjna. Where has she gone? No real mother would curse her sons as if they are worthless fools." Afraid to be cursed by the Sun, Chaya confessed and told him the whole story.

Then the Sun went to the house of Vishvakarma looking for Samjna. When he asked Vishvakarma about Samjna, he said, "My daughter couldn't take your brilliance. You are really way too hot and bright to bear. If you really want her back, you will let me cut your brilliance down a bit." The Sun agreed, so Vishvakarma put him on his lathe and began to cut him down to a bearable brilliance.

14. Chitra (23° 20' Virgo - 6° 40' Libra)

Meaning:	"the bright" "the multicolored" or "a work of art"
Symbol:	a shining jewel
Shakti:	the power to accumulate good karma or merit (punya cayani shakti)
Basis above:	law
Basis below:	truth
Desire:	to have wonderful children

Deity: Tvashtar, the shaper, the celestial craftsman (later called Vishvakarma, the celestial architect), signifies the craftsmanship of weapons making. He thereby insures security and safety. He also made celestial chariots for the gods. He is the maker of both the thunderbolt and the chalice of Soma. He has the power to give both long life and prosperity. He gives the shape to male and female bodies in preparation for marriage. He rules over the development and shaping of the embryo in the womb. He rules over all forms. He sometimes envies and sometimes admires the skill of the other celestial craftsmen. His grandchildren are the gods of agriculture, the Ashwins.

In later stories, when Tvashtar came to be called Visvakarma, the celestial architect, he designed and built the universe. After he was finished, he ritually offered himself in order to complete his work.

Vishvakarma's Father was Prabhasa, one of the eight Vasus. His Mother was Varastri, who was the sister of Brihaspati. She was a celibate who had yogic powers. Visvakarma was born to these illustrious parents and became the celestial craftsman. He invented all the different kinds of handicrafts. He was the architect of the gods, the maker of ornaments, and the most famous sculptor. He also made chariots for the gods that flew through the air. In one story, Vishvakarma made a special flying chariot that he gave to Arjuna. Arjuna used it in his battle against the Kauravas. He also built the palaces of Varuna and Yama, and made a special bow for Shiva.

Interpretation: Chitra brings skill and craftsmanship. Those falling under its influence become adept at whatever they do. They are very creative and make good poets, artists and musicians. They love aesthetics and have a natural eye for beauty, especially the beauty of forms, shapes and spaces. This nakshatra is related to natural mechanical ability so Chitra people are natural architects, arrangers, builders, and engineers.

The symbol of Chitra is a shining jewel, so it produces brilliance. Chitra people have a tendency to be charming, beautiful and charismatic. They are articulate, dynamic speakers and tend to be in the public eye. They love children and want their offspring to also shine. They are prone to speaking first without thinking, and sometimes regret what they blurt out. They sometimes criticize out of self-righteousness. When this happens, neither friends, nor family are immune to their criticism. (See the story of Visvakarma cursing his daughter that follows.) They shine in their chosen field of work, where they become highly skilled. Occasionally they can become caught up in their own brilliance and become jealous of their competitors or those who may outshine them.

Chitra is generally a very auspicious nakshatra and things started under its influence tend to endure. The Chitra person is also highly capable of becoming virtuous and has great capacity to accumulate good karma, both through spiritual practices and selfless service. As the deity suggests, Chitra people have a certain martial quality as well. The thunderbolts and weapons fashioned by Tvashtar (Visvakarma) may represent a warrior attitude, which makes Chitra people prepared to fight, or at least speak out, for what they think is right. They create the structures and forms to re-establish dharma, and to vanquish evil. Sometimes they take up a fight against a powerful opponent, (see the story about Indra invading Tvashtar's house). Note: Mahatma Gandhi had his Ascendant in Chitra. He stood up to the English, forbidding them to stay in his country. Like the story of Tvashtar and Indra, the English continued for some time to take what they wanted by force. Ultimately, of course, Gandhi prevailed. In the process, he performed "ritual sacrifice" by adopting the life of an acetic and fasting many times. He finally sacrificed his own life as Vishvakarma did in his sacrificial ritual of creating the universe.

Stories Related to Chitra:

Visvakarma and Rohini

Tvashtar (Vishvakarma) once cursed the Moon for spending too much time with one of his daughters, Rohini. (See the story of Rohini under Rohini nakshatra.)

Indra Breaks into Tvashtar's House

Tvashtar kept the ambrosia of the gods, soma, in his house for the purpose of giving it to Indra. Once Indra killed Tvashtar's son in order to take Tvashtar's cows. Tvashtar got angry and would not let Indra enter his house to get the soma. Indra broke in to Tvashtar's house and took the ambrosia by force.

Vishvakarma and the Horse's Head

Once the demon, Hayagriva, did intense austerities and received a boon from the goddess that he could never be killed, except by someone with the head of a horse. This made him very confident and egotistical and he started making problems for righteous people and also for the gods. As a result, Mahavishnu decided to kill him. Because of the boon, however, Mahavishnu and all the gods could not defeat Hayagriva. After many years of intense fighting, Mahavishnu became very tired and decided to rest. In order to wake him up, Brahma created termites and put them at the end of Mahavishnu's bow, which was laying beside him as he slept. When the termites ate the end of the bow, the bowstring snapped so hard that it hit Mahavishnu and cut off his head. Vishvakarma cut off a horse's head and placed it on Vishnu. In this way Vishnu was able to defeat Hayagriva. Note: Mahavishnu is part of the Vedic trinity of Brahma, Vishnu and Shiva. He expresses himself as the principle of maintenance and re-establishment of dharma or righteousness. In the story, Vishvakarma provides the necessary structure (tool) through which Vishnu expresses himself.

Vishvakarma Curses his Daughter

Vishvakarma's daughter, Citrangada, was once bathing in a river, when a young and handsome prince came down to the river. It was love at first sight. So in spite of the advice of her servants, she let the prince seduce her. When Vishvakarma found out, he cursed his daughter saying, "Because you have swerved from the path of righteousness, you will not have a husband or a child in your lifetime." With this the Saraswati River rose up and dragged the prince a long way down the river. When this happened, Citrangada fainted. When she awoke, she jumped into the river and was swept away. The current carried her deep into the forest. A celestial being who was traveling through the sky saw Citrangada and asked her what she was doing in the middle of such a dangerous forest. When she told him, he told her to go to a certain temple and seek help from the presiding deity. She did this, and as soon as she was finished with her oblations, a hermit who knew the mantras of Samaveda came to her and asked her what happened. When she told him, the hermit got angry and cursed Vishvakarma saying, "Let Vishvakarma, who has behaved in such a cruel way toward his own daughter, become a monkey!" For this reason, Vishvakarma spent hundreds of years as a huge monkey, making mischief in the forests. After many adventures and a great deal of mischief, Vishvakarma was allowed to regain his original form on the condition that he first father a son by a celestial nymph named Ghrtaci. He gladly obeyed and had a son, Nala. Nala was later the monkey who built the bridge to Lanka which helped Rama (an incarnation of Vishnu) retrieve Sita and slay Ravana, thus re-establishing dharma.

Note: The desire for righteousness sometimes takes the form of self-righteousness, which has its own consequences. In the end, however, even self-righteousness can sometimes serve the cause of supporting dharma. "All's well that ends well," yet too much adherence to structure and form can cause a person to miss the spirit of the truth.

Vishvakarma, as Nala, Builds a Bridge for Rama

Nala, the monkey king, is said to be a partial incarnation of Vishvakarma. In the *Ramayana*, when Rama was trying to cross the ocean to Sri Lanka to rescue Sita, Nala helped him. Nala had the ability to float stones on the water by chanting the name of Rama. He built a bridge for Rama by floating stone after stone out into the ocean toward Sri Lanka.

15. Swati (6° 40' Libra - 20° 00' Libra)

Meaning: "the independent one"
Symbol: a young sprout or shoot swaying in the wind
Shakti: the power to scatter like the wind (pradhvamsa shakti)
Basis above: movement in different directions
Basis below: changing form
Desire: to have the freedom to move as I wish in all the worlds

Deity: Vayu (deified wind). Wind is said to be the breath of the gods. Vayu represents divine breath. He is the fundamental element of speech. He is an explorer, a wanderer and the messenger of the gods who leads their sacrifices. He is also considered to be a purifier. Another meaning for Vayu is "pervader." He is considered to be all-powerful. Without Vayu, a person cannot live. He is also considered to be the king of the celestial musicians. He rules the Northwest direction.

Interpretation: Swati people are independent. Like the sprout, the symbol of the nakshatra, they grow slowly but surely into their individualized form, persevering against the elements. In the beginning, they sometimes experience wavering, uncertainty, indecisiveness or self-doubt. Sometimes the Swati person's attempt at creating a new beginning appears tenuous or even futile. Nevertheless, Swati's strength lies in perseverance. Continuing their efforts over a long period of time often gives them the success they desire.

Like the young sprout, the Swati person is sensitive. And like the deity, Vayu, the king of the celestial musicians, the Swati person usually loves music and sometimes shows talent in this direction. Saraswati, a goddess related to knowledge and music is also sometimes associated with this nakshatra, so Swati people have a double dose of aptitude for creative and artistic pursuits.

This nakshatra is restless, like the wind, so Swati people like to travel and wander freely, whether in the world or in the mind. This nakshatra is related to speech, so Swati-types are communicators. They are messengers as well, and enjoy sharing the stories of their various wanderings. They are also naturally connected to the breath and can benefit from anything that helps to regulate breathing such as pranayama, deep breathing and aerobics. Malefics placed in Swati, if supported by other afflictions to the second house, can suggest bad breath or harsh speech, while benefics will suggest sweet speech and/or fresh breath. Also, Swati people tend to have "windy" problems, such as gas or belching, and other issues that are connected to vata in Ayurveda.

The shakti of this constellation is the power to scatter like the wind, so Swati has a scattering effect on the planets placed within it. Mars placed here, for example, may create unfocused or scattered actions. Having a planet that represents a particular relative located in Swati, may make that relative a vata type, and in some cases the person may be unfocused, scattered, or ungrounded.

Stories Related to Swati:

Vayu Blows the Top off Mount Meru

Narada once asked the wind to blow off the summit of Mount Meru, so Vayu blew up a storm that lasted for a year. But Vishnu's bird, Garuda (wings of speech), shielded the mountain from the wind. Then Vishnu suggested that Vayu try again after the bird was gone. He did this, and he blew off the top of the mountain. It landed in the sea and became the island of Ceylon.

Vayu and the Silk-Cotton Tree

In ancient times, a silk-cotton tree grew high in the Himalayas. It had grown to be quite large and its branches sprawled out in all directions. As a result, birds nested in its branches, monks rested in its shade and the tree began to feel conceited. One day, the great sage, Narada, came by and noticing the magnificent tree, he praised it saying, "How wonderfully big and sturdy this tree is. Even the storms do not move it!" This caused the tree's ego to swell even more and he said, "You are right, the storms are my servants."

Later, Narada related this comment to Vayu. Vayu became furious and went to the tree and said, "You stupid tree, you think that I am afraid of you and that this is why I keep still when I am around you. Nothing could be further from the truth. What really happened was that in the old days when Brahma was creating the universe, he rested for a while under your branches. This is why I have given you special consideration. But if you still believe that you are so powerful, come and fight me!" The tree became indignant and accepted Vayu's challenge.

The next day the fight began. Vayu changed into a storm and blew all the leaves, flowers and fruits off the tree. As a result, the tree stood bare and humiliated. His pride was curbed.

Note: Bhisma told this story to Yudhisthira in the *Mahabharata*. He was using it as an example to demonstrate that if you give help to your enemy, he will only become arrogant. However, in the context of the constellation of Swati, a slightly different meaning can be derived from the story. The young sprout swaying in the wind, the symbol of the constellation, represents initial doubts. The gigantic tree in this story shows the possibilities inherent in the tenuous beginnings symbolized by the sprout. It sometimes happens, though, that a person who starts out lacking confidence becomes successful, only to later become arrogant, which is the flip side of an unhealthy ego. Perhaps the story illustrates an important principle that contains valuable "food for thought" for the Swati person. Even though time may change the young, insecure sapling into a giant tree, it is wise for the tree to remain conscious that he is, ultimately, the servant of the Divine, and not the other way around.

Shiva's Hair

Shiva's hair is said to be Vayu, who is supposed to be a form of Soma. It is the mythological source of the Ganges River, which represents the offering of soma that comes from Shiva's head.

16. Vishakha (20° 00' Libra - 3° 20' Scorpio)

Meaning: "the forked one"
Alternative name and meaning: Radha, "the delightful one"
Symbol: a gateway covered with leaves
Shakti: the power to achieve many goals in life (vyapana shakti)
Basis above: to cultivate
Basis below: reaping the harvest *[handwritten: may be farmers or gardeners or from farm families]*
Desire: to gain the greatest splendor among the gods

Deity: Indragni is actually a pair of deities; Indra, the king of the gods, and Agni, the fire god. Agni represents the pure fire of consciousness within everything. He is the chief deity among the elements (Vasus). Indra is might personified. He is the all-powerful ruler of heaven. Indra represents the manifestation of outer power. Indragni links Indra to his fiery source and symbolizes awesome might, force and power. (For more about Agni, see Krittika nakshatra. For more about Indra, see Jyeshtha nakshatra.) Through worshipping Indragni, one becomes brilliant, intelligent, strong, healthy and beautiful.

Interpretation: Vishakha, "the forked," symbolizes two optional routes, like a "fork in the road." Down one road, Vishakha gives incredible power. It suggests the potential for great achievement and success. The gateway is a symbol of this success. The power of Indra is the power of the thunderbolt. This allows Vishakha people to express their ambition with great force. Sometimes this takes the form of vanquishing an opponent or competitor while in pursuit of personal success and glory. Vishakha people have a strong desire to be the most successful among their peers. The second road leads Vishakha to the ritual fire, Agni. From the ancient Vedic point of view, the entire universe is a ritual sacrifice. Agni is the purifying, burning fire of consciousness, through which the Vishakha person makes his life a ritual of surrender, detachment, and austerity. Instead of personal ambition for worldly success, he becomes consumed by a one-pointed desire for freedom. His ambitious energy is redirected toward the goal of burning the seeds of ignorance in the fire of knowledge. This type of Vishakha person can also experience great achievement, but the fruits come in the form of spiritual awareness, insight and knowledge.

In either case, Vishakha people tend to succeed by their own efforts and power. Vishakhas love the truth and they pursue it courageously. They are courageous in other ways as well, often willing to go beyond physical, emotional and mental boundaries in order to accomplish their goal. They are intense, and often suffer from isolation and alienation. This may be partially due to their tendency to disregard the feelings of others for the sake of their ambitions.

In spite of their self-reliant and competitive approach to achievement, Vishakha people have a strong desire to partner. Indragni, the deity of the nakshatra, is a dimorphic pair, two gods in one body. Vishakha people are usually very concerned about their partnerships and relationships. They are intense and passionate, and sometimes this brings volatility in their relationships.

Stories Related to Vishakha:

Radha and Mythology

The alternative name for this nakshatra is Radha, who was the playmate, lover and ultimate devotee of Krishna. The name, Radha, is related to success and achievement, the shakti of this nakshatra. Radha's relationship with Krishna was also a very passionate one, which is reflected in the fiery power and intense relationship-orientation of the constellation.

Radha and Krishna Make Love

Once Krishna met Radha at Rasamandala and they made love for one day of Brahma. Then Krishna picked a good astrological time and discharged his semen into Radha's womb. Radha was very tired because all the lovemaking. She was also shaken up due to receiving Krishna's hot semen. So she started to perspire and breathe very slowly. As a result, her sweat covered the whole universe. Her sighs became the Goddess of the Life-Giving Breaths of all created animals.

For more information on Vishakha, see the stories under Indra (Jyeshtha nakshatra) and Agni (Krittika nakshatra).

17. Anuradha (3° 20' Scorpio -16° 40' Scorpio)

Meaning: "additional Radha"
Symbol: a gateway covered with leaves, a lotus, or a staff
Shakti: the power of worship (radhana shakti)
Basis above: to ascend
Basis below: to descend
Desire: to be regarded as a friend in all the worlds

Deity: Mitra rules the bond of friendship. In ancient times, friendship was considered to be the highest of all virtues. Mitra embodies the sacred commitment of giving one's word. He is warm and benevolent, yet he makes men honor their promises, commitments and contracts. These commitments and contracts make it possible for people to live together in social groups. He is an enemy of violence or disputes. Mitra was married to Revati (prosperity).

Interpretation: Anuradha is a nakshatra of friendship, and gives the capacity for understanding human relationships to whomever it influences. If focal planets are placed here, the person will honor his commitments and will also expect others to do the same. "My word is my bond" might be an appropriate slogan for this nakshatra. The Anuradha person is a natural and reliable friend. He is goal-oriented, like the Vishakha person, but instead of accomplishing his goals by sheer force of will, he gains success through the alliances and friendships he creates along the way. Anuradha gives leadership abilities as well as the ability to work in teams. It also gives the person a natural tendency to prefer to work with a partner. Similarly, the Anuradha person prefers marriage to being single, and understands the commitments involved in marital bonding.

The relationship of Anuradha to Radha, the consort of Krishna, suggests success. Radha means "success." It also suggests the pleasure of sharing in relationship and the creative fulfillment that results. Krishna wanted to be able to experience the pleasure of love, but he couldn't because he was alone. So he manifested himself in dual form. The story of Radha and Krishna is the story of the union of Supreme Man (Purusha) with Nature (Prakriti) and the resultant birth and evolution of the universe.

Other qualities associated with this nakshatra are wealth, living far from one's birthplace, travel, and wandering.

Stories Related to Anuradha:

Mitra, Varuna and the Nymph

Mitra and Varuna (the god of the sea) were always together. In fact their spirits shared the same body. One day they saw a celestial nymph named Urvasi. They both got excited and separated into two different bodies. Varuna made advances toward Urvasi, but she rejected him. Instead, she accepted Mitra and had intercourse with him. But Varuna was still lusting after Urvasi. In the heat of his desire he had a seminal discharge. The semen was kept in a kumbha (pot). When Urvasi saw this, she was filled with both sympathy and passion, causing the semen in her womb to ooze out and fall on the ground. This was also taken and put in the same pot as Varuna's semen. Out of this pot, Vasistha and Agastya, two great sages were born.

Mitra and the Nectar of Vitality

Once a great king named Prithu saw that the earth had lost dharma, so he became upset. He decided to destroy the world. The earth became afraid, took the form of a cow and ran away. The king chased the cow for a long time until it finally gave up the chase and surrendered itself to the king. Then the king asked the cow to take care of the needs of all beings. The cow agreed. Then various gods came and milked the cow, producing lots of good things like grains, virtue, and silver. Mitra was one of the gods who milked the cow. When he milked it, the cow produced the nectar of vitality in a pot of gold.

Another Radha

Even though the deity of this nakshatra is Mitra, the name Anuradha means "additional Radha" or "after Radha." So an understanding of Radha can be helpful in understanding the nakshatra. In Anuradha, myths depicting Radha as the embodiment of devotion are probably the most appropriate.

18. Jyeshtha (16° 40' Scorpio – 30° 00' Scorpio)

Meaning: "the eldest"
Symbol: a circular talisman, also an earring
Shakti: the power to rise, overcome, conquer (arohana shakti)
Basis above: to attack
Basis below: to defend
Desire: to gain supremacy among the gods

Deity: Indra, the king of the gods, the ruler of the heavens. He throws the thunderbolts during storms. He is the companion of Vayu, the wind. He is "might" personified. He is also perpetually young looking. He is the great and generous hero. As the ultimate warrior, he is both aggressive and willing to be of service, but he is not afraid to use force, if necessary, in order to prevail. His arrows are the thunderbolts and his bow is the rainbow. Indra loves his pleasures. He gets intoxicated drinking soma. He also likes to dance. He steals the soma from his father and goes out and performs great deeds. He is a great lover, who has many sexual encounters. He is passionate and frequently commits adultery. He is symbolized by a bull. His place is in the East. Arjuna, the hero of the *Mahabharata*, is said to be a partial incarnation of Indra.

Interpretation: Jyeshtha is the constellation of seniority and authority. People born in this nakshatra have leadership ability and frequently occupy positions of authority. They also have a sense of their own power. Like Indra's thunderbolt, this power can be used for good or for personal gain. As in many of the myths about Indra, however, the personal use of power without regard for others has serious consequences. The sense of power can bring ego and self-importance. As in the story about Durvasas, the Jyeshtha person must be ever conscious of the impact of his power and charisma on those around him. He must remember to show proper appreciation to those who serve and revere him.

Jyeshtha is a sign of sexual potency and power. This can be used for good or ill. If the Jyeshtha person learns to conserve and channel this power it becomes the key to knowledge, success and wisdom. If he becomes a seducer, he only produces suffering and loneliness for himself.

Other Indra-like qualities associated with Jyeshtha include courage, enthusiasm, exuberant energy, fame, and daring. Jyeshtha people desire to reign supreme among their peers. As mentioned in several myths, this nakshatra can also occasionally be associated with financial losses, setbacks, and later recovery. Ultimately, however, nothing can really keep the Jyeshtha person down. Even when they occasionally find life leading them into the "belly of the serpent" (see the story of Indra in the "Belly of the Serpent" that follows), they have a unique ability to emerge unharmed. They are naturally "protected," as the symbol of this nakshatra suggests.

Stories Related to Jyeshtha:

Indra Seduces the Wife of a Saint

Mukunda, the wife of a great seer, was attracted to a king named Rukmangada. So Indra disguised himself as King Rukmangada in order to seduce Mukunda. He succeeded in seducing her, but he caused himself great suffering as a result.

Indra, The Thousand-Eyed One

Indra also seduced the wife of Sage Gautama. The Sage, in turn, threw his wife out of the house, made her invisible, and then cursed Indra. His curse caused Indra to have a thousand vaginas covering his body. In order to overcome the curse, he had to perform spiritual practices for many years. As a result of his penance, the vaginas became eyes, so Indra is now called "the thousand-eyed one."

Indra Insults a Great Sage

Durvasas, a great sage, gave Indra a garland. Indra made light of it, and the sage was insulted so he cursed Indra. As a result, Indra was defeated in a battle and became so impoverished that he even had to beg for butter. In the end, those who had beaten him in the battle became inattentive to their duties and Indra recovered his possessions.

Indra, the First Teacher of *Yajur Veda*

Indra was celibate for many years. As a result he was able to achieve supreme knowledge. Through Indra, spiritual knowledge was brought into the human world. He became the first teacher of the *Yajur Veda*. He also brought us the science of healing.

Indra in the Belly of the Serpent

Once Indra, the king of the gods, and Vritra, the king of the serpents, fought a great battle. Vritra threw a huge bludgeon made of black iron at Indra. Indra threw a bolt made of a hundred joints and destroyed the bludgeon as well as Vritra's hand. Vritra came at Indra with his jaw opened so wide that the lower part touched the earth and upper part touched the heavens. With his jaw open, he flicked out his serpent-tongue and bared his huge fangs. He looked like the god of death, swallowing the three worlds as he swallowed both Indra and his elephant Airavata.

When the gods, sages and protectors of the worlds saw this, they cried out loud, "Oh no! How unfortunate." It seemed that all was lost. The king of the gods had been swallowed by a serpent of seemingly infinite strength and power.

Indra, however, was not afraid. He was protected by a special blessing from Lord Narayana called the Narayana Kavacha. Because of this yogic power, he stayed alive in the belly of the serpent. Then in one powerful stroke, he ripped open the stomach of the demon and emerged unharmed. He quickly cut off Vritra's head, and then began to slice his neck up and down on all sides. It took 360 days for Vritra to completely fall to the ground and die, which is the number of days it took the Sun to complete its course in those days.

The Narayana Kavacha can be invoked through the use of mantras to Lord Vishnu. Although the Vedic ritual for this purpose is more involved, one can invoke this protective energy simply by chanting the mantra "Om Namo Narayanaya" and "Om Visnave Namah." At the same time, visualize and feel that you are surrounded by the protective energy of lord Vishnu.

19. Mula (0° 00' Sagittarius - 13° 20' Sagittarius)

Meaning:	"the root"
Symbol:	tied up roots
Shakti:	the power to destroy or damage (barhana shakti)
Basis above:	to break
Basis below:	to crush
Desire:	to find the root of all progeny

Deity: Nirriti (misery), also Prajapati, (the lord of progeny). Nirriti is a form of the deity Dhumavati (the smoky goddess), who represents the dissolution of all things at the end of the universe. She rules witchcraft and magical powers. She is the daughter of Adharma (non-righteousness). She also protects people who are mentally or physically disabled. She rules over poverty, frustration, despair, and misfortune. Her direction is the Southwest. In later myths she was replaced by Kali, the consort of Shiva, who scares away the demons, thereby removing suffering and ignorance from the world. She dispels fear, rules over time and also sleep.

Interpretation: Mula is a constellation at the center of the Milky Way galaxy, so Mula people have the tendency to go to the very core or center of things. This enables them to become intensely and deeply interested in their chosen subject. They can become researchers, investigators or philosophers. They may also take an interest in the occult, or any subject that can potentially uncover secret knowledge.

The roots in the symbol are tied up, so Mula symbolizes the concept of binding or tying things together. Mula people sometimes do well in occupations that involve bundling, bunching, tying, and binding. Sometimes they tie things together figuratively, as in tying together ideas, so they can be good at grouping and organizing.

As the deity, Nirriti, suggests, Mula is a nakshatra that can be associated with problems, losses and disappointments of different kinds. Although Mula people sometimes become wealthy, this nakshatra is usually problematic for financial matters, so Mula people should not borrow or loan money. Nirriti, however, can also protect the Mula person from various types of problems. For this, righteous living, charity and strict non-violence (ahimsa) are required. Sometimes, the Mula person experiences a sense of utter loss and dissolution at some point in life. In many cases, this becomes a catalyst for deep spiritual surrender and acceptance, leading to righteous living and the re-establishment of material equilibrium. However, many Mula people naturally tread a narrow path of right living and virtue. These types tend to become more successful as a rule. Wealth and abundance are not outside the grasp of people who have dominant planets in this nakshatra, provided they take care to remain in Nirriti's graces.

Nirriti, who became Kali in later mythology, is one of the most misunderstood goddesses in the Hindu pantheon. Normally she is thought of as a goddess of misery and suffering. In fact, she is a goddess who protects and heals people who are going through misery and suffering. As a result, Mula has deep healing energy. The roots, which symbolize this nakshatra, can be understood as representing medicinal herbs. Mula people sometimes become successful herbalists, Ayurvedic practitioners, psychologists, crisis counselors, or emergency room doctors. They also pursue other occupations that help remove the misery of others.

Like Kali, the Mula person is not afraid of looking fear in the face and scaring it away. Mula prominent in the chart suggests that the person is a warrior by nature. Sometimes this is difficult for female Mula-types to accept. Females are programmed by the culture to be sweet and gentle. In spite of the evolution of consciousness regarding female gender stereotyping in recent decades, assertive or angry females are still not acceptable in our culture. Females with Mula prominent in their charts commonly try to hide or suppress this side of themselves, sometimes feeling that there is something secretly wrong. In fact, the best way to find peace with this placement is simply to claim and become the inner warrior, the inner Kali.

Although this nakshatra is usually associated with Nirriti or Kali, it has ancient connections to Prajapati, the Creator. This gives the Mula person the desire to procreate, producing a healthy dose of sexual energy and creative energy. In the creative (or procreative) realm, however, they are looking for a profound experience to link them to the core or root of creative energy.

Stories Related to Mula:

Kali Dances on the Battlefield

Once the gods got into a great battle with the demons, and were being defeated. So they ran to Shiva and asked him to help. Shiva became upset and commanded Karttikeya, the god of war, to go help. He also sent Kali into the battle. They say Kali's eyes looked like red lotuses as she fought the demons. She took ten million elephants and men into her hand, laughed and put them in her mouth. Later in the same battle, Karttikeya was wounded and fell unconscious. Kali took him on her lap and brought him near Shiva. Shiva revived him. Then Kali went back to the battlefield and roared like a lion. She laughed wildly, taunting the demons. Then she grew fangs, took off all her clothes, drank wine and danced on the battlefield. In this form she ate the demons' flesh and drank their blood.

Note: In mythology Kali is depicted as dancing on the battlefield and laughing. This symbolizes her supreme power over everything in the universe. With one of her four hands she removes fear. With another she gives true happiness, which can only be realized when fear is totally conquered. She is also usually naked which represents the "nakedness" that is unveiled when all things in the material universe ultimately dissolve. She is black, which is the absence of color, symbolizing the void, the transcendental abyss where no relative quality can exist. She is the ultimate reality, completely beyond duality.

Nirriti and Lakshmi

At the churning of oceans, Nirriti appeared first. Then Lakshmi, the goddess of fortune, finally rose from the ocean. Nirriti is older than Lakshmi. Legend has it that Nirriti lives in a sacred fig tree called the pippala tree. Every Saturday, Lakshmi comes to visit her and pay her respects.

20. Purva Ashadha (13° 20' Sagittarius - 26° 40' Sagittarius)

Meaning: "the former undefeated" also "early victory"

Symbol: a winnowing basket (used for separating grain from the husk)

Shakti: the power to invigorate or energize (varchograhana shakti)

Basis above: strength

Basis below: connection

Desire: to gain the sea upon wishing for it

Deity: Apas, (deified water). It represents all pervasiveness, flexibility, patience, invincibility, and creative energy.

Interpretation: This constellation represents success and victory. Those born with focal planets here tend to succeed quickly. They also have the patience necessary for longer perseverance. Like water, they flow around obstacles, into all the nooks and crannies, eventually overcoming all odds. Also like water (or semen), they have a reservoir of creative energy. This creativity can take traditional forms, such as artistic or musical talent, or simply the ability to creatively solve problems. It also gives them a strong procreative urge and sex drive, which may be why they seem to be lucky in attracting a loving spouse and good friends. Purva Ashadha people usually have a strong attraction to water and a desire to be near it. The desire of the constellation is "to achieve the ocean at a wish," which might be interpreted literally, giving a desire to live near the water or to participate in water activities. This can also be interpreted symbolically, indicating a spiritual desire to merge with the transcendent ocean of pure consciousness.

The winnowing basket symbolizes the quality of discrimination.

NAKSHATRAS

[handwritten: They were two of a kind. Megan is Ascendent in Bharani, Yama, her deity is the judge]

"Separating the wheat from the chaff" is a strength of Purva Ashadha people. They have the ability to judge good and bad, positive and negative, desirable and undesirable. This gives them the ability to make choices that enhance and support their lives, contributing to their success in life. On the other hand, this same tendency sometimes takes the form of prejudice, elitism, self-righteousness, or religious dogmatism. This side of Purva Ashadha has given it a reputation for starting wars (or simply arguments).

The shakti of this nakshatra is the power to energize. Purva Ashadha people tend to invigorate and energize whatever they contact. The medium for transmitting this energy may be indicated by specific connections in the chart. The ruler of the third house (the hands) placed here, for example, might give the ability to energize through the hands. Similarly, a key planet, placed in the fourth house in this constellation, can give the person an ability to energize homes or environments through activities such as interior design, gardening, Vastu, or Feng Shui.

Stories Related to Purva Ashadha:

In the Beginning

"This existence desired, 'May I be many and procreate'; and he created the Fire-That-Is-Thought (tejas). This Fire wished, 'May I be many and procreate' and from it the causal waters (ap) appeared. Therefore, when men are warm, they perspire. From heat springs forth water. This water wished, 'May I be many and procreate,' and it gave birth to food grains. Therefore, when it rains food grains multiply." (*Chandogya Upanishad* 6.2.3-4. {463})

"The Lord of progeny (praja-pati), verily, was longing for issue. He warmed himself. Having warmed himself, he produced a pair, water (semen) and breath, thinking, 'These will procreate for me many kinds of beings. The Sun, verily, is his breath of life; The Moon, indeed, is these waters. From the waters everything is made, both what is manifest and what is unmanifest. Therefore, all manifestation is water.' " (*Prasna Upanishad* 1.4-5. {464} Alain Danielou, *Myths and Gods of India*)

21. Uttara Ashadha (26° 40' Sagittarius - 10° 00' Capricorn)

Meaning: "the latter undefeated" or "later victory"
Symbol: the tusk of an elephant
Shakti: the power to give an unstoppable victory (apradhrisya shakti)
Basis above: the strength to win
Basis below: the goal that can be won
Desire: to gain victory that can never be lost

Deity: The ten Visvadevas. They are the Ten Universal Principles, the sons of Dharma and the Goddess, Vishva. Their names are Goodness, Truth, Will Power, Skillfulness, Time, Desire, Firmness, Ancestor, Brightness, and Summit.

Interpretation: Uttara Ashadha, like Purva Ashadha, is a nakshatra of victory. In this case "later victory" suggests more patience and perseverance than the previous nakshatra. The tusk of the elephant, the symbol for this nakshatra, suggests a connection to Ganesha, the elephant-headed god who is worshiped at the beginning of all new ventures as the remover of obstacles. Ganesha's blessing assures success. The symbol evokes an image of great power for accomplishing any undertaking. This symbol, coupled with the basic desire and shakti of the constellation, gives the Uttara Ashadha person a tendency to achieve success that endures.

The deities of Uttara Ashadha, the Visvadevas, suggest a wide range of qualities necessary for success in life. Uttara Ashadha people usually have strong desire, backed up by strong will, mental brightness, power, skill, and patience over time. This formula brings them to the summit or fulfillment of their desires. They become successful and prosperous. In the process of achieving their goals, they naturally respect and show gratitude for the traditions of the past, their predecessors and elders. They have many friends. They also have a strong sense of purpose or duty in life.

Ganesha is depicted as having a single tusk. The number "one" symbolizes maya, the relative material world. The tusk itself is a symbol of the absolute, un-manifest reality. So the single tusk represents both the manifest and the un-manifest simultaneously. Through this symbol, the Uttara Ashadha person is challenged to live, act and succeed in the world while remaining unattached, constantly absorbed in transcendent being.

Stories Related to Uttara Ashadha:

Brahma Tells Daksha to Procreate

One of the most important of the Visvadevas is Daksha (ritual skill), who is also called the lord of progeny. Brahma ordered Daksha to procreate. Attempting to comply with Brahma's wish, Daksha mentally produced ten thousand sons. In turn, Daksha told them also to procreate. But Narada talked them into renouncing the world and becoming celibates. So Daksha produced another ten thousand sons. But they also followed Narada and became celibates. This time Daksha got mad and cursed Narada saying that from this time onward Narada would never stay in one place. After that, Brahma got Daksha to calm down, and Daksha decided to try physical procreation. So he and his wife, Asini, had sixty daughters. Thirteen of these daughters were married to Kasyapa (vision). These daughters in turn were the mothers of all living beings on earth.

Lust Tries to Distract Shiva

Another important Visvadeva is Kama (lust). Once Kama was sent by the gods to get Shiva out of his meditation because they were afraid of Taraka, a demon who had become too powerful. Shiva got angry when Kama disturbed him and sent a flash of fire out of his third eye. So Kama became disembodied and was reborn as the son of Krishna.

Ganesha

Even though this nakshatra is ruled by the Vishvadevas, the elephant tusk symbol creates a relationship to Ganesha, the elephant-headed god.

Ganesha is Born and Loses His Head

Parvati (Shiva's consort) was taking a bath. She was rubbing her body, but worrying that she didn't have a servant to guard the door. Some of the scales from her skin, which were floating in the water, gathered together and formed into a baby. She called him Ganapati (Ganesha) and told him to guard the door for her. Later, Shiva wanted to come into the house and Ganapati tried to keep him out. Shiva sent his attendants against Ganapati. There was a battle and Ganapati's head was cut off. Parvati was very sad about this, so Shiva cut off the head of the first living being that passed by, which happened to be an elephant, and put it on Ganapati's body.

Ganesha as the Remover of Obstacles

Once a great prince named Abhinandana had a great ritual sacrifice to which he invited all the gods except Indra (the king of the gods). Indra got angry and told Time to stop the ritual. Time became a demon named Obstruction, who was the embodiment of blockages and obstacles. He not only interfered with Abhinandana's ritual offering, but also went on a rampage, obstructing other ritual sacrifices wherever he went throughout the world. The great sage, Vasishta, asked Brahma (the Creator) what to do about Obstruction. Brahma told him to pray to Ganesha to conquer obstruction, because the only one who is beyond Time is Ganesha, and no one can conquer him. Ganesha conquered Obstruction, who in turn put himself under the protection of Ganesha and from that time on has been his servant. This is how Ganesha became associated with the removal of obstacles and why he is worshiped before starting any new work.

22. Shravana (10° 00' Capricorn - 23° 20' Capricorn)

Meaning: "the ear"
Symbol: three footprints
Shakti: the power to connect (samhanana shakti)
Basis above: seeking
Basis below: paths
Desire: to hear people say good things about me

Deity: Vishnu (the pervader). He is said to hold the universe together. He dwells in everything. He is the principle of duration. He is the universal intellect, the planner of the universe. The moral codes and theologies of religion that keep life in order are related to Vishnu. He rules sattva guna, the cohesive tendency. He is represented with four arms that are related to the four directions, the four aims of life (kama, artha, dharma, and moksha), the four castes, the four ages of human history, and the four *Vedas*. He rides on a great bird named Garuda (wings of speech), whose body is said to be *Sama Veda*.

Interpretation: Shravana is a nakshatra of listening. It rules oral communications of all kinds. Those who have focal planets placed here tend to be talkative and frequently become articulate, effective speakers, as well as good listeners. Shravana people have a great capacity to learn and an ability to develop wisdom in life.

Vishnu, the deity of Shravana, brings an interest in religion and theology, especially those that have oral traditions. Hence, Shravana people become virtuous, knowledgeable, and philosophical. They also tend to become prosperous and famous. This nakshatra gives the ability to link or connect diverse elements, such as concepts, people, or things.

The footprint symbolizes walking. Shravana people like walking, hiking, running, and traveling in general. If the ruler of the ninth house is placed in this nakshatra, for example, the person may travel around the world, just as Mahabali covered the three worlds in three strides. By the same token, if the lagna lord or any of the significators of the feet or legs is afflicted in this nakshatra, the possibility of limping (even if only temporarily) arises. One translation of the name Shravana means "to limp." Limping is an uneven or unbalanced form of conveyance. Expanding this idea, if the ruler of the fourth house (car) is afflicted and in Sravana, there might be a tendency for the person's car to run unevenly or to have a flat tire during that planet's dasha.

The three footprints, which symbolize this nakshatra, also make the myth of Vamana particularly important to the Shravana person. In the story, Vamana restored order and balance to the Universe by kicking the demons out of heaven and putting the gods back in heaven. The gods symbolize the highest values in life such as spirituality, ethics, morality, and virtue. The demons represent basic desires such as greed, ambition, lust, and pride. The myth shows the capacity of the Sravana person to restore order and balance to life by re-establishing his highest ideal as a priority.

If the ruler of the tenth house is placed in Sravana, for example, the person might "kick the demons out of heaven" through remodeling his career. Sometimes this means quitting a job where greed and ambition are the leading motivations in order to pursue work where higher motivations rule. In another senario, the person could cut back on his work hours in order to give more attention to family, spirituality, health or other domains of life, thus creating greater balance in life. A key planet placed in Shravana in the seventh house can bring about a revamping of priorities in the area of marriage. The person "kicks the demons out of heaven" by getting rid of a relationship that is based on lower motivations, rather than selflessness and unconditional love. This placement could also suggest that the spouse likes to run, walk, bike or hike, and expresses other Shravana traits as well.

Dramatic metamorphosis for the purpose of creating greater balance is not always a necessary element of Shravana. The Shravana person sometimes practices the art of maintaining priorities as a constant feature of life. Instead of overthrowing a relationship or a career because ideals and priorities have been undermined by more basic desires, the attentive Shravana person constantly reprioritizes in small doses. Ever vigilant to stay true to his highest good, he weeds the garden of his career, relationship, health, and spiritual program daily. He always remembers what is really important and lets those values guide his life.

Shravana people like to have good reputations and are often well liked or popular in some way. This stems from the basic desire of the nakshatra, which is "to hear people say good things about me." The Shravana person often actively participates in building his reputation and creating his own fame. In negative cases, however, the person becomes overly concerned with his reputation and image. Whether the desire for good reputation expresses itself in a negative or positive way, of course, depends on the disposition of multiple factors in the chart.

Stories Related to Shravana:

Vamana, the Dwarf Incarnation of Vishnu, and His "Three Footsteps"

Long ago, Mahabali, the king of the demons, conquered all the three worlds, heaven, earth and the underworld. The demons were living in the heavens and the gods were living in the underworld. Everything was backwards, so Aditi, the mother of all the gods, prayed to Vishnu that her sons be restored to their rightful place in the heavens. Vishnu was pleased with her prayers, so he blessed her by giving her a son who was an incarnation of Vishnu. Aditi's son was named Vamana and he was a dwarf. One day Mahabali was performing a horse sacrifice on the north bank of the Narmada River. Vamana came into the sacrificial hall holding an umbrella, a rod and a pot filled with water. Nobody knew Vamana's identity, but the priests who were performing the sacrifice were so impressed by him that they suspected that he might possibly be a god in disguise. Mahabali, who was a giant demon, looked way down at Vamana, greeted him, and told him to make a wish. Vamana said, "My dear king, you speak so sweetly. Just give me three paces of the land in your domain that I will measure with my feet. This is all I want." Mahabali was surprised to hear such an insignificant request coming from his tiny visitor, but he agreed.

Shukra (Venus), the guru of the demons, was very skeptical about Vamana, and saw through his disguise. He secretly told Mahabali not to make any promises because this person was actually Vishnu. Mahabali, however, had already given his word, and refused to go back on it. So Shukra cursed him saying, "You brag about your wisdom and learning, but you are actually a dimwit! As a result, all your prosperity will be destroyed."

Yet, even after this curse, Mahabali honored his word. His queen, Vindhyavali had brought a golden pot full of water. Mahabali took the pot and washed the feet of Vamana, who instantly began to grow. Vamana became so big that it was unimaginable, and Mahabali saw many wondrous things on his giant body such as the elements, the senses, the mind, deities and even the whole universe.

After growing so large, Vamana took the first step and covered the whole earth. With the second step he covered the rest of the three worlds. Then Vamana said, "You promised to give me three paces of land. I have taken two. But there is no more room left in the entire universe for the third step. Therefore, you cannot keep your promise to me, so you should go to the underworld." Mahabali asked Vamana to put the third step on his head, which he did, pushing Mahabali down into the underworld.

After that, Vamana brought back Indra, the king of the gods, and installed him as the ruler of heaven.

Brighu Curses Vishnu

Once the demons were defeated by the gods. Then the demons asked Brighu Maharishi's wife, Puloma, to protect them. She agreed and started doing austerities in order to destroy the gods. Vishnu saw her doing this and threw his discus at her and killed her. As a result, Brighu got very angry and cursed Vishnu saying, "Because you have killed my wife, you will have to be born as a man and suffer the pain of being separated from your wife for many years." This is why Vishnu later incarnated as Rama. The Ramayana tells the story of how his wife was stolen by the demon, Ravana, and how Rama got her back again. (For stories of Vishnu in the form of Rama, see the *Ramayana*.)

See Rohini nakshatra on Vishnu competing with Brahma.

23. Dhanishtha (23° 20' Capricorn - 6° 40' Aquarius)

Meaning: "the wealthiest"
Symbol: a musical drum
Shakti: the power to give wealth and fame (khyapayitri shakti)
Basis above: birth
Basis below: prosperity
Desire: to revolve around the summit of the gods

Deity: The eight Vasus. Vasu can be defined as "the good" or "the wealthy." It also means "that which surrounds" or "to dwell," so it signifies that which dwells in something, or that in which something dwells. The Vasus are the spheres of existence and the deities of the spheres. They are forms of Brahma, the Immense Being. The root word "vas" means "to shine." The Vasus are Earth in which Fire (digestion) resides, Space in which Wind (life) resides, Sky in which the Sun (intellect) resides, and the Constellations in which the Moon (immortality) resides.

Interpretation: As the name suggests, this constellation signifies wealth. Even though wealth can't be determined by a single factor in a horoscope, focal planets placed here give the person a natural edge in attaining prosperity. Also, planets ruling houses that signify particular relatives, if placed here, may suggest that the relative becomes prosperous. This nakshatra also rules precious things such as gemstones and other valuables.

Dhanishtha's symbol, the drum, signifies music. Hearing music, especially rhythmic music, is part of the nakshatra's domain. Related to this, an alternative name for the constellation is Sravistha, which means "the most famous." Sravistha actually comes from the verb, sru, "to hear." Hearing, of course, is an important element of music. It can also symbolize being "heard of," so it also represents reputation or fame. The basic desire of this nakshatra is "to revolve around the summit of the gods," so the Dhanishtha person aspires to the highest and most dignified position. He desires to be among the chosen few who live life in the wealthiest condition and are held in the highest esteem.

On the negative side, this constellation is sometimes related to problems in marriage. This may be more problematic in male charts, and if other indications in the chart agree, may produce a negative attitude toward women. It can also produce a sense of superiority and elitism.

Stories Related to Dhanishtha:

The Sky Incarnates As a Man

Because of a curse, the Sky had to take birth as a man, so he was born as Bhisma, the father of heroes.

The Earth Feeds a King

The Earth is considered the support of all creatures and the nourisher of life. She is represented as a goddess or as a cow that feeds all beings with her milk. The first king whose name was Prthu and who was the inventor of agriculture, forced the earth, who was reluctant, to yield her treasures and feed men.

Note: Stories of other Vasus are given under these other nakshatras: Wind (Swati), Fire (Krittika), Sun (Hasta), Moon (Mrigashira), and Water (Purva Ashadha).

24. Shatabhisha (6° 40' Aquarius - 20° 00' Aquarius)

Meaning: "possessing (or requiring) a hundred physicians"
Symbol: an empty circle
Shakti: the power of healing (bheshaja shakti)
Basis above: all-pervasiveness
Basis below: support for everything
Desire: to be firm and not unsteady

Deity: Varuna, "the coverer" or "the binder." Varuna rules the relationship of man to the gods. So he represents the mysteries and the laws of the gods. He rules the invisible, so his behavior can't be predicted. He rules magical power. He represents the inner reality of things, higher truth and order, which are beyond the understanding of man. His power comes during the night. In the *Rig Veda* he says, "I am Varuna, these magic powers were first given to me." He rules over the Adityas. He maintains natural and moral laws as expressions of cosmic order. In later texts Varuna appears as the lord of waters, ruling the sea and underground waters. He gives rain and rules over rivers. The nagas are his subjects. He is the lord of destiny and rules over the West.

Interpretation: Shatabhisha is symbolized by a circle that covers and hides, so this nakshatra represents things that are hidden or mysterious. People with focal planets here may have an interest in esoteric subjects and the occult, or they may simply have a desire to uncover hidden secrets. For this reason, Shatabhisha is sometimes found to be a prominent influence in the charts of astrologers and metaphysicians, as well as modern researchers in science or technology. Extending this symbolism, planets falling in Shatabhisha may make certain characteristics of the houses they rule mysterious or hard to uncover. On a higher level, however, Shatabhisha people strive to uncover the transcendental truths of life and to live by the natural laws that govern man's relationship to the Divine. The circle also represents a holding-in or a containing of things. The ruler of the fourth house (the home) placed in Shatabhisha, for example, might suggest that the person's house might be fenced-in or located in an enclosed or hidden place.

Varuna, the deity of this nakshatra, rules over the oceans, so this constellation brings an affinity for water, the ocean, rivers and lakes. It brings other connections to water as well. Malefics in this nakshatra, however, sometimes cause a fear of the ocean or water. This is particularly true when Rahu or Ketu are placed in Shatabhisha along with (or aspected by) Saturn or Mars.

Varuna's association with Shatabhisha also produces a natural sense of morality and cosmic law. The Shatabhisha person has a strong sense of what is right, just and fair. This gives him clarity, inner stability and integrity. He values these qualities because they make him firm and steady.

The meaning of the nakshatra, "a hundred physicians," is also noteworthy. In many cases a focal planet placed here will promote an interest in alternative healing, possibly leading the person to become a healer. In other cases the person seeks out "a hundred physicians" or takes "a hundred medicines" in the process of trying to improve health and vitality. If this nakshatra is afflicted and if other factors in the chart agree, the person sometimes gets a disease that is hard to diagnose or hard to cure. In this case the meaning, "requiring a hundred physicians," is more applicable, but may also suggest that a cure may come after trying many different healing modalities. The mysterious nature of this nakshatra suggests that resorting to healing modalities that are "magical" in some way may be helpful. The myth about Harischandra's son (see story that follows), also suggests the necessity of sacrifice (or healing crisis), as a prerequisite of healing.

The shakti of Shatabhisha is the power of healing. This not only gives the person the power to heal themselves, but the general ability to heal others. If there are other factors in the chart that agree, then the Shatabhisha person might do well in a healing profession. Usually the Shatabhi-

healer prefers to use multiple healing modalities instead of just one. He is also most effective when he asks his patients to make a sacrifice (see the Harischandra myth) or a commitment to their healing process.

Stories Related to Shatabhisha:

Varuna, Mitra, and Vasistha

Varuna initiated Vasistha, the great Vedic seer, into his mysteries. It is said that Varuna knows a hundred thousand remedies. He makes the Sun shine, the Moon walk in brightness, and the stars disappear when dawn comes. Varuna and Mitra were always found together. They jointly fathered Vasistha, who was born in a kumbha (a pot), which is the Sanskrit name for the sign of Aquarius in which this nakshatra resides.

Varuna Kidnaps Bhadra

Soma had a daughter, Bhadra, who was very beautiful. Varuna was very attracted to her, but she married Utathya, who was the son of a great sage. One day, when Utathya was gone, Varuna kidnapped Bhadra and took her away with him to his home in the ocean. When Utathya came home and found his wife missing, he went to Narada, who told him that Varuna was the culprit. Utathya asked Narada to ask Varuna to return Bhadra. Narada spoke to Varuna, but Varuna refused. As a result, Utathya flew into a rage and drank up the ocean. Varuna didn't budge. So Utathya dried up all of Varuna's lakes. At this, Varuna began shaking in fear, returned Bhadra, and bowed at the feet of Utathya. Utathya forgave him and returned his oceans and lakes.

Kasyapa Steals Varuna's Cow

Once Kasyapa wanted to perform a sacrifice. He got everything ready, but he needed a cow and wasn't able to get one in time. So he stole Varuna's cow and began his ritual. Varuna found out and went to Kasyapa and demanded that he give back the cow. Kasyapa refused. So Varuna went to Brahma to see if he could persuade Kasyapa. But Brahma was also unable to get Kasyapa to return the cow. So Brahma and Varuna cursed Kasyapa that he would have to be reborn as a caretaker of cows. As a result, Kasyapa was reborn as Vasudeva (the father of Krishna).

Varuna Tells King Harischandra to Sacrifice His Son

Harischandra, had a hundred wives, but none of them could give him a son. So he went to the Ganges River and prayed to Varuna. After some time, Varuna appeared and said that Harischandra would have a son, but in return, he must sacrifice the son as a ritual offering to Varuna. Harischandra reluctantly agreed, and soon his wife Chandramati got pregnant. When their son was born, they named him Rohitasva. Harischandra loved him very much, so he postponed giving Rohitasva to Varuna by continually making up excuses. Finally, Varuna cornered him and made him agree to turn Rohitasva over to Varuna at the age of eleven, after his sacred thread ceremony.

The boy's eleventh birthday came. Preparations were being made for the sacred thread ceremony, when Varuna arrived. Unfortunately, however, Rohitasva found out about his father's promise to Varuna and ran away. When Varuna asked Harischandra to turn over his son, Harischandra couldn't find his son. So Varuna cursed him and he got the disease called dropsy.

In a state of utter despair, Harischandra went to the great sage, Vasistha and asked him what to do to be cured. Vasistha told him that he would have to fulfill his promise to Varuna and sacrifice his son. He pointed out to Harischandra that he hadn't listened carefully Varuna's words. Varuna words were "a son" not "that son," he said. Vasistha continued, "Sons are of ten types. Sons that are purchased are also sons. So go find a Brahman who is willing to sell his son and sacrifice him to Varuna. If you please Varuna in this way you will be healed." Harischandra followed Vasistha's advice, purchased a child and sacrificed him to Varuna. In the meantime, Visvamitra had taught the poor child a Varuna mantra that he chanted during the sacrifice. In the end the child's life was spared and Harischandra was cured.

25. Purva Bhadrapada (20° 00' Aquarius - 3° 20' Pisces)

Meaning: "the front lucky feet (of a funeral bed)"
Symbol: the front end of a funeral bed
Shakti: the power of spiritual fire, which elevates consciousness (yajamana udyamana shakti)
Basis above: that which is good for people
Basis below: that which is good for the gods
Desire: to gain radiance and the splendor of spiritual knowledge

Deity: Aja Ekapada, "the one-footed goat" or the "unborn one." According to the *Vishnu Purana*, along with Ahirbudhnya, Aja Ekapada was one of the four sons of Vishvakarma. He is said to be one of the preservers of all the gold in the world. The one-footed goat symbolizes the three qualities of nature or Prakriti. He is "the unborn one," the source of life, also called "the victorious" (Jayanta) and "the divider" (Ravi). Also represented as a lifeless egg, he is the transcendent fire at the source of everything that exists in the universe. Aja Ekapada is also a form of Shiva. The one-footed goat is a symbol of both silence and motionlessness. He is also seen as a sea serpent, a symbol of the kundalini, which gives the power of elevated consciousness.

Interpretation: Purva Bhadrapada is a constellation that represents the unmanifest fire of consciousness (Aja Ekapada), which is at the basis of everything. It can therefore be related to the deepest aspect of cosmic awareness, burning within the person whose Moon or Ascendant falls in this nakshatra. The funeral cot in India is a vehicle for cremation, the final purification ritual. In this way, Purva Bhadrapada represents the fiery purification process that brings about eventual transcendental awareness. On the material level, it represents burning or heat.

This constellation brings the fire of passion and strong desires that may lead to problems in life. Its negative side suggests anger, greed, deceit, lack of generosity, nervousness, fear, and general attraction to the dark forces of life. By extension, if the constellation is afflicted, it may bring the ripening of past life karmas which produce anguish and suffering. The symbol of the funeral bed can also have an obvious relationship to death, funerals, mortuaries, mourning, and sadness.

Stories Related to Purva Bhadrapada:

Aja Ekapada stories are scarce. See the stories of other serpents under Uttara Bhadrapada and Ashlesha nakshatras.

26. Uttara Bhadrapada (3° 20' Pisces - 16° 40' Pisces)

Meaning: "the back lucky feet (of a funeral bed)"
Symbol: the back end of a funeral bed
Shakti: the power to bring rain (varshodyamana shakti)
Basis above: the raining of clouds
Basis below: the growth of planets
Desire: to find a foundation

Deity: Ahirbudhnya (the serpent of the deep) is connected with fertility of the earth and sky. Like Aja Ekapada, the deity for the previous nakshatra, he is related to Rudra, a form of Shiva. He is a son of Vishvakarma (the deity of Chitra nakshatra).

Interpretation: Like Purva Bhadrapada, this nakshatra is related to heat and burning. In fact, these two nakshatras together are sometimes called "the scorching pair" and represent things that are hot or burning. This brings a good deal of passion and desire, as well as spiritual fire to both nakshatras. The serpent of the deep symbolizes the kundalini energy, which is itself symbolized as a coiled serpent at the base of the spine. This gives the Uttara Bhadrapada person a natural ability to awaken the kundalini energy through meditation and other spiritual practices. On the mundane level, the symbol represents the tendency of the Uttara Bhadrapada person to develop a deep interest in certain subjects and to go to profound or deep levels with various pursuits. Similarly, the relationship of the deity to water brings greater ability to temper or quell the fires of passion and therefore, more benevolence is associated with this nakshatra. People with focal planets located here tend to be selfless and generous. They are also talkative, they love the ocean, they tend to have good children, and live righteous lives.

The shakti of Uttara Bhadrapada is "the power to bring the rain." This represents an ability to bring release and cleansing after a buildup of tension. Bringing the rain has emotional connotations as well. In the evaporation/condensation cycle in nature, water changes form as it evaporates from the ocean and rises to the heavens. When it finally condenses, rain returns the water to its source. This cycle is also seen in the Uttara Bhadrapada person. Here the ocean can be defined as symbolizing consciousness. The evaporation process suggests the ability to project consciousness into the heavens in the form of emotion, imagination, or inspiration. The Uttara Bhadrapada person runs on inspiration and imagination and has the ability to dream lofty dreams. Projected inspiration and imagination sometimes lacks stability, however, bringing the need to return to the self. After some time spent in the rarified air of inspirational or imaginative thinking, the Uttara Bhadrapada person may use tears and emotional release as a mechanism, which returns his awareness to the here and now. A more negative form of this cycle can bring mood swings from inspiration to sadness, along with a feeling that the alternating moods are somehow a sign that something is wrong. The person desperately holds on to inspirational states and is averted to states of sadness or depression. In the more aware Uttara Bhadrapada person, alternating moods are simply experienced as the natural cycle inspiration and release of emotion. Instead of holding on to inspiration and avoiding sadness, the person realizes that the cycle is only the inevitable play of consciousness. Their greatest desire and ultimate destination is to find a foundation, which transcends the emotional ups and downs. That foundation is the ocean of pure consciousness, realized when the kundalini (the serpent of the deep) is finally awakened.

Story Related to Uttara Bhadrapada:

Story from the *Mahabharata*

Once Duryodhana put snake poison in the food of Bhima. Bhima ate the food and then went to take a bath in the river. When the poison took effect, Bhima passed out and fell flat in the river. Then Duryodhana tied him up with ropes and put him into deeper water. Bhima sunk to the bottom where he was bitten by many water snakes. Instead of killing him, however, their poison acted as an antidote. Bhima recovered and killed the serpents. (Note: Although this story is not specifically about Ahirbudhnya, it is about serpents of the deep. In keeping with the tone of this nakshatra, the story illustrates the beneficial effect of serpent energy. When correctly channeled, Uttara Bhadrapada's energy can produce much good.)

27. Revati (16° 40' Pisces - 30° 00' Pisces)

Meaning: "wealthy"
Symbol: a drum
Shakti: the power of nourishment (kshiradyapani shakti)
Basis above: cows
Basis below: calves
Desire: to become lord of the animals

Deity: Pushan, the Nurturer, or Nourisher. He is the protector of the cattle of the gods. He gives prosperity and also symbolizes security. He protects the roads and is considered the god of safe travel. He gives good vehicles. He is also the finder of lost things and lost animals. He is worshiped by those who do magic and by those who wish to find stolen items. He is associated with semen, soma, and the chalice of immortality. He is connected with the marriage ceremony. He loved his sister, Surya (the solar one). Pushan is toothless and feeds on a type of gruel, so all oblations offered to him must be ground up.

Interpretation: Revati is a constellation that is related to prosperity. Those whose Moon or Ascendant falls in this nakshatra naturally focus on abundance. They also like to travel and tend to have good luck while traveling. Their journeys are protected and their routes are illuminated by Pushan, the god of safe travel. Also like Pushan, the Revati person tends to have a generous and protective spirit. He is willing to give nourishment, sustenance and protection to the street person, the traveler, or those in need. Pushan was also the caretaker of souls as they went from the land of the living to the land of the dead, so Revati people are good at lending support to people who are dying. They are also drawn to animals and sometimes re-enact the stories of Pushan by displaying such qualities as the ability to find lost animals, or even heal animals that are sick. Focal planets in this constellation along with a strong sixth house indicate that the person will have a pet. This is truer in cultures such as the United States, where people commonly have pets. Multiple malefic influences here can sometimes create a fear of animals or problems due to animals.

Revati also has a connection to food and nourishment. In the story that follows, Pushan's teeth were knocked out for eating the sacrificial offering. This can symbolize the need to recognize the value of discrimination regarding food, diet, and nutrition. Afflictions to health-related planets here can cause nutritional deficiencies or imbalances stemming from improper or excessive dietary habits. Understanding the value of sacrificing or sublimating the attachment to food and adopting a moderate approach to diet, can also be a key to health and happiness in the life of a Revati person. Similarly, afflictions to this nakshatra as well as to the second house can also represent dental problems.

The drum, the symbol of this nakshatra, is an instrument used for keeping time. As a result, Revati is a nakshatra related to time and other kinds of rhythmic measurements. Revati people may have a natural sense of rhythm, be musical, or like to get into a rhythm in their work. Similarly, they are better off when they establish routines that allow the natural body rhythms such as rest, sleep, eating and exercise to take place at regular intervals.

Story Related to Revati:

Shiva Breaks Pushan's Teeth

Pushan broke his teeth while eating the offering in a sacrifice held when Rudra attacked Prajapati to prevent him from committing incest with his daughter. In another version, Rudra became enraged and attacked the gods who were present at Daksha's sacrifice. First he knocked out Bhaga's eyes. Then he saw Pushan eating the offering, so he broke his teeth.

Author's Journal:

The Swami and the Dead Girl

I have always contended that the best form of astrology is that which is practiced by an enlightened astrologer, one for whom the subtle energy channels called nadis have opened. For this kind of astrologer, the chart becomes unnecessary and astrology becomes an entirely internal matter. My friend and spiritual teacher Swami Sivanandamurthy is such an astrologer. He studied astrology deeply in his teenage years and gained a reputation in his twenties and thirties as an outstanding astrologer. He practiced astrology as a form of service, not as a profession. Somewhere in his forties, after many years of meditating six hours a day, he became self-realized. After that, he gave up the practice of formal astrology.

Swamiji always enjoys talking about astrology, however, and when I visit his ashram, he usually turns the conversation towards astrological topics. On one occasion, we were walking in the garden in front of his house. He lives in a simple, but beautiful house, in a small fishing village on the east coast of India. It was a warm, starry night and we had just come back from the evening meditation in the Ganesha Temple. Swamiji looked up into the sky and said, "There is Jupiter in Revati. Look there. You will see the constellation of Purva Bhadrapada. Over here in the shape of a cart is Rohini." He effortlessly navigated the constellations giving anecdotes and astrological commentary as he went, displaying an observational astronomical prowess that is possessed by very few astrologers.

Swamiji has always encouraged me in my practice of astrology, saying that astrology is a form of sadhana. "Astrology is better for the astrologer than it is for the client," he says frequently. After many years of practice, combined with regular meditation, the astrologer no longer needs the horoscope, due to an awakening of the internal astrological nadis.

It is from this angle that I relate the following story told to me by a devotee of Swamiji. I had been talking to Swamiji one afternoon in his home. As usual, the discussion spanned a wide range of subjects. At one point, Swamiji mentioned a trip that he had taken recently to Scotland and that he had many devotees in Scotland. Immediately my curiosity was peaked. "Scotland?" I thought. "Why Scotland?" I have nothing against Scotland, in fact I think it is a very attractive country, but I had never heard of any big proliferation of Vedic culture, yoga, meditation or even New Age spirituality there. Maybe I am simply ignorant, but I simply was curious how an Indian spiritual teacher was well received in Scotland.

After the conversation was over, I cornered Swamiji's assistant and asked, "How is it that Swami Sivanandamurthy has such a big following in Scotland?" He told me that many years ago, Swamiji had a lady disciple here in India. She once asked him if she would have any children and he predicted that in a certain month and year she would have a baby girl. He told her that this girl would grow up to be healthy and happy and live a long productive life.

A few years later, the lady and her husband moved to Scotland. While they were there, the child was born exactly at the time predicted by Swamiji. When the child was three years old, however, she suddenly became seriously ill. The mother rushed her to the hospital, where she died on the emergency room table. The mother was completely confused and upset and immediately got on the phone to India. "Swamiji," she said, "my daughter has died on the emergency room table. You told me that she would live a long, happy life. How can this be?" In a gentle voice, Swamiji said, "The girl is not dead!" "But Swamiji," the mother said, "she has just been pronounced dead by the attending doctor. She is dead!" Again in a calm voice Swami Sivanandamurthy said, "Get a second opinion!"

The mother was frantic. Who could she ask? It was the middle of the night and no other physicians were in sight. She rushed down the hall of the hospital, going from room to room until she found a cardiologist. She begged the doctor to look at her child and give a second opinion. The cardiologist examined the child and told the mother that the girl was indeed dead. She begged him to do something, anything to revive her daughter. At this point nearly twenty minutes had gone by. Out of sympathy for the mother, the doctor agreed to open the chest of the girl and examine the heart. He told her that this would not bring the girl back, but might at least provide some information about the condition of the heart. The mother agreed and the doctor cut open the girl's chest, exposing the heart. Immediately, the heart began to beat again. The girl recovered fully, in spite of being clinically dead for twenty minutes.

Glossary

Aditi – mother of all the gods, primary mother goddess
Agni – Hindu deity of fire
Angular Houses – houses 1, 4, 7, & 10
Anuradha – seventeenth Nakshatra
Aprarigrah – principle of non-attachment
Aquarius – eleventh sign of the zodiac
Ardra – sixth Nakshatra
Aries – first sign of the zodiac
Artha – one of the four goals or aims of life
Artha Houses – houses 2, 6, & 10
Ascendant – Rising sign or first house, also called lagna
Ashlesha – ninth Nakshatra
Ashwini – first Nakshatra
Aspects – relationships between planets that show how planets influence each other
Ayanamsha – distance in degrees and minutes between the tropical and sidereal zodiacs
Ayurveda – the Vedic medical system, used with Vedic astrology

Bhadra Yoga – the Mahapurusha Yoga for Mercury
Bharani – second Nakshatra
Bhava – house
Bhava Chart – house chart
Brahma – the Vedic god of creation; part of the Hindu trinity
Brihaspati – Jupiter

Cancer – fourth sign of the zodiac
Capricorn – tenth sign of the zodiac
Chandra – the Moon
Chesta Bala – motional strength of a planet; used in Shadbala
Chitra – fourteenth Nakshatra
Combustion – planet closely conjunct the Sun
Conjunction – planets placed in the same sign
Constellations – a grouping of stars; another term for Nakshatras

Dashas – major planetary periods
Debilitation – the weakest sign placement for a planet

Deity – a god or goddess
Dhana Bhava – second house
Dharma Bhava – ninth house
Dharma – law, duty, or purpose; one of the four goals or aims of life
Dharma Houses – houses 1, 5, & 9
Dig Bala – directional strength of a planet; used in Shadbala
Drekkanas – one third of a sign
Drik Bala – aspect strength of a planet; used in Shadbala
Dusthana – the challenging 6, 8, or 12 houses of the horoscope
Dusthana Houses – houses 6, 8, & 12

Electional Astrology – Muhurtha, astrology to select auspicious times for events
Equanimity – state in which various positive and negative vibrations of consciousness are stilled
Exaltation – the best sign placement for a planet

Four Aims of Life – dharma (purpose), artha (material wealth), kama (desire), and moksha (spiritual freedom)

Ganesha – elephant-headed god who removes obstacles
Ganita – astronomical and astrological calculations branch of Vedic astrology
Gola – observational astrology branch of Vedic astrology
Graha – planet, means "grasper"
Guru – Jupiter; or a spiritual guide

Hamsa Yoga – the Mahapurusha Yoga for Jupiter
Hasta – thirteenth Nakshatra
Horary Astrology – Prashna; creating a chart for the time a question is asked
Houses – twelve divisions of the zodiac

Indra – king of the gods, ruler of the heavens
Indragni – the pair of deities, Indra (king of the gods) and Agni (fire god)
Ishta Devata – one's personal deity

Jaimini – Jyotishi of the past who developed a unique system of Vedic astrology
Jainism – an ascetic religion of India
Jataka – natal astrology

Jyeshtha – eighteenth Nakshatra
Jyotish – Vedic astrology, the science of light

Kala Bala – temporal strength of a planet; used in Shadbala
Kalatra Bhava – seventh house
Kali - dark form of the goddess; related to Saturn
Kali Yuga – age of darkness
Kama – desire, pleasure, affection, emotion; one of four goals or aims of life
Kama Houses – houses 3, 7, & 11
Kapha – water dosha of Ayurveda
Karma Bhava – tenth house
Karttikeya – war god, son of Shiva; related to Mars
Kendra – angles of the horoscope
Kendra Houses – houses 1, 5, & 9
Ketu – south node of the Moon, considered a planet in Vedic astrology
Kona Houses – houses 1, 5, & 9
Krittika – third Nakshatra
Kriyamana Karma – new karma created this lifetime by our own freewill

Labha Bhava – eleventh house
Lagna – Ascendant or rising sign
Lakshmi – Hindu goddess of prosperity and beauty; related to Venus
Leo – fifth sign of the zodiac
Libra – seventh sign of the zodiac

Magha – tenth Nakshatra
Mahapurusha Yoga – planetary combination that involves either Mercury, Venus, Mars, Jupiter or Saturn located in an angle house or its exalted sign
Malavya Yoga – the Mahapurusha Yoga for Venus
Mantras – sacred sounds
Minor Dusthana Houses – houses 3 & 11
Moksha – liberation or spiritual freedom; one of the four goals or aims of life
Moksha Houses – houses 4, 8, & 12
Moolatrikona – portion of a sign in which a planet placed there is particularly strong
Moon – Chandra
Mrigashira – fifth Nakshatra

Glossary

Mrityu Bhava – eighth house
Muhurta – electional astrology; selecting an auspicious time to begin an undertaking
Mula – nineteenth Nakshatra

Nagas – deified serpents
Naisargika Bala – inherent strength of a planet; used in Shadbala
Nakshatra – 27 lunar constellations, each a 13° 20" section
Natal Astrology – Jataka, interpretation of the birth chart
Natural Benefics – the planets Jupiter, Venus, Mercury, and a waxing Moon
Natural Malefics – the planets Saturn, Mars, Rahu, Ketu, and a waning Moon
Navamsha chart – ninth divisional chart
Nimitta – branch of Vedic astrology that works with omens

Observational Astronomy - Gola
Omens - Nimitta

Parashara – great sage considered by some to be the father of Vedic astrology, compiled the important astrological work Brihat Parashara Hora Shastra
Pisces – twelfth sign of the zodiac
Pitris – ancestral spirits; deities related to Magha Nakshatra
Pitta – fire dosha of Ayurveda
Planetary War – two planets (except the Sun and Moon) placed within one degree of each other
Prarabdha Karma – portion of karma that is set in motion this lifetime, the karma reflected in the horoscope
Prashna – horary astrology; creating a chart for the time a question is asked
Purnarvasu – seventh Nakshatra
Purva Ashadha - twentieth Nakshatra
Purva Bhadrapada – twenty-fifth Nakshatra
Purva Phalguni – eleventh Nakshatra
Putra Bhava – fifth house
Puvapunya – accumulated merit from past lives
Pushya – eighth Nakshatra

Rahu – north node of the Moon, considered a planet in Vedic astrology
Raja Yoga – combination of planets that denotes a royal or kingly status

Rashi – astrological sign
Rashi Chart – birth chart
Retrograde – the apparent backward movement of a planet, which gives a stronger dose of the planet's significations
Revati – twenty-seventh Nakshatra
Rig Veda – sacred text of India
Roga Bhava – sixth house
Rohini – fourth Nakshatra
Ruchaka Yoga – the Mahapurusha Yoga for Mars
Rudra – fierce form of Shiva

Sagittarius – ninth sign of the zodiac
Sahaja Bhava – third house
Samadhi – state of total absorption in the absolute stillness of pure consciousness
Sanchita Karma – total pool of karma stored up from past actions
Sattva – spiritual or pure in nature
Scorpio – eighth sign of the zodiac
Seva – spiritual service
Shadbala – six-point system used to judge the strength of a planet
Shakti – energy or essence
Shaktipat – awakening of kundalini
Shasha Yoga – the Mahapurusha Yoga for Saturn
Shatabhisha – twenty-fourth Nakshatra
Shiva – the destroyer god; part of the Hindu trinity
Shravana – twenty-second Nakshatra
Shukra – Venus
Siddhis – psychic powers
Sidereal Zodiac – zodiac used in Vedic astrology
Sthana Bala – positional strength of a planet; used in Shadbala
Sukha Bhava – fourth house
Surya – the Sun
Swati – fifteenth Nakshatra

Tara – wife of Jupiter (Brihaspati)
Taurus – second sign of the zodiac
Thanu Bhava – first house
Trik Houses – dusthana houses 6, 8, & 12
Trikona Houses – houses 1, 5, & 9
Trine – houses 1, 5, 9
Trine Houses – houses 1, 5, & 9

Tropical Zodiac – zodiac oriented to the seasons, used in Western astrology

Upachaya Houses – growing houses 3, 6, 10, & 11
Uttara Ashadha – twenty-first Nakshatra
Uttara Bhadrapada – twenty-sixth Nakshatra
Uttara Phalguni – twelfth Nakshatra

Vargottama – the same sign position of a planet in the natal chart and the Navamsha chart
Varuna – god of the waters
Vata – air dosha of Ayurveda
Vayu – deified wind, related to Swati Nakshatra
Vedanga – auxiliary disciplines or limbs of the Vedas
Vedas – sacred scriptures of India
Vedic Astrology – Jyotish
Vidya – spiritual science
Virgo – sixth sign of the zodiac
Vishakha – sixteenth Nakshatra
Vishnu – the preserver of the universe; part of the Hindu trinity
Vyaya Bhava – twelfth house

Yagya – Vedic ceremony used as a remedy to improve certain conditions
Yama – god of death; related to Bharani Nakshatra
Yogakaraka – planet that rules both an angle and a trine house at the same time; the planet of power for six of the Ascendants
Yugas – world ages

Zodiac – constellations of the stars

Bibliography
Path of Light, Volumes I & II

CLASSICAL TEXTS

Burgess, Rev. Ebenezer. (trans.) *Surya Siddhanta* (Delhi, India: Motilal Banarsidass 1997)
Chidbhavananda, Swami (commentator). *The Bhagavad Gita* (Tirupparaitturai, Tiruchirappalli District, Tamil Nadu, India: Sri Ramakrishna Tapovanam, Secretary 1992)
Dhundiraj, Pt. *Jatakabharnam* Girish Chand Sharma (trans.) (New Delhi, India: Sagar Publications 1998)
Dikshita, Vaidyanatha. *Jataka Parijat, Volumes 1 - 3* V. Subramanya Sastri (trans.) (New Delhi, India: Ranjan Publications 1932)
Griffith, Ralph T. (trans.) *Rig Veda* (Delhi, India: Motilal Banarsidass 1992)
Kalidasa. *Uttara Kalamrita* P. S. Sastri (trans.) (New Delhi, India: Ranjan Publications 1994)
Mahadeva. *Jataka Tatva* S. S. Sareen (trans.) (New Delhi, India: Sagar Publications 1987)
Mantreswara. *Phala Deepika* S. S. Sareen (trans.) (New Delhi, India: Sagar Publications 1992)
Mukhopadhyaya, Satyamsu Mohan, et al. (trans.) *Vamana Purana* Anand Swarup Gupta (ed.) (Varanasi, India: All India Kashiraj Trust 1968)
Parasara, Maharishi. *Brihat Parasara Hora Sastra Volumes I & II* Girish Chand Sharma (trans.) (New Delhi, India: Sagar Publications 1995)
Parasara, Maharishi. *Brihat Parasara Hora Sastra, Volumes I & II* R. Santhanam (trans.) (New Delhi, India: Ranjan Publications, 1992)
Pargiter, F.E. (trans.) *Markandeya Purana* (Asiatic Society of Bengal & Shamsher Bahadur Singh 1995)
Raja, Punja. *Sambhu Hora Prakasha* R. Santhanam (trans.) (Delhi, India: R. Santhanam Associates 1995)
Rao, B. Suryanarain. *Sri Sarwarthachintamani* (Delhi, India: Motilal Banarsidass 1996)
Santhanam, R. (trans.) *Hora Ratna* (Delhi, India: R. Santhanam Associates 1995)
Sareen, S.S. (trans.) *Chamatkar Chintamani of Bhatt Narayana* (New Delhi, India: Sagar Publications, 1986)

Bibliography

Sattar, Arshia (trans.) *The Ramayana Valmiki* (Bombay, India: Penguin Books 1996)

Satyacharya, Sage. *Satya Jatakam* (New Delhi, India: Ranjan Publications 1979)

Shastri, P.S. (trans.) *Brihat Jataka* (New Delhi, India: Ranjan Publications 1996)

Subramaniam, Kamala (trans.) *Mahabharata* (Bombay, India: Bharatiya Vidya Bhavan 1995)

Tagare, Ganesh Vasudeo (trans.) *Ancient Indian Tradition and Mythology (Volumes 1 - 62 of The Puranas)* (Delhi, India: Motilal Banarsidass 1970)

Bhagavata Purana, Part 2, Volume 8
Bhagavata Purana, Part 3, Volume 9
Bhagavata Purana, Part 4, Volume 10
Bhagavata Purana Part 4, Volume 11

Brahmanda Purana, Part 1, Volume 22
Brahmanda Purana, Part 2, Volume 23

Brahma Purana, Part 1, Volume 33

Siva Purana, Part 2, Volume 2
Siva Purana, Part 4, Volume 4

Agni Purana, Part 2, Volume 28
Agni Purana, Part 3, Volume 29

Kurma Purana, Part 2, Volume 20
Kurma Purana, Part 2, Volume 21

Narada Purana, Part 3, Volume 17
Narada Purana, Part 4, Volume 18

Skanda Purana, Part 1, Volume 49
Skanda Purana, Part 2, Volume 50
Skanda Purana, Part 3, Volume 51
Skanda Purana, Part 7, Volume 55
Skanda Purana, Part 11, Volume 59
Skanda Purana, Part 12, Volume 60

Padma Purana Part 7, Volume 45
Padma Purana, Part 9, Volume 47
Padma Purana, Part 10, Volume 48

Varaha Purana, Part 1, Volume 31
Varaha Purana, Part 2, Volume 32

Taluqdar of Oudh, A. (trans.) *The Matsya Puranam* (Delhi, India: Oriental Books Reprint Corp. 1980)
Varahamihira. *Brihat Jataka* B. Suryanarain Rao (trans.) (Delhi, India: Motilal Banarsidass 1996)
Varahamihira. *Brihat Jataka* Swami Vijnanananda (trans.) (Delhi, India: Oriental Books Reprint Corp. 1979)
Varma, Kalyana. *Saravali, Volumes 1 & 2* (New Delhi, India: Ranjan Publications 1996)
Vijnanananda, Swami (trans.) *Srimad Devi Bhagavatam* (India: Munshiram Manoharlal 1996)

CONTEMPORARY TEXTS

Bhat, M. Ramakrishna. *Fundamentals of Astrology* (Delhi, India: Motilal Banarsidass 1979)
Braha, James. *Ancient Hindu Astrology for the Modern Western Astrologer* (N. Miami, Florida: Hermetician Press, 1986)
Charak, Dr. K.S. *Elements of Vedic Astrology, Volumes 1 & 2* (New Delhi, India: Vision Wordtronic 1995)
Charak, Dr. K.S. *Essentials of Medical Astrology* (New Delhi, India: Vision Wordtronic 1994)
Danielou, Alain. *The Myths and Gods of India* (Rochester, Vermont: Inner Traditions 1991)
deFouw, Hart, and Robert Svoboda. *Light on Life* (London, England: Penguin Arkana, 1996)
Dowson, John. *A Classical Dictionary of Hindu Mythology* (London, England: Routledge & Kegan Paul Ltd. 1979)
Feuerstein, Georg, Subhash Kak, and David Frawley. *In Search of the Cradle of Civilization* (Madras, India: Quest Books 1995)
Frawley, David. *The Astrology of the Seers* (Salt Lake City, Utah: Passage Press 1990)
Gerson, Scott. *Ayurveda, The Ancient Indian Healing Art* (Rockport, MA: Element Books Limited 1997)
Gupta, Anima Sen. *Classical Samkhya: A Critical Study* (Delhi, India: Munishiriam Monoharlal Publishers Pvt. Ltd. 1982)
Gupta, Anima Sen. *The Evolution of the Samkhya School of Thought* (Delhi, India: Munishiriam Monoharlal Publishers Pvt. Ltd. 1986)
Hillebrandt, Alfred. *Vedic Mythology* (Delhi, India: Motilal Banarsidass 1981)
Iyer, H. R. Seshadri. *New Techniques of Prediction* (Bangalore, India: Janapriya Prakashana 1963)

O'Flaherty, Wendy Doniger. *Karma and Rebirth in Classical Indian Traditions* (Delhi, India: Motilal Banarsidass 1990)
Ojha, Pandit Gopesh Kumar. *Predictive Astrology of the Hindus* (Delhi, India: D.B. Taraporevala and Sons 1990)
Rajaram, Navaratna S. and David Frawley. *Vedic Aryans and the Origins of Civilization* (New Delhi, India: Voice of India 2001)
Raman, B.V. *Graha and Bhava Balas* (Bangalore, India: P.N. Kamat 1979)
Raman, B.V. *How to Judge a Horoscope, Volumes 1 & 2* (Bangalore, India: P.N. Kamat 1980)
Raman, B.V. *A Manual of Hindu Astrology* (Bangalore, India: P.N. Kamat 1980)
Raman, B. V. (translator). *Prashna Marga, Volumes 1 & 2* (Delhi, India: Motilal Banarsidass 1994)
Rath, Sanjay. *The Crux of Vedic Astrology* (New Delhi, India: Sagar Publications 1998)
Rath, Sanjay. *Varga Chakra* (New Delhi, India: Sagar Publications 2002)
Reichenbach, Bruce R. *The Law of Karma* (Honolulu, Hawaii: University of Hawaii Press 1990)
Santhanam, R. *Practical Vedic Astrology* (Delhi, India: R. Santhanam Associates 1997)
Svoboda, Robert. *The Greatness of Saturn* (Tulsa, Oklahoma: Sadhana Publications 1997)

Index

A

Adisesa 359, 360, 361, 362
Aditi 89, 352, 353, 354, 370, 401, 418
Adityas 352, 369, 405
Agni 89, 336, 337, 338, 339, 344, 348, 382, 383, 384, 418, 419
Ahirbudhnya 409, 411, 413
Ahorata 409, 411, 413
Aja Ekapada 409, 411, 413
Amavasya Tithi 365
Angular Houses 418
Anuradha 418
Apas 418
Aprarigrah 418
Aquarius 32, 33, 75, 76, 116, 137, 146, 152, 282, 317, 403, 405, 407, 409, 418
Ardra 347, 348, 349, 418
Aries 31, 32, 33, 53, 54, 116, 136, 148, 279, 317, 329, 336, 418
Arjuna 256, 271, 338, 339, 376, 388
Artha 26, 129, 130, 399, 419
Artha Houses 130, 418
Aryaman 353, 369, 370
Ascendant 18, 53, 55, 82, 83, 135, 136, 141, 204, 217, 218, 219, 220, 316, 317, 318, 319, 320, 321, 330, 364, 370, 376, 409, 414, 418, 420
Ashlesha 358, 359, 360, 410, 418
Ashwini 15, 90, 327, 329, 330, 331, 343, 418
Ashwini Kumaras 90, 329, 330, 331
Aspects 20, 22, 24, 25, 27, 67, 69, 91, 103, 109, 147, 155, 169, 180, 194, 204, 250, 252, 255, 267, 281, 283, 285, 298, 300, 315, 318, 319, 320, 321, 359, 364, 370, 418
Astrological Calculations 25, 418
Astronomy 22, 24, 26, 30, 34, 355, 421
Asuras 100, 360
Atharva Veda 24, 25
Ayanamsha 32, 33, 418

Ayu 238, 248, 250
Ayurveda 238, 248, 250

B

Benefics 119, 133, 141, 161, 198, 199, 238, 248, 250, 305, 313, 316, 317, 320, 321, 367, 380
Bhadra Yoga 149, 238, 248, 250, 277, 280, 418
Bhaga 353, 366, 367, 368, 370, 373, 415
Bhagavad Gita 256, 271
Bharani 333, 334, 418, 423
Bhava Chart 418
Brahma 35, 36, 92, 94, 100, 107, 112, 122, 331, 332, 335, 338, 340, 342, 343, 345, 346, 347, 350, 356, 359, 361, 365, 373, 377, 381, 384, 397, 398, 402, 403, 407, 418
Brighu 323, 324, 325, 402
Brihaspati 97, 98, 100, 101, 163, 346, 355, 356, 357, 375, 418, 422
Brihat Parashara Hora Shastra 421
Buddhism 29, 269

C

Cancer 31, 50, 59, 60, 116, 124, 125, 126, 127, 136, 137, 142, 150, 281, 317, 352, 355, 358, 418
Capricorn 73, 74, 116, 126, 137, 145, 152, 270, 279, 282, 317, 321, 396, 399, 403, 418
Causal Body 44, 45, 46, 86
Chandra 341, 344, 346, 347, 365, 418, 420
Chatushpad Drekkanas 218, 219, 220
Chaya 109, 153, 154
Chaya Graha 109, 153, 154
Chesta Bala 113, 418
Chitra 375, 376, 377, 411, 418
Combustion 119, 418
Conjunct 119, 309, 418
Constellation 403, 418

INDEX

Constellations 403, 418
Cyavana 330, 331

D

Daksha 337, 341, 345, 347, 350, 353, 361, 397, 415
Danielou, Alain 87, 328, 372, 395
Dashas 418
Debilitation 115, 116, 418
Deity 329, 333, 336, 340, 344, 348, 352, 355, 358, 363, 366, 369, 371, 375, 379, 382, 385, 388, 391, 394, 396, 399, 403, 405, 409, 411, 414, 419
Dhana Bhava 155, 419
Dhanishtha 403, 404
Dharma 26, 73, 129, 130, 131, 133, 254, 256, 264, 271, 276, 376, 377, 378, 386, 399, 419
Dharma Bhava 254, 419
Dharma House 129, 419
Dharma Houses 129, 419
Dig Bala 113, 118, 419
Diksha 263
Directional Strength 118, 419
Divisional Charts 18, 20, 127
Drekkanas 218, 219, 220
Drik Bala 113, 419
Dusthana 11, 118, 134, 135, 419, 420
Dusthana Houses 134, 135, 419, 420
Dwapara Yuga 34

E

Eighth House 67, 118, 132, 134, 135, 144, 159, 172, 185, 199, 214, 228, 229, 238, 239, 240, 241, 242, 243, 244, 245, 246, 247, 248, 249, 250, 251, 252, 253, 260, 261, 275, 276, 291, 306
Electional Astrology 419
Eleventh House 145, 160, 173, 186, 201, 216, 230, 245, 262, 277, 286, 287, 288, 292, 293, 294, 295, 296, 297, 298, 299, 307
Enemy's Sign 115
Equal House 127
Equanimity 23, 46, 47, 49, 105, 122, 151, 287, 350

Exaltation 114, 115, 150, 152, 321

F

Fifth House 142, 157, 171, 183, 194, 195, 197, 202, 203, 204, 205, 206, 207, 213, 227, 242, 259, 274, 289, 304
First House 139, 140, 147, 148, 149, 150, 151, 152, 153, 156, 169, 181, 195, 211, 225, 240, 257, 272, 288, 302
Four Aims of Life 129
Fourth House 82, 108, 118, 126, 132, 142, 157, 170, 180, 181, 182, 183, 184, 185, 186, 187, 188, 189, 190, 191, 192, 193, 194, 197, 212, 213, 226, 227, 242, 258, 259, 273, 289, 304, 319, 320, 321, 345, 349, 395, 400, 406
Frawley, David 7, 21, 328
Friend's Sign 115

G

Ganapati 398
Gandhiji 38, 39, 40, 41, 42, 84, 85
Ganesh 106, 107
Ganesha 396, 397, 398, 416, 419
Ganita 25, 419
Garuda 106, 333, 359, 380, 399
Gayatri Mantra 371
Gemini 31, 57, 58, 63, 97, 116, 125, 127, 136, 137, 141, 149, 277, 280, 317, 319, 344, 348, 352
Gola 25, 419, 421
Graha 419
Grahas 25, 84, 85
Guru 38, 51, 97, 99, 100, 103, 130, 133, 173, 200, 215, 250, 254, 258, 260, 261, 263, 264, 265, 266, 267, 268, 269, 270, 276, 292, 307, 346, 356, 357, 401

H

Hamsa Yoga 150, 281, 419
Hans Baba 322, 323, 325, 326
Hasta 335, 371, 372, 404, 419
Hemmed In 119, 321
Holy Science 33
Horary Astrology 25, 29, 421

Horoscope 17, 18, 23, 25, 28, 47, 48, 49,
    51, 56, 58, 77, 86, 88, 89, 94, 97,
    99, 121, 124, 129, 130, 133, 134,
    135, 140, 149, 183, 228, 259, 309,
    318, 324, 349, 364, 403, 416, 419,
    420, 421
Horoscopes 52
House Occupants 315
House Rulers 128
Houses 124, 129, 130, 131, 132, 133, 134,
    135, 136, 137, 140, 156, 169, 181,
    195, 211, 225, 240, 257, 272, 288,
    302, 315, 321, 418, 419, 420, 422

I

Immortality 330
Indra 100, 111, 112, 122, 330, 338, 339,
    346, 356, 357, 376, 377, 382, 383,
    384, 388, 389, 390, 398, 402, 419
Indragni 382, 383, 419
Influx 9, 44, 46
Ishta Devata 195, 419

J

Jaimini 28, 419
Jain 38, 39, 40, 50, 81, 82
Jataka 25, 419, 421
Jupiter 11, 25, 70, 77, 97, 99, 100, 116,
    119, 121, 122, 141, 149, 150, 163,
    164, 165, 176, 183, 190, 204, 205,
    219, 220, 226, 227, 228, 233, 249,
    250, 257, 261, 266, 277, 281, 288,
    289, 291, 292, 296, 297, 301, 303,
    305, 307, 311, 312, 315, 316, 317,
    318, 319, 320, 346, 355, 356, 367,
    370, 416, 418, 419, 420, 421, 422
Jyeshtha 382, 384, 388, 389, 419
Jyotish 9, 24, 25, 26, 27, 28, 43, 48, 49,
    52, 84, 89, 129, 130, 318, 323,
    324, 325, 355, 419, 423
Jyotishis 9, 28

K

Kala Bala 113, 420
Kalaprakashika 26
Kalapurusha 52
Kalatra Bhava 223, 421

Kali 33, 35, 36, 37, 391, 392, 393, 420
Kali Yuga 33, 35, 36, 37, 420
Kalpa 35, 163
Kama 26, 129, 399, 419
Kapha 91, 96, 99, 102, 147, 303
Karma 19, 21, 23, 43, 44, 45, 46, 47, 48,
    55, 64, 79, 86, 94, 99, 100, 111,
    132, 133, 195, 210, 239, 243, 252,
    259, 270, 284, 302, 356, 375, 376,
    420, 421, 422
Karma Bhava 270, 420
Karmic Bondage 43, 44, 45, 46, 47, 79,
    110, 301
Kartari Yoga 119, 321
Karttikeya 336, 337, 338, 393, 420
Kendra 11, 118, 133, 420
Kendra Houses 133, 420
Ketu 25, 110, 111, 113, 119, 153, 154,
    166, 167, 178, 179, 192, 193, 207,
    208, 221, 222, 236, 237, 253, 269,
    284, 285, 299, 300, 305, 309, 314,
    315, 316, 372, 406, 420, 421
Kona Houses 133, 420
Krishna 28, 29, 36, 106, 184, 256, 271,
    338, 339, 365, 383, 384, 386, 397,
    407
Krishna Paksha 365
Krita Yuga 35, 36
Krittika 336, 337, 338, 382, 384, 404, 420
Kriyamana Karma 420
Kundalini 69, 93, 132, 153, 238, 244, 246,
    250, 252, 261, 306, 314, 358, 359,
    360, 409, 411, 412, 422

L

Labha Bhava 286, 420
Lagna 81, 83, 317, 420
Lahiri Ayanamsha 32
Lakshman 338
Lakshmi 112, 113, 340, 351, 393, 420
Laksmana 335
Leo 31, 61, 62, 116, 124, 125, 126, 128,
    136, 142, 317, 321, 363, 366, 369,
    420
Libra 65, 66, 116, 126, 137, 138, 144, 150,
    152, 223, 282, 316, 317, 318, 319,
    320, 375, 379, 382, 420
Longevity 104, 240

INDEX

M

Magha 363, 364, 365, 369, 370, 420, 421
Mahabharata 28, 29, 381, 388, 412
Mahapurusha Yoga 141, 148, 149, 150, 183, 228, 277, 418, 419, 420, 422
Maha Raja Yoga 295
Mahamrityunjaya 112
Mahavira 40
Mahayugas 35
Malavya Yoga 150, 282, 420
Malefics 111, 119, 133, 135, 143, 145, 146, 203, 207, 221, 259, 262, 264, 277, 280, 285, 286, 298, 305, 309, 316, 317, 321
Mantras 24, 25, 39, 99, 100, 110, 111, 195, 198, 199, 202, 204, 206, 208, 303, 361, 371, 372, 378, 390
Manu Samhita 33, 34
Manvantara 35, 36, 361
Maraka 226
Mars 25, 50, 53, 93, 94, 95, 111, 116, 117, 119, 141, 148, 162, 163, 170, 175, 176, 183, 189, 203, 218, 219, 228, 232, 248, 265, 277, 279, 280, 295, 310, 316, 317, 319, 320, 321, 380, 406, 420, 421, 422
Mercury 25, 57, 63, 91, 96, 97, 98, 116, 117, 119, 122, 141, 148, 149, 163, 171, 176, 183, 189, 203, 204, 219, 228, 232, 233, 249, 265, 266, 277, 280, 295, 296, 310, 311, 315, 316, 317, 319, 320, 321, 418, 420, 421
Midpoint 127
Minor Dusthana Houses 135, 420
Mitra 353, 385, 386, 387, 407
Moksha 26, 81, 85, 110, 111, 129, 132, 140, 181, 238, 253, 301, 302, 312, 399, 419
Moksha Houses 132, 420
Moolatrikona 115, 116, 420
Moon 25, 53, 82, 89, 91, 92, 97, 98, 113, 114, 115, 116, 119, 120, 122, 147, 162, 175, 188, 202, 203, 217, 218, 219, 220, 221, 231, 232, 247, 248, 258, 264, 279, 292, 294, 295, 308, 309, 315, 316, 317, 319, 330, 338, 341, 344, 345, 346, 347, 349, 356, 361, 364, 365, 367, 370, 372, 377, 395, 403, 404, 407, 409, 414, 418, 420, 421
Mrigashira 344, 345, 346, 347, 356, 404, 420
Mrityu Bhava 238, 419
Muhurta 420
Mula 391, 392, 393, 420

N

Nagas 358, 360, 362, 420
Naisargika Bala 113, 420
Nakshatra 4, 18, 418, 419, 420, 421, 422, 423
Nakshatras 20, 327, 418
Narada 338, 350, 380, 381, 397, 407
Narayana 350, 351, 357, 390
Natal Astrology 25, 419
Natural Benefics 11, 119, 315, 421
Natural Malefics 421
Navamsha 117, 421, 422
Navamshas 27
Nimitta 10, 25, 26, 50, 51, 421
Nimitta Karan 50, 86
Ninth House 118, 119, 130, 131, 132, 133, 144, 145, 159, 160, 162, 172, 173, 185, 186, 199, 200, 215, 229, 244, 254, 255, 256, 257, 258, 259, 260, 261, 262, 263, 264, 265, 266, 267, 268, 269, 270, 276, 286, 291, 292, 306, 307, 400
Nirriti 391, 392, 393

O

Observational Astronomy 421
Omens 421

P

Panchami Tithi 362
Papa 44, 45, 132
Papa Karma 132
Papa Kartari Yoga 119, 321
Parashara 28, 421
Pisces 33, 77, 78, 79, 116, 137, 146, 150, 281, 282, 317, 409, 411, 414, 421
Pitris 363, 364, 365, 369, 370, 421
Pitta 421

431

Planetary Friendship 116
Planetary Strength 114
Planetary War 120, 421
Planets 18, 20, 25, 26, 31, 50, 53, 59, 82, 84,
    85, 86, 87, 94, 104, 107, 114, 115,
    118, 120, 122, 127, 133, 134, 135,
    138, 139, 143, 175, 183, 198, 214,
    224, 225, 228, 238, 239, 250, 255,
    259, 270, 274, 286, 292, 295, 303,
    305, 307, 315, 316, 317, 318, 319,
    320, 321, 328, 334, 337, 340, 349,
    355, 356, 358, 359, 364, 367, 369,
    370, 372, 380, 385, 392, 394, 399,
    403, 406, 411, 412, 415, 418, 421
Prajapati 340, 349, 350, 368, 391, 393, 415
Prakriti 386, 409
Prarabdha Karma 10, 47, 421
Prashna 25, 26, 29, 419, 421
Prashna Marga 26, 29
Precession of the Equinox 9, 32
Punya 44, 45, 46, 375
Puranas 328, 344, 351, 362
Purnarvasu 421
Purnima 345
Purva Ashadha 394, 395, 396, 404, 421
Purva Bhadrapada 409, 410, 411, 416, 421
Purva Phalguni 366, 367, 368, 370, 421
Purvapunya 133, 149, 195, 259
Pushan 344, 414, 415
Pushya 355, 356, 421
Putra Bhava, 194, 421

Q

R

Rahu 25, 108, 109, 111, 113, 119, 152,
    153, 166, 178, 192, 206, 207, 221,
    235, 236, 248, 252, 268, 269, 283,
    284, 285, 298, 299, 305, 309, 314,
    316, 367, 372, 406, 421
Raja Yoga 118, 184, 185, 197, 243, 246,
    261, 276, 295, 305, 306, 307, 421
Rama 29, 184, 335, 338, 342, 378, 402
Raman, Dr. B.V. 19, 32
Ramayana 342, 378, 402
Rashi 117, 421
Rashi Chart 117, 421
Rashis 52
Ravana 422
Retrograde 117, 421
Revati 385, 414, 415, 416, 421
Rig Veda 24, 28, 29, 355, 405, 421
Ritam Bhara Pragya 195
Roga Bhava 209, 422
Rohini 340, 341, 347, 377, 402, 416, 421
Ruchaka Yoga 148, 279, 422
Rudra 35, 342, 345, 347, 348, 349, 350,
    360, 368, 411, 415, 422

S

Sage Markandaya 36
Sagittarius 70, 71, 77, 116, 126, 128, 137,
    145, 150, 237, 281, 316, 317, 319,
    321, 391, 394, 396, 422
Sahaja Bhava 168, 422
Samadhi 422
Sama Veda 24, 399
Samjna 373, 374
Sanchita Karma 422
Sati 347
Sattva 35, 399
Saturn 25, 82, 90, 104, 105, 106, 108, 114,
    116, 119, 121, 141, 146, 147, 151,
    152, 164, 165, 170, 177, 178, 183,
    191, 205, 206, 220, 221, 228, 234,
    235, 251, 252, 266, 267, 268, 277,
    280, 282, 283, 292, 298, 309, 311,
    313, 314, 316, 317, 319, 320, 321,
    367, 406, 420, 421, 422
Satya Yuga 34
Savitar 371
Scorpio 67, 82, 83, 93, 116, 126, 137, 144,
    148, 159, 237, 279, 317, 321, 382,
    385, 388, 422
Second House 124, 125, 126, 130, 131,
    137, 141, 155, 156, 157, 158, 159,
    160, 161, 162, 163, 164, 165, 166,
    167, 169, 182, 196, 211, 212, 225,
    226, 241, 257, 258, 272, 273, 286,
    288, 303, 316, 318, 380, 415
Seva 422
Seventh House 143, 158, 171, 184, 199,
    214, 223, 224, 225, 228, 231, 232,
    233, 234, 235, 236, 243, 260, 275,
    290, 305

INDEX

Shadbala 113, 114, 418, 419, 420, 422
Shakti 132, 328, 329, 333, 336, 340, 344, 345, 348, 352, 355, 358, 363, 364, 366, 367, 369, 370, 371, 375, 379, 380, 382, 383, 385, 388, 391, 394, 395, 396, 399, 403, 405, 406, 409, 411, 412, 414
Shasha Yoga 152, 422
Shatabhisha 221, 405, 406, 407, 422
Shat Panchasika 26
Shiva 35, 95, 100, 103, 106, 112, 334, 335, 336, 337, 342, 345, 347, 348, 349, 350, 351, 355, 356, 372, 373, 376, 377, 381, 391, 393, 397, 398, 409, 411, 420, 422
Shravana 354, 399, 400, 401, 422
Shubha Kartari Yoga 119, 321
Shukra 346, 401, 422
Siddhis 69, 195, 250, 261, 365, 371
Sidereal Zodiac 422
Sign Chart 127, 128
Signs 18, 20, 26, 31, 41, 50, 51, 52, 59, 64, 74, 79, 81, 114, 115, 120, 124, 125, 126, 136, 137, 152, 282, 327
Sign Strength 116
Sita 338, 378
Sixth House 128, 130, 134, 135, 143, 158, 171, 184, 198, 209, 210, 211, 212, 213, 214, 215, 216, 217, 218, 219, 220, 221, 222, 223, 227, 243, 259, 260, 274, 275, 290, 305, 316, 320, 415
Soma 92, 100, 330, 332, 377, 381, 388, 414
Sravistha 403, 404
Sthana Bala 113, 422
Sukha Bhava 180, 422
Sun 25, 31, 32, 33, 53, 61, 83, 88, 89, 91, 106, 113, 114, 116, 119, 120, 128, 147, 161, 162, 174, 175, 187, 188, 202, 217, 218, 219, 220, 221, 231, 246, 247, 263, 264, 278, 279, 293, 294, 302, 308, 309, 317, 319, 329, 330, 331, 334, 343, 348, 349, 364, 367, 370, 371, 372, 373, 374, 390, 395, 403, 404, 407, 418, 421, 422
Surya 25, 89, 90, 106, 371, 372, 373, 414, 422

Surya Siddanta 25
Swati 379, 380, 381, 404, 422, 423

T

Taittiriya Brahmana 328
Tara 97, 98, 122, 346, 356, 422
Taurus 55, 56, 116, 128, 136, 141, 150, 282, 317, 336, 340, 344, 422
Temporal 45, 316, 317, 319, 320, 321, 420
Tenth House 145, 160, 173, 186, 200, 215, 229, 245, 261, 270, 272, 277, 278, 279, 280, 281, 282, 283, 284, 292, 307
Thanu Bhava 139, 422
Third House 141, 157, 168, 169, 170, 174, 175, 176, 177, 178, 182, 196, 212, 226, 241, 258, 273, 288, 303
Treta Yuga 33, 35, 36
Trik 134
Trikonas 133
Trine 118, 305, 317, 423
Tropical Astrology 31
Tropical Zodiac 31
Tvashtar 375, 376, 377
Twelfth House 146, 161, 174, 187, 201, 216, 230, 246, 263, 278, 293, 301, 302, 308, 309, 310, 311, 312, 313, 314

U

Unoccupied Houses 321
Upachaya Houses 135, 422
Upanishads 254
Uttara Ashadha 396, 397, 422
Uttara Bhadrapada 410, 411, 412, 422
Uttara Phalguni 369, 370, 422

V

Vamana 354, 400, 401, 402
Vana Parva 36
Varahamihira 28, 30
Vargottama 117, 422
Varuna 342, 353, 376, 386, 405, 406, 407, 408, 422
Vasus 375, 382, 403, 404
Vata 96, 102, 108, 153, 207, 225, 380
Vayu 379, 380, 381, 388, 423

Vedanga 9, 25, 423
Vedas 24, 25, 27, 28, 46, 256, 399, 423
Vedic Astrology 3, 9, 24, 25, 140, 9, 19, 52, 156, 195, 19, 168, 29, 210, 224, 240, 256, 272, 287, 302, 423, 181
Venus 25, 55, 65, 100, 102, 103, 116, 117, 119, 128, 134, 138, 141, 150, 151, 164, 165, 177, 183, 190, 191, 205, 220, 225, 226, 227, 228, 229, 230, 231, 234, 243, 250, 251, 266, 267, 277, 281, 282, 297, 306, 308, 312, 313, 315, 316, 317, 318, 319, 320, 321, 345, 346, 367, 401, 420, 421, 422
Vidya 423
Vipareeta Raja Yoga 118, 243, 246
Virgo 63, 64, 96, 116, 124, 125, 126, 137, 143, 149, 209, 280, 317, 318, 319, 320, 369, 371, 375, 423
Vishakha 382, 383, 384, 386, 423
Vishnu 35, 112, 113, 163, 184, 342, 347, 350, 351, 353, 354, 359, 360, 365, 377, 378, 380, 390, 399, 401, 402, 409, 423
Visvadevas 396, 397
Visvakarma 374, 375, 376, 377
Vyaya Bhava 301, 423

W

X

Y

Yagya 347, 359
Yajur Veda 24, 390
Yama 333, 334, 335, 363, 373, 374, 376, 423
Yami 334
Yogakaraka 317, 320, 423
Yugas 33, 34, 35, 36, 423
Yukteshwar, Sri 32, 33

Z

Zero Degrees 116
Zodiac 26, 31, 32, 33, 68, 74, 77, 90, 124, 137, 141, 142, 143, 144, 145, 146, 270, 327, 355, 418, 419, 420, 421, 422, 423

The Author

James Kelleher has been a full-time Vedic astrologer since 1980. He was introduced to Vedic astrology in 1975 by M. K. Gandhi, a world-renowned Vedic astrologer and spiritual adept. Gandhi gave Jim his first astrology reading in which he predicted that Jim would become an astrologer, and encouraged him to begin reading about the subject. Gandhi offered to train Jim in the Vedic system of astrology, and later invited him to become his personal assistant.

After studying astrology in India, Jim worked as a professional astrologer in London for five years, assisting Gandhi with his diverse international clientele. In 1984 he returned to the United States and quickly became one of the country's leading Vedic astrologers. He is the co-founder of the American Council of Vedic Astrology and the American College of Vedic Astrology. He is also an adjunct professor at Hindu University of America located in Orlando, Florida. He has been awarded the titles of *Jyotish Kovid* and *Jyotish Vachaspati* by the Indian Council of Astrological Sciences. Jim maintains a busy private practice in Los Gatos, California.

james@jameskelleher.com
www.jameskelleher.com

Path of Light

Volume II

The Domains of Life

James Kelleher

Volume II of this remarkable set is available from
www.jameskelleher.com

NINE PLANETS

VEDIC ASTROLOGICAL MANTRAS

Nine Planets Mantra CD — $18

The Nine Planets Mantra CD provides a great resource for those wishing to benefit from the chanting of planetary bija mantras. These mantras were imparted to James Kelleher by his guru. Chanted by a traditional South Indian Vedic pundit, the mantras are beautifully recorded against the droning sound of a tambura. They can be easily learned and chanted by anyone. Listening to them and chanting them regularly will lead to greater prosperity, success and fulfillment in every domain of life.

"As part of a large-scale reorganization, my entire department at Boeing was laid off. On your recommendation, I began chanting the Venus mantra. After 3 days of chanting the mantra, I got a call from my boss. He said there had been a change. They had decided to lay off the entire department, except for me! This seemed to be more than a coincidence."
— S.M., Seattle, WA

"I have been chanting the Ketu mantra for the past year and have found that it makes me feel very smooth and seems to increase my intuition."
— T.S., New York, NY

Now available at www.jameskelleher.com

ABOUT THE TYPE

This book was set in Garamond, a typeface based on the types of the sixteenth-century printer, publisher, and type designer Claude Garamond, whose sixteenth-century types were modeled on those of Venetian printers from the end of the previous century. The italics are based on types by Robert Granjon, a contemporary of Garamond's. The Garamond typeface and its variations have been a standard among book designers and printers for four centuries.

Composed by JTC Imagineering, Santa Maria,CA
Designed by John Taylor-Convery